Democracy and the Claims of Nature

Critical Perspectives for a New Century

EDITED BY
BEN A. MINTEER AND
BOB PEPPERMAN TAYLOR

ROWMAN & LITTLEFIELD PUBLISHERS, INC.
Lanham • Boulder • New York • Oxford

ROWMAN & LITTLEFIELD PUBLISHERS, INC.

Published in the United States of America
by Rowman & Littlefield Publishers, Inc.
4720 Boston Way, Lanham, Maryland 20706
www.rowmanlittlefield.com

12 Hid's Copse Road
Cumnor Hill, Oxford OX2 9JJ, England

British Library Cataloguing-in-Publication Information Available

Library of Congress Cataloging-in-Publication Data

Democracy and the claims of nature : critical perspectives for a new century / edited by Ben A. Minteer and
    Bob Pepperman Taylor.
        p. cm.
    Includes bibliographical references and index.
    ISBN 0-7425-1522-2 (Cloth : alk. paper)—ISBN 0-7425-1523-0 (Paperback : alk. paper)
        1. Environmental ethics. 2. Environmentalism. 3. Environmental policy. 4. Democracy. I. Minteer, Ben
    A., 1969– II. Taylor, Bob Pepperman.

    GE42 .D46 2002
    179'.1—dc21

                                                                                              2002001810

Printed in the United States of America

♾™ The paper used in this publication meets the minimum requirements of American National
Standard for Information Sciences—Permanence of Paper for Printed Library Materials,
ANSI/NISO Z39.48-1992.

If all were as it seems, and men made the elements their servants for noble ends! If the cloud that hangs over the engine were the perspiration of heroic deeds, or as beneficent as that which floats over the farmer's fields, then the elements and Nature herself would cheerfully accompany men on their errands and be their escort.

—Henry Thoreau, *Walden*

We are still under the sway of the destructive and thoroughly vain belief that man is the pinnacle of creation, and not just a part of it, and therefore everything is permitted to him.

—Vaclav Havel, *The Art of the Impossible*

Contents

PART THREE: ENVIRONMENTALISM AND THE BOUNDARIES OF DEMOCRATIC DISCOURSE

PART FOUR: DEMOCRACY AND ENVIRONMENTAL MOVEMENTS

Preface

Democracy and the Claims of Nature is a sustained and urgent conversation, provocative, engaging, and constantly informed by the art and discernment of Ben Minteer and Bob Pepperman Taylor. It reflects the fact that contemporary environmentalism is multifaceted and full of conflict, no coherent doctrine and perhaps not even a persuasion, but certainly a deliberation of the grandest sort. Moreover, Minteer and Taylor recognize that environmentalism involves a paradox. In one sense, it is intensely contemporary, driven by the dynamics of technology and global economics, caught up in struggles over policy and in party politics. In fact, environmentalism, one of the few successes of the left in recent civic education, is the major contemporary political challenge to the creed of the market, a force for change mirroring concern for the future. Yet at the same time, environmentalism is deeply conservative, zealous to preserve an inheritance—"conservation," in the older language of Progressivism. And *Nature*, invoked by Minteer and Taylor, is incomparably ancient, a matter of first things and, just as Thoreau reminded us, correspondingly linked to classical literature and thought.[1]

Environmental politics, Minteer and Taylor note, is bound up with an enduring challenge to democracy: Are democracies and democratic peoples capable of foresight? Can they detect and control dangers before they become overwhelming? Among the American Framers, Alexander Hamilton was not alone in suspecting that the public will fail that test; general goods and long-term projects, he argued, will chiefly be perceived and dealt with by "speculative men," while ordinary citizens will not step far beyond what is close at hand.[2] Hamilton's argument only becomes more persuasive as politics grows in scale and complexity, as the pace of change makes the future ever more immediate, and as citizens, baffled and overwhelmed, are tempted to withdraw into private life. Even in Hamilton's republic, however, elites were to be elected, ultimately dependent on public opinion and sentiment, and as Minteer and Taylor write, contemporary politics confronts us with the question *Will democratic publics limit themselves in response to environmental crises?* Can democracy "learn a kind of humility about its own power and authority"?

The auguries are not promising. Affluent Americans, after all, chafe at suggestions that they sacrifice any of their superfluities. In response to the crisis of international terrorism, President Bush urged Americans to go to the mall and called for lower taxes.

And in the intellectual world, as Minteer and Taylor indicate, a fashionable version of democratic theory argues that democracy resists all external constraints, insisting on the public's right to construct its own world. These difficulties, however, only underline the fact that environmentalism points, unwaveringly, to great issues of political theory.

The basic vocabulary of environmentalism makes that clear enough. An *environment* surrounds or encompasses something, entailing a distinction between the environment and the environed. Applied to human affairs, we can argue whether the environment confines human beings (as in the Enlightenment project for mastering nature) or embraces them (as in Romanticism); what is not at issue is that the term implies a view that is centered on human beings conceived as separate from their environs. By contrast, *nature*, Minteer and Taylor's preferred term, suggests something not merely around us but pervasive. We are not *in* it but *of* it; nature is a whole of which we are so many parts. Nature, so understood, indicates not only a distinct human place but a role and responsibility within the whole. And it would not be hard to argue, following ancient teaching, since nonhuman nature has sound but not speech, that human beings—*zoon logistikon*, Aristotle said, animals who talk—have a special duty to be the voice of the voiceless, to discover and articulate the claims of nature. This collection stands as a fine example of the effort to fulfill that obligation.

Minteer and Taylor have built this book, I think, around the recognition that democratic government rests on, and has a corresponding need to acknowledge, the claims of nature. In a democracy, citizens rule, but also are ruled by the laws they make, of course, but more fundamentally by nature. Democracy proclaims that all citizens are equal despite their differences, that they are equal by nature, their very diverse experiences and achievements aside, that—as Americans have held from the beginning—they are "created equal" under "the laws of Nature and of Nature's God." Minteer and Taylor and their contributors are invaluable in helping us appreciate that enduring teaching.

Wilson Carey McWilliams
Rutgers University

Notes

1. Thoreau, *Walden and Other Writings* (New York: Modern Library, 1950), 91.
2. Hamilton, *The Federalist*, no. 17.

Introduction

Bob Pepperman Taylor and Ben A. Minteer

This volume contains new essays addressing the relationship between democracy and environmentalism. The authors of these essays are philosophers, political theorists, and social scientists, and their papers highlight the tensions and sympathies between democratic ideals and procedures on the one hand, and environmental values and practices on the other. The book itself has grown from the editors' conviction that it is important for those writing in the field of environmental ethics to engage in dialogue with those writing about environmental politics, and that both of these groups exchange views with those who are primarily concerned with democratic political theory. Readers familiar with the past thirty years of environmentalist thinking know that the intersection of these fields has produced a lively, if not always cohesive, literature ranging from work on environmental justice to ecofeminist and green and ecocentric political theory to the more recent development of pragmatic environmental ethics. The purpose of this volume is to provide a number of the leading thinkers in these and related fields the opportunity to reflect upon where we stand in our understanding of the relationship between democracy and the claims of nature. We hope that these reflections will help in the ongoing process of clarifying the understanding of our environmental and democratic commitments, and the relationship between the values these commitments represent.

The book is divided into four sections. The first of these, "Democracy and Environmental Values," addresses a number of the most important debates in contemporary environmental ethics. The section begins with chapters by Bryan Norton and Ben Minteer promoting, on democratic and philosophical grounds, a pragmatic approach to environmental ethics. Robyn Eckersley's chapter provides an indirect response to this view, arguing that radical environmental and political critique requires an ecocentric environmental ethics. Taking the perspective of democratic political theory, Joe Bowersox warns both environmental ethicists and environmental administrators of the dangers of what he fears is a common and insufficiently political perspective on environmental concerns. The section concludes with an essay by J. Baird Callicott explaining what he understands to be the relationship between the hierarchy of values that include both environmental ethics and democratic commitments. As an appendix to this section, Callicott responds to criticisms of his work raised in the Norton,

1

Minteer, and Bowersox contributions. In so doing, he highlights some of the key choices facing those who seek to link environmental ethical argument with democratic values and procedures.

If section 1 approaches political concerns from the perspective of environmental ethics, section 2, "Environmentalism and Democratic Citizenship," begins to reverse the relationship. Here the discussion centers more on the question of how democratic citizenship is to be informed and practiced in light of more specific environmental considerations. The answers given to these questions differ noticeably among the contributors. Catriona Sandilands opens the section with a provocative discussion of the way environmental issues can create the opportunities for a new, active, and liberatory democratic citizenship. John Barry investigates the way in which democratic citizens can best think of their relationship to nature in the context of their democratic deliberations, and Andrew Light considers how restoration ecology can be used as a vehicle to promote environmental and democratic citizenship. Bob Pepperman Taylor completes the section with a reading of Aldo Leopold as a model educator of democratic citizens.

The third section, "Environmentalism and the Boundaries of Democratic Discourse," raises the thorny question of the fair and proper inclusion of human and nonhuman stakeholders and interests in democratic deliberations over environmental policy. Peter Wenz evaluates the justice, and the prospects for justice, in the effects of democratic environmental decisions made in the United States on people and the environment in poor and undeveloped nations. Luis Vivanco provides an important case study of the impact of rain forest conservation, driven primarily by individuals and nongovernmental organizations (NGOs) originating in the United States, on citizens in Costa Rica. Tim Hayward brings us back to considerations of domestic justice by defending constitutionally mandated environmental rights for citizens, and John O'Neill discusses the epistemic, moral, and political problems and prospects for representation of nonhuman nature in democratic deliberation.

The final section, "Democracy and Environmental Movements," begins with Robert Paehlke's assessment of the relationship between the past generation of environmental policy and democratic politics. Timothy Luke provides an argument about the relationship between environmentalism and populist social and political movements generally, while Robert Gottlieb looks closely at the relationship of environmentalism, justice, and one particular social movement: the drive for community food security. Charles Rubin completes this section by looking at the "civic environmentalism" literature and assessing the relationship of these local, community-based movements to democratic politics. In a very real sense, Rubin's paper completes not only this section, but the book as a whole, through its evaluation of what we learn about democratic theory and practice by looking at this environmentalist case study. With this chapter, the book has moved from environmental ethics to democratic theory to the politics of environmental movements and, finally, to a consideration of one type of environmental politics and what it can teach us about the relationship between democratic political theory and democratic political practice as a whole.

Readers of this volume familiar with the literature of environmental ethics and environmental politics will not be surprised at many of the themes found in the essays. As in much of the environmentalist and environmental ethics literature from the past few decades, there are discussions here of the proper understanding of democratic politics and its relationship to a satisfactory environmentalism. There are discussions of the relationship of environmentalism and science, and how this relationship may or may not influence our politics and ethics for better or worse. There are debates, in a number of different forms, between "reform" or liberal and radical environmentalism, and between pragmatic and principle-driven approaches to environmental valuation and decision making. There are attempts to explain how a green politics may or may not be the conceptual link between a number of our political values, most importantly democracy and justice and rights, and the political link between movements as diverse as food security and respect for civic diversity. There are discussions that should influence debates between those who stress rural and wilderness environmentalism, and those who promote an urban environmentalism. In short, there is material here that grows out of and reflects the continued evolution of debates and literatures that are recognizable to anyone who has followed the environmental ethics and politics of the past generation.

Naturally, we hope this volume contributes to the work of moving these debates and literatures ahead in a useful and compelling way, and that it captures some of the best current thought about the relationship between democracy and environmentalism. But we also believe the arguments in these papers evoke a number of broader philosophical and political themes. For example, anyone who has studied nineteenth- and twentieth-century debates between reform and revolutionary socialists will find the debates between liberal and radical environmentalists recognizable territory indeed. For another example, one of the main lines of argument in the present dispute between J. Baird Callicott, on the one hand, and Bryan Norton and Ben Minteer, on the other, is essentially a contemporary version of an older and more general disagreement about the place of philosophical claims within a democratic polity.[1]

This second issue, the ancient tension between the special languages of philosophy and the deliberations of a democratic political community, raises a general problem at the heart of democratic political theory; we might call it the problem of *limits*. This problem has always been understood to be raised by the possible asymmetry between democratic willing and moral principle. Plato famously lampooned democrats as lacking all ability for self-governance,[2] and every serious democratic theorist has had to explain, in response to such criticisms, how a democratic polity could be expected to control such excesses, either through constitutional mechanism or civic education.[3]

Alexis de Tocqueville, a friendly but tough critic of democracy, puts the problem like this. Democratic equality and liberty seem to have the effect of making democratic citizens deeply preoccupied with themselves. "I am convinced that in the long term democracy turns the imagination away from all that is external to man to fix it only on man."[4] The regard that democracy encourages for the importance of every citizen not only tends to encourage a radically humanistic moral sensibility, however; it also promotes a radical individualism and materialism as well. Democratic equality "tends to isolate them [citizens] from one another and to bring each of them to be occupied with himself alone"[5] through its subversion of all social authorities and hierarchies that traditionally bound communities together. Tocqueville is blunt about what he thinks is the narrowness of the moral vision promoted by democracy: "In democratic societies each citizen is habitually occupied with contemplating a very small object, which is himself."[6]

One consequence of this individualism, he fears, is that these self-preoccupied citizens become passionately committed to material prosperity: "The taste for well-being forms the salient and indelible feature of democratic ages."[7] Thus, the moral world of democracy becomes profoundly constrained, narrow, and uninspiring. Democracy makes "each man forget his ancestors" and "hides his descendants from him and separates him from his contemporaries; it constantly leads him back toward himself alone and threatens finally to confine him wholly in the solitude of his own heart."[8]

This inclination that Tocqueville emphasizes as fundamental to understanding the nature of democracy, the turning of democratic citizens from all knowledge and concerns beyond the interests and wills of individuals, is the inclination that distinguishes much democratic theory and practice from classical conceptions and practices of politics. Classical political theory conventionally relies upon a conception of nature to provide the normative limits for political life, as when Aristotle argues that man is a creature who by nature lives in a polis.[9] Such a claim defends a particular kind of politics, in all its complexity, on the grounds that it reflects and cultivates human nature in its most admirable form(s). The truth or falsity of the entire political theory stands or falls with the conception of nature upon which it is built. In this sense, the classical political tradition represents a contest between differing conceptions of nature itself, with all its normative implications.

In response to this tradition, the greatest of all democratic theorists, Jean-Jacques Rousseau, famously cut the cord between a just political order and nature, arguing that justice and ethics are entirely conventional, that democratic legitimacy depends upon an equal respect for the individual wills of citizens rather than the conformity of political life with a natural order, that natural liberty and moral (and political) liberty are radically distinct and incommensurable.[10] Such a move is tremendously liberatory, of course; Richard Rorty points out that democracy rebels against all external constraints and insists upon constructing a world in which there is nothing more divine than men and women and the world they freely construct together.[11] It also, however, conceives of human wills and interests as all important, and threatens thereby to create and justify a world without moral restraint.[12] Democratic legitimacy, so conceived, depends entirely upon the legitimacy of the democratic process, and seems potentially deaf to normative evaluation independent of such processes. As Tocqueville put it, "those who regard universal suffrage as a guarantee of the goodness of choices make a complete illusion for themselves. Universal suffrage has other advantages, but not that one."[13]

Tocqueville thought the only hope for softening the negative and narrowing moral effects of democracy was religion. At least in nineteenth-century America, the primary focus of his observations, religion mitigated the humanism, materialism, and individualism of democratic citizens. "Their passions, needs, educations, circumstances—all in fact seem to cooperate in making the inhabitants of the United States incline toward the earth [i.e., toward materialism]. Religion alone, from time to time, makes him raise passing, distracted glances toward Heaven."[14] Almost all the habits promoted by democracy, in fact, are challenged by religion.

> The greatest advantage of religions is to inspire almost wholly contrary instincts. There is no religion that does not place man's desires beyond and above earthly goods and that does not naturally raise his soul toward regions

much superior to those of the senses. Nor is there any that does not impose on each some duties toward the human species or in common with it, and that does not thus draw him, from time to time, away from contemplation of himself. This one meets even in the most false and dangerous religions.[15]

If democracy cannot provide the antidote for its own vices, at least democratic societies like the United States are friendly toward religions; and these religions can promote modest alternative moral educations.

While few scholars and intellectuals today, at least outside of certain conservative circles, place their hopes for the moral reform of democratic society on the promotion of religion, it is remarkable to note the similarity between Tocqueville's analysis and the trends in much environmentalist writing from the past generation. Like conventional critics of democracy, much environmentalism has feared the humanism and materialism and individualism of democratic society. And, like Tocqueville and other critics, environmentalists not uncommonly promote a view of nature that will teach moral truths beyond this humanism, materialism, and individualism.[16] Instead of appealing to conventional religious or philosophical teleologies, however, these environmentalist critics appeal to a modern and scientifically informed philosophy of nature. For many, an "ecological education" has come to replace the traditions of religion and classical philosophy as the locus of moral limits on individual will and desire.

To investigate the relationship between democracy and nature, then, is to touch upon an old and fundamental concern about the moral integrity of democracy in new but sometimes surprisingly recognizable ways. The contemporary environmental movement is by no means alone in raising serious doubts about the ability of American democracy, or any other modern liberal democracy, to (morally) control its own will and desires, especially (but not only) when confronted with capitalist promises of seemingly endless economic riches.[17] But it does raise these doubts in particularly poignant forms, growing from very real environmental problems and the public policy challenges they represent: it is as though the natural environment has come to embody, through its deterioration and destruction at the hands of democratic society, the very flaws critics have always assumed to be endemic to democracy. If the problem in the past has often been framed by friends of democracy as how to think about the impact of the natural world on democratic society and politics, the problem now is at least initially reversed: what is the impact of democratic society and politics on the natural world, and how does this in turn speak about the moral and practical potential of democratic politics?

The answers that are given to this question are many and complex and frequently incompatible. Especially during the 1970s it was not uncommon for some environmentalists to argue that only authoritarian forms of government would be able to contend with the severe problems of resource scarcity that were foreseen.[18] Today, antidemocratic arguments are no longer heard in the way they were less than a generation ago,[19] but environmentalists differ significantly in their assessment of the responsiveness of contemporary liberal democracies to environmental problems, the possibility and desirability of more participatory democratic forms for the sake of the environment, the democratically most desirable way of thinking about environmental obligations, and so forth, as the contributions to this volume amply illustrate.

What is important to note here, however, is not just the variety or cogency of answers that are given to the question of the relationship between modern democracy and the natural world. It is also of great interest and importance to observe the way a political movement growing from very particular policy problems (pollution and public health, resource scarcity, species extinction, the destruction of wild areas at alarming rates, etc.) has led to a new way of thinking about a very old and very crucial problem: can a democratic society learn to discipline its own wants and impulses? can it respect a natural world beyond its own creation? can it learn a kind of humility about its own power and authority? As much as anything else, the answers given to these questions define the differences between the contributors of this volume, and those writing in the field at large. And as much as anything else, these questions are not only problems for environmentalists, but for anyone concerned about the health and practice of democracy in the twenty-first century—and beyond.

We would like to express our gratitude to Cheryl Brownell, Elizabeth Corley, Jan Feldman, Tom Mazza, Patrick Neal, Tim Smith, Fran Pepperman Taylor, and Alan Wertheimer for their advice about this project. The contributors must also be thanked for their patient good humor and commitment to seriously addressing the relationship between environmental and democratic values. Finally, thanks to Stephen Wrinn, of Rowman & Littlefield, for his enthusiastic support of and good sense about this volume.

Notes

1. See Michael Walzer, "Philosophy and Democracy," *Political Theory* 9, August 1981, 379–99.

2. "A man who didn't have the experience [of the democratic city] couldn't be persuaded of the extent to which beasts subject to human beings are freer here than in another city. The bitches follow the proverb exactly and become like their mistresses; and, of course, there come to be horses and asses who have gotten the habit of making their way freely and solemnly, bumping into whomever they happen to meet on the roads, if he doesn't stand aside, and all else is similarly full of freedom." Plato, *Republic*, Book VIII, 563c, in Allen Bloom, ed., *The Republic of Plato*, 241–42.

3. Compare, on the one hand, James Madison in *Federalist*, number 10, with John Dewey in *Democracy and Education* on the other.

4. Alexis de Tocqueville, *Democracy in America*, Harvey C. Mansfield and Delba Winthrop, eds. (Chicago: University of Chicago Press, 2000), 460.

5. Ibid., 419.

6. Ibid., 464.

7. Ibid., 422.

8. Ibid., 484.

9. *Politics*, Book 1, chapter 2.

10. "This passage from the state of nature to the civil state produces quite a remarkable change in man, for it substitutes justice for instinct in his behavior and gives his actions a moral quality they previously lacked." Rousseau, *On The Social Contract*, Book 1, chapter 8, in *Jean-Jacques Rousseau: The Basic Political Writings* (Indianapolis, Ind.: Hackett, 1987), 150.

11. See Richard Rorty, *Achieving Our Country* (Cambridge, Mass.: Harvard University Press, 1998), chapter 1.

12. Leon Wieseltier comments that "People who think they have created themselves are dangerous people, because they have an exaggerated sense of the malleability of things. They think they can begin again." Leon Wieseltier, *Kaddish* (New York: Knopf, 1998), 381.

13. Tocqueville, *Democracy in America*, 190.

14. Ibid., 430.

15. Ibid., 419.

16. Deep Ecology is just one of the many strains of environmental thought that illustrates these points.

17. Tocqueville observed that "in their doubt of opinions, men in the end attach themselves solely to instincts and material interests, which are much more visible, more tangible, and more permanent in their nature than opinions." Tocqueville, *Democracy in America*, 180.

18. Most famously, see William Ophuls, *Ecology and the Politics of Scarcity* (San Francisco: Freeman, 1977).

19. Although there are active and secretive groups like the Earth Liberation Front (ELF) that commit terrorist acts in the name of environmental principles and commitments.

Part 1

DEMOCRACY AND ENVIRONMENTAL VALUES

CHAPTER 1

Democracy and Environmentalism
FOUNDATIONS AND JUSTIFICATIONS
IN ENVIRONMENTAL POLICY

Bryan G. Norton

A New Fault Line in Environmental Ethics?

My reading in the field of environmental ethics today suggests that there is a major, and at least somewhat new, "fault line" emerging in the field. This new fault line may be difficult to discern because it is layered upon the long-standing and dominant division between anthropocentrists and nonanthropocentrists. This new fault line may run quite close to the older one, but this is not obvious, because the arguments recently offered are at first glance so different from the meta-ethical arguments typical of disagreements between anthropocentrists and nonanthropocentrists. To avoid begging important questions, I will try to present the new division, and the arguments regarding it, as a distinct issue having to do with the role of philosophers and of philosophical reasoning in the public process of environmental policy formation and implementation. The question to be addressed in this chapter, accordingly, is: What is an environmental ethicist's job in a reasonably well-functioning democracy?

The new fault line has been initially characterized—perhaps this will remain apt after careful scrutiny—as marking a difference between pragmatists and others—but, again, I want to avoid too-quick generalizations before examining the arguments that indicate the true location of the fault line. I therefore start by examining recent plaints that pragmatists are trying to "silence" philosophers. Clarifying these concerns about philosophers' voices may help us to understand the real separations that pull environmental philosophers apart over this particular fault line. These exchanges will illuminate differences in the way professional philosophers view their tasks, and also raise important questions about public discourse in the postmodern age. I hope I am forgiven if I begin this chapter, which is intended to make a more general point about public environmental discourse, by analyzing internecine quarrels among environmental ethicists.

In part I, I address J. Baird Callicott's recent charge that pragmatists—specifically Ben Minteer and I—have undertaken to silence philosophers, because we reject "foundationalism."[1] Here, I explore a key ambiguity in foundationalism—in an effort to better understand Callicott's idea of the role of philosophers in the search for improved environmental policies. In part II, I explain why Minteer and I, besides rejecting strong, epistemological foundationalism as philosophically unsupportable, also see claims of foundational knowledge by philosophers as dangerous for democracy and democratic discourse, by illustrating the role that strong epistemological foundationalism can play in antidemocratic arguments such as those of Laura Westra. Finally, in part 3, I suggest a more pragmatic approach to environmental philosophy, an approach that claims no special privilege for philosophical discourse, but that emphasizes the analysis of procedural fairness in a pluralistic society of equals. This approach, which has been called "discourse ethics" by European pragmatists such as Jürgen Habermas, provides a useful starting point for seeking cooperative policy decisions in a diverse democracy.

I. The (Feared) Silence of the Philosophers

J. Baird Callicott has recently argued that pragmatists such as Ben Minteer and I wish to silence philosophers: "Minteer's effort to purge foundationalism from environmental philosophy is, in my opinion, tantamount to an effort to silence philosophers, who play an important role in public, and yes, in democratic debate."[2] Callicott suggests that philosophers will be plunged into silence if they are not allowed to appeal to "foundations," thereby implying that appeal to foundations is essential to philosophers' role in public policy. For example, in criticizing my own views Callicott says that my policy views are either based on some foundation or they are "wholly arbitrary."[3] Since Callicott—and also Holmes Rolston, III—have reacted vehemently to cautions about their insouciant appeals to "foundations," I start by exploring what they mean by this concept and why it is so important to them.

Just prior to the urgent plea for a foundational voice for environmental ethicists just quoted, Callicott says: "According to Minteer, most environmental philosophers, Rolston and I especially, are foundationalists; he of course is not. But these repeated expressions of commitment to democracy and democratic values expose Minteer's foundationalism, which is more insidious and disingenuous because it is cryptic."[4] Apparently Callicott understands "being a foundationalist" as roughly equivalent to "having some basic beliefs to which one would appeal if questioned," for he goes on to argue that everyone, myself included, who offers any arguments or analysis are committed "cryptically?" to a foundation of some sort.

Callicott simply responds to Minteer's criticisms without defining the foundationalism he defends, but we can piece together what he means from a couple of passages in which he describes the activities of philosophers and their contributions to public discourse. First, he explains that foundational thinking is essential to what philosophers have been doing for 2,500 years. He describes philosophers as having "constructed great systems of thought integrating an epistemology, ontology, ethics and politics in a coherent whole." He acknowledges that these systems, "denying, as many of them did, the full reality of the world as most of their contemporaries experienced it," were considered "weird," and "few, including the philosophers themselves, ever took such intellectual constructs seriously enough to base public policy on them." The value of these systems, rather, "was to subtly undermine conventional ideas," by presenting an alternative to the accepted point of view in the society.[5]

Callicott then mentions a second traditional role for philosophers, which is to articulate "at-first-bizarre" ideas that are beginning to emerge in the culture. Philosophers serve as midwives to new ideas that have worked their way into the community and may eventually transform it. Here, Callicott refers to his nonanthropocentrism as an illustration. "Today the Western Weltanschauung is being colonised by ideas that were first articulated by (frankly) foundational environmental philosophers." Articulated, he says, but not invented: philosophical midwives merely "bring to light ideas that are gestating in some mysterious way in the dialectic of cultural discourse," and in this case, foundationalists are on the verge of once more transforming society by articulating the "idea that nature has intrinsic value."[6]

These traditional explorations are apparently what Callicott understands as foundationalism: "philosophers expose the conceptual foundations of conventional assumptions. Some do so straightforwardly by asserting conventional assumptions—universal human rights, for example—and providing foundational justifications for them," while others assert unconventional positions and provide foundations for them.[7] This explanation, however, leaves crucially ambiguous what Callicott claims, epistemologically, for foundations and this ambiguity in turn leaves unclear what contribution philosophers can make to public policy discourse. Given the modest claims Callicott makes for philosophical midwives, it appears that philosophers' main task is to examine emerging worldviews, to clarify their structure, and to identify "basic" principles that support that structure—what formalists might call "axiomatizing" the system by identifying core beliefs and separating these from "theorems" that follow from the axioms by inference. Since some people in the culture already believe these ideas, the philosopher need take no role in *justifying* either the principles or the axioms—this explicative activity merely helps nonphilosophers to better understand what they already believe.

What is surprising, terminologically, is that Callicott treats these modest activities of philosophical "midwives" as somehow dependent on "foundationalism," a term usually taken by philosophers to refer to a particular—and highly controversial—theoretical position in epistemology. It is therefore surprising also to learn that cautions regarding enthusiastic endorsements of foundationalism by environmental ethicists actually conceal a nefarious plot by pragmatists to "privilege their own cryptic foundational beliefs and forestall any critical discussion of them or the proposal and justification of any alternatives." Whew! Did we really do all that? A more calm reading of the situation might call for a bit of clarity about what, exactly, is meant by "foundationalism," since—according to Callicott—even antifoundationalists must necessarily be foundationalists, and liars to boot! What has gone wrong here? To put the point simply, those of us who have criticized foundationalism in environmental ethics mean something much narrower, and something with much more epistemological bite than the kind of "let-me-articulate-my-culture's-emerging-ideas" method that Callicott finds essential. A brief historical look at the idea of foundationalism will clarify this difference.

Foundationalism, most basically, is the belief that knowledge has a two-tier structure in which some beliefs are supported without inference and others are justified by inference from these noninferential beliefs.[8] Typically, this question is raised in the context of theories of epistemological justification; the nature of justification has of course been a central issue in the history of modern philosophy and modernism more generally. Advocacy and criticism of foundationalism has centered on two issues: (1) What is the nature of foundational beliefs, and what gives them epistemological authority? and (2) What is the nature of inferences that are sufficient to transfer that authority from foundational beliefs to inferential ones?

According to Descartes, one could embrace modern science and the scientific method, and at the same time avoid the religious heresy of doubting God's fairness—if and only if we have unquestionable reasons to believe in the evidence of our senses. God could not, he reasoned, have held human spirits responsible for choosing between good and evil actions in the physical world, unless the senses are capable of transferring reliable knowledge about that world to mental substance. What was distinctive about Descartes's account of reliable knowledge was that he insisted that our beliefs—to be supported at all—must be supported *by deduction* from a *self-evident base*, from an a priori, reason-based "foundation." Here, we have an example of what could be called "strong epistemological foundationalism," the view that true knowledge must be certain knowledge and certainty can only be obtained if its foundations are indubitable/self-evident and all inferences from these foundational beliefs are by deduction.

From this starting point, modern epistemology became a battleground between "foundationalist" believers and skeptics. Initially, the battle lines formed across the English Channel, and the main issue was the *source* of the foundational knowledge base. In this early period of modernism, the battle was not over *whether* there are foundations for certain knowledge but *which* foundation—reason and intuition or the evidence of the senses—should be adopted as "THE" foundation of knowledge. Locke, no less than Descartes, was committed to a rational reconstruction of the everyday beliefs on which we base action; he merely proposed to rebuild Descartes's edifice of knowledge on sensory input rather than a priori principles. Only with Hume, the implacable skeptic and coldly consistent empiricist, did it become clear that empiricist foundations could not support the Cartesian edifice of certainty about everyday beliefs on a foundation of sense experience. Since the empiricists had thoroughly rejected innate ideas and rational intuition as the basis for our knowledge of the world, Hume's skeptical conclusion seemed unavoidable.

Immanuel Kant, however, responded that, while skepticism seemed unavoidable if knowledge were built up from bits of sensation, "transcendental arguments" could reestablish the primacy of reason and banish skepticism. Kant took it that certain knowledge is possible and necessary, and then asked: what would be required to support such knowledge? His answer included his famous "categories"—the foundations of order and reason that were understood to be implicit in the very structure of knowledge itself. While Kant's brilliant analysis changed philosophy forever, turning epistemological analysis inward and seeking the foundation of objective certainty in the subjective acts of knowers, his analysis did not resolve the deepest problems of Cartesian rationalism—its difficulties in claiming self-evident knowledge and the iron-clad connection Descartes saw between epistemological uncertainty and moral chaos.

Eventually, Kant's subjectivist turn became a linguistic turn and, languages being highly varied and idiosyncratic, the grand, rationalist strategy of Kant was reduced to empirical exercises in linguistic anthropology. Empirically derived categories would, of course, be unacceptable to Kant, who demanded that the categories be derivable from reason in order for them to be interpreted as "necessary and universal." Treating the Kantian categories as relative to culture and based on anthropological observation represents the final, if protracted, death of Cartesian rationalism and a priori epistemological foundationalism.

Once rationalist foundationalism proved untenable, twentieth-century analytic philosophers, especially the logical atomists and logical positivists, experimented with various reconstructions of our knowledge by reduction of complex beliefs to logico-linguistic constructs built from "observation sentences" or "sense data" reports, treating the latter as unquestionable starting points for rebuilding our knowledge. So far, all of these attempts have failed to provide a convincing linguistic reduction of common beliefs to directly observable, foundational bits of experience. While some philosophers continue to struggle to articulate an empirically based foundational position, most contemporary analytic philosophers, following Willard Van Orman Quine and Wilfred Sellars, have concluded that it is impossible to use sense data reports as incorrigible bases to arrive at unquestionable inferences about the external world.[9] It is worth surveying these complex arguments briefly, because they place a heavy burden of proof on any contemporary epistemological foundationalism.

Responding to linguistic versions of foundationalism favored by logical positivists, who proposed various definitional/logical reductions of beliefs to "incorrigible" observations, Quine argued that there is no sharp distinction between sentences that are true by virtue of the "meaning" of words and sentences that are validated by experience alone. Second, Quine argued that attempts at logical reduction to empirical foundations were, similarly, unable to yield noninferential truths with warrant that is transferable across languages.[10] Having argued that it is impossible to separate an observational component in our belief systems from the logical and semantic relations of the linguistic system, Quine persuasively established that the goal of empiricist foundationalism was a pipe dream—one can extract necessity and universality from language only if the world presents itself as necessarily organized, prelinguistically, into objects and natural kinds. But that form of necessity, what Quine called "essentialism," cannot be established by experience.

Quine, following pragmatists and citing them explicitly, took essentialism to be dead. Languages are systems of conventions and the "ontologies" so created are internal to the interpretation of that system of meanings and beliefs.[11] Corrections in our belief system cannot involve the simple substitution of a true for a false belief, taken independently. In fact, since experience sometimes causes us to change the categories and meanings of our terms (when, for example, scientists changed from defining whales as fish to defining whales as mammals on the basis of physiological observations and changes in taxonomic systems), empiricism can place no ultimate *epistemological* weight on analyticity of sentences or meanings of words. This conclusion led pragmatists to embrace conventionalism (the view that languages are best understood as tools, created consciously or unconsciously for the purpose of real-world communication). Language does not *picture* reality in a representational sense; it *reflects* reality, but only through the mirror of our language, as our observations are shaped by the words we choose to express them.

What is important to realize, however, is that Quine did not give up empiricism as the touchstone of knowledge, or as a corrective to inadequate beliefs—nor did he give up on experience-based objectivity for our knowledge. Once one renounces essentialism, which appeals clandestinely and illegitimately to prelinguistic necessity in the real world, Quine argued, we need not fall into skepticism because the conventionalist can still claim to learn from experience by comparing our entire belief system to expected observations. Experience will eventually "correct" our belief system, provided we are open to it, and are open to linguistic innovations as well as to new experience. Quine, thus, advocates a form of "holistic empiricism," whereby experience can (eventually) force us to change our views as to what is true, but it cannot dictate what the correct view is.[12] This limited form of objectivity, pragmatists find, is adequate to fend off subjectivity and skepticism, but it leads away from foundationalism and toward a holistic process carried on by a community of truth seekers. The idea of community is key, since being a member of a communicative community exposes our beliefs to new experiences as we must engage in discourse with others, who see the world from a different perspective.

The best way to explain this pragmatist alternative to foundationalism and skepticism remains a clever analogy, due to the sociologist, Otto Neurath, in the 1920s.[13] Neurath likened our total belief system to a ship which, for whatever reason, may never leave the water for dry dock. It would be possible, Neurath notes, for the crew to repair parts of the ship, one or a few at a time, replacing each plank as it weakens with age or rot, standing on strong planks in order to execute repairs. In this way, given enough time and enough repairs, the ship might gradually be entirely replaced, board by board. Such changes might not be one-for-one exchanges of parts as problem areas are more radically redesigned during repairs, so that the "same" ship remains afloat, and might even be "improved," even as it is continually used. The ship as a whole remains afloat as long as a significant portion of the planks are, at any given time, deemed solid enough for now, and can support the crew and allow repairs in weak areas. By analogy, Neurath argued, one can avoid skepticism if one believes that experience can gradually force the modification of each one of our beliefs. On this view, there is no fixed set of beliefs, no "foundation" or "intellectual dry dock," that is itself "solid" and indubitable. We must rely on consensual acceptance, in particular problematic situations, of some beliefs shared by participants as an adequate basis for experimentation and improvement of beliefs in remaining areas of doubt and disagreement. This approach allows progress in improving the entire set of our beliefs, without relying on self-evident truths.

The key to Quine's argument against empirical foundationalism is the recognition that all observation by humans—if it is to function within a complex system of meanings and inferences within any communicative language—is to some degree theory bound. It cannot, then, serve as a "foundational" (noninferentially known) base for those beliefs, because it requires some of those beliefs for its own meaning and justification. The lesson of modern philosophy, in a nutshell, has been that essentialism, the view that the world consists of prelinguistically existing individuals and natural kinds, is unsupportable; when essentialism became untenable, the claims of strong, epistemological foundationalism, which relied upon appeal to a priori access to prelinguistic truth, likewise became untenable. Attempts to reestablish necessity by appeal to linguistic form or semantic relations could not overcome the variability of language and apparent inseparability of what one senses from the way one talks about it.

I find these arguments persuasive; I do not know if Callicott does. If he does not, this chapter is not the place to take up the issue, for my point is not that foundationalism is necessarily false, but only that anyone who undertakes to defend a strong, categorical foundationalism, claiming that our assertions can be derived from a noninferential and prelinguistic knowledge base, must somehow answer these, as yet unanswered, criticisms. Alternatively, one can accept conventionalism about objects and categories, and recognize that the basic principles/foundations of any belief system are relative to the conceptualizations that constitute that system. If one accepts the conventionalist alternative, however, one must, on pain of inconsistency, give up claims to the presystematic "truth" or universal "objectivity" of any given set of such foundational principles.

On this nonessentialist interpretation of the relationship between "ontology" and language, ontology—the choice of which objects to make our basic theoretical entities— is relative to language and to the purpose for which a language is developed or chosen. To go from the fact that some people speak of "intrinsic value in nature" to the conclusion that "nature has intrinsic value," would be impossible. An ontology supported in this way is simply a figment of a language which is used in some particular cultural context, hardly the basis for cross-cultural and robust arguments that we should, for example, stop feeding people and protect ecosystems.

It is now possible to explain why I find Callicott's championing of foundationalism so surprising. Given its history in the wars against skepticism throughout the modern period, it is natural to interpret Callicott's endorsement of foundations as a strong, epistemological position that will allow deduction of unquestionable conclusions about the way things are and what ought to be done about it from some self-evident premises that are unavoidable by all rational beings. Here, then, is the crucial decision point for Callicott the foundationalist. Does he endorse and defend strong epistemological foundationalism (which would be the most normal and reasonable interpretation of his remarks that foundationalism is essential to philosophical reasoning)? Or, does he mean to introduce an alternative to the traditional meaning, and defend a less universalistic and less absolutist version of foundationalism?

Remember that the definition of foundationalism in a philosophical dictionary stressed the "two-tier" nature of knowledge as the defining mark of foundationalism. Historically, we noted, the "foundation" of knowledge was argued to be knowable a priori and the foundations were assumed to be self-evidently knowable and universally applicable across cultures and linguistic barriers. As rationalism became more and more difficult to defend, logical empiricists and others have experimented with atoms of sensation as the foundations of absolute and certain knowledge, as complex and less immediate everyday beliefs were construed as logical "constructs" out of sensory atoms. As noted, however, this route to certain knowledge through empiricist means was apparently blocked by Quine's argument that, while the categories of our logic and language can imbue nature with a structure, such structures depend on the language chosen; linguistic forms reveal not essences that might anchor thought to a prelinguistic reality beyond language and our linguistic characterization of it. And so Callicott's confident endorsement of foundationalism, which, if it commits him to anything, commits him to the separation of belief and knowledge systems into two "tiers" with different epistemological status, teeters on this ambiguity regarding the epistemological status of those claims located in the foundational tier. The ambiguity can be dramatized in the following two choices, with one of the choices allowing two versions:

CHOICE 1: STRONG EPISTEMOLOGICAL FOUNDATIONALISM

Version 1A: Rationalist Foundationalism

Elements of the foundational tier of knowledge that support inference to second-tier (inferred) knowledge are knowable without experiential evidence—they are self-evident and knowable a priori. Foundational truths, on this version of strong epistemological foundationalism, are necessary and presuppositionless, and need not be relativized to a particular culture or worldview; they are objectively and universally true for all rational beings.

Version 1B: Experience-Based
(Positivist) Epistemological Foundationalism

The foundational tier of knowledge is composed of pretheoretical, prelinguistic, and presuppositionless units of sensory experience. On this view, most of our everyday beliefs are (at least in principle) verifiable by reference to these foundational units of experience, which are to be combined through linguistic and logical rules, and allow the in-principle derivation of complex beliefs from those experiential units plus recursive applications of symbolic logic.

CHOICE 2: EXPLICATIVE FOUNDATIONALISM

This choice retains the idea that belief and knowledge systems have a two-tier structure and that, in any such system, there will be "basic" beliefs that function to justify and support less basic beliefs, but explicative foundationalism differs from strong epistemological foundationalism in dropping the claim that foundational truths are necessary, certain, or incorrigible in any general, system-independent sense. This weaker form of foundationalism endorses the view that, for any system of beliefs, it is possible to identify some set of basic beliefs or principles that are not themselves to be justified within the system. The special role of foundations cannot be that they are epistemologically privileged and presuppositionless; the claim for them, apparently, is the psychological one that advocates of the system in question do not, in fact, provide justifications for these beliefs, but use them as starting points in justifications for nonfoundational beliefs. This means that the foundational beliefs cannot be supported within the system. Unlike the two versions of strong epistemological foundationalism, explicative foundationalism makes no claims to the universality of foundational beliefs and principles. Identifying foundations is simply to reveal the structure of a belief system and to suggest the proper flow of argumentation within the system. Asserting that some belief or principle is foundational in this sense is to make a psychological statement about the thought processes of a group of people who endorse a belief system or a worldview. The explication of foundations, therefore, provides no reason for anyone who does not already accept the foundational belief in question to accept it.

While it is not my place to make the decision for him, neither of Callicott's choices seem very attractive. If Callicott chooses to defend strong epistemological foundationalism, he faces formidable epistemological obstacles, obstacles that have caused pragmatists and many others to call into question both the possibility and the necessity of such strong knowledge as the basis of right action. If Callicott opts for either of the versions of the first choice, I will simply sit back and request arguments to show how such a bold move can avoid hitherto unanswered skeptical questions.

If one judges from Callicott's previous publications, one would expect him to endorse the second choice—indeed, strong epistemological foundationalism would be completely out of intellectual character. For example, in his "deconstruction" of Rolston's concept of intrinsic value—which seems to exemplify one or both of the versions of strong epistemological foundationalism—Callicott criticizes Rolston for not questioning the Cartesian dichotomy between subject and object and for going "the whole nine yards and [putting] a free-standing natural being's state of motion *and* intrinsic value in space and time, on the objective side of the Cartesian schism, and its color in a perceiver's sensorium, on the subjective side!"[14] In contrast, he insists that intrinsic valuation also requires a valuer, and hence intrinsic value for Callicott is relational—it emerges from a relationship between an observer and an object. Accordingly, intrinsic value has no reality outside the system of assumptions adopted by the nonanthropocentrist because: "The act of observing changes the observed phenomena; to know nature—at least at the sub-atomic level—is to affect it, to participate in shaping its being."[15] From this and other textual evidence, one would infer that Callicott intends to defend only explicative foundationalism and that he rejects epistemological absolutism based either on necessary, a priori truths or on appeals to presuppositionless observation.

Epistemologically, the difference between explicative and strong epistemological foundationalism is crucial; if environmental ethicists and environmentalists were to endorse strong, epistemological foundationalism, then they would consider themselves armed with universally applicable arguments that can be used to support their positions, both descriptive and practical, because they take the objects and categories of their position to reflect, essentially, the true nature of reality. Their arguments would be *categorically* applicable to all rational beings, because they are based on necessary and universal beginning points, and are derived by deduction. Categorical arguments, then, differ radically from the sorts of arguments that would result from an exercise in explicative foundationalism. Explicative foundationalists can make no claims for the extra-systematic truth of their foundational assertions or for the essentialist nature of categories and individuals—their ontology and their genealogy have validity only within the belief system as it has evolved and has been explicated by its midwives.

The results of an explicative foundational analysis, then, are only hypothetical upon particular starting points and basic commitments. No claim is made for the generality of any foundations explicated from new or emerging frameworks. Explicative foundationalism, in this sense, has no epistemological bite outside the circle of people who believe in the foundational principles of a given, particular belief system or worldview; it simply provides a psychological description of what a group's basic commitments happen to be. Any arguments based on explicated foundations of an emerging worldview provide at best hypothetical arguments about what to do: "if you accept this foundational belief, then you should . . . " Any foundations generated by explication are, then, persuasive only to those people who have already adopted the foundational beliefs of the worldview in question.

This is not of course to say Callicott could not offer *both* hypothetical *and* categorical arguments—hypothetical arguments for those who have already become nonanthropocentrists and more generally applicable categorical arguments to convince the nonbelievers. If he wishes to construct more robust arguments regarding what to do based on new or emerging "foundations," he can argue in ways that will be persuasive to nonbelievers in his emerging worldview. Here, however, Callicott simply faces the problem of foundations at a deeper level. Is there a foundation lying deeper than the basic assumptions of his particular worldview? Is there, after all, an *essential* organization of nature, independent of language, worldview, and culture? So Callicott faces the same choice as above: Will he argue for the foundations of his new worldview by appeal to deeper and more universal foundations? Or, will he concede that his "foundational" explorations have no universal, epistemological warrant, which limits his contribution as a philosopher to mere explication of the views of others?

Again, it is not my intent to argue that Callicott is committed to either of these rather unattractive versions of foundationalism. My point, rather, is that Callicott's invocation of foundationalism as essential to his practice as a philosopher can only be understood and evaluated if he clarifies where he stands on this crucial, historically posed dilemma. If, on the one hand, he claims foundational thinking gives him access to certainty and absolute knowledge, contemporary epistemologists will of course object that he must shore up the implicit claims of essentialism, a task that seems impossible given current arguments. If, on the other hand, he endorses, as he seems to do in his critique of Rolston, a more relational, naturalistic, and open-ended epistemology that eschews claims of certainty and incontrovertibility, Callicott seems thereby to have moved much closer to pragmatists regarding how we know and how we should justify our beliefs. But once one makes this move to a more relational conception of perception and knowing, it's not clear what role the original claim of foundationalism, that knowledge has a "two-tiered" structure, retains. What are called foundations on the explicative view are highly relative to particular belief systems and their internal structure which, in turn, are legitimized only by the psychological appeal of certain basic and unquestioned principles espoused by some members of current society.

To return to the question of whether philosophers who follow pragmatists and forsake the historically popular idea that knowledge has a two-tiered structure, one must clarify what role a philosophical voice might play in deliberating, choosing, and implementing an improved environmental policy. If one adopts a very limited role for philosophers in public policy discussions, that of articulating, explicating, and clarifying worldviews advocated by others, as Callicott suggests, the practice of explicative foundationalism apparently has a very limited epistemological role. To identify a belief as foundational within a system is just to say that that belief is basic and unquestioned by some group of speakers who have accepted these beliefs. Such an identification, while perhaps comforting or even revelatory to individuals who already accept the worldview in question, provides no basis for justifying either the foundational belief or any derivative, inferred belief taken to follow from those foundations. What appears to have happened (assuming for the moment that Callicott is defending only explicative foundationalism) is that Callicott has rejected the epistemological warrant usually thought to be the kernel of foundationalism, while retaining the husk of foundationalism in the form of a two-tier structure. But this husk, once cleared of its epistemological kernel, is mostly worthless if we turn to the real task of environmental policy—to find policies—democratically—that can be supported by stakeholders and participants who may have very different worldviews and belief systems.

What environmental activists *want* from philosophers, of course, are arguments that provide reasons, reasons based on premises for which warranted assertability can be claimed, arguments that will convince judges in endangered species cases, arguments that make sense to sympathetic but wavering members of Congress, and so on. The activist wants, that is, arguments that can reasonably be expected to convince other participants in a rational process of deciding how to manage the environment. Callicott, by limiting philosophers' methods to explicative foundationalism, seems to have abdicated any role for philosophers in convincing participants in the policy process who are not already convinced of the truth of emerging ideas such as the idea that nature has intrinsic value.

Pragmatists have severed the modernists' connection between knowledge and essence, and seek arguments for facts, for values, and for the usefulness of particular concepts, all on the single basis of experience. They have broken free of the dilemma of foundationalism by challenging modernist epistemology, not from a Humean, skeptical viewpoint, but from a Darwinian, evolutionary perspective. Pragmatists seek objectivity, but they do so more holistically, as Quine advocated, rather than by responding inadequately to Cartesian demands for prelinguistic and universal foundations for either morals or knowledge. Pragmatists recognize only a single method, and advocate a unified "logic" based ultimately on experience. The core of this method is a commitment to the corrective effects of broadening experience through communication. There is no special "a priori" method that ensures philosophers, as experts on reason, have some special access to truth. Following Quine, pragmatists recognize that everything we encounter, from immediate sensation to abstract theory, is ultimately based in experience. The world is through-and-through contingent. As noted, this does not mean that there is no advance of knowledge—holistic comparisons of current belief systems with new experiences yield gradual improvement. What is lost is the essentialist idea that truth is correspondence of utterance to priorly existing, sentence-sized "facts" that inhabit a shadowy, prelinguistic world. What is lost also, as Quine recognized, is any claim that philosophy is an independent discipline with its own subject matter.[16] Philosophy occupies the abstract end of a continuum of discussions of more-or-less empirical and contingent claims; philosophy, in a world that countenances only experience and no a priori truths or categories, is continuous with the scientific disciplines, not separate from the sciences.

What, then, are we to make of the claim that pragmatists wish to silence philosophers? First, pragmatists must agree with Callicott that their more limited and holistic approach to comparing our belief systems, in action, with our experiences and the communicated experience of others with different interests and worldviews, leaves no important role for the two-tiered approach of foundationalists. Further, the pragmatic recognition that recognizing only the unified "logic" of experience—and rejection of an epistemological role for a priori reasoning—undermines the claims that philosophers have a *special* role as an overriding voice in public discussion. Philosophers, like other participants, can appeal only to experience.[17] This does not mean philosophers are not important contributors to public discourse—their training and special skills in abstraction and the role of language in thought prepare them to work with experience in ways few other participants can. So philosophers are neither silenced nor devalued on the pragmatist understanding, but philosophers' voices are voices comparable to those of other participants by claiming no special access to "foundations" from which they can derive certain and incorrigible truths not accessible to nonphilosophers. In the next section, I will explain why this more humble understanding of philosophical discourse is important for protecting democracy.

Following Dewey, pragmatists also recognize no sharp dichotomy between fact and value. All assertions must, taken with our other beliefs, stand up to our future experience. In ordinary discourse—where all deliberation about what to do in political contexts must take place—there is no separation of facts from values. We can, by creating specialized languages, purge values from our language; however, such languages, ipso facto, are not rich enough to allow deliberation regarding what to do. In a democratic society, the question of what to do must be a public question. It cannot be resolved by pure science alone, nor can philosophers provide a priori principles for setting and judging values and goals. Pragmatism engages both facts and values within a problematic context, a context in which people with differing values and differing moral and worldview commitments endorse different facts and different models of environmental change. For pragmatists, however, who encounter both science and ethics in the value-laden situations in which real-world interests vie to affect policy, the relevant language cannot be the specialized languages of either a narrow, disciplinary science or of a narrow theory about what is meant by a small subset of the society.[18]

II. Democracy or Environmental Protection?

A number of political philosophers and scientists have questioned whether protection of resources can be achieved by democratic means. Some serious scholarship, and interesting speculation, has centered on the question whether population growth and resource depletion (or failures of sinks for pollution) might become so severe that democratic implementation of environmental policies will become impossible, invoking fears of a future ruled by the iron fist of dictatorship, husbanding resources for the rich, and starving all marginal populations. It is important, however, to distinguish two quite different attitudes present in the literature on the incompatibility of democracy and environmental protection. One group of writers wonders whether democracies will be sufficiently supple to respond to warning signals that resource-producing systems are stretched thin and in danger of collapse; these writers express fear that, at some point in the future, overuse of resources, overpopulation, or environmental degradation will force a choice between resource degradation due to open access and overuse of resources, making democracy untenable *in the future*.[19]

Another, smaller group of scholars, however, goes beyond offering cautions regarding the future. These writers, far from seeing environmental dangers as a threat to democracy, see democracy itself as a threat to environmental values. For example, the philosopher Laura Westra (1998) explicitly argues that "democracy is insufficient to contain or eliminate the repeated threats to which we are exposed."[20] She believes that (a) democracy is necessary, but not sufficient, to protect the integrity of nature, so (b) we should "supplement" democracy with "second-order principles," which are based on a "law of peoples,"[21] and which override any democratic process. According to Westra, her second-order principles—principles she explicitly refers to as "non-negotiable," are to be enforced "even by coercive means."[22] This apparent confusion of the demands of legality with those of morality includes no discussion of who, exactly, should exert the force in defense of this "law of peoples." In practice, one might worry that "supplementing" democracy with unnamed individuals who will coercively enforce their own view of right and justice, overriding democratically formed policies, is a bit like "supplementing" a democratic republic with a führer and storm troopers.

Westra's cavalier dismissal of the hard-won commitment to democracy is supported with an extremely skewed interpretation of the facts. She argues, for example, that "in some sense the plight [of residents of North American cities] is even worse" than the plight of peoples in developing nations under dictatorships. "Democracies are no different," Westra says, "from, say, military regimes or other nondemocratic states in terms of the severity of the environmental threats to which their citizens are exposed, although the threats themselves may be different in different communities."[23] These rash claims flout obvious observational evidence from the Soviet Union and Eastern Europe with regard to dictatorships of the Left. Similar evidence against the environmental benignity of right-wing dictatorships also abounds, witness Nigeria in the 1990s.

In fact, of course, given the evidence, both democrats and antidemocrats must admit that their favored forms of government—democracies usually and dictatorships, apparently, always—have failed miserably in improving environmental policies and protecting environmental assets. The question, then, is: which system is more susceptible to reform and correction? On this point, I think there is no doubt; for all its imperfections, democracy has sustained itself by its ability, often exercised only episodically, to "throw the bums out," and to effect a change in the public and political sphere of action.

This reasoning forces us to choose: we must decide whether we are, first and foremost, environmentalists or, first and foremost, democrats (while admitting its many and varied weaknesses). And there is no point in fooling ourselves, as Westra does, that an environmentalist gestapo would enforce her particular, nonnegotiable view of Right, in a way that is either more humane or more protective of nature's integrity than a democratic government would. We do in fact face a choice. Either we are willing to flout democracy, manipulate political institutions, and turn to coercion when all else fails to achieve nonnegotiable demands, or we can embrace democracy, recognize its weaknesses and accept the undeniable evidence that some democracies are environmentally destructive, at least in the short run, and set out to educate, to improve process, and to strive to improve policy through democratic means. For my part, given these alternatives, I choose democracy. I suppose that most Westerners will agree with me on this point, and I do not expect Westra's strident antidemocratic stance to gain many followers. This extreme position can, however, help us to see the connection between the concern about silencing philosophers and epistemological foundationalism. The dangers of the latter position, I hope, can be more clearly seen when we examine Westra's extreme position and how it relates to democratic discourse.

To see the connection, notice that Westra closes the book discussed above by discussing—in a very positive light—a quotation from Kant:

> But kings or king like peoples which rule themselves under laws of equality should not suffer the class of philosophers to disappear or to be silent, but should let them speak openly. This is indispensable to the business of government.[24]

"The work of philosophers," Westra comments in response, " is viewed [by Kant] as the only possible antidote to that of politicians, who lack moral theories and do not even possess 'the practical science they boast of.'" She goes on to endorse Kant's "plea for the inclusion of philosophers in public policy decisions," while admitting that she lacks Kant's "optimistic view of philosophers in general."[25] So Westra seems to end her book by simply requesting that philosophers be included in the policy process—and who could object to that? Certainly not I—I believe in a completely open policy process, and welcome a variety of voices, from philosophers—even philosophers with National Socialist leanings—to migrant laborers.

Given the passages quoted above, however, one cannot help but think this simple plea for inclusion to be a bit disingenuous; if philosophers are merely to be "involved" in public policy process like everyone else, how does it happen that their "second-order principles" can override democratically derived policies? As her comment on Kant, above, clearly suggests, what "politicians" lack—and what (some?) philosophers can supply—is a correct moral theory from which one can deduce what *must* be done, regardless of the outcome of democratic processes of deliberation and decision making. Her position seems to be that, while not all philosophers ("in general") can be trusted (pace Kant), some philosophers (she and who else?) are in a position to interpret the universal (though admittedly vague) Principle of Integrity and determine which laws it allows to be implemented and which should be overridden.

The most striking aspect of the antidemocratic position is the apparent confidence with which its advocates assert—based upon moral principle and moral reasoning—the superiority of their positions to the outcomes of democratic processes. How can they be so certain of their principles? How can they be so certain of their principle-based policy positions that they will turn to coercion and even violence if legitimate democratic authorities fail to institute the policies they favor? A moment's reflection on these questions makes it apparent that rather strong epistemological premises are necessary to support the view that individuals and small groups, once convinced that a harm is being perpetrated by the policies of a democratically legitimate government, can be justified in using coercive means to override democratic decisions.

Westra can, I believe, claim democracy should be suspended when democratic outcomes fail to protect ecological integrity only if she has some reason to believe that her philosophical beliefs about what is right are more certainly true than the deliberated and aggregated values and viewpoints of "ordinary" participants (nonphilosophers) as they are registered in the political process. I emphasize the certainty aspect of foundations here because the alternative—to claim philosophers and their views have *moral* priority in public decision making—could only be viewed as an unjustified moral claim of privilege for philosophers. If, for example, Westra could claim that her principle of integrity and its moral value follow by deductive steps from indubitable principles (or, perhaps, that it *is itself* an indubitable principle), then she could argue as follows: "Since the policy I think we should follow is a deductive consequence of an indubitable principle, I cannot be wrong in advocating my policy. Because other participants have arrived at their viewpoints by calculating their self-interest or by appealing to nonphilosophical principles, the outcome of the public process is clearly flawed, because it conflicts with my indubitable principles. Since I cannot be mistaken in my reasoning, I am justified in countermanding policies that do not accord with my principles."

If one is troubled by the seeming arrogance of this epistemological argument, or troubled by the possibility that different philosophers might appeal to different, and incompatible, principles, consider Westra's alternatives. Either philosophers have some special means to determine morally correct policy outcomes or they don't. If they don't, then it seems obvious that, within a diverse, democratic society in which multiple viewpoints and interests are expressed, philosophers should participate on the same basis as other disciplines and members of the public through speeches, writings, discussion, and advocacy of their views. Their special skills, however, should not trump the ideas and arguments of other participants. If philosophers give their best arguments, and criticize the arguments provided by economists and others, point out how important moral considerations of various sorts are to the decision at hand, and yet they do not prevail, philosophers should accept the outcome, and perhaps go into retreat to reconsider how their arguments can be made more persuasive for the next go-round. On the other hand, if philosophers believe they may override a democratically legitimate decision, then certainty is key.

From this reasoning I draw the following lesson. Fears about philosophers being silenced can be understood in two ways. On the one hand, one can say that philosophers have as much right, certainly, as do any other citizens to contribute actively to public discourse about what to do. On this view, however, philosophers have no special privileges, such as the right to trump democratic outcomes of which they do not approve. In short, philosophers participate, perhaps with distinct viewpoints and skills, in public discourse, but they do so on the same terms as other participants. Let me say unequivocally, with regard to this first understanding, that I strongly endorse the right—indeed the obligation—of philosophers to participate in public deliberation and decision processes on these terms. This follows from a broader commitment to keeping the decision process open to all groups and "voices" in the society. What concerns me, on the other hand, is the fear that philosophers may somehow be excluded or "silenced" in the policy process is too often a smoke screen for the much less defensible view that philosophers, because of some special skill or ability to see the truth, should not only be heard when they express their opinion within the give-and-take of public discourse, and when they vote on candidates and policies as do other participants in a democracy, but also that they should be "heard" in the sense that their voice should be privileged and should override democratic outcomes they do not accept. In my view, this latter form of silence would be, as they say, "golden."

III. An Ethics for Environmental Policy Discourse

The deeper issue that emerges from concerns about the silencing of philosophers—once the confusions about foundationalism have been cleared away—is the question whether philosophers engage in a distinct discourse, an abstract, universal discourse in which one can deduce conclusions about what policies are moral from unquestionable principles or whether philosophical discourse is, or should be, embedded in the maelstrom of policy discourse, asking what to do in problematic, real-world situations. In the latter case, one is less likely to "apply" a universal principle to deduce a conclusion, and more likely to organize a conference where scientists, philosophers, and stakeholders can discuss the goals for a watershed—what I have called "practical" philosophy.[26]

What bothers me is that when philosophers emphasize general, meta-ethical theories, and claim too much for the "foundations" these theories identify, they turn their attention away from policy details and away from efforts to resolve differences by ongoing dialogue and deliberation involving an open public discourse. In the worst case, philosophers carry this elitism to an extreme, claiming special privilege to override, rather than trying to repair, democratic processes. This extreme viewpoint strikes at the very heart of democratic thought by creating a "priesthood" or "kinghood" of philosophers. Accordingly, what I find most objectionable in Westra's antidemocratic stance is her suggestion that her "second-order" principles are "nonnegotiable." To make this claim is to exempt herself (and other philosophers?) from the conventions of public discourse, which demand respect for the viewpoints of others even when they clash with one's own. These conventions require willingness to seek compromise and partial solutions based on consensus in order to achieve cooperative solutions to shared problems.

Elsewhere, I argue that environmental ethicists are missing an opportunity to locate their kind of analysis within the European tradition—deeply affected by the American pragmatists—of "discourse ethics."[27] Discourse ethicists concentrate on the conditions of actual discourse and how these conditions compare to the requirements of an "ideal" discourse, focusing attention on the preconditions of discourse itself, which requires respect for the opinions of others and openness to new ideas and criticisms. These preconditions, the discourse ethicists argue, are essential to modern democratic process, and to the inclusive discourse that would be required if rational individuals were to submit themselves to democratically derived law. As Jürgen Habermas has so insightfully argued, law in modern states must, somewhat paradoxically, have the dual aspects of coercive force and moral legitimacy.[28] Rational individuals, exercising practical reason, will submit to coercion provided only that they believe they had a voice in the determination of law and that, viewed prospectively, the law is legitimate only when the process remains open. Democracy almost always depends on acceptance of outcomes some individuals oppose; and this acceptance—"legitimacy"—depends on the open-ended nature of the legislative and policy process. Citizens can accept the coercion of law if, when new evidence or new arguments are introduced into public discourse, it is in principle possible for the democratic balance to shift the other way, reversing laws and policies that have passed previous tests of public discourse and practical reason. Notice, however, that refusal to negotiate with others with whom one disagrees is to violate a central premise of any speech community that legitimates itself democratically according to those conventions.

I have agreed with Callicott that philosophers have a role in public discourse, but I am not yet clear what Callicott believes that role should be. If I understand him correctly, Callicott describes a hypothetical role for philosophers, allowing them to help advocates strengthen and clarify inferential relationships among their existing beliefs, explaining values already embraced. Philosophers might, also, help out by making new, emerging world-views and theories of ethics more acceptable by rationalizing and clarifying their foundations, and helping in spreading the ideas, although that may well be a very slow, perhaps multigenerational, process. What I do not know is whether Callicott also believes in a truly foundational, distinctively philosophical discourse from which he can derive, by deduction from an indubitable base, arguments that would convince any rational person, even if they have not had a "conversion" to the minority idea that nature has intrinsic value. If he admits that he is making no universal claims for intrinsic value, but only sees them as expressions used to describe the experience of one subset of one culture, or perhaps subsets of many cultures, it seems that his position essentially nullifies any use of intrinsic value as a basis for policies in situations where there are usually many competing claims, a number of competing values, and diverse worldviews represented.

Was Callicott correct in linking pragmatism to his concern about the silencing of philosophers? Yes, at least in one sense. He was correct that, *if* his position is that philosophers should be allowed to appeal to true foundations—in the Cartesian sense, or something resembling this—then pragmatists would oppose him, based on the Quinean arguments summarized above. But he has no need to assert any such strong form of foundationalism in order to assume the duties of midwife to a new worldview, and if Callicott is content, trapped in Humean skepticism, able to advance only hypothetical, explicative arguments, and leaves the epistemology to others, we have no disagreement. No disagreement, except that we pragmatists consider it a tragedy, because we need his contribution to good arguments in controversial situations demanding action today.

If Callicott were to adopt a pragmatist epistemology, and a more pluralistic approach to understanding environmental values as they express themselves in the public process, he could avoid the dilemma of foundationalism. Philosophical pragmatists reject not just epistemological foundationalism, we also reject the Cartesian assumption that justification of actions and policies requires deduction from incorrigible first principles. Whatever Callicott wants to say about intrinsic value can easily be said within a pragmatist epistemology—he is clearly predicting, as Leopold speculated, that references to intrinsic value will emerge as dominant in a new culture, one that gradually eliminates error through experimental science and experimental, adaptive management.[29] If Callicott's intention is to contribute to the policy process, it seems it would be desirable also to develop a practical epistemology, one that works in the trenches, by helping us to improve the arguments available to convince today's participants, who endorse varied viewpoints and approaches to evaluation of environmental change. Rejecting the Cartesian method of justification, pragmatists do not retreat into silence, they work to develop policies that serve multiple social values, including both anthropocentric and nonanthropocentric values.

Pragmatists reject both dogmatism and self-evidence on the one hand, and skepticism about value-based justifications on the other, because they believe that, while there are no necessary truths, more and more varied experience will eventually call into question those false beliefs and inadequate values that people assert and try to apply in real situations. They adopt a Darwinian epistemology according to which knowledge emerges through the constant testing of our beliefs when we put them to the test of guiding action. By analogy to natural selection of adaptive traits, less successful beliefs are gradually winnowed from public belief systems as broader and broader experience—understood as active attempts to apply beliefs to solve concrete problems—drives a cultural evolution of ideas which, while many times faster than genetic evolution, mimics genetic evolution and eliminates unproductive ideas of selection. Further, as we learn to sort out unproductive ideas, it is possible to develop and gradually improve the methods of gathering and storing new information; hence pragmatists express confidence in logic and methodology to improve our ability to marshal experience as it is necessary in problematic situations.[30] On this Darwinian model of knowledge, then, diversity of viewpoints and experience coming from different interest groups is a boon to improved understanding. Pragmatists believe that each of our beliefs must eventually be tested by acting upon it; they believe that diversity of viewpoints and values can, through communication, expand the range of collective experience of the community of truth seekers. Believing in the efficacy of a method based on expanding experience—whether observational, experimental, or by accessing the experience of others through communication—pragmatists believe in the possibility of gradually rooting out error because the method of experience exposes our beliefs to more and broader experience, through communication with people who occupy different roles and who have very different worldviews. The key to avoiding the hopeless dilemma of modernism, of course, is to reject Descartes' unreasonably high demand that all justification must be certain, deducible from self-evident principles, in order to count as good reasons to act in particular situations. The fear of moral chaos as a result of epistemological skepticism, as exemplified by Descartes and Kant, was based on an unreasonable standard—necessity and universality—in the foundations of knowledge.

Conclusion

If the above explanations clear away some of the disagreements between Callicott and pragmatists as based on differences in our usage of the term *foundationalism*, there may be a possibility for a broad rapprochement between Callicott's view from environmental ethics and the somewhat broader, pragmatic approach that seeks a general theory of environmental evaluation as a part of an adaptive management effort. Callicott sees his task as developing and disseminating a new worldview, a process that is ongoing as worldviews clash and change, accommodate, assimilate, and recycle ideas and ideologies. These issues are important in Callicott's work, and I do not deny their eventual importance, nor Callicott's contribution to this ongoing dialogue. But if environmental philosophy is limited to a long-term war against failing assumptions of modernism, where will we find answers to day-to-day decisions about how to manage ecosystems? Identification, and justification of a new basic, abstract philosophical foundation for an evolving worldview, such as Callicott seeks, is a slow, perhaps multigenerational process. What we need is a quick-and-dirty epistemology of environmental action, one that tests abstract ideas in the maelstrom of adaptive environmental management.[31]

One way toward rapprochement between Callicott and pragmatists then, would be to recognize that language is more basically a communicative tool than a pure system of descriptions of the world. On this view it is possible to use many different linguistic tools in different communicative situations, with language being asked to do many tasks besides describing and predicting. In more practical, problem-oriented situations, appeals to intrinsic value in nature have had little effect because these ideas are connected, most directly, to questions of worldview change, psychology, and worldview dynamics, subjects that connect closely to the languages of persuasion, emotion, and motivation. The problem is that, at least so far, advocates of intrinsic value in nature have not provided specific, observable, and measurable goals for nonanthropocentric management. The problem, I believe, occurs at least partly because connections between the concept of intrinsic value and the descriptive languages of management science are at present too loose to use the concept in environmental science.

Perhaps it is wrong to expect a term that finds its natural habitat in the mainly emotive and literary discussion of intellectual change through time to provide guidance in the philosophy of management. The multifarious ideas of intrinsic value theory may, then, prove useful in the long-term discussion of how our culture should evolve, and how our future worldviews will develop as human experience expands; on this view, however, the idea should not be expected to resolve policy differences today, before specific details of emerging worldviews are formed, criticized, and re-formed. Even advocates for the development of a new, nonanthropocentric worldview—recognizing the urgency of the threats and the slowness of worldview change—should accept the need for a more case-based discourse for linking values and policy goals. This discourse would emphasize the activist and practical, problem-oriented aspects of environmental management—as well as the crucial role of values in the management process—but would think of environmental values more in a consensualist mode.

I am encouraged to see that Callicott has now endorsed the convergence hypothesis. This empirical hypothesis states that we should expect, given evolutionary and ecological similarities between humans and other animal species, that what is good for humans—as long as it includes the whole breadth of human values projected over indefinite time—will converge with ecosystem policies to protect wildlife and ecosystems that form their habitat—with what might be called a nonanthropocentric viewpoint. If we agree on this, we are on the same track regarding policy—we should try to achieve a sustainable human society, recognizing that achieving this goal would require also the protection of wildlife and ecosystems. This means we can justify the same policies with multiple premises, therefore widening the political appeal of environmentally sound policies. I could even accept that, once we are headed in the right general direction toward sustainable human culture, that Callicott, by then, having gained more converts to an intrinsic value theory and having clarified the policy demands of intrinsic value theory, may well be able to point out some instances where divergence has occurred and sustainable development is harming nature. Until we achieve policies that are sustainable from a human viewpoint, however, I think we need to concentrate on specifying the empirical conditions that would be required for sustainable living, which requires a practical discourse, not appeals to controversial, "foundational" ideas. Nonanthropocentrism would then become less relevant in immediate policy discussions, even as it retains its possibly central role in the ongoing, long-term, and parallel discussion of cultural change, especially in post-modern, western societies.

What I am suggesting is a form of intellectual "zoning," which recognizes that, while some regions of intellectual discourse are tightly tied to observation and to empirical disciplines, other regions are related more closely to poetry, literature, and worldview examination. The empiricist zone of discourse is most relevant to immediate problems of what to do in the face of real and observable environmental problems; the more emotive realm of discourse, often removed from any base in today's science, addresses our relation to nature as it unfolds over generations of human culture. One might even say that these two zones of discourse change at very different temporal scales. If we adopt this zoned view of the problems of environmental philosophy, pragmatist epistemology seems to me to be well suited to serve as a philosophy of environmental science and management, while intrinsic value theory finds its role in speculative, emotive discussions about the possibility and desirability of certain worldview changes. It may therefore turn out that philosophers can have a greater and more effective voice if they accept, at least temporarily, that there are multiple discourses within environmental ethics, discourses that "connect," semantically and thematically, to different zones of intellectual and public discourse. In this case, discourse about what to do, given the best available science, seems quite disconnected from the zone of discourse that examines possible worldview changes. Indeed, they seem to be discourses that are engaged with a different scale of cultural time. But herein lies the opportunity for rapprochement between pragmatists and intrinsic value theorists (provided the latter abandon strong epistemological foundationalism); questions of long-term changes in worldviews and guiding principles can be thought of as inhabiting a zone of discourse that is more connected to literature and psychology. Pragmatic philosophy of the environment, on the other hand, occupies that zone of discourse where science, values, and policy quandaries all intersect within the context in which policy choices must be made.

Notes

1. J. Baird Callicott, "Silencing Philosophers: Minteer and the Foundations of Anti-Foundationalism," *Environmental Values* 8, no. 4 (November 1990): 499–516.

2. Ibid., 511.

3. Ibid., 509.

4. Ibid., 510.

5. Ibid., 513.

6. Ibid.

7. Ibid., 511.

8. P. K. Moser, "Foundationalism," in *The Cambridge Dictionary of Philosophy*, ed. Robert Audi (Cambridge, U.K.; Cambridge University Press, 1995), 276–78.

9. Willard Van Orman Quine, "Two Dogmas of Empiricism," in *From a Logical Point of View* (New York: Harper and Row, 1963), 20–46; and Wilfred Sellars, "Empiricism and the Philosophy of Mind," in *Minnesota Studies in the Philosophy of Science* 1 (Minneapolis: University of Minnesota Press, 1956).

10. Quine, "Two Dogmas."

11. Rudolf Carnap, "Empiricism, Semantics, and Ontology," supplement to Carnap, *Meaning and Necessity* (Chicago: University of Chicago Press, 1956), 205–21; and Sellars, "Empiricism and Philosophy."

12. Quine, "Two Dogmas"; also see Willard Van Orman Quine, *Ontological Relativity and Other Essays* (New York: Columbia University Press, 1969).

13. Neurath's example is mentioned by Quine, *From a Logical Point of View*, 79, and discussed in W. V. Quine, *Word and Object* (Cambridge, Mass.: Cambridge University Press, 1960), 3f.

14. J. Baird Callicott, "Rolston on Intrinsic Value: A Deconstruction," *Environmental Ethics* 14, no. 2 (summer, 1992): 129–43 (quotation from 140).

15. Callicott, "Rolston on Intrinsic Value," 139.

16. Quine, "Epistemology Naturalized," in *Ontological Relativity*.

17. Ibid.

18. S. Funtcowicz and J. Ravetz, "Science for the Post-Normal Age," in *Perspectives on Ecological Integrity*, ed. Laura Westra (Dordrecht, The Netherlands: Kluwer, 1995), 146–61.

19. Bruce Hannon, "World Shogun," *Journal of Social and Biological Structures* 8 (1985): 329–41; Robert Heilbroner, *An Inquiry into the Human Prospect* (New York: Norton, 1974); William Ophuls, *Ecology and the Politics of Scarcity: A Prologue to a Political Theory of the Steady State* (San Francisco: Freeman, 1977; William Ophuls, *The Politics of Scarcity Revisited: The Unraveling of the American Dream* (New York: Freeman, 1992); D. Ludwig, R. Hilburn, and C. Walters, "Uncertainty, Resource Exploitation, and Conservation: Lessons from History," *Science* 260 (April 2, 1993): 17–19.

20. Laura Westra, *Living in Integrity: A Global Ethic to Restore a Fragmented Earth* (Lanham, Md.: Rowman & Littlefield, 1998), 57; also see Garrett Hardin, "Who Shall Care for Posterity?" in L. Pojman, *Environmental Ethics: Readings in Theory and Application*, 3d ed. (Belmont, Calif.: Wadsworth, 2001), 278–83. Hardin takes a hard line, especially with less-developed countries. He argues that it has always been privileged minorities who save and preserve for the future: "Well-fed soldiers acting egoistically (to preserve their institutional right to be well fed) can protect posterity's interests against the egoistic demands of today's hungry people. It is not superior morality that is most likely to serve posterity but an institutional design that makes wise use of special privilege" (282).

21. Westra, "Living," 68.

22. Ibid., 72.

23. Ibid.

24. Quoted from Kant, *Perpeptual Peace*, appendix I, by Westra, in "Living," 255.

25. Ibid., 255.

26. Bryan Norton, "Applied Philosophy vs. Practical Philosophy: Toward an Environmental Policy Integrated According to Scale," in *Environmental Policy and Environmental Activism*, ed. D. E. Marietta and L. Embree (Lanham, Md.: Rowman & Littlefield, 1995).

27. Bryan Norton, *Constructing Sustainability* (in preparation).

28. Jürgen Habermas, *Between Facts and Norms: Contributions to a Discourse Theory of Law and Democracy*, trans. W. Rehg (Cambridge, Mass.: MIT Press, 1988).

29. See Bryan Norton, "Leopold as Practical Moralist and Pragmatic Policy Analyst," in *The Essential Aldo Leopold: Quotations and Commentaries*, ed. C. Meine and R. L. Knight (Madison: University of Wisconsin Press, 1999).

30. Bryan Norton, "A Pragmatist Epistemology for Adaptive Management," in *Bioethics and Pragmatism*, ed. Jozef Keulartz, Michiel Korthals, Maartje Schermer, and Tsalling Swierstra (Dordrecht, Netherlands: Kluwer, forthcoming).

31. Bryan Norton, "Pragmatism, Adaptive Management, and Sustainability," *Environmental Values* 8 (1999): 451–66.

CHAPTER 2

Deweyan Democracy and Environmental Ethics

Ben A. Minteer

Justifying Democracy in Environmental Ethics

Are environmental philosophers' "claims of nature" undemocratic? This question was on my mind a few years ago when I was writing a paper.[1] In the article, I criticized several of my fellow environmental ethicists, specifically, J. Baird Callicott, Holmes Rolston, and Eric Katz, for engaging in what I suggested were democratically objectionable philosophical arguments in support of their normative environmental projects. My intent was to start what I thought was a necessary conversation about the relationship between the practice and mission of environmental ethics and broader democratic values and commitments. In their rebuttals, however, Rolston and Callicott were very skeptical of my advocacy of a democratic pragmatism in constructing and justifying environmental ethical claims and policy arguments. Rolston, for his part, challenged me to demonstrate how such a pragmatic approach to environmental values could account for the "moral considerability" of nonhuman nature.[2] This is certainly an important question, even if I believe it has been overemphasized in the field's discourse at the expense of more significant conversations. In an effort to clarify my thinking on this matter, and as a partial response to Rolston's judgment that pragmatic approaches to environmental valuation are necessarily committed to the flimsiest forms of instrumentalism, I recently put forth an argument for a reconstructed notion of intrinsic value along pragmatic lines; an argument that I believe is consistent with John Dewey's contextual approach to moral deliberation.[3]

Callicott, in a later reply to my paper, also issued an intriguing challenge, one that I believe touches on a more significant issue than the normative question posed by Rolston. Specifically, in his rebuttal Callicott objected to the fact that, despite my paper's call for a more democratic temperament in environmental ethical argument, I offered no reasons "for a commitment to democracy."[4] Moreover, he thought that my motivations for seeking to place such considerations front and center in environmental ethics were "cryptic," and therefore "insidious" and ironically *un*democratic, given the context. "Minteer assumes," Callicott wrote with a noticeable skepticism, "that democracy and democratic values are unquestionably good things, but in pretending to eschew foundations, he slyly puts the foundations of democracy and democratic values beyond discussion and debate."[5]

I take Callicott's remarks here as a provocative request for me to offer some sort of *justification* for a commitment to democratic values and practices—that is, a global philosophical claim from which democratic principles and institutions like freedom of speech, thought, self-determination, and so on may be deduced with total certainty. Indeed, as his remarks here and elsewhere suggest, Callicott appears to be looking for me to provide a general metaphysical argument—that is, one about the essence of human nature, or the existence of certain natural rights—that may be evoked to support our intuitive, shared understanding of democratic principles and institutions. Unfortunately, I do not think there is a convincing and coherent philosophical defense of democracy to be made along these lines. But this is a modest concession and should not frighten democrats—in environmental ethics or elsewhere—into abandoning our principles because they lack a metaphysical, "valid-in-all-possible-worlds" justification. It does nothing to warrant skepticism toward democracy; nor does it call into question the particular status and legitimacy of democratic values and practices in environmental ethics. Rather, I would suggest that it only challenges the presupposition that such metaphysical claims are in fact *necessary* to the justification of democratic values and decision making (and democratic environmentalism) in the first place.

Thankfully, metaphysical founding is not the only way to go about justifying democracy as a shared experience, or a "way of life" as John Dewey so memorably put it. One alternative strategy, appealing to many of the postmodern persuasion, would be to suggest that our commitment to democratic practices and norms is nothing more than a historically contingent set of attitudes that has, better than any alternative, allowed us to "cope" with social existence in the modern era. On this reading, democratic values and principles rest upon nothing more than constructed cultural conventions (especially, linguistic practices) and the "social hopes" of individuals qua democratic citizens. This is, of course, the sort of strong antifoundationalist move preferred by "neopragmatists" such as Richard Rorty and Stanley Fish, theorists who wish to completely dispense with the idea that our democratic politics require *any* sort of philosophical justification, especially (but not only) metaphysical "backup." As I will go on to discuss, I am not persuaded by their position, mostly because I do not think that they are consistent with the very pragmatic tradition they rely on in advancing their deconstructive arguments. So if I am to respond to Callicott's challenge to justify a commitment to democracy in environmental ethics, I must turn to something other than this.

What, though, remains if we want to avoid the fruitless search for democracy's metaphysical foundations, yet we find the reduction of democratic commitments to an airy therapeutic vocabulary too close to moral nihilism for comfort? I think there is another path—one perhaps between these two poles—open to us. It would find us looking for the justification of our democratic values and beliefs in something more substantial than Rorty's and Fish's ungrounded linguistic practices, but in something less objectionable than a philosophical foundation posited to exist outside (and prior to) human experience. I believe that this type of support is found in Dewey's pragmatism, though my understanding here is clearly at odds with Rorty's and others' claiming of

Dewey as special kind of radical antifoundationalist *and* radical antiformalist—that is, a pragmatist "without method." In particular, I think that in many places in his work, Dewey offers, among other justifications, a powerful and persuasive *instrumental* (or, more precisely, "logical") defense of democratic commitments and institutions. I would suggest that it is an even more convincing argument in the environmental context, especially to the degree that we are searching (as I believe we should be in environmental ethics) for effective ways to resolve specific environmental disputes and dilemmas.

Before I discuss this justification of democracy found in Dewey, however, I will provide a quick sketch of the recent pragmatic awakening in environmental ethics and claim the special relevance of Dewey's moral and political thought for this movement among environmental philosophers. From there, and as anticipated in my remarks above, I will discuss how the question regarding the political consequences of philosophical pragmatism (focusing on Dewey's project) has created an interesting rift in contemporary pragmatic philosophy—that between, on the one hand, "neopragmatists" such as Rorty and Fish, and, on the other, "paleopragmatists" (to borrow a term from Robert Westbrook), such as James Gouinlock and Hilary Putnam. I do not hesitate to take sides in this debate. As mentioned above, I believe the latter camp has pretty much got Dewey right, and I will attempt to defend this interpretation by providing a short overview of Dewey's instrumentalist theory of inquiry and its connection to democratic values and institutions. With this piece in place, in the final section I will highlight the critical differences between Deweyan democracy as I understand it (and the method of inquiry that supports and is reinforced by it) and the approach to environmental valuation and policy argument commonly taken by environmental ethicists.

Environmental Ethics, Pragmatism, and Dewey

Over the course of its short professional history, environmental ethics has been dominated by various nonanthropocentric positions consumed with identifying and dismantling the "arrogant humanism" of Western ethical attitudes toward the natural world. Early and historically influential papers by Routley and Rolston paved the way for much of the field's subsequent development along these nonanthropocentric lines; in the following decades, sustained normative arguments in monographs by Paul Taylor, Rolston, and Callicott drove this message home to an expanding group of students interested in exploring the moral and metaphysical dimensions of the human–nature relationship.[6] Uniting these approaches was the view that environmental problems were the consequence of a faulty anthropocentric metaphysics and ethics, philosophical failures that needed to be corrected by the adoption of an axiology able to account for the intrinsic value of nature within a biologically or ecologically defined "worldview." One of the more significant conclusions drawn by nonanthropocentrists was that many of the resources of the Western philosophical tradition, hobbled by an exclusivist concern with the "interests" or "moral considerability" of human beings (at the expense of nonhuman nature), were incapable of underwriting sufficiently respectful environmental attitudes and practices, at least in their conventional humanist forms.

Given this context, it is not all that surprising that "environmental pragmatism," whose namesake evokes the "anthropocentric" philosophical tradition represented by Charles Sanders Peirce, William James, and John Dewey, should only now be emerging as a viable alternative to the field's historically dominant nonanthropocentrism. In their important 1996 anthology, environmental philosophers Andrew Light and Eric Katz outlined what they took to be the main tenets of the new pragmatism in environmental ethics. As they understood it, there were roughly four major forms that pragmatic environmental ethics could take in the field:

1. Examinations into classical American philosophical pragmatism and environmental issues;
2. The articulation of practical strategies for bridging gaps among environmental theorists, policy analysts, activists, and the public;
3. Theoretical investigations into the overlapping normative bases of specific environmental organizations and movements, for the purposes of providing grounds for the convergence of activists on policy choices, and among these theoretical debates;
4. General arguments for theoretical and metatheoretical moral pluralism in environmental normative theory.[7]

It is clear that Light and Katz favor a very broad and loose accounting of the commitments that qualify one for membership in this new pragmatic movement. Given the relative youth of the field, not to mention the diversity of the classic American pragmatists' projects, this seems a wise decision. But it also results in some lumping and splitting problems that, to my mind, call into question such a "big tent" understanding of environmental pragmatism. Indeed, a strong case may be made that, of the four forms of pragmatism in environmental ethics offered by Light and Katz, only the first fully deserves the pragmatic label, at least in a robust philosophical sense. The second and third versions might be more appropriately thought of as environmental "coalition building" or political strategies—strategies that may or may not take on pragmatic forms in particular contexts. Similarly, with respect to the last version, a normative or metaethical pluralist need not be a pragmatist in the classical sense. One thinks here of a philosopher like W. D. Ross, whose "prima facie duties," while undeniably pluralistic, were wrapped within a deontological ethical approach that couldn't be more at odds with the experimentalism and moral contextualism of pragmatists like Dewey (and James, for that matter).

I do not wish to impugn Light and Katz's characterization of environmental pragmatism, nor am I looking to devote too much energy to patrolling the camp's semantic boundaries. I would only like to point out that their inclusivist approach must be viewed with a healthy degree of caution. Indeed, we have to look no farther than Katz himself to see how this philosophical ecumenism toward "environmental pragmatism" threatens to blur what should be critical distinctions. Katz's long-standing advocacy of a holistic noanthropocentrism and his commitment to a pronounced metaphysical dualism between nature and human culture—decidedly nonpragmatic convictions, in my opinion—are well known to any who have followed his work in the field over the past two decades.[8] In spite of this, in a recent paper Katz has claimed to be a "metaphilosophical environmental pragmatist," because he now recognizes how anthropocentric principles, argued in certain environmental contexts, can prove effective in promoting rational environmental behaviors and policies.[9] One really wonders if the term *pragmatism* possesses any philosophical punch if it can win the endorsement of so non-pragmatic a theorist as Katz. Of course, Katz can claim to be whatever he wants to be. But those concerned with the integrity of the tradition of Peirce, James, and Dewey might have reason to be more than a little suspicious about such projects conducted in pragmatism's name.

Consequently, I would suggest that if pragmatism in environmental ethics is to develop as a legitimate and philosophically coherent alternative to foundational nonanthropocentrism in the field, it can do no better than to turn directly to Dewey's interpenetrating arguments in ethics, logic, and democratic theory for its philosophical resources. Dewey's reliance upon a common method of inquiry in all areas of experience (including the moral and political), and his linkage of this cooperative activity with democratic culture and society, is a valuable inheritance for environmental pragmatists. I also believe that his focus on the reconstruction of problematic situations—and the practical, problem-solving emphasis running through his philosophical project—provides inspiration for pragmatists wishing to make more lasting contributions to public environmental policy and deliberations over natural resource management. As mentioned above, elsewhere I have discussed how Dewey's value theory and his understanding of the unity of inquiry bring a new dimension to environmental philosophers' debates over "intrinsic value" in nature and its place in environmental policy arguments.[10] In the rest of this chapter, I would like to highlight the general connection between Dewey's democratic thought and his theory of inquiry ("logic," in his own shorthand), a discussion I hope will provide one possible justification for a commitment to democracy in cultural experience. If I am right, there are very powerful reasons to support democratic values and practices, especially in the environmental context, where our ability to resolve the conflicts and conundrums of the human–nature relationship might very well depend on the institutional conditions secured by our democratic commitments.

Pragmatists and Democracy: A House Divided

The ongoing revival of pragmatism in social, philosophical, and legal circles (if *revival* is an appropriate term for a movement that has historically waxed and waned rather than completely disappeared from the Anglo American intellectual scene) owes much to the high-profile efforts of Richard Rorty to elevate Dewey and the pragmatists' intellectual stature in Western philosophy. His somewhat idiosyncratic interpretation of Dewey as a thoroughgoing historicist and radical relativist (though Rorty eschews the latter term), however, has risen more than a few hackles among Dewey scholars. This tension has only been exacerbated by Rorty's unlikely claiming of Dewey as a fellow traveler of "post-Nietzschean" European philosophers such as Heidegger and Wittgenstein, and the French postmodernists Derrida and Foucault. To my mind, though, and as indicated above, one of the most significant objections raised against Rorty and his postmodernist makeover of Dewey is his desire to decouple Dewey's politics—his "re-nascent liberalism" and democractic faith—from his philosophical views, particularly those relating to Dewey's writings on logic and his theory of inquiry. According to Rorty, Dewey never attempted to justify his unflagging commitment to democratic principles and practices—certainly not, at least, in any meaningful philosophical sense. Instead, Rorty suggests that Dewey offered only "inspiring narratives and fuzzy utopias,"[11] a political vocabulary articulating nothing more than a purely conventional "anti-ideological liberalism."[12]

Rorty thus claims that Dewey "saw democracy not as founded upon the nature of man or reason or reality but as a promising *experiment*,"[13] an endeavor whereby Dewey "asks us to put our faith in ourselves—in the utopian hope characteristic of a demo-cratic community—rather than ask for reassurance or backup from outside."[14] Rorty's characterization of democracy as an ungrounded "experiment" is interesting, and I will have more to say about this shortly. For now, though, the significant point to make is that Rorty thinks Dewey's adherence to democratic values and politics has very little to do with his possessing particular *philosophical* beliefs, including not only metaphysical and epistemological claims, but also, as we shall see momentarily, notions about the logical method of experimental inquiry.

Rorty's dismissal of attempts to read Dewey, and pragmatic philosophy more gener-ally, as justifying or entailing a particular political project (democratic or otherwise) is wholeheartedly embraced by the literary theorist Stanley Fish, whose forays into legal and social theory have shown him to be an even more rabid deconstructive neopragmatist than Rorty. In his provocative recent book, *The Trouble With Principle*,[15] Fish cautions us to remember that pragmatists' deep commitment to fallibilism cuts both ways. "If prag-matism points out that its rivals cannot deliver what they promise—once-and-for-all an-swers to always relevant questions," he writes, "pragmatism should itself know enough not to promise anything. If pragmatism is true, it has nothing to say to us; no politics follows from it or is blocked by it; no morality attaches to it or is enjoined by it."[16] As his remarks here suggest, Fish favors a view of pragmatism that emphasizes its radical contingency and antiformalism, and his work vigorously rejects all attempts to found and apply lawlike, al-gorithmic principles to existential situations. Pragmatists, Fish believes, inevitably must slide down a slippery slope to complete epistemic and moral relativism. To his mind this is an unarguably good thing: "Once you start going down the anti-formalist road (with pragmatism or any other form of antifoundationalist thought)," he surmises, "there is no place to stop. Once contextualism is given its head and apparently firm meanings are made to shift and blur whenever a speaker is reimagined or a setting varied, no mecha-nism, not even the reification of context itself, will suffice to put on the breaks."[17] Like Rorty, Fish wants to deny the necessity, as well as the desirability, of having our politics underwritten by theoretical arguments *of any kind,* especially the dreaded "neutral prin-ciples" to which Fish believes the philosophical justification of political and legal practices must ultimately resort. "If democracy has to some extent worked," he concludes, "it is be-cause certain political structures are firmly in place and not because its citizens have in-ternalized the sayings of Emerson, Dewey, and James."[18] Our political experience comes first, and it is composed of only a set of (unjustified) public practices that we happen to have adopted within our liberal culture at a particular time and place.

What may be said of this neopragmatic skepticism toward the relationship between pragmatism and democracy? For starters, Rorty's and Fish's claims appear, at least to many "paleopragmatist" observers (and I count myself among them), to completely miss the core of Dewey's project: his tireless commitment to the logical refinement and practical application of a unified method of inquiry to moral, social, and political life. The philosopher James Gouinlock has made one of the more persuasive and consistent cases for this reading of Dewey's work:

> In Dewey's ideal, experimental inquiry and democratic behavior become fused. The nature of their combination can best be suggested by thinking of them as a union of certain moral and intellectual virtues—with the distinction between moral and intellectual less fixed than it seemed to be for Aristotle. The virtues include a willingness to question, investigate, and learn; a determination to search for clarity in discourse and evidence in argument. There is also a readiness to hear and respect the views of others, to consider alternatives thoroughly and impartially, and to communicate in a like manner in return. One is not irrevocably committed to antecedent conviction but is ready to qualify or change his views as a consequence of inquiry and communication. . . . These might be viewed as the virtues of the experimental inquirer, but they are also virtues in the process of collective moral deliberation. What makes democratic behavior more than free speech and counting votes is that the participants use *scientific intelligence* in determining the nature of their situation and in formulating plans of action, and they are not stuck on foregone conclusions.[19]

This "fusing" of norms of experimental inquiry and democratic practice and the reliance of inquiry on what Gouinlock refers to as "scientific intelligence" are the very moves and commitments Rorty and Fish would like to read out of the pragmatist canon. As we shall see below, Rorty is not at all comfortable with Dewey's attention to and high opinion of scientific method; a hostility doubtless owing to Rorty's strong efforts to de-privilege the epistemic authority of science as producing "special" truths corresponding to an objective, external world. But as we shall also see, Dewey's articulation of method and inquiry avoided this criticism by firmly grounding itself within the practices of concrete human experience.

I believe the textual evidence shows that Dewey was quite clear and consistent about the connection between the method of inquiry (inclusive of, but not reducible to, those forms employed in the natural sciences) and democracy. Consider, for example, the following places (and these are only a smattering of quotes from an overwhelmingly vast corpus of work) where Dewey spoke directly to this connection:

> From *The Public and Its Problems* (1927):
> There can be no public without full publicity with respect to all consequences which concern it. Whatever obstructs and restricts publicity, limits and distorts public opinion and checks and distorts thinking on public affairs. *Without freedom of expression, not even methods of social inquiry can be developed.* For tools can be evolved and perfected only in operation; in application to observing, reporting and organizing actual subject matter; and this application cannot occur save through free and systematic communication.[20]

From "Ethics" (1932):
The alternative method [to dogmatism] may be called experimental. It implies that reflective morality demands observation of particular situations, rather than fixed adherence to *a priori* principles; that free inquiry and freedom of publication and discussion must be encouraged and not merely grudgingly tolerated; that opportunity at different times and places must be given for trying different measures so that their effects may be capable of observation and of comparison with one another. It is, in short, *the method of democracy*, of a positive toleration which amounts to sympathetic regard for the intelligence and personality of others, even if they hold views opposed to ours, and of *scientific inquiry into facts and testing of ideas*.[21]

From *Liberalism and Social Action* (1935):
The method of democracy—insofar as it is that of organized intelligence—is to bring these conflicts [conflicting private and social interests] out into the open where their special claims can be seen and appraised, where they can be discussed and judged in the light of more inclusive interests than are represented by either of them separately.[22]

Democracy has been a fighting faith. When its ideas are *reinforced by those of the scientific method and experimental intelligence*, it cannot be that it is incapable of evoking discipline, ardor and organization.[23]

From "Creative Democracy—The Task Before Us" (1939):
For what is the faith of democracy in the role of consultation, of conference, of persuasion, of discussion, in formation of public opinion, which in the long run is self-corrective, except *faith in the capacity of the intelligence of the common man to respond with commonsense to the free play of facts and ideas which are secured by effective guarantees of free inquiry, free assembly and free communication?*[24]

From *Freedom and Culture* (1939):
It is of the nature of science not so much to tolerate as to welcome diversity of opinion, while it insists that inquiry brings the evidence of observed facts to bear to effect a consensus of conclusions—and even then to hold the conclusion subject to what is ascertained and made public in further new inquiries. I would not claim that any existing democracy has ever made complete or adequate use of scientific method in deciding upon its policies. *But freedom of inquiry, toleration of diverse views, freedom of communication, the distribution of what is found out to every individual as the ultimate intellectual consumer, are involved in the democratic as in the scientific method.*[25]

If Rorty is looking to purge Dewey's thought of any discussion of the relationship between democratic commitments and scientific inquiry, he certainly has his work cut out for him. As these few excerpts show, in Dewey's view democracy and the scientific method significantly overlap; they share a set of common virtues characteristic of properly conducted, controlled inquiry. These virtues—toleration, openness, free communication, a nondogmatic, fallibilist attitude toward held beliefs, and so on—describe the normative constraints of sound scientific investigation. They also describe many of the normative requirements and constraints of democratic deliberation. Indeed, by "securing effective guarantees of free inquiry, free assembly and free communication," democratic institutions and their articulated moral principles provide the experiential matrix in which intelligent, socially organized inquiry and cooperative problem solving can occur.

This need to provide a suitable environment for social inquiry, where "conflicts are brought out into the open"—and which terminates in warranted public knowledge ("which in the long run is self-corrective")—is thus part of the justification for the existence of democratic values and practices: an "instrumentalist" justification of democracy. In a society where public speech and free communication are curtailed or denied, where openness and publicity are replaced by secrecy and the suppression of information, and where the freedom to assemble in the streets and the meeting hall is discouraged or withheld from citizens, there can be no meaningful or effective intelligent inquiry into social problems. As Hilary Putnam has succinctly put it, democracy for Dewey "is not just one form of social life among other workable forms of social life; it is the *precondition for the full application of intelligence to the solution of social problems*."[26] Democratic institutions are justified, in other words, by the "requirements of scientific procedure in general: the unimpeded flow of information and the freedom to offer and to criticize hypotheses."[27] While democracy obviously rests upon additional commitments as well—for example, the moral conviction that individual citizens have a presumptive "right" to contribute to the ongoing shaping of values and goals guiding the community—this instrumentalist/methodological justification plays a major part in Dewey's thinking about the pressing need for basic democratic freedoms and protections. Furthermore, this relationship between democracy and the experimental method of inquiry is a two-way street: the practice of inquiry turns back on and enriches democratic practices and principles by assisting in the effective resolution of politically divisive public problems and dilemmas.

Rorty, not surprisingly, remains unconvinced by such talk. Responding to Gouinlock's argument about the central role of the experimental inquiry in Dewey's writings, Rorty concedes the point, but downplays its significance. "Granted that Dewey never stopped talking about scientific method, I submit that he never had anything very useful to say about it," he quips. Furthermore, Rorty issues a challenge to Gouinlock and his other paleopragmatist opponents on this front: "Those who think I am overstating my case here should, I think, tell us what this thing called 'method'—which is neither a set of rules nor a character trait nor a collection of techniques—is supposed to be."[28] Rorty's remarks here essentially restate the views expressed in his earlier paper, "Pragmatism without Method," where he explicitly spelled out his objection to those claiming the significance of Dewey's theory of inquiry for his philosophical and political thought. As he wrote in that paper, "If one takes the core of pragmatism to be its attempt to replace the notion of true beliefs as representations of "the nature of things" and instead to think of them as successful rule of action," (as Rorty clearly does) "then it becomes easy to recommend an experimental, fallibilist attitude, but hard to isolate a "method" that will embody this attitude."[29]

Rorty is quite correct that Dewey never offered a distinct method encapsulating the experimentalist attitude if by "method" he means an a priori, formal process set down in schematic detail. Such an unwieldy instrument would not have been compatible with Dewey's emphasis on the creative role of deliberation within problematic situations; nor would it, I think, have fit with his elevation of the place of unique contextual considerations within moral and political experience. But if we relax the definition of "experimental method" to refer to something less than a rigid set of formal procedures guiding inquiry—or a collection of specialized techniques—then Dewey clearly has much to say about the method of intelligent inquiry. Moreover, his instructions here are significantly more substantial and rigorous than the modest endorsement of the need for individuals to display "reasonable" and "tolerant" characters in their cooperative problem-solving activities. Dewey devoted his monumental 1938 work, *Logic: The Theory of Inquiry*, to the elaboration of this method and the pattern he believed all successful inquiries assumed. In summary form, this pattern was defined by a progression of operational stages: (1) the formulation of a "problematic situation," or the judgment that a particular "indeterminate" situation—that is, one characterized by a perceived instability or disturbance—requires investigation; (2) the contextual analysis and generation of various action-guiding hypotheses; (3) the reasoning through, rehearsing, and testing of these hypotheses; and (4) the construction of a reflective and terminating judgment resolving the problem at hand (though a terminating judgment still open to revision and replacement in the light of future inquiry).[30]

In arguing that this pattern of inquiry be implemented in social, moral, and political experience, Dewey avoided charges of vulgar "scientism" and positivism by making it clear that he was not suggesting that scientific methods (as employed in the natural sciences) simply be lifted root and branch and transplanted to other realms of human culture:

> When we say that thinking and beliefs should be experimental, not absolutistic, we have then in mind a certain logic of method, not, primarily, the carrying on of experimentation like that of laboratories. Such a logic involves the following factors: First, that those concepts, general principles, theories and dialectical developments which are indispensable to any systematic knowledge be shaped and tested as tools of inquiry. Secondly, that policies and proposals for social action be treated as working hypotheses, not as programs to be rigidly adhered to and executed. They will be experimental in the sense that they will be entertained subject to constant and well-equipped observation of the consequences they entail when acted upon, and subject to ready and flexible revision in light of observed consequences.[31]

The method of inquiry Dewey had in mind was inclusive of science, to be sure, but he saw it also as a general pattern of problem solving to a lesser degree operational in the arts, historical analysis, jurisprudence, and other "nonscientific" domains of experience. Dewey's argument was simply that the method he described worked better than any other in resolving social problems, wherever they occur, and that if the method was authoritative, it was so not because of any "correspondence" to a metaphysically defined reality, but rather because experience had shown it to outperform its rivals:

> We know that some methods of inquiry are better than others in the same way in which we know that some methods of surgery, farming, road-building, navigating or what-not are better than others. It does not follow in any of these

> cases that the "better" methods are ideally perfect, or that they are regulative
> or "normative" because of conformity to some absolute form. They are the
> methods which experience up to the present time shows to be the best meth-
> ods available for achieving certain results, while abstraction of these methods
> does supply a (relative) norm or standard for further undertakings.[32]

So Rorty can be reassured that a reliance on the method of inquiry does not throw us into the fires of foundationalism, representationalism, metaphysical dualism, or any of the other philosophical nightmares that keep him awake at night. For Dewey, the method of inquiry arose from reflective study of *actual* successful inquiries in the arts and sciences and the consideration of their constituent elements and processes, not from some transcendental realm "outside ourselves." It was not a rationalistic instru-ment to reveal the hidden order of the cosmos, nor was it a special philosophical tool to make the universal voice of nature articulate. It was instead an evolving and fallible social process for transforming problematic situations into ones that are more settled and secure. And the continual revision and refinement of this method, guided by in-formal logic and substantively infused with the empirical failures and achievements of particular experiments in social life, kept Dewey's model free from the more objec-tionable formalistic trappings and maintained a significant, if not critical link between reflective activity—thought—and the world of lived experience.

What is curious is that, as his remarks above suggest, Rorty does in fact recognize that Dewey viewed democratic life through the lens of inquiry: "Dewey saw democ-racy not as founded upon the nature of man or reason or reality but as *a promising ex-periment*."[33] But after making this observation, Rorty mistakenly concludes that the "promising experiment" Dewey finds in democracy rests only upon ungrounded "so-cial hope" and his "fuzzy" utopian vision of democratic culture. I think he's missed the heart of Dewey's project. The elaboration and defense of the method of inquiry as ap-propriate to the whole of human experience, including moral and political life, is an unmistakable preoccupation of Dewey's work. While he offered much more than the instrumental justification outlined here, this justification is, I believe, powerful in Dewey's project, despite Rorty's and Fish's postmodernist attempts to expunge it from pragmatic accounts of democratic politics and values.

Dewey and the Claims of Nature

So Dewey reminds us that if effective inquiry into our common social problems is to be realized, we must see to it that the social institutions and practices necessary for un-dertaking this inquiry are put into place and vigorously defended. Democracy, in this reading, is therefore a requirement of the general method of intelligent problem solv-ing and dispute resolution, a method we see most fully expressed in the experimental sciences. Over time, and by its fruits, this method has shown itself to be the best means available for transforming our myriad problems and conflicts in the sciences and tech-nical arts into settled, stable, and secure situations. Dewey thus concludes that the ap-plication of the experimental method to the improvement of the moral and political realms of the human estate is warranted by such past experience. The task, therefore, is for citizens to develop the proper intellectual habits and supporting social conditions capable of promoting this method in all aspects of daily life.

Robyn Eckersley, in her evenhanded critique of the pragmatic approach in environmental philosophy appearing in this volume, suggests that classical and contemporary pragmatists' focus on this activity of problem solving results in a toothless, piecemeal politics incapable of developing a sufficiently radical critique of our social problems, including the environmental predicament. "The greatest weakness of such an orientation [pragmatic problem solving] is that it has a tendency to be conservative, *to take too much as given*, to avoid any critical inquiry into 'the big picture' and to work with rather than against the grain of existing structures and discourses (such as those that are prevalent in real-world liberal democracies)."[34] But this conclusion is challenged by Dewey's own *radical* conception of democracy, his reconstructed liberalism that favored a communal understanding of economic life and politically coordinated social action:

> Liberalism can be true to its ideals only as it takes the course that leads to their attainment. The notion that organized social control of economic forces lies outside of liberalism shows that liberalism is still impeded by remnants of its earlier *laissez faire* phase, with its opposition of society and the individual. The thing which now dampens liberal ardor and paralyzes its efforts is the conception that liberty and development of individuality as ends exclude the separate and competing economic action of individuals as the means to social well-being as the end. We must reverse the perspective and see that socialized economy is the means of free individual development as the end. . . . The attainment of a state of society in which a basis of material security will release the powers of individuals for cultural expression is not the work of a day. But by concentrating upon the task of securing a socialized economy as the ground for and medium for release of the impulses and capacities men agree to call ideal, the now scattered and often conflicting activities of liberals can be brought forth to effective unity.[35]

Dewey is not John Locke; nor is he Adam Smith. Far from an endorsement of "existing structures and discourses," Dewey's project of socialized liberalism requires the planned transformation of productive life to a more "democratic" order; one where each citizen can experience "effective liberty": the positive freedom defined by the institutional encouragement of the growth of our cultural selves in a socially organized manner. Dewey's sharp critique of the metaphysical atomism and methodological individualism of classical liberalism is often overlooked by political theorists, even though the reclamation of his radical democratic credentials has been underway for some time now.[36] Contrary to Eckersley's judgment, Dewey was seriously concerned with the "big picture" of American political economic structures; moreover, his call to fully democratize such structures was a necessary move if the method of social intelligence he advocated could be effectively brought to bear on vexing public problems.

I now return to where I began this chapter: Callicott's challenge to justify democracy. I have attempted to offer just such a defense of democracy; or, more accurately, I have highlighted and endorsed what to my mind is one of Dewey's most compelling arguments in support of democratic values and practices. As mentioned earlier, I believe that this particular, instrumental justification of democracy also holds a special connection to environmental ethical inquiry, or at least my view of how such inquiry should be conducted. Given the empirical evidence supporting the existence of robust public-value pluralism toward the environment,[37] as well as the undeniable complexity and scientific uncertainty surrounding environmental problems, it seems wise to adopt an experimental and fallibilist approach to environmental ethical and policy inquiry. Indeed, the thorny intergenerational normative and empirical aspects of many environmental problems, not to mention the *intra*generational social value conflicts and scientific disagreements playing into discussions surrounding issues like environmental risk assessment, regional and international biodiversity protection, global climate policies, and the like, suggest that we would do well to assume a more explicitly pragmatic attitude toward our environmental goals and polices, as well as the moral claims offered in support of them. I think that there is every reason to believe that the adoption of this attitude will render our institutions and communities more dynamic and therefore more effective and responsive to environmental perturbations. I also believe that it promises to stimulate the kind of social learning necessary for intelligent and adaptive environmental management and problem solving, learning achieved through the practice of collective inquiry and public deliberation over alternative environmental values and policy goals.

It seems, however, that many environmental philosophers do not see moral inquiry and policy choice in these terms. Ethicists like Callicott and Laura Westra, for example, rather than adopting the sort of experimental and provisional attitude toward their normative claims I am advocating here, prefer to cling to a single moral "end" (intrinsic natural value)—an end advanced prior to moral deliberation and cooperative social inquiry—and attempt to anoint it as the *sole* principled ground for defending our environmental decisions policy choices. "One wants to offer the *right reasons* for doing the right thing—as well as to get the right thing done—irrespective of pragmatic considerations," Callicott writes.[38] Westra writes in a similar vein: "Even reaching a right decision on wrong principles may not be sufficient, if the principles are such that they would permit a morally bad decision on another occasion."[39] In their adherence to absolute "right reasons" and "right principles," in the philosophical justification of environmental decisions, philosophers like Callicott and Westra display their commitment to a class of privileged universal ethical claims (roughly, those comprising nonanthropocentric holism), claims advanced as the "correct" moral justifications for all environmental public policies and practices. This almost Kantian preoccupation with purity of moral motivation (which is somewhat surprising for an avowed Humean like Callicott) is, I would suggest, unhelpful for actual environmental problem solving and dispute resolution. In fact, I believe that these results-driven enterprises will politically founder if environmental philosophers are successful in constraining the public debate over environmental policy alternatives to the uniquely authoritative "real reasons" they deduce from their metaphysical arguments about the human "embeddedness" in nature.[40] In rejecting "pragmatic considerations," they and other like-minded environmental philosophers turn their backs on the arguments that have proven historically successful in safeguarding environmental health and integrity—from hunters' support for protective wetland legislation, to recreationists' efforts to defend roadless areas in national forests, to citizens' concerns for the environmental inheritance of their children and grandchildren. An environmental ethics that seeks to de-privilege these and other "pragmatic reasons" for supporting the environmental agenda is one committed to staying on the policy sidelines.

This is regrettable because I think that environmental philosophers can, in fact, make significant contributions to the task of democratic and effective environmental problem solving and policy argument. For example, we can participate in the identification and clarification of public environmental value claims, and help to target ecological indicators that track such values over time and space. We can also help develop and refine better and more inclusive methods of social inquiry and valuation, and work within our communities to help our neighbors identify and articulate coherent and well-integrated social and environmental goals and objectives. When criticism is necessary (and this will be often), philosophers can provide it as politically engaged *citizens*, rather than dogmatic metaphysicians—or worse, environmental philosopher kings. While environmental ethicists may have special skills that will prove useful in specific public policy deliberations (e.g., the ability to make well-reasoned arguments), we do not have a special *knowledge* of the moral and metaphysical "truths" that must govern communities' relationship with their natural and social environments.

In the end, I suspect that environmental philosophers like Callicott and Westra simply see the mission of environmental ethics very differently than I do. They think it is to provide the metaphysical and moral premises that will save us from our political mistakes by philosophically guaranteeing the correct environmental policy agenda. I am wary of such guarantees and think that environmental philosophers should stick to a humbler task: the facilitation of improved methods of inquiry into specific environmental problems and the shoring up of the democratic social institutions that allow these methods to run free in daily life. Callicott thinks that this means I wish to "silence philosophers." I do not. I do, however, wish to make philosophical environmental inquiry more democratically accountable and more experimental—and thus more publicly useful. Otherwise, I fear that, rather than building public coalitions for collectively agreed upon environmental policy goals, environmental ethicists will end up only preaching to our philosophical choirs. That this would be a most regrettable development is a conclusion on which I think all of us in environmental ethics, despite our differences, can agree.

Notes

1. Ben A. Minteer, "No Experience Necessary? Foundationalism and the Retreat from Culture in Environmental Ethics," *Environmental Values* 7 (1998): 338–48.

2. Holmes Rolston III, "Saving Nature, Feeding People, and the Foundations of Ethics," *Environmental Values* 7 (1998): 349–57.

3. Ben A. Minteer, "Intrinsic Value for Pragmatists?" *Environmental Ethics* 23 (2001): 57–75.

4. J. Baird Callicott, "Silencing Philosophers: Minteer and the Foundations of Anti-Foundationalism," *Environmental Values* 8 (1999): 511.

5. Ibid., 512.

6. Richard Routley, "Is There a Need for a New, an Environmental Ethic?" *Proceedings, 15th World Congress of Philosophy* 1 (1973): 205–10; Holmes Rolston III, "Is There an Ecological Ethic?" *Ethics* 85 (1975): 93–109; Paul Taylor, *Respect for Nature* (Princeton, N.J.: Princeton University Press, 1986); Holmes Rolston III, *Environmental Ethics* (Philadelphia: Temple University Press, 1988), and *Conserving Natural Value* (New York: Columbia University Press, 1994); J. Baird Callicott, *In Defense of the Land Ethic* (Albany, N.Y.: SUNY Press, 1989), and *Beyond the Land Ethic* (Albany, N.Y.: SUNY Press, 1999).

7. Andrew Light and Eric Katz, eds., *Environmental Pragmatism* (London: Routledge, 1996), 5.

8. See, for example, the chapters appearing in Eric Katz, *Nature as Subject: Human Obligation and Natural Community* (Lanham, Md.: Rowman & Littlefield, 1998).

9. Eric Katz, "A Pragmatic Reconsideration of Anthropocentrism," *Environmental Ethics* 21 (1999): 377–90.

10. Minteer, "Intrinsic Value for Pragmatists?"

11. Richard Rorty, *Philosophy and Social Hope* (London: Penguin, 1999), 120.

12. Richard Rorty, *Objectivity, Relativism, and Truth* (New York: Cambridge University Press, 1991), 64.

13. Rorty, *Philosophy and Social Hope*, 120, emphasis added.

14. Ibid., 119–20.

15. Stanley Fish, *The Trouble with Principle* (Cambridge, Mass.: Harvard University Press, 1999).

16. Ibid., 295.

17. Ibid., 294.

18. Ibid., 301.

19. James Gouinlock, "What Is the Legacy of Instrumentalism? Rorty's Interpretation of Dewey," in *Rorty & Pragmatism: The Philosopher Responds to His Critics*, ed. H. J. Saatkamp (Nashville, Tenn.: Vanderbilt University Press, 1995), 88, emphasis added.

20. John Dewey, *The Public and Its Problems* (1927; reprint, Athens, Ohio: Swallow Press, 1991), 167, emphasis added.

21. John Dewey, "Ethics," in *The Later Works, 1925–1953*, ed. Jo Ann Boydston, 12 (1932; reprint, Carbondale: Southern Illinois University Press, 1989), 329, emphasis added.

22. John Dewey, *Liberalism and Social Action* (1935; reprint, Amherst, Mass.: Prometheus, 2000), 81, emphasis added.

23. Ibid., 91, emphasis added.

24. John Dewey, "Creative Democracy—The Task before Us," in *The Later Works, 1925–1953*, ed. Jo Ann Boydston, 14 (1939; reprint, Carbondale: Southern Illinois University Press, 1991), 227, emphasis added.

25. John Dewey, *Freedom and Culture* (1939; reprint, Buffalo, N.Y.: Prometheus, 1989), 81, emphasis added.

26. Hilary Putnam, *Renewing Philosophy* (Cambridge, Mass.: Harvard University Press, 1992), 180, emphasis added.

27. Ibid., 188.

28. Richard Rorty, "Response to James Gouinlock," in *Rorty & Pragmatism*, ed. H. J. Saatkamp (Nashville, Tenn.: Vanderbilt University Press, 1995), 94.

29. Rorty, *Objectivity, Relativism, and Truth*, 65–66.

30. John Dewey, "Logic: The Theory of Inquiry," in *The Later Works, 1925-1953*, ed. Jo Ann Boydston, 12 (1938; reprint, Carbondale: Southern Illinois University Press 1991).

31. Ibid., 202–3.

32. Ibid., 108.

33. Rorty, *Philosophy and Social Hope*, 120, emphasis added.

34. Robyn Eckersley, "Environmental Pragmatism, Ecocentrism, and Deliberative Democracy: Between Problem-Solving and Fundamental Critique," chapter 3 of this book, emphasis in original.

35. Dewey, *Liberalism and Social Action*, 90–91.

36. See, for example, Robert Westbrook, *John Dewey and American Democracy* (Ithaca, N.Y.: Cornell University Press, 1991).

37. Ben A. Minteer and Robert E. Manning, "Pragmatism in Environmental Ethics: Democracy, Pluralism, and the Management of Nature," *Environmental Ethics* 21 (1999): 191–207, and "Convergence in Environmental Values: An Empirical and Conceptual Defense," *Ethics, Place and Environment* 3 (2000): 47–60.

38. Callicott, *Beyond the Land Ethic*, 244, emphasis added.

39. Laura Westra, "Why Norton's Approach Is Insufficient for Environmental Ethics," *Environmental Ethics* 19 (1997): 293.

40. Callicott, *Beyond the Land Ethic*, 51.

CHAPTER 3

Environmental Pragmatism, Ecocentrism, and Deliberative Democracy

BETWEEN PROBLEM-SOLVING AND FUNDAMENTAL CRITIQUE

Robyn Eckersley

The debate over the virtues of ecocentric theory (moral monism) versus environmental pragmatism (moral pluralism) provides an occasion to reflect upon the democratic character of these respective environmental philosophies and their associated political practices. Environmental pragmatists have been generally critical of monistic philosophies, which they understand ecocentrism to be, on the grounds that they are dogmatic, insensitive to diverse cultural and moral contexts, and therefore too inflexible to be of any assistance in the practical resolution of environmental problems and conflicts.[1] Environmental pragmatism, on the other hand, is defended as more tolerant, open-minded, and ecumenical in its respect for moral pluralism and cultural diversity and more democratic in its defense of environmental policy deliberation by the affected parties. It is also defended as more effective when it comes to practical environmental problem solving.

In response, ecocentric philosophers (most notably J. Baird Callicott) have argued that the pragmatists' embrace of moral pluralism carries with it the danger of lapsing into indecisive relativism. In particular, the refusal by environmental pragmatists to privilege any substantive environmental values in advance of policy dialogue is seen as problematic insofar as it can lead to philosophical contradictions and dubious political outcomes that may not necessarily protect the environment.[2] According to this construction, ecocentric theorists and activists are the fearless environmental justice advocates, standing up for the interests of the environmental victims of economic development, including both humans and nonhuman species.

On the face of it, environmental pragmatism would appear to be able to boast better democratic credentials than ecocentrism insofar as it does not seek to shape or determine environmental policy in advance of democratic deliberation among the affected parties. While ecocentric philosophers, such as J. Baird Callicott, have offered a spirited defense of moral monism, they have not yet offered any sustained defense of the *democratic* credentials of ecocentrism against the charges of environmental pragmatists. This is somewhat surprising, given the embrace of deliberative democracy by so many ecocentric political theorists.[3] Moreover, this embrace of deliberative democracy draws considerable inspiration from critical theory (particularly that of Jürgen

Habermas), and provides a fertile point of connection and engagement with environmental pragmatism, which defends the virtues of practical deliberation following the classical tradition of American pragmatism.

In this chapter, I seek to defend the democratic credentials of ecocentrism and offer a sympathetic critique of environmental pragmatism. I also suggest that the different philosophical approaches and strategic practices preferred by environmental pragmatism and ecocentrism may be understood as two different and necessary "democratic moments" in the processes of environmental policy making, which carry with them different purposes, strengths, and weaknesses. I shall call the pragmatists "the mediators" and ecocentric theorists and activists the "advocates." (I apply these labels equally to theorists and activists in each camp, on the view that public philosophical reflection and communication is no less political than practical political engagement and activism.) The environmental mediators are good listeners who are flexible and open-minded. They are respectful of the diversity of different human modes of interacting with and valuing ecological communities and they seek to reduce conflict by focusing on immediate, practical environmental problem solving. Often this may require deftly sidestepping intractable and heated moral conflicts in order to concentrate the minds of the parties on common practical problems. In contrast, the environmental advocates are the relentless critics of the status quo who are deeply committed to particular environmental values, worldviews, and policy goals. They are the activists and long-term visionaries who seek to inspire, move, persuade, and cajole others in order to shift cultural understandings by a variety of different forms of political communication and engagement (such as political rhetoric, satire, science, logic, poetry, literature, art, and practical example). They are prepared to challenge and disrupt conventional norms and policy discourses, generate political conflict, and sometimes they may refuse to engage in formalized democratic deliberation if it is likely to compromise their values and goals.

These distinctions may be understood as two different ideal types, which means that not all environmental pragmatists and ecocentrics would necessarily conform exactly to the respective criteria. Moreover, these ideal types are not entirely mutually exclusive, in that both the mediator and the advocate support democratic deliberation, at least in principle. However, as we shall see, there are tensions associated with how democratic deliberation is understood and best realized. I therefore enlist the figures of the pragmatic mediator and the activist advocate in order to draw out these differences and illuminate the necessary and potentially productive tensions between these different types of democratic engagement. Indeed, these tensions resonate with a more general tension in political thought and practice about the relative importance of, and relationship between, justice and democracy. On the one hand, we are familiar with the claim that justice should be the "first virtue" of political thought and practice and therefore prior to, or at least determinative of, democracy while, on the other hand, we find claims that justice is simply that which emerges from a fair democratic dialogue. Posing the tension in these stark terms would suggest that ecocentrics understand environmental justice to be the necessary starting point of political inquiry and practice, while environmental pragmatists would accord this status to democracy since it provides the fairest means of reconciling value pluralism. However, this is not meant to suggest that ecocentrics are necessarily undemocratic nor that environmental pragmatists are not concerned about environmental justice. Rather, the different starting points merely illuminate different entry points and objectives that inform different understandings of the *relationship* between justice and democracy. In any event, in recent debates in political theory there seems to be a growing acknowledgment that neither justice nor democracy should be understood as the prior virtue, that justice and democracy presuppose each other and are therefore mutually defining.[4] The real debate, as we shall see, concerns how environmental justice and democracy are mutually related, in theory and practice.

While both approaches have their strengths and drawbacks, ultimately I will be arguing that environmental pragmatism ought to take a more critical and less instrumental approach to deliberation and that such a move would enable more opportunities for creative (as distinct from destructive) engagement between the figures of the advocate and the mediator. I show that the contemporary environmental pragmatists' and ecocentric political theorists' understandings of deliberation diverge in some significant respects and suggest that the differences between pragmatic mediation/conflict resolution and ecocentric advocacy can be understood in terms of the distinction between a "problem-solving" versus a "critical" orientation to environmental deliberation and policy making. In order to develop this argument, in the following discussion I evaluate environmental pragmatism from the perspective of the (ecocentric) environmental advocate, although in the concluding discussion I also expose some of the limitations of the more adversarial advocate role.

Environmental Pragmatism

The environmental pragmatists' commitment to open-ended inquiry and practical democratic engagement is grounded in the insights of the classical American pragmatists, the chief pioneers of whom were C. S. Peirce (1839–1914), William James (1842–1910), and especially John Dewey (1859–1952). As a philosophical movement, the early pragmatists were concerned "to improve the methods by which human beings can acquire new knowledge and understanding of their environment, both in an ordinary life context and, in a more organized way, through science."[5] Common and related themes developed by the "classical pragmatists" included an emphasis on the tentative and provisional character of knowledge, the self-corrective character of inquiry as an ongoing experiential process, and the interpretation of ideas, meaning, and truth through their practical consequences. According to this radical empiricist approach, truth is interpreted not in any abstract or absolutist way but rather from the standpoint of particular agents in relation to their experience of particular problems, an experience that includes agents' beliefs and utilities. John Dewey, in particular, reinterpreted pragmatism as instrumentalism and interpreted truth as "warranted assertability."

Socially and politically, the classical pragmatists were humanists and democrats who emphasized the importance of the social construction of knowledge and social learning through democratic inquiry. As Parker puts it, "For the pragmatist, 'participatory democracy' is a political expression of the metaphysical idea that reality is involvement and transformation."[6] That is, humans are active experimenters who constantly reorder their understanding of and orientation to the world as a result of their constructed and reconstructed experience *in* the world. John Dewey, in particular, believed that science advanced because it was self-corrective by virtue of its method of testing scientific claims and counterclaims against experience. By a parity of reasoning, he hoped that society would progress by means of the "deliberative testing" of public policies against experience. As a democrat, he also argued that deliberation should be socially inclusive, not elitist.

Contemporary environmental pragmatists likewise defend inclusive democratic deliberation that is respectful of the plurality of existing environmental values, beliefs, and lived experiences within particular communities. Indeed, Light and Katz—editors of the first comprehensive volume of environmental pragmatist thought—speculate that one of the reasons for the failure of much environmental philosophy to influence public policy is its "methodological and theoretical dogmatism."[7] In particular, they accuse nonanthropocentric moral monism of forcing a premature closure in environmental philosophical discourse and they seek to counteract this with a more ecumenical method of inquiry which they claim is more sensitive to the fact of moral pluralism. Historically, they point out that environmental philosophy is still a relatively young field of inquiry—a stage that they argue justifies multivocality and an opening out of inquiry, not stabilization or closure.

For some environmental pragmatists, the human perspective is the only thing we know as humans and therefore the human perspective becomes the measure of all things by default.[8] For committed Deweyians, it is meaningless to talk about the value of something in the absence of a human valuer, although this need not rule out the valuing of nonhuman entities for their own sake by human subjects. Indeed, respect for moral pluralism necessarily entails respect for those cultures and traditions that value nonhuman nature in moral, aesthetic, or spiritual terms. But it also necessarily entails respect for those cultures and traditions that do not. Some pragmatists go so far as to reject the ends-means distinction in environmental ethics along with the notion of any fixed and final end. From this perspective, it makes no sense to say that an entity is intrinsically valuable in the sense that its value is self-sufficient, abstracted from its relations with other entities. Values are weblike, interrelated, and specific to particular human/environment contexts and cannot be meaningfully defended outside such real-world evaluations and choices where different clusters of values must always be related to each other.[9]

The relational ontology, constructivist epistemology, and radically empiricist methodology of environmental pragmatism support a social and political philosophy of justice that is essentially proceduralist.[10] Environmental pragmatists may therefore be included among those political philosophers who have taken the dialogic turn in justice theory, where instead of developing substantive principles of justice and associated policies in advance of particular problems, the preoccupation is with "attempting to specify the conversational conditions under which citizens can begin to negotiate their political difference."[11] That is, environmental pragmatists are concerned to discover the most appropriate democratic procedures in which a constructive environmental dialogue and practical problem solving might take place. Just solutions to social and ecological problems must be understood as provisional, dialogical, and context specific in relation to a particular community of inquirers rather than fixed, monological, and universal.

Although I have so far introduced environmental pragmatism as essentially a method of environmental policy making rather than as a substantive environmental philosophy, there are some environmental pragmatists, such as Bryan Norton, who have developed pragmatism in a more substantive direction, insofar as they have defended the principle of sustainability as philosophically consistent with environmental pragmatism. That is, sustainability is defended on the grounds that it keeps open options and opportunities for future generations and is consistent with a Darwinian emphasis on practical survival and a pragmatic conception of truth. For Norton, pursuing the practical path of sustainability is more likely to guarantee the survival of the community of inquirers and their descendants than any rival philosophy, and is therefore "destined, in the terms of Peirce, to be adopted as the conclusion of all rational inquirers, as they struggle through many experiments to make coherent sense of human experience."[12] The principle of sustainability is also defended as especially amenable to social learning: it is open-ended and therefore requires social interpretation and experimentation before it can find expression in practical policies in response to practical problems.

However, for Andrew Light and Eric Katz, environmental pragmatism is defended primarily as a methodology rather than a substantive environmental philosophy.[13] This approach involves starting with existing environmental problems and conflicts and understanding, and working with the experience, beliefs, values, and "baggage" that real people carry with them in particular contexts. Given their keen sensitivity to context, most environmental pragmatists are reluctant to specify in advance exactly how constructive dialogues might be fashioned, other than to acknowledge the fact of moral and cultural pluralism and urge the parties to look for creative ways of maintaining respect for moral and cultural difference in the processes of deliberation and decision making. Although environmental pragmatists *personally* wish to see more environmental protection, in privileging method over substance they cannot allow their personal desires to distort or derail the processes of constructive dialogue. Insofar as environmental pragmatists find themselves embroiled in real environmental conflicts as distinct from philosophical ones, we would still expect them to assume the figure of the mediator in seeking to pacify the parties and facilitate the democratic resolution of practical problems. Their "tools" are being respectful, listening, remaining open-minded, experimenting, working creatively with the moral and cultural resources at hand, and seeking only the minimum necessary common ground for the purposes of practical problem solving. In this context, the tactful avoidance of deep-seated moral, religious, cultural, and social differences is defended as more productive than allowing unnecessary heated debate about deep-seated differences. As a method of environmental problem solving, environmental pragmatism is necessarily flexible and cannot offer any further specificity. No "how-to-do-it" manuals or institutional designs are offered, only loose heuristic guidelines, since the point is to leave the clarification of issues, agenda setting, practical problem solving, and adaptive learning and management to real stakeholders who constitute the relevant "community of inquirers" that must live with, and learn from, the consequences of their decisions. Under these circumstances, compromise, incremental change, and even "muddling through" are preferable to grand social engineering.[14] In this they follow the Popperian tradition according to which "grand social engineers" are the "enemies" of the open society.

Against this background, we can see why both ecocentric theorists and activists might be portrayed by those sympathetic to environmental pragmatism as "the self-appointed guardians of an uncompromising ideology . . . indulging in a fantasy of Platonic education."[15] That is, ecocentrics (as advocates of deeply held convictions about the green good life) appear to wish to "foist" their vision on others without regard to religious, cultural, and philosophical differences. From this perspective, if ecocentric political activists were to capture state power, liberal democracy would be in danger of giving way to ecoauthoritarianism. Environmental pragmatism may thus be seen as joining forces with green liberalism in defending the freedom of individuals to choose their own environmental destinies. If forced to choose between the unpalatable alternatives of the liberal distopia of a global Manhattan or the green distopia of the ecoauthoritarian state, green liberals would choose the former.[16]

Environmental pragmatism also shares with liberalism what political philosophers refer to as a "right over good" conception of justice. In the case of environmental pragmatism, only the fair rules of dialogue are expected to trump different conceptions of the good life (including those of deep ecologists) to the extent to which such conceptions conflict with such rules. Indeed, the primary appeal of "right over good" theories of justice—or what Agnes Heller has called "an incomplete ethico-political concept of justice"—is that they seek to avoid the tyranny of perfectionism and promote toleration of difference while providing a fair framework and procedure for making legitimate decisions.[17] Legitimate decisions are never perfect, correct, or absolute. They are merely decisions that parties can "live with" for the time being because they accept the processes of decision making as fair, even though they might have personally preferred a different outcome.

In the philosophical debates, we see this commitment to moral pluralism and an "incomplete ethico-political concept of justice" at work in the distinction made by environmental pragmatists between "applied" and "practical" philosophy. Whereas applied environmental philosophy seeks to deduce particular policies from general environmental principles that are determined in the abstract, in advance of practical problems, practical philosophy seeks a reconciliation of real-world moral pluralism by developing principles and strategies in the context of specific practical problems. Deliberation, creative conflict mediation, and social learning thus replace any quest for ethical perfection. For Bryan Norton, moral monism (such as nonanthropocentric environmental ethics) and applied philosophy typically go together. That is, moral monists are "armchair philosophers" who develop and defend particular universal principles from which policy makers and others are expected to "derive" particular policy options. In contrast, practical philosophers seek to generate workable principles from practice rather than work out practical policies from general principles.[18]

Paul Thompson has taken Norton's critique of applied philosophy a step further in questioning the role of environmental philosophy if all it does is clarify and articulate the different ethical arguments (utilitarian, Kantian, contractarian, egalitarian, and so on) underpinning the perspectives of competing stakeholders in environmental policy conflicts. He has suggested that attempts to understand stakeholders' conflicts as representing applications of different moral theories is more likely to exacerbate any standoff between the protagonists, sharpening formerly inchoate views and intuitions into more articulate and entrenched views, adding to the levels of self-righteousness of opposing parties, and foreclosing the possibility of agreement.[19] Instead of constructing philosophical principles in advance of application, Thompson argues that we need to deconstruct philosophical abstractions in order to prepare the ground for more creative practical thinking. As he explains, "Pragmatic deconstruction is a form of moral pedagogy that goes before reconstruction, and hence before any attempt at prescription."[20] Indeed, Thompson maintains that once we have stripped away the philosophical gloss, environmental problems can typically be boiled down to a question of incompatible *use* of a particular resource or ecosystem by different stakeholders.[21] Once understood in these terms, it is possible to sort out a program of action based on the requirements of *pragmatic necessity*—an approach he believes will produce a response that is more likely to be "serviceable" in relation to the specific problem facing the relevant community of inquirers than abstract philosophical inquiry.

The Limitations of "Practical Problem-Solving"

So far, we have outlined the environmental pragmatist understanding of how a "genuine environmental democracy" ought to function. That is, environmental pragmatists hold to a regulative ideal of democratic deliberation that is respectful, ecumenical, and directed toward practical problem solving. As appealing as this regulative ideal may be, I nonetheless want to highlight three major, interrelated limitations and/or undeveloped dimensions of environmental pragmatism. The first is that its narrow focus on problem solving makes it insufficiently critical and emancipatory when examined from the perspective of oppressed and marginal groups and classes or nonhuman species. From this perspective, environmental pragmatism runs the risk of being too accommodating of the existing constellation of social forces that drive environmental degradation. The second limitation is that it is too instrumentalist in the way that it seeks to close off noninstrumental democratic encounters and the opportunity for the parties to engage in dialogue for dialogue's sake—a possibility that can sometimes work to build mutual respect and trust as much as it can deepen antagonisms. Moreover, although environmental pragmatists seek to avoid moral reductionism, their *method* of inquiry is reductionist in the sense that it seeks to filter out arguments that do not address questions of practical necessity—effectively reducing collective deliberation to deliberation about competing utilities. The third criticism is that there is ultimately nothing especially *environmental* about the kind of democratic inquiry defended by environmental pragmatists, in the sense that environmental pragmatism ultimately rests on a liberal humanist moral premise rather than any explicit environmental values. And as we shall see, many ecocentric political theorists have taken issue with the moral foundations of liberal democracy on the grounds that it is not pluralist or inclusive enough.

Too Accommodating, Not Critical Enough

To remain consistent with their methodological approach, we would expect environmental pragmatists to approach environmental conflicts by recommending practically oriented deliberation and mediation among the parties or their representatives. We would also expect them to counsel against anything that that might lead to an escalation of conflict, since conflict stands in the way of practical problem solving. Now there certainly are many circumstances when such a strategy is likely to be prudent and effective. Indeed, the concern to unify disparate political actors around a common problem is one of the greatest strengths of environmental pragmatism, which has suggested some tactful and creative methods that might, in some instances, serve to soften or shelve such deeply held moral convictions in order to achieve practical outcomes.[22]

However, deeply held moral, religious, and/or cultural convictions may not be the only reasons why the respectful and practical democratic disposition hoped for by pragmatists may be found in short supply. In real-world democracies, differences in income, wealth, status, knowledge, and "communicative power" are widespread. In their effort to acknowledge and work with *moral* pluralism, environmental pragmatists have tended to neglect a wider range of *other* reasons for conflict, intransigence, or noncooperation by particular parties to environmental disputes. For example, it may be because of poverty and economic necessity brought about by capital flight, debt, or corruption. It may be because certain parties have other, more "effective" means of force at their disposal to achieve their goals other than the force of argumentative persuasion, such as the public coercive power of the state, the private power to make threats or inducements, or even the more subtle power that comes with simply belonging to the dominant cultural or ethnic group in a particular society. Or it may be because certain parties or their advocates do not believe they will achieve a fair or meaningful hearing precisely because the forces arrayed against them are more powerful and/or because the outcome of any cooperative dialogue may serve to deflect attention away from deeper and more systemic "background injustices," including social and economic structures and the social dispositions they foster. This is a situation that regularly confronts the unemployed, indigenous peoples, women, people of color, and those advocates who seek the protection of endangered and threatened species and their habitats. In their otherwise laudable practical concern to work creatively with the diverse moral orientations of the parties in particular policy dialogues in response to particular problems, structural injustices and the powerful social agents and dominant discourses that serve to reproduce them are necessarily placed in the background. Of course, environmental pragmatists would doubtless be aware of, and troubled by, such structural problems. However, my point is that there is nothing in their practical *method* of problem solving that would encourage or facilitate a shift toward a more general political or economic critique precisely because such a move would detract from reaching a practical agreement in response to particular and immediate problems. These limitations of environmental pragmatism are neatly encapsulated in Robert Cox's distinction between problem-solving theories and critical theories. As Cox explains, "whereas the problem-solving approach leads to further analytical sub-division and limitation of the issue dealt with, the critical approach leads toward the construction of a larger picture of the whole of which the initially contemplated part is just one component, and seeks to understand the processes of change in which both parts and whole are involved."[23] A roughly similar distinction can be found in the critical rationalism of Karl Popper as compared to the critical theory of the Frankfurt School, particularly in the "second wave" work of Jurgen Habermas.[24]

However sympathetic and inclusive environmental pragmatists may be in relation to the powerless, their focus on procedural questions, rather than substantive questions of justice, provides only a minimal means of bridging the discrepancy between those who possess "communicative power" (along with other forms of power) and those who do not. Nor does the otherwise commendable ecumenical ethos of environmental pragmatism provide any assurance to advocates of marginalized and oppressed groups (including those advocates who act as the political representatives of nonhuman species) that their deepest concerns will be addressed. Moreover, the reluctance of environmental pragmatists to specify or institutionalize the kinds of procedures, decision rules, and devices that might provide a practical embodiment of their method of dialogical justice, leaves marginalized groups without any institutional safeguards to ensure a fair and informed hearing—other than the goodwill of the parties and the generic skills of any pragmatist mediators who happen to be present. In short, the more radically open are democratic procedures, the more they are susceptible to abuse as well as good use.

The problem of broader discourses and structures that transcend the local policy making community raises considerable institutional challenges for environmental pragmatism, which has not engaged in any critical analysis of macro policy developments at the national and global level, such as the ascendancy of neoliberalism and the increasing salience of the rights of corporations relative to citizens, which condition and constrain the negotiating margins of local and regional environmental policy making. As is typically the case in an increasingly globalized world, local and even regional conflicts cannot always be practically solved by the immediate parties in dispute because they rarely have control over the broader structures, social forces, and decisions that have helped to generate environmental degradation. Of course, this problem cuts both ways. Given that local stakeholders are rarely the only ones affected by the spatial and temporal consequences of their decisions, their decision making should be "layered" into broader, macro-policy frameworks. For example, local policy-making communities should be guided by international environmental treaty commitments, while at the same time be given the opportunity to influence such treaty negotiations.

Bryan Norton is an exception here in drawing attention to the multiscalar dimensions of environmental problems as part of his pluralistic, integrative framework for ecological management. According to this normative framework, local stakeholders ought to consider impacts on larger spatial and temporal dynamics and scales.[25] Such an approach avoids the limitations of a narrow problem-solving approach while also being explicitly environmental if not critical. Such an approach also departs significantly from the strictly methodological/procedural focus of most of the environmental pragmatist literature by offering a substantive normative framework that is defended on the basis of "a broadly Darwinian approach to epistemology and morality."[26]

In other words, such a framework is defended as likely to be accepted by policy makers because it provides "useful knowledge" about how humans might best survive in a changing world. While the broad direction (if not the philosophical underpinnings) of this framework would doubtless appeal to many ecocentric advocates, Norton, as a pluralist, has not fully grappled with the question of how his normative insights might be institutionalized in local, regional, and global policy-making processes. Moreover, there is also a need to engage critically with the limited time horizons and forms of political representation in real-world liberal democracies, social and economic structural inequalities, and the powerful social agents and dominant discourses that serve to reproduce them, that stand in the way of reform. Of course, any such move would necessarily entail a shift from the figure of the pragmatic mediator, who acknowledges and respects the values and interests of environmentalists and developers alike, to the figure of the critical advocate as a committed political actor seeking change.

For methodological pragmatists, however, the commitment to pluralism provides the very basis for defending a strictly proceduralist conception of democracy, since there is no background of shared moral beliefs to give any substantive moral purpose to the political order or provide any overarching constraints on democratically determined decisions, save those that recognize and protect the political equality of each of its members and their rights to participate in the democratic processes. That is, we have no basis for agreement other than the need for "fair" procedures.[27] Thus those political rights that are necessary for democracy are *constitutive*; all other rights and substantive claims, including environmental ones should not serve as *constraints* on democracy.

From the point of view of those who advocate change on behalf of the "environmentally disempowered," such a methodological focus is too narrowly conceived. Approaching environmental problems and conflicts with the open-minded, respectful, and practical disposition suggested by pragmatists can be positively foolhardy when there are more powerful forces arrayed around the negotiating table, and especially when their arguments resonate with dominant economic discourses. Indeed, maintaining a narrow problem-solving focus runs the risk of perpetuating structural injustices by, for example, ameliorating environmental side effects for particular local communities and making the structural injustices a little easier to live with. This problem is generally recognized by new social movements and radical democratic theorists and requires difficult and ongoing practical judgments about whether to cooperate in policy dialogues or adopt more confrontational strategies, which may extend to civil disobedience in those cases where the relevant legal and policy regimes are believed to be manifestly unjust.

Boycotting the processes of negotiation in order to highlight more systemic injustices may be more politically and strategically beneficial than participating in negotiations, even when such negotiations may carry the promise of producing compromises and incremental policy shifts in favor of such groups in particular cases. That such tactics are regularly employed by environmental justice and wilderness advocates is testimony to, among other things, the political frustration experienced by those with limited resources and limited control over agenda setting.

Of course, a cynic might suggest that refusing to continue a formal dialogue because it is not "free enough" is really just a code for saying that the dialogue is not running in the direction that the environmental advocate might wish. While this accusation is necessarily true (and therefore frequently made) in real-world liberal democracies, it also trivializes or fails to acknowledge the systemic injustices and associated discourses that constrain the parameters of policy deliberations in such democracies. When differences in communicative power distort democratic communication, both justice and democracy are more likely to be served by persisting with critical advocacy rather than "submitting" to mediation and narrow problem solving. This is not to say that successful mediation cannot or does not occur. Rather, it is merely a reminder that it has sometimes served as a strategic tool for developers and therefore has ambiguous potential.[28]

Introducing strategies of empowerment can therefore help to "correct" democratic processes. Similarly, devising special forms of representation for those who are systematically underrepresented can help to ensure communicative equality.[29] After all, what Cohen calls a "favorable associative environment" does not always arise naturally. It has to be actively constructed by the use of public powers—a move that itself requires deliberation and is invariably contested by those social forces that stand to lose. However, such strategies can be justified in democratic grounds. That is, for so long as organized public power is not fully democratic, then justice advocates may resort to strategic rather than communicative action in order to establish the conditions for fair and free deliberation. From a Habermasian perspective, "[s]trategic action would appear justified only as long as it seeks to establish conditions that allow communicative rationality to unfold its potential, not insofar as it anticipates the possible outcomes of praxis as discourse."[30] While opting to "walkout" and engage in further strategic or communicative action elsewhere may seem petulant and uncompromising from the point of view of the frustrated mediator who is concerned to achieve a practical outcome rather than a stalemate, from the perspective of the advocate it is a continuation of democratic deliberation by other means.

Now some environmental pragmatists may well object to my argument by pointing out that environmental pragmatism has the potential to develop in a much more critical direction. After all, if economic and political structural inequalities stand in the way of a more robust democracy, then as democrats, pragmatists ought to challenge those structural inequalities and therefore incline toward a more critical pragmatism. Indeed, Dewey emphasized the need for institutional criticism. And as Michael Walzer has shown, those who reject abstract and universal moral theory in favor of democratic dialogue that is respectful of moral and cultural pluralism can still play the role of social critic by enlisting and critically interrogating the shared meanings that are local and internal to particular communities.[31] This would apply especially where members of particular communities are excluded from participating in the construction of shared social meanings within that community.

While I accept that there is plenty of room for environmental pragmatists to travel in this direction, such moves would tend to divert attention away from practical problem solving toward more of a Big Picture analysis and critique of social structures (of the Coxian kind). This would necessarily weaken some of the claimed advantages of the pragmatist method of inquiry, namely, that it is practically efficacious because it focuses on immediate problem solving by reconciling competing environmental uses and bracketing more fundamental differences in environmental values and worldviews. Moreover, as we have seen, this Big Picture critique will invariably have global dimensions, with social meanings that now operate well beyond local, territorially based communities and cultures. This, in turn, makes the defense of cultural particularism in local communities more challenging. Now none of these points represent insuperable barriers for environmental pragmatism, although if it took a more critical turn it would need to change its "marketing." That is, it cannot claim to offer a method of environmental problem solving that is efficacious from an instrumental point of view while also remaining consistently critical of broader social structures. Indeed, I do not believe any political theory can reasonably make such a claim!

Too Instrumentalist

Even where environmental pragmatists are at their strongest in suggesting that intractable debates about deeply held moral convictions might be deftly sidestepped in order to focus on the practical problems at hand, I have suggested that this is a recipe that is likely to work only some of the time. One of the reasons for this is that not all environmental conflicts can or ought to be reduced to a simple question of incompatible *use* of nonhuman nature by differently situated humans. This is because environmental conflicts are also manifestations of deeper social and political controversies concerning lifestyle, identity, cultural dispositions, and modes of relating to others. Under these circumstances, practical conflicts cannot and ought not be isolated from these deeper social and political conflicts because any resolution of particular problems usually serves as a precedent for future policy making, in which case much more is at stake than merely solving the *particular* practical problem at hand. In such circumstances, what Thompson calls "the force of necessity" is therefore unlikely to bring together the relevant community of inquirers and allow them to let go of their fundamental convictions in order to reach an effective pragmatic resolution of the immediate environmental problem/conflict.

Yet there is a deeper, and somewhat ironic, point to be made against the instrumentalist, problem-solving orientation of environmental pragmatism. For those sympathetic with the work of Hannah Arendt and also the Frankfurt School, keeping the dialogue alive in order to ask more and deeper questions is ultimately more valuable and important than resolving immediate, narrowly defined practical problems. From an Arendtian perspective, democratic exchange is an intrinsically valuable end in itself rather than a mere means to other ends while for the Frankfurt School the challenge is merely to prevent instrumental reason from dwarfing or displacing other forms of human reason.[32] The irony here is that approaching deliberation in a less goal directed way may turn out to be more "instrumental" in fostering mutual trust and mutual understanding of difference *precisely because the pressure of practical imperatives is lifted*. After all, it is difficult *simultaneously* to listen and open oneself outward in order to understand differently situated others while also making instrumental assessments and calculations of one's environmental claims in relation to others.

In defending the virtues of noninstrumental democratic deliberation, Douglas Torgerson has carried Arendt's insights to their extreme conclusion in arguing that maintaining a relentlessly questioning dialogue in the "green public sphere" is ultimately more important than maintaining a green political *movement*, which is mostly oriented toward achieving environmental results.[33] While this seems to me to be carrying the point too far in providing a justification for endlessly foreclosing any practical policy action, Torgerson nonetheless helps us to see the inevitable tensions that can arise between the unconstrained moment of dialogue (where parties seek mutual understanding freed from the force of practical necessity) and the constrained moment of decision making under the pressure of reaching a decision with decisive consequences (where not all perspectives, interests, and values can be equally accommodated).

There is, of course, a more familiar dimension to the ecocentric critique of instrumentalism. A common feature of the variety of different ecocentric philosophies is a rejection of a purely instrumentalist posture toward the human and nonhuman worlds. This is not a denial of the use–value of ecosystems, merely a refusal to *reduce* the human relationship with human and nonhuman others to a purely instrumental one. Now environmental pragmatists, as we have seen, also acknowledge and respect the variety of different human modes of relating to nature (instrumental, moral, aesthetic, religious) and some have gone so far as to reject the instrumental value versus intrinsic value distinction on the grounds, rightly I believe, that values are weblike, interrelated, and specific to particular human/environment contexts. However, when it comes to making practical policy decisions, the radically empiricist epistemology of environmental pragmatism is one that ultimately calls on the parties in a policy deliberation to privilege instrumental evaluations over noninstrumental ones on the grounds that this is the most efficacious way of reaching practical agreement. However, behind this instrumental argument lies a deeper set of claims: that humans must necessarily construct a uniquely human environment out of the materials of nature, one that serves and expands human survival and human purposes.[34]

Now the appeal of this approach is that it concentrates the discussion on what it is we all have in common. That is, whatever else we may value or desire, we are all instrumentally dependent on ecosystems for our survival and well-being and this is indeed a point of convergence among all humans, whether environmentalists or not. Moreover, this pragmatic focus manages to avoid the crude utilitarian calculations of neoclassical economists, who take individual preferences as given and merely seek to aggregate them for the purposes of cost-benefit analysis. In contrast, environmental pragmatists seek the reflexive, collective scrutiny and evaluation of practical consequences within a deliberative setting in a way that is able to facilitate societal learning.

While such an approach may often work to achieve a greater measure of unity among environmentalists, whether preservationists or conservationists, in relation to complex problems such as global warming and species extinction (where instrumental and noninstrumental arguments increasingly converge), the plain fact is that the policy-making community is not made up of environmentalists alone.[35] What this means is that in deliberative encounters between environmentalists and developers, environmentalists would always have to show that preserving and protecting nature is more instrumentally valuable to present and future human generations than exploiting and transforming it. As Callicott puts it, environmentalists would find themselves having "to compete head-to-head with the economic values derived from converting rainforest to lumber and pulp, savannahs to cattle pasture, and so on."[36] Enlisting Norton's principle of sustainability as a guide to environmental policy deliberations will not necessarily steer policy deliberations toward environmental protection, since the principle leaves it open to the parties to determine *what* is to be sustained (natural capital or the total capital stock, made up of natural and human made capital?) and *for whom* (human or nonhumans) and over what time period (how many generations?). For those parties who are ready to accept that human-made capital can substitute for natural capital, to satisfy the sustainability principle it is enough to hand on to the next generation a capital stock that is no less than that enjoyed by the previous generation, even though this may be made up of an ever diminishing proportion of natural capital.

In the light of such anticipated dangers, the deployment by radical environmentalists of the language of the "intrinsic value" of nonhuman nature, or "the rights" of nonhuman nature serves as a strategically useful, though somewhat imperfect and clumsy, attempt to force a more systematic consideration of nonhuman interests and hopefully "trump" competing arguments that favor exploitation on grounds of utility. While there may be better ways of achieving such systematic consideration (for example, I have argued elsewhere for the constitutional entrenchment of the precautionary principles as a mandatory procedural requirement in policy making),[37] the resort to the language of "rights," "intrinsic value," or "inherent dignity" of nature may be understood, among other things, as a strategic attempt to tap into an emancipatory vocabulary. Historically, the successive struggles to extend rights have been struggles to deepen and extend recognition to hitherto excluded social classes and groups (slaves, the working class, women, ethnic minorities). Such struggles have also been struggles over social power and the "social construction of reality," including the power to define what is "real" and who/what should count as "normal" and morally considerable. More recently, however, new social movements and a diverse range of linguistic, ethnic, and religious minorities have introduced an identity/difference politics that has challenged the liberal democratic "color-blind constitution" along with homogenizing models of political identity and citizenship.[38] Such movements and groups have challenged the idea of "extending" political recognition on the basis of criteria that does not reflect their own experiences and identities.

Similar problems arise with the method of "humane extensionism" that has been employed by many environmental philosophers and activists, which seeks to incorporate nonhuman others and ecosystems into human moral frameworks by analogy with humans. Despite well-meaning intentions, such a method serves to privilege similarity with humans over difference.[39] This sets artificial limits on the range of values and reasons why we might respect nature, creating a web of incorporations and inclusions that leaves us unable to respect "unassimilated otherness."[40] Ironically, some environmental pragmatists, such as Weston, have recognized this problem, but have not seen the need to explore how the unassimilated otherness of nonhuman nature might be acknowledged and respected in its own right by the environmental policy-making community.[41] Yet, ultimately, there seems to be no nonquestion begging a moral standpoint from which to justify exclusion of any nonhuman others from the moral horizons of environmental policy making. Epistemological and experiential limitations on human understanding of nonhuman nature certainly make the challenge a difficult one but, as we shall see, these limitations should not be used as a basis for withholding prima facie recognition.

Liberal Humanism, Not Pluralist Enough?

As we have seen, environmental pragmatists purport to celebrate moral pluralism and reject nonanthropocentric theory as monistic and reductionistic. Yet if the environmental pragmatists' embrace of moral pluralism is to avoid arbitrary or indecisive relativism then pragmatists must ultimately privilege *some* moral values over others, if only to justify their pragmatic democratic procedures. Any approach that understands justice in dialogic terms—as fair dialogue—necessarily presupposes a prior moral theory of what is fair. As we have seen, environmental pragmatism ultimately comes to rest on the basic (monistic?) liberal humanistic principle of respect for individuals and their right to participate in the determination of their collective fate. Ecocentric democratic theory may be understood not as rejecting this principle but rather as seeking to extend it (by vicarious means as I explain below), on the ground that the moral pluralism of environmental pragmatism is not quite pluralist enough. That is, it calls for a more inclusive moral and procedural framework that acknowledges and seeks to reconcile not just conflicting human values and interests but also conflicts between human and nonhuman interests in ways that ensure special advocacy on behalf of nonhuman interests. If this is still monism, as pragmatists aver, then it is at least a more encompassing monism than liberal humanism.

Now we have seen that environmental pragmatists recognize that some individuals and cultures value nonhuman nature for its own sake. In view of the ecumenical spirit of environmental pragmatism, where such preferences and values are held by particular stakeholders in environmental policy conflicts, they must be acknowledged and brought into the policy deliberations. Here, it must be noted that some of the "methodological environmental pragmatists" (such as Eric Katz and Andrew Light), seem to be more agnostic than the committed Deweyians about the sources of value and are prepared to extend pluralism to encompass nonanthropocentric intuitions about value.

However, this only arises when such preferences or values happen to be held by particular stakeholders in particular conflicts. There is nothing in the environmental pragmatist method of inquiry that would guarantee any special representation rights to nonhuman species—*as a matter of procedure or due process*—where their fate may be imperiled in those circumstances where there are no self-appointed nonhuman advocates in the relevant human stakeholder community.

By way of clarification, it should be pointed out that the argument that there is ultimately nothing especially environmental about the kind of democratic inquiry defended by environmental pragmatists is directed to the liberal humanist premises of environmental pragmatist thought (i.e., to the ultimate values that an environmental pragmatist democracy is supposed to serve and uphold), not to the pragmatic arguments that are offered in support of practical deliberation as a method of environmental policy making. This is because an ecocentric case can also be made that democratic deliberation, through its requirement of publicity and the giving of reasons acceptable to others, is more conducive to the protection of common or generalizable interests—such as ecological interests—than the "distorted" and strategic political communication that is characteristic of liberal democracies.[42] However, unlike environmental pragmatists, many ecocentric political theorists have looked more critically at deliberative democracy in order to explore how the moral foundations, procedures, and forms of democratic representation might be widened to acknowledge nonhuman others. This is not a question that has been seriously entertained by environmental pragmatists since it does not make sense in terms of their constructivist and radically empiricist epistemology.

Indeed, it is this epistemological question about how we come to *know* nature that has been central to the general resistance to ecocentric efforts to transcend anthropocentrism or human chauvinism in policy making. To borrow Kate Soper's terminology, are we seeking to emancipate "nature" or Nature?[43] That is, are we seeking to liberate the "nature" we have constructed, or Nature as extra-discursive reality? Now some deep ecologists have resisted social constructivism and have sought to invoke the authority of science to buttress their moral arguments for, say, wilderness preservation and species protection.[44] But it is not necessary to subscribe to a naïve realist epistemology in order to argue the moral case for considering the interests of nonhuman others in policy making. Indeed, to accept that reality is socially constructed, and that "truth" is standpoint dependent, is necessarily to acknowledge that there are many "realities" and "standpoints," human and nonhuman, even though they may be incommensurable with our own experience, and therefore not easy to grasp. Yet this "difficult to grasp" argument is too often used as a shield against ecocentric moral claims. Here, environmental pragmatists effectively rely on their radically empiricist epistemology, which interprets ideas, meaning, and truth through their practical consequences for humans, as a justification for restricting moral considerability to humans. No positive moral argument is advanced in defense of this posture. It is mostly arrived at by default as if it were somehow "natural" in terms of their Darwinian emphasis on practical survival. But even this argument could be enlisted on behalf of nonhuman others, who likewise possess an interest in their own survival.

A postpositivist, constructivist epistemology does not deny the existence of Nature as an extra-discursive reality; it simply acknowledges that we do not have any *shared* access to this reality other than through human frameworks of understanding. The distinctive political project of ecocentrism, as I understand it, is to enable the flourishing of Nature in the knowledge that we must always necessarily grapple with the fact that we only have access to Nature through our own discursive maps (whether based on scientific or customary/vernacular knowledge), which are approximate, provisional understandings of so-called real Nature. If we understand the problem in this way, then there ought to be no necessary *moral* objection to proceeding with the project of enabling and promoting a flourishing nonhuman Nature. Indeed, the acknowledgment that the only Nature we know is a provisional, socially constructed "map" that is at best an approximation of the "real territory" provides the basis of a number of cautionary tales as to how the "emancipatory project" might be pursued. Such an argument might run as follows: if we want to enable the nonhuman to flourish and if it is acknowledged that our understanding of nature is incomplete, culturally filtered, and provisional *then* we ought to proceed with care, caution, and humility rather than with recklessness and arrogance in our interactions with "nature." In short, we must acknowledge that our knowledge of Nature and its limits is itself limited (and contested). Practically, these arguments provide support for a risk-averse posture in environmental and technology impact assessment and in environmental policy making generally.

If the foregoing arguments are accepted, then we have reason to question the pluralist credentials of environmental pragmatism in the same way that William Connolly has challenged the pluralist credentials of liberal pluralism. According to Connolly, conventional liberal moral pluralism serves to constrain the ongoing pluralization of moral values and is therefore too cramped and stingy. That is, despite its celebrated tolerance of diversity, liberal pluralism sustains consolidated identities, congealed moralities, barriers, and notions of normality/abnormality that serve to suppress and oppress the other, reducing the other to what some "we" already is.[45] Connolly has argued that we ought to be both generous and critical in encountering new political movements and their claims. As he explains, "The ethos of critical responsiveness pursued here does not reduce the other to what some 'we' already is. It opens up cultural space through which the other might consolidate itself into something that is unaffected by negative cultural markings."[46] Connolly's arguments join force with the aspirations of ecocentric theorists who are concerned to recognize "unassimilated otherness" in nonhuman nature and find ways of acknowledging such otherness in deliberative dialogue without distorting or assimilating that "otherness" in the process. As advocates, the point is to widen the "terms of contestation" rather than to prevent contestation.[47]

Conclusion

As is so often the case, the very strengths of a particular philosophical approach can, when examined under a different light, emerge as weaknesses. The greatest strength of the problem-solving approach of environmental pragmatism is that it is practically minded and focused only on that which is strictly necessary to resolve a problem in order to keep conflict to a minimum. The greatest weakness of such an orientation is that it has a tendency to be conservative, *to take too much as given*, to avoid any critical inquiry into "the big picture" and to work with rather than against the grain of existing structures and discourses (such as those that are prevalent in real-world liberal democracies) and facilitate "interest accommodation" in the context of the prevailing alignment of social forces. It accepts the path dependency of institutional design, and prefers incrementalism over any radical overhaul of social institutions precisely because the latter is disruptive and likely to generate conflict of a kind that makes agreement much more difficult.

By the same token, while ecocentric advocates avoid the limitations of pragmatism by keeping "the big picture" in view and pursuing relentless critical inquiry, the downside of this is that they can indeed become uncooperative, deaf to criticism, and often responsible for thwarting well-meaning efforts to reach practical policy compromises over pressing environmental problems. Because of their deep-seated moral commitment to overcoming environmental injustices, they tend to be more concerned with their own desired policy outcomes than reaching consensus. And since environmental advocates typically find themselves working in inhospitable contexts that fall short of their demanding ideals, they are often forced to act strategically and not necessarily communicatively in the Habermasian sense of the term, sometimes utilizing material and even coercive levers to bring about their desired end. On this score, sympathetic critics are right to suggest that the environment movement ought to be more reflexive, and more attentive to the importance of communicative action, both within its own ranks as well as with the broader society.[48]

Indeed, *both* pragmatist mediators and ecocentric activists must operate in a political context that falls short of their mutually informing ideals of justice and democracy (albeit in different ways)—a brute fact that requires difficult strategic political choices about where to direct intellectual focus and political energy. In this context, the choice as to whether to "weigh in" as an advocate (and therefore become a relentless critic of those who disagree) or a mediator (in an effort to generate respect and trust and find common ground) is always a difficult one. However, in view of the respective strengths and limitations of critical advocacy and pragmatic mediation, I suspect we would find our "real-world democracy" even poorer if it were made up of only mediators, or only advocates. This is because the tension between the advocate and the mediator ought to be understood as a healthy, constitutive tension in any democratic society because, among other things, it serves to steer democratic deliberation away from policy paralysis, on the one hand, and policy complacency, on the other. Democracy is about *arguing* as well as *making decisions* and advocates and mediators play different but invaluable roles in each of these phases. Now, in theory, the tensions between environmental pragmatism and ecocentrism might be narrowed or possibly even resolved by the development of a more *critical* pragmatism if some of my criticisms are taken on board. However, ultimately—in practice—I do not believe they can, or ought, to be eliminated in any "real-world" democracy.

Notes

1. This is the predominant view of the contributors to Andrew Light and Eric Katz's edited collection, *Environmental Pragmatism* (London: Routledge, 1996). Much of the environmental pragmatists' critique, particularly that of Bryan Norton, has been directed against the nonanthropocentric moral monism of J. Baird Callicott. See, for example, Bryan Norton, "Integration or Reduction: Two Approaches to Environmental Values," in *Environmental Pragmatism*, ed. Andrew Light and Eric Katz (London: Routledge, 1996),105–38.

2. See, for example, J. Baird Callicott (1990), "The Case against Moral Pluralism," *Environmental Ethics* 12, no. 2: 99–124; and Callicott, "Environmental Philosophy Is Environmental Activism: The Most Radical and Effective Kind," in *Environmental Philosophy and Environmental Activism*, ed. Don E. Marrietta Jr. and Lester Embree (Lanham, Md.: Rowman & Littlefield, 1995).

3. See, for example, Freya Mathews, ed., *Ecology and Democracy* (London: Frank Cass, 1996); Brian Doherty and Marius de Geus, eds., *Democracy and Green Political Thought: Sustainability, Rights and Citizenship* (London: Routledge, 1996); Andrew Dobson, "Critical Theory and Green Politics," in *The Politics of Nature: Explorations in Green Political Theory*, ed. Andrew Dobson and Paul Lucardie (London: Routledge, 1993); John Dryzek "Green Reason: Communicative Ethics for the Biosphere," *Environmental Ethics* 12 (1990): 195–210; Robyn Eckersley, "Habermas and Green Political Theory: Two Roads Diverging," *Theory and Society* 19 (1990): 739–76; Robyn Eckersley, "The Discourse Ethic and the Problem of Representing Nature," *Environmental Politics* 8 (1999): 24–49; Robyn Eckersley, "Deliberative Democracy, Ecological Representation, and Risk: Towards a Democracy of the Affected," in *Democratic Innovation: Deliberation, Association and Representation*, ed. Michael Saward (London: Routledge, 2000); and Angelika Krebs, "Discourse Ethics and Nature," *Environmental Values* 6 (1997): 269–79.

4. Carol Gould, *Rethinking Democracy* (Cambridge, U.K.: Cambridge University Press, 1988); Iris Marion Young, *Justice and the Politics of Difference* (Princeton, N.J.: Princeton University Press, 1990); Mark Kingwell, *A Civil Tongue: Justice, Dialogue, and the Politics of Pluralism* (University Park: Pennsylvania State University Press, 1995); Seyla Benhabib, *Democracy and Difference: Contesting the Boundaries of the Political* (Princeton, N.J.: Princeton University Press, 1996).

5. Bryan Magee, *The Great Philosophers: An Introduction to Western Philosophy* (Oxford, U.K.: Oxford University Press, 1987), 29.

6. Kelley A. Parker, "Pragmatism and Environmental Thought," in Light and Katz, *Environmental Pragmatism*, 27.

7. Andrew Light and Eric Katz, "Introduction: Environmental Pragmatism and Environmental Ethics as Contested Terrain," in *Environmental Pragmatism*, ed. Andrew Light and Eric Katz (London: Routledge, 1996), 2, 3.

8. Parker, "Pragmatism and Environmental Thought," 33.

9. Anthony Weston, "Beyond Intrinsic Value: Pragmatism in Environmental Ethics," *Environmental Ethics* 7, no. 4 (1985): 321–40, reprinted in Light and Katz, *Environmental Pragmatism*, 285–306 (subsequent page references refer to the reprinted version).

10. Exceptions are noted below.

11. Mark Kingwell, *A Civil Tongue: Justice, Dialogue, and the Politics of Pluralism* (University Park: Pennsylvania State University Press, 1995), 26.

12. Norton, "Integration or Reduction," 122–23.

13. "For us, environmental pragmatism is an open-ended inquiry into the specific real-life problems of humanity's relationship to the environment," Light and Katz, "Introduction," 2.

14. Norton, "Integration or Reduction," 124.

15. Bob Pepperman Taylor, "Democracy and Environmental Ethics," in *Democracy and the Environment: Problems and Prospects*, ed. William Lafferty and James Meadowcroft (Cheltenham, U.K.: Edward Elgar, 1996), 96.

16. This, at any rate, is the view defended by Marcel Wissenburg in *Green Liberalism: The Free and the Green Society* (London: UCL Press, 1998).

17. Agnes Heller, *Beyond Justice* (Oxford, U.K.: Basil Blackwell, 1987), 221.

18. Norton, "Integration or Reduction," 108. Similarly, Daniel Farber has argued that "A convincing analysis should be like a web, drawing on the coherence of many sources, rather than a tower, built on a single unified foundation." See Daniel A. Farber, *Ecopragmatism: Making Environmentally Sensible Decisions in an Uncertain World* (Chicago: University of Chicago Press, 1999), 10.

19. Paul B. Thompson, "Pragmatism and Policy: The Case of Water," in *Environmental Pragmatism*, ed. Andrew Light and Eric Katz (London: Routledge, 1996), 205.

20. Thompson, "Pragmatism and Policy," 203.

21. Ibid. 204.

22. Cass Sunstein has also defended agreements on outcomes and narrow or low-level principles on which people can converge from diverse foundations. He argues that such "incompletely theorised agreements" are a distinctive solution to social pluralism. See Cass Sunstein, "Deliberation, Democracy and Disagreement," in *Justice and Democracy: Cross-Cultural Perspectives,* ed. Ron Bontekoe and Marietta Stepaniants (Honolulu: University of Hawaii Press, 1997), 115. As Andrew Light has shown, Arne Naess has also defended the deep ecology platform along these lines. See Andrew Light, "Callicott and Naess on Pluralism," in *Beneath the Surface: Critical Essays on the Philosophy of Deep Ecology,* ed. Andrew Light and David Rothenburg (Cambridge, Mass.: MIT Press, 2000).

23. Robert W. Cox, "Social Forces, States and World Orders: Beyond International Relations Theory," *Millennium: Journal of International Studies* 10, no. 2 (1981): 126–55, 129.

24. For an illuminating discussion of these differences, see John Dryzek, *Discursive Democracy: Politics, Policy and Political Science* (Cambridge, U.K.: Cambridge University Press, 1990), 32–33.

25. Norton, "Integration or Reduction," 129, 132.

26. Ibid., 133.

27. Joshua Cohen, "Procedure and Substance in Deliberative Democracy," in *Deliberative Democracy: Essays on Reason and Politics,* ed. James Bohman and William Rehg (Cambridge, Mass.: MIT Press, 1997), 409.

28. Dryzek, *Discursive Democracy,* 46.

29. Cohen, "Procedure and Substance in Deliberative Democracy," 426–27.

30. Jurgen Haacke, "Theory and Praxis in International Relations: Habermas, Self-Reflection, Rational Argument," *Millennium* 25, no. 2 (1996): 255–89, 279.

31. Walzer, Michael, *Spheres of Justice: A Defence of Pluralism and Equality* (Oxford, U.K.: Blackwell, 1983). I thank Bob Pepperman Taylor for reminding me of Walzer's contribution to this debate.

32. See, for example, Hannah Arendt, *The Human Condition* (Chicago: University of Chicago Press, 1958); Theodor Adorno and Max Horkheimer, *The Dialectic of Enlightenment,* trans. John Cummings (London: Verso, 1979); and Jürgen Habermas, *Toward a Rational Society: Student Protest, Science and Society,* trans. Jeremy Shapiro (London: Heinemann Educational Books, 1971).

33. Douglas Torgerson, *The Promise of Green Politics: Environmentalism and the Public Sphere* (Durham, N.C.: Duke University Press, 1999).

34. As Bob Pepperman Taylor has shown, John Dewey was no different from Locke, who saw nature as something that was to be used for "the support and comfort" of humans. According to Pepperman Taylor, "Dewey's naturalism, his rebellion against the dualisms of conventional, Lockean, liberal epistemology, does not lead to a rejection of the values that inform these earlier dualisms—the values of a human-dominated world." See Bob Pepperman Taylor, "Democracy and Environmental Ethics," in *Democracy and the Environment: Problems and Prospects,* ed. William Lafferty and James Meadowcroft (Cheltenham, U.K.: Edward Elgar, 1996), 181.

35. Norton's plea for a pluralistic integration of environmental values, bringing together Conservationists and Preservationists, is directed to environmentalists, not the broader community. See Bryan Norton, *Toward Unity among Environmentalists* (New York: Oxford University Press, 1991).

36. Callicott, "Environmental Philosophy Is Environmental Activism," 22.

37. Eckersley, "Deliberative Democracy, Ecological Representation and Risk."

38. As Benhabib explains, "Contemporary Western liberal democracies are being challenged by groups who insist upon their unassimilatable difference and who want to use their experience of alterity to demystify the rationalist and identitary illusions of these liberals democracies." See Benhabib, *Democracy and Difference,* 5.

39. See, for example, John Rodman, "The Liberation of Nature?" *Inquiry* 20 (1977): 83–145; and Brian Luke, "Solidarity across Diversity: A Pluralistic Rapprochement of Environmentalism and Animal Liberation," in *The Ecological Community: Environmental Challenges for Philosophy, Politics, and Morality*, ed. Roger S. Gottlieb (New York: Routledge, 1997).

40. Val Plumwood, *Feminism and the Mastery of Nature* (London: Routledge, 1993), 52.

41. Weston, "Beyond Intrinsic Value," 289.

42. John Dryzek, *Rational Ecology: Environment and Political Economy* (London: Basil Blackwell, 1987); Dryzek, "Green Reason"; Robert Goodin, "Enfranchising the Earth, and Its Alternatives," *Political Studies* 44 (1996): 835–49; Dobson, "Critical Theory and Green Politics"; Eckersley, "Deliberative Democracy, Ecological Representation and Risk."

43. Kate Soper, *What Is Nature?* (Oxford, U.K.: Blackwell, 1995).

44. See the contributions to Michael E. Soule and Gary Lease, eds., *Reinventing Nature: Responses to Postmodern Deconstruction* (Washington, D.C.: Island Press, 1995).

45. William Connolly, *Ethos of Pluralization* (Minneapolis: University of Minnesota Press, 1995).

46. Ibid., xvii.

47. William Connolly, *Identity/Difference: Democratic Negotiations of Political Paradox* (Ithaca, N.Y.: Cornell University Press, 1991).

48. Torgerson, *The Promise of Green Politics*; and Robert J. Brulle, *Agency, Democracy and Nature: The U.S. Environment Movement from a Critical Theory Perspective* (Cambridge, Mass.: MIT Press, 2000).

CHAPTER 4

The Legitimacy Crisis in Environmental Ethics and Politics

Joe Bowersox

The Paradox Defined

I have been preoccupied with a paradox. It began twelve years ago while rereading William Ophuls's *Ecology and the Politics of Scarcity*. One of Ophuls's central points is that ethical change is insufficient and perhaps irrelevant for addressing our contemporary environmental ills:

> Individual conscience and the right kind of cultural attitudes are not by themselves sufficient to overcome the short-term calculations of utility that lead men to degrade their environment. Real altruism and genuine concern for posterity may not be entirely absent, but they are not present in sufficient strength to avert the tragedy. Only a government possessing great powers to regulate individual behavior in the ecological common interest can deal effectively with the tragedy of the commons.[1]

Soon after rereading this passage, my graduate institution hosted philosopher Tom Regan for a lecture on animal rights. After completing his disquisition, Regan faced stiff questioning from the audience regarding the meaning and implication of such rights: how did such rights compare to the rights of humans? How would they affect political and legal structures? Would such negatively defined rights require certain positive duties of humans and human political institutions toward animal communities? Ultimately, the ethicist shrugged and threw up his hands, uttering, "I am only a moral philosopher. I don't worry about those things."[2]

These are the dimensions of the paradox: politics—that realm of human social behavior in which we debate the social and political goals for our society—seems to presume that ethical debate is neither necessary nor even relevant to that project, while ethics—the philosophical study of right conduct and the good life—acts as if its pronouncements on such subjects need not concern itself with political effects. In fact, to we children of the Enlightenment, this bifurcation between politics and ethics might not only seem natural, but necessary: has it not been the case throughout human history that when we start mixing politics with truth claims (whether they be religious—

such as in the European religious wars of the sixteenth and seventeenth centuries—or ethical, such as during the French Revolution's Reign of Terror) blood has been spilled in copious quantities? Faced with such sanguinary historical experiences of mixing politics and ethics, like Locke[3] and Madison[4] we might assume that the best way to avoid political violence would be to construct a politics that did not depend upon apodictic truth claims regarding right conduct and the good life. Indeed, we might even argue along with Boorstin[5] that the true *genius* of American politics is its ability to function *without reference* to a particular set of comprehensive claims that one might associate with an ideology or philosophy.

But let us consider just what politics and ethics do: both are about channeling and potentially altering human behavior to achieve particular individual and collective ends. Yet, one—politics—assumes that such channeling is best done through external incentives and sanctions, while the other—ethics—assumes such incentives and sanctions are best executed internally. Both, in essence, want to prevent murder, lying, and the destruction of ecosystems. Politics assumes the best way to do this is through social, political, and economic policies—a system of external incentives and sanctions. Ethics assumes such goals are best achieved via the sanctions of conscience. Given this understanding of the common purpose of politics and ethics, I maintain that their continued divorce ultimately leads to the illegitimacy of both, and the increasing reliance of individuals and policy makers upon "standards" apparently provided them by two other human creations, science and economics. Both science and economics appear to provide not only reasonable individuals concrete guidance in day-to-day life, but also solid, indisputable criteria for persuasion. Both assertions—that the bifurcation of ethics and politics undermines their social legitimacy and that economics and science have become surrogate modes of analysis—spell trouble not only for environmental protection and restoration but for democratic society as well. The balance of this essay will be devoted to examining this bifurcation in environmental ethics and politics, its origins, and its implications for environmental protection and democratic practice. I begin by examining the work of two authors, J. Baird Callicott and Christopher Foreman. While both have their own positive projects and hence are unique, their predispositions toward ethics and politics portray a general problem. I conclude with a brief discussion of legitimacy and the role deliberative democracy may play in its formation.

Ethics (and Science) over Politics: Callicott

To be sure, the stark contrast I have illustrated above between ethics and politics generally and in environmental debates particularly is perhaps an overstatement. Many environmental policy analysts and environmental ethicists explicitly say they see the logical and even necessary connections. J. Baird Callicott for one, argues that "in thinking, talking, and writing about environmental ethics, environmental philosophers already have their shoulders to the wheel, helping to reconfigure the prevailing cultural worldview and thus helping to push general practice in the direction of environmental responsibility."[6] Callicott quite rightly maintains that the world of ideas—

of normative claims about the way the world works, of questions of duty and the good life—*does* shape the way we view and act within the world of pocketbooks, mortgages, and video games. Callicott draws attention to two cogent examples of such—the role the Enlightenment conceptions of humanism and rights doctrine as "articulated by Hobbes, Locke, Bentham, and Kant, among others"[7] played in the abolition of slavery over the last four hundred years, and the role that Lynn White's critique of theological justifications of environmental exploitation played in making the "stewardship inter-pretation of the God-"man"-nature relationship . . . [the] semiofficial religious doc-trine" of the three major monotheistic religions.[8]

Oddly, however, Callicott seems to suggest that ethics are primary in this world transformation, and he provides no hint about the relation of his preferred "holistic, nonanthropocentric environmental ethic" to practical politics. I think this is the case for two reasons, both of which illustrate the contemporary bifurcation of ethics from politics. One reason has to do with the content of his holist ethic, the other is implicit within his assumptions about the nature of human agency discussed in Callicott's more recent analyses.

Callicott's Normative Ethical Theory

For over two decades now Callicott has been articulating a philosophically robust de-fense of a holist, nonanthropocentric codification of Aldo Leopold's land ethic. While noting that the famous conservationist's ethical musings were more aphoristic than sys-tematic, Callicott has reinterpreted Leopold's maxim via the subjectivist axiology of David Hume and Adam Smith, the evolutionary and biological origins of ethics argued by Charles Darwin and more contemporary writers like E. O. Wilson, the ecological models of ecosystem pioneers Charles Elton and Arthur Tansley, and the Copenhagen interpretation of Quantum Physics.

A brief discussion of these constituent parts is necessary. Hume and Smith provide the basis for a subjectivist axiology that though based in "self love,"[9] posits a theory of moral sentiments in which human values are the result less of reason and more of per-sonal attachments to people and things we love or desire. Callicott summarizes Hume thus: "moral value . . . is in the eye of the beholder."[10] However, Callicott claims that such a radical subjectivity is "fixed" by Darwin:

> Hume suggests that the values . . . are not arbitrary, but arise spontaneously in you because of the "constitution of your nature." The affective constitu-tion of human nature, Darwin plausibly argued, is standardized by natural selection. . . . [C]ertain sentiments were naturally selected in a social envi-ronment which permitted and facilitated growth in the size and complexity of society. The social sentiments, however, though fixed by natural selection, are open-ended.[11]

Thus, moral values (or what Callicott calls "moral-like limitations"[12]) may be partially subjective, but not radically relative.[13] According to Callicott, values are only perceived as relative (by emotivists and intuitionists, for example) due to "the nearly universal inattention of philosophers 'to . . . the "biologization of ethics"'" by sociobiologists like E. O. Wilson. For Callicott, value judgments may not be objectively right or wrong, but a "functional equivalent" of objectivity is derived from a "consensus of feeling":

> Human feelings, like human fingers, human ears, and human teeth, though both individually variable and open to information by cultural manipulation, have been standardized by natural selection. . . . Hence, radically eccentric value judgments may be said to be abnormal or even incorrect in the same sense that we might say that someone's radically curved spine is abnormal or incorrect.[14]

After reducing ethics to functional systems of "moral-like" sentiments somewhat standardized through natural selection, Leopold's land ethic, according to Callicott, appears as a culturally represented evolutionary adaptation for inclusive fitness.[15] Then, relying heavily on the ecosystems interpretations of Charles Elton and Arthur Tansley (not necessarily in vogue in science circles these days[16]), Callicott maintains that "ecology inclines its students toward a more holistic vision of the world," and makes "it possible to apprehend the same landscape as an articulate unity (without the least hint of mysticism or ineffability)."[17] Callicott further argues that just as Heisenberg's uncertainty principle breaks down the purported objectivity of the scientific observer by demonstrating a subject's physical properties are to some extent affected by the presumptions of the observer, by analogy quantum physics acts also as a solvent for a crucial obstacle to holist ecological thought by dismantling the Cartesian subject/object dichotomy existing between valuing humans and valued or unvalued Nature.[18]

Having now established roots in a Humean axiology and the biologization of ethics, Callicott then combines these developments with the holistic premise of the expansive ecological self gleaned from ecology and quantum theory:

> If we assume (a) . . . that nature is one and continuous with the self, and (b) with the bulk of modern moral theory that egoism is axiologically given and that self-interested behavior has a prima facie claim to be at the same time rational behavior, then the central axiological problem of environmental ethics, the problem of intrinsic value in nature may be directly and simply solved. . . . If the self is intrinsically valuable, then nature is intrinsically valuable.[19]

This brief sketch of Callicott's normative project allows us to observe several *antipolitical* tendencies within his reasoning. First, by utilizing Hume to establish a subjective axiology, which is then "fixed" or standardized via Darwin and contemporary sociobiology, Callicott simply suggests that the moral "sight" of each isolated "beholder" over time converges on a standard that results not so much from deliberation, debate, and consensus formation (how one might *assume* that value conflicts may be settled consciously and rigorously[20]), as from the rather nonpurposive, undirected trial and error of evolution: those who employ "incorrect" values in their decisions are simply eliminated ad hoc from the human species.[21] This would occur with or without conscious social decisions: the mechanism of ethical convergence is *independent* of any perceived political or social system, or the postulation of substantive political and ethical discourse (though that mechanism does, in effect, render judgment on the fitness of political, social, and economic systems[22]). In fact, the whole structure here is reminiscent of laissez-faire economics: members of the biotic community "depend upon one another economically," and species "optimize their populations" in accordance with (food) supply and (predator) demand.[23] In all, atomistic individuals find that in the sociobiological marketplace some of their actions are rewarded (shunning fratricide improves overall clan fitness) while others are sanctioned (intolerance of social deviance wipes out plague-resistant genes). The "hidden hand" keeps the system in balance and promotes the greatest good despite the inattention of individuals to the conscious formation of that greatest good:

> Each of the myriad living forms, while pursuing its own interests, performs a function which contributes to the overall flow of materials, services, and energy within the system. . . . In general, each thing has a certain role or function in the natural economy.[24]

Who needs politics when biology—via the economy of nature—does the job more keenly? Indeed, Callicott's description of "natures' economy" is insightful, yet it does very little to tell us as moral and political agents how to value the "whole" or its "parts." But like economic laissez-fairism, it seems to mystically entail reason upon all actions (albeit after the fact) as we shrink away from actual social responsibility for our judgments and actions, submitting to the "larger scheme of things." The ecological "market" decides.

Callicott's holism is problematic on another account. Apparently,[25] the New Physics requires us to recognize that, in essence, the subject and the object are one, thus utilizing the axiological primacy of the self (assumed in Callicott's Humean starting point) to attribute not only value to nature (part of the greater self), but also to explain duties toward nature. In his most pointed discussions, Callicott makes the implications of this movement clear—the self and nature are collapsed into one:

> If quantum theory and ecology imply in structurally similar ways in both the physical and organic domains of nature the continuity of self and nature, and the self is intrinsically valuable, then nature is intrinsically valuable. If it is rational for me to act in my own interest, and nature and I are one, then it is rational for me to act in the best interest of nature.[26]

Callicott has retained his vision of unity in later writings as well, though he has on occasion softened the "unity" to a description of "one reality, with objective and subjective poles."[27] Clearly, Callicott recognizes the advantages of a stronger unity of nature and self: environmental protection truly becomes a matter of self-interest and of altruism. This allows Callicott to accomplish what other environmental theorists have been unable to do—posit intrinsic value of nature without fundamentally challenging the axiologically privileged position of the self in modern society.[28] Furthermore, since our expansive and environmentally inclined moral sentiments are the result of natural selection (to promote the well-being of this larger self) one can speculate, as Callicott appears to do, that "deviant," anti-ecological behavior is as much an abnormality as genetic spine disorders.[29]

This move toward unity fundamentally eliminates and effaces the distance and distinction needed for ethical judgment and political action. One is left with the ethics and politics of a single abstract self: can the index finger of the hand act immorally against the thumb of the same? Can the third finger and pinky form a political community? Ethos and polis necessitate a plurality voices, of entities.[30] Thus, Callicott misses the point entirely when he attempts to defend his theory against claims of "fascism" by suggesting that holist ecocentrism does not mean that one would go around depopulating the world of humans in order to provide more *Lebensraum* for endangered species:[31] The problem is much deeper than any single egregious action. Rather, the problem is that his model of holist ecocentrism is the totalitarian ideal: a single organism, unified in purpose and motive and in no need of dialogue or debate, for there can be only one authentic voice from the whole. Plurality is itself a sign of sickness, of biological unfitness.[32]

Callicott's Practice

Besides these antipolitical aspects inherent within Callicott's normative theory, Callicott's personal vision of social change also demonstrates an indifference to politics. He describes his own move from being "Joe Bioregionalist"[33] living the life of personal transformation (while others around him continued to live lives of excessive consumerism), to professional ethicist concerned about going to conferences and getting papers published in academic journals. The lesson Callicott learns from this experience is that personal transformation is not enough—broad social change must occur. Single individuals eating homegrown vegetables and riding their bikes around town is simply not enough: "The incremental approach—you change, I change, the next person changes, after awhile we all will have changed our environmental behavior—seems futile."[34]

Yet Callicott makes clear that it is not his jet travel to professional conferences to defend holist ecocentrism that will change society. This is not really the source of the "cultural ether" within which we live.[35] Nor is its source collective political action.[36] Rather, Callicott suggests it is once again science that saves the day: the same scientific revolution that gave us the New Physics (and the effacement of the subject/object and fact/value dichotomies discussed above) is key to changing the preferences of contemporary individuals from hard path technologies and agro-industrial food stuffs to microwave ovens, photovoltaic cells, and organic produce. Computers inculcate systemic—even ecosystemic—thinking.[37] In the end, these "postmodern" technologies not only reduce anthropogenic impacts on the environment, but are also the source of the real "ether" that will trigger a cultural shift:

> I believe that [these technologies] will communicate the post-Modern holistic, systemic, dynamic, concept of nature with us smart monkeys as creative, interactive, components in it. Hopefully that will set the stage for a positive feedback cultural process: more holistic-systemic-interactive thinking leading to more technological innovation in the same motif and esprit

leading to more thinking in the same vein and so on. Ultimately, we should hope to see corresponding changes in politics, economics, agriculture, medicine, and other primary aspects of civilization.[38]

It would seem that what we need are fewer environmental ethicists and more electrical engineers. Indeed, Callicott suggests that real change may have little (if anything) to do with conscious theorizing: "The new systemic understanding of nature, human nature, and the human-nature relationship along with its associated values may *trickle down* [my emphasis] into the popular mind less through its direct and didactic representation in books and TV documentaries than through its embodiment in post-Modern solar-electronic technology and organic-ecological agriculture."[39] With statements like this, one wonders how in the world Thoreau, Emerson, and Greeley ever thought to overcome slavery with mere words and collective action unsupported by a truly "post-slavery" technology.

The language of "trickle down" economics is telling. Callicott's ruminations on practical change exude no lack of confidence in science or an economistic understanding of human societies and nature. Furthermore, when Callicott *does* mention politics, it is in reference to overcoming Hardin's[40] tragedy of the commons via "mutual coercion mutually agreed upon."[41] This too is telling, for the tragedy of the commons is not a political model, but an economic one: isolated individuals make resource allocation choices based upon their own self-interest and the anticipated *but unknown* choices of other consumers of a common pool resource. The tragedy occurs *because* there is no social/political mechanism by which those individuals overcome their isolation to communicate directly regarding possible common interests: the only information they receive are market signals regarding supply, demand, consumption, and scarcity.[42] As was problematic in Hardin's own analysis,[43] the proffered solution, "mutual coercion mutually agreed upon," requires the existence of an efficacious politics that is precluded by the market assumptions of the tragedy itself. Hardin simply suggests that the information cues provided by a failing market will be so overwhelming they cannot be ignored: the exploiters of the common pool resource will simply be shocked out of their splendid atomistic isolation and resort to "politics."

Ironically, the individuals Callicott wishes to inculcate into a holist ecocentric ethic to avert the tragedy of the commons are just as atomistic and isolated. In a now too-common ploy, Callicott argues that these isolated individuals may simply recognize a similar fait accompli as that posited by Hardin: facts about the natural world cannot be ignored, and the "Darwinian-Einsteinian-Leopoldian" understanding of humans' interrelation with nature may gain sway over our minds—and hence our values—via "universal ecological literacy."[44] Truly a son of the Enlightenment, Callicott thus suggests that change will occur if we simply "dare to know." Yet, as noted above, he seems more inclined to suggest change that may lead to the *political* conditions necessary for "mutual coercion mutually agreed upon" will occur via market exposure—taking their cues from the post-Modern goods available to them, isolated consumers will set aside their atomistic lives to become engaged citizens. Startlingly, Callicott—the primary spokesperson of holist ecocentrism—places more hope in science and economics than ethics and politics.

Politics over Ethics: Foreman

In political writings on environmental issues, there are examples of scholars who do take ethics and values seriously, explicitly noting relationships between normative claims and political consequences.[45] But many are still reluctant to claim much relevance for ethics in their examinations,[46] while others even suggest that somehow claims about moral duties and conceptions of the good life sully the waters of rational policy deliberations.[47] Christopher Foreman's examination of the environmental justice movement[48] exemplifies the dilemma.

In his recent work on the environmental justice (EJ) movement, Christopher Foreman develops a sophisticated analysis of a movement that is clearly arguing first and foremost for a change in personal and public values. Responding to the work of activists like Lois Gibbs,[49] scholar/activists such as Robert Bullard,[50] and groups like the United Church of Christ's Commission on Racial Justice,[51] Foreman rightly characterizes the EJ movement's general impetus as a "normative belief in citizens and communities having a more significant voice in everything from scientific assessment to facility permitting" in managing exposure to hazardous or nonhazardous pollutants.[52] Foreman also notes the movement's overarching egalitarian orientation, critiquing corporate capitalism and traditional interest-group pluralism, and favoring a more redistributive and participatory politics.[53] Hence, though Foreman often criticizes local EJ groups as simply a racial or class variant on the NIMBY (Not In My Back Yard) syndrome,[54] he is clearly aware that the environmental justice movement, by combining elements of the ethically charged civil rights movement with environmentalism, poses a serious ethical challenge to the existing political and social order.[55]

Foreman seems on the whole sympathetic with the basic goals of the EJ movement—he *seems* indeed to wish that communities of color and persons of lower socioeconomic status were less vulnerable to health and environmental hazards, and Foreman also expresses the desire to raise the overall quality of life of the nation's most desperate communities, and improve their participation in public decision making.[56] Yet Foreman consistently argues that resolute commitment to such a "fanciful"[57] set of normative values is not only counterproductive, but also dangerous.[58]

Foreman's argument against the political manifestation of such "raw" and perhaps inappropriate ethical commitments is instructive not simply because he demonstrates another example of the subordination of ethics to politics, but also because of the way his image of politics represents a particularly economistic understanding of public dilemmas. This is indeed reminiscent of the economistic predilections displayed by Callicott, and symptomatic of the biases exhibited in much of the contemporary environmental policy literature.

The Inferiority and Threat of Ethics to Politics

Foreman's subordination of ethical impulses to "political realism" is a curious yet common phenomenon in contemporary political analysis, whether one is examining environmental issues, welfare reform, or abortion. He doesn't deny the authenticity of the values—communities of color and lower socioeconomic status *do* feel alienated and dispossessed, and *do* distrust government and business, which *do* appear to conspire to place the least desirable economic activities in the least empowered communities. Nor does Foreman deny the authenticity of their commitment to egalitarianism and participatory democracy. Rather, Foreman suggests such ethical commitments, when they are given unmediated expression by grassroots activists and other well-intentioned citizens in the public sphere, short circuit the requisite "cool headed" and "objective" rationalism necessary to substantively address problems of toxic exposure and even political and economic equity and opportunity issues:

> [M]ovement rhetoric argues that no community should be harmed and that *all* community concerns and grievances deserve redress. Scholar-activist Robert Bullard proposes that "the solution to unequal protection lies in the realm of environmental justice for all Americans. . . . When pressed about the need for environmental risk priorities, and about how to incorporate environmental justice into priority setting, Bullard's answer is a vague plea for nondiscrimination. . . . This is symptomatic of a movement for which untrammeled citizen voice and overall social equity are cardinal values. Bullard's position also epitomizes the desire . . . to avoid speaking difficult truths.[59]

For Foreman, it is clear that one such "difficult truth" is that fundamental value commitments, as apodictic statements about the way the world (or at least the social world) *ought* to work, are disruptive to the preference aggregation and subsequent political compromise demanded of pluralist democratic politics. Following the predisposition of classical liberals from Locke to Berlin[60] before him, Foreman assumes that values and ethical impulses are radically subjective and incommensurable, and hence not a legitimate or even useful basis of politics. Though such impulses may be the source of some people's political awakening, effective political participation, policy formation—and indeed the stability of democratic politics generally—requires one to set aside raw ethical impulses (what Foreman calls one's intuition) to pursue a rational policy process dominated by cost-benefit analysis, risk assessment, and the concomitant trade-offs.[61]

The general tenor of Foreman's critique parallels a *normative* vision of democratic politics as nonideological, empirically oriented, problem solving reminiscent of Boorstin's classic thesis of the benefits of ideological shallowness and nonnormative debate,[62] and Dahl's polyarchy, in which competition among minority preferences produces public policy compromise and encourages social moderation.[63] Foreman, in fact, appears nostalgic, desiring a return to the stability of a pluralist politics dominated by two parties that negotiate between interests (like organized labor and business), striking deals that provide economic satisfaction (or a semblance of such) for most parties involved.[64] While few believe that we can put the "New Politics" genie back into its proverbial bottle, it is not uncommon for analysts like Foreman to suggest that a more appropriate, less controversial, and hence more efficacious politics may emerge if participants checked their "boundaryless" and incoherent values at the door.[65]

The problem, of course, is that the reason the "Old Politics" worked was because it reflected an implicit (though not universal) consensus on the importance of political and ethical moderation, compromise, and economic growth for maintaining political stability: if political stability would be endangered by ardent ethical or religious convictions, the latter ought to give way.[66]

Rationalism—Narrowly Defined

Foreman is convinced that the values and goals of EJ proponents cast doubt upon their ability to participate effectively in the development of rational public policies addressing their substantive commitments.[67] Yet for Foreman it is clear that "rational" public policy requires risk assessment and benefit/cost analysis. Only through the use of these techniques can citizens and decision makers make policy-relevant distinctions between actual and perceived risks, legitimate fears and unfounded panic, nebulous, abstract goals and realistic priorities.[68]

Foreman cites approvingly Associate Justice Stephen Breyer's *Breaking the Vicious Circle: Toward Effective Risk Regulation*[69] as a model of "rational" thinking regarding risk. Of particular interest to Foreman is Breyer's critique of "the last 10%," in which it is implicitly argued that environmental cleanup or risk reduction past a certain threshold is economically inefficient: compared to the marginal costs of achieving the last increment of risk reduction to the total cost of all increments before it, money and time may be better spent elsewhere.[70] Ultimately, Breyer provides Foreman a succinct and compelling argument for viewing environmental protection and risk reduction as an amenity purchased (rather than protected) by societies, and such purchase implies associated opportunity costs:

> [E]nvironmental justice activism generally fails to confront the inevitable tradeoffs between economic opportunity and environmental risks. These risks are, in the grand scheme of things, mostly relatively low and manageable. Easy slogans do not adequately speak to the fates of communities that certainly want to avoid undue risk but that also need industrial development to provide jobs and local opportunity.[71]

For Foreman, risk assessment and benefit-cost analysis become the means by which to "rationalize" the incoherent and emotive desires of antiscientific, parochial activists,[72] and inoculate the body politic from extremism, thus encouraging a more technocratic politics that subordinates ethics to political realism. In this desire Foreman is also not alone: risk assessment is appealing particularly to classical liberals trying to escape the divisiveness and apparent overselling and exaggeration by activists seeking greater environmental protection and regulation.[73] Throughout his work, Foreman also reflects this bias, and acts as if there is such a consensus on the utility, objectivity, and hence legitimacy of risk assessment that the necessity of its application is beyond question. There is literally *no* discussion of the implicit value assumptions that undergird risk assessment and benefit-cost analysis, assumptions that suggest markets are the proper determinants of value, that no human, resource, or ethical commitment is "priceless," or beyond negotiation, and that by maximizing economic efficiency one maximizes personal as well as collective welfare.[74]

Ultimately, Foreman vividly illustrates a potent and pervasive paradox of contemporary politics and political analysis: by proffering an implicitly value-laden version of political rationality, Foreman claims objectivity and neutrality for "tools" that are actually an alternative set of values and beliefs. Yet because these are tools rather than value claims, constructive and comprehensive criticism of their application to a given situation is short-circuited. Who opposes a tool other than a Luddite or a saboteur? Aren't we all interested in getting the best information and arriving at the best outcome? In short, Foreman subordinates the *explicit* ethical arguments of EJ activists (for placing priority on safety, equity, and participation) to the *implicit* ethical claims sneaking into public policy debates in the Trojan Horse of risk assessment and benefit cost analysis.

Undermining Legitimacy

In his advocacy of "rational" techniques for policy determination, Foreman wishes to empower professionals, not necessarily activists: while communities may have some legitimate concerns about equity and participation, ultimately professionals must determine the *actual* risks faced by a community and balance the trade-offs accordingly. Sure, there should be "dialogue" with community members, and professionals ought to instruct community members regarding the *actual* risks. Yet Foreman notes with approval Justice Breyer's call for a new "group of civil servants" spanning across agencies, the courts, and legislatures with the requisite training and competence to rationalize environmental and risk management policies.[75]

Foreman thus simply misses the point. Yes, it is important for policy choices to be informed by and executed by competent professionals. Furthermore, within certain constraints, risk assessment and benefit-cost analysis can provide information relevant to addressing social goals.[76] Nevertheless, EJ activists and others that act *because of* their value orientations, may not believe that *any* trade-off is acceptable.[77] And rather than being naïve and parochial, the value positions of activists often may be the result of contextual comparison, analysis, and testing. Responding to Foreman's disparagement of activists' values, Gary Abraham has noted that

> The perspective of local opponents . . . is not as restricted as Foreman suggests. Local opponents compare their communities with others not burdened by risks of accidental and unavoidable discharge of toxics or other specific adverse impacts on the environment, and to this extent local opponents adopt a regional and national perspective. Indeed *comparison* is at the heart of local judgments . . . [and] prompts the typical questions opponents insist on injecting into siting decisions. Why is a landfill being sited here, far from the source of the waste? Why are there no chemical factories in wealthier suburban communities? . . . Are such facilities really necessary?[78]

Abraham suggests that "rationalists" like Foreman often do not consider economic, educational, and psychological obstacles that citizens may face when trying to participate in arenas where the rationalists' rules and languages of engagement are operative.[79] Someone who argues that X under no circumstances may be diminished or put at risk is simply beyond ken for the advocates of Foreman's political realism: their proper tools require that preferences be expressed in potential trade-offs. Hence, "political realists" and "ethical idealists" are literally speaking two different languages of value. Ironically, it is the activists' values that are more transparent, while the rationalists' are opaque—hidden in the assumptions of the tools of political realism.

It is also ironic that risk assessment and benefit-cost analysis, originally advocated in the 1970s and 1980s as the means by which to restore consensus and legitimacy to public policy, now may be undermining political legitimacy. Perhaps this should not be too surprising, given the application of these tools in the most partisan of ways.[80] But the impact upon policy legitimacy is much broader than this observation.

In essence, Foreman, like Callicott, argues that the *only* values worth asserting in politics and policy making are those beyond question and contestation, like those apparently derived from and perpetuated by science and economics (just as in an earlier age such may have been derived from religion). The problem is, in a democratic age, such an assertion (even in the guise of objective tools) seems disingenuous. This is the rub: we expect our value claims to be open to dialogue and debate at the same time we nervously anticipate that such contestation may weaken our belief in and commitment to them.

Political Legitimacy and the Flight to Science and Economics

For both Callicott and Foreman there is a curious dependence upon science, both (1) as an alternative to often misplaced and subjective ethical impulses (Foreman), and (2) as a substitute for political agency and basis for values (Callicott). It probably shouldn't be all that surprising: as children of the Enlightenment, they (and we) have become wary of both ethics and politics, assuming both are arenas of subjective and ultimately incommensurable claims about the way the world *is* and *ought* to work. Science, and to a lesser extent that "dismal" social science, economics, may purportedly give us empirical bases for both facts and values. Yet, when confronted with such *scientistic* assumptions, I am reminded of J. S. Alper's reflections on the role of biological science in decision making:

> If biological facts are to be used in moral decisions, it must be assumed that biological facts are relevant in making ethical decisions. This premise itself is of course a value judgement. Biological facts have relevance in ethical decision-making only if we choose to allow them to have relevance.[81]

I believe that Alper's observations are just as applicable to the use of science generally, not only in ethics but also in politics. Science and the scientific method are perhaps an inevitable "spackle" with which we would try to fill the void left by the collapse of objective religious and philosophical truth claims, particularly since it was science that did so much to undermine theology and philosophy. In turn, economics, which claims to do for the social world what science does for the natural world (that is, provide objective understanding of human behavior—the quintessential "rational actor") also pretends to this role.

Nevertheless, the practice of science (as well as economics) is rife with theoretical assumptions that are necessary even for the formation of falsifiable hypotheses.[82] Hence, by the time we get to claims like those made by Callicott and Foreman, any reliance upon science or economics is *shot through* with value assumptions privileging certain types of evidence and logical structure, as well as visions of what human action *ought* to exemplify or maximize—things like efficiency, rationality, individual action, self-interest, and so forth. *Some* of these might indeed be things we want to emphasize, but, following Alper, it is probably the case that we often avoid *conscious* and explicit deliberation over such. And that is where the question of legitimacy once again becomes central, and where we can return to the necessity of bringing ethical and political dialogue back together.

Legitimacy Reconsidered

I am often struck by what insights are gained in the classroom. For about ten years now I have been teaching an environmental ethics course at my university, and on numerous occasions something like the following has occurred: we are reading a piece in animal rights or ecocentrism or ecofeminism, and after laying out the philosophical reasoning of a position, I ask a student, "Well, what do you think? Do you think author X is right to suggest that we, as humans, must give moral consideration to nonhuman entities?" The conversation often goes something like this:

> Student: "Well, my religious faith says that only humans have souls. I don't believe what the author says."
>
> Bowersox: "Good. Then based upon your apodictic and coherent faith, you must believe that the author is a bad person for maintaining the position that they do."
>
> Student: "Well, they can believe any way they wish. It is just that according to my beliefs nonhumans don't have souls and therefore I don't have to treat them differently than I currently do."

Such exchanges demonstrate to me what has happened to our ability to make normative arguments: my student is a private moral authoritarian (her faith is apodictic and commanding for her) yet a public nihilist (no agreement is possible or necessary between her, the author, or anyone else in the class). My students and most people commonly assume that normative arguments are merely individual whims masquerading as categorical imperatives—radically subjective opinions incommensurable with the evaluations of others. Each "is orthodox to himself."[83] Indeed, as Rawls noted some years ago, this seems to be one of the foundational political commitments of the Enlightenment:

> [A]s a practical political matter no general moral conception can provide a publicly recognized basis for a conception of justice in a modern democratic state. The social and historical conditions of such a state have their origins in

the Wars of Religion following the Reformation and the subsequent development of the principle of toleration, and in the growth of constitutional
government and the institutions of large industrial market economies. . . .
[A] workable conception of political justice . . . must allow for a diversity of
doctrines and the plurality of conflicting, and indeed incommensurable, conceptions of the good affirmed by members of existing democratic societies.[84]

Callicott and Foreman assume this essential Lockean and Rawlsian position of incommensurability, yet rely upon science and economics to "force" consensus: Callicott
does so by suggesting convergence upon the land ethic is biologically inevitable, which
will then establish the necessary preconditions for efficacious political action. Foreman
seeks to silence or at least marginalize normative argument in favor of political realism
and pragmatic management. Both are dangerous strategies.

They are dangerous because they continue to foster the sublimation of key normative assumptions open to challenge and refutation. Cloaking normative argument
in science or economics doesn't make them any more apodictic, just more abstract and
obscure. Given the coercive limits of even the most totalitarian of states,[85] the compliance levels necessary to achieve the goals of most environmental regulations will require high levels of voluntary support via social consensus. Social consensus is only
possible to the extent that these assumptions are consciously exposed to deliberation,
critique, confirmation, and possible refutation.

Returning to the idea that both ethics and politics are two ways of channeling human
behavior to achieve individual and collective ends, and given the dangerous consequences
of avoiding normative argument over such things as the relative worth of species (human
and nonhuman) or the equity effects of the siting of a hazardous waste incinerator, we
must recognize that it is time for us as children of the Enlightenment to get over the unnecessary bifurcation of the two. While the separation of politics and ethics made sense to
our seventeenth- and eighteenth-century predecessors, four hundred years of skepticism
has thoroughly undermined the categorical claims of both. No amount of science or social science is going to reestablish either systems' claims to self-evidence. Hence, it is time
for politics and ethics to join forces, recognizing not only their shared outcomes, but also
a common method of inquiry. The method may be referred to as deliberative democracy,
in which claims about how the world works, what one ought to do, and the nature of the
good life are contested, amended, and contingently agreed upon. Rather than hiding behind science and economics, values become the explicit subject of politics and the conscious starting point for all policies. Perhaps here we can find a useful space between our
private moral authoritarianism and our public moral nihilism. By doing so, we may yet
escape the inherent subjectivity imposed upon our politics and ethics since the Enlightenment, basking in the dull glow of intersubjective agreement.[86]

Deliberative Democracy—Necessarily

This image of deliberative democracy is not new to environmental thought: while early
writers such as Ophuls, Heilbroner,[87] and others suggested that the path to environmental salvation led through the valley of authoritarianism, a veritable cottage industry
has developed around normative defenses of the role of democracy (albeit in various

forms) in environmental disputes. This volume, in essence, is a product of that industry and its political commitments. But while many laborers in this cottage maintain that they are here by choice—that is, they have a normative commitment to the defense and advancement of democratic forms of politics—I would argue that there is no practical, defensible, and viable alternative to democracy, *even if* there are theoretically possible alternatives out there, such as some sort of green theology that would inculcate a new relation with the natural world via personal recognition of and reverence for the divine.[88] While I think that such a "green theology" is the most likely alternative to a "green politics," and one that *may eventually* find acceptance in the religious ethos of our society,[89] that acceptance itself is most likely going to be the result of experiencing a *political conversation* and not necessarily a religious *conversion* experience.[90]

As skeptical children of the Enlightenment, we are unlikely to accept simple pronouncements of "one ought to do X" or "one ought to believe Y," whether the source of such statements is one's professor, priest, or president. Before one adopts the proffered belief or perogative, most will demand further explanation: over the last four hundred years or so we have simply knocked out the metaphysical struts propping up apodictic reasoning, whether it be reasoning regarding the status of one's soul or the status of one's exam grade. Of course there is a "downside" to this condition: sometimes we would like our interlocutors to simply "do as we say," whether we cloak our statements in science, economics, or religion. But the *self-evident authority*, the necessary recognition of such statements as givens, has evaporated.[91]

Happily, deliberation—and deliberative democracy—can be part of the solution, not simply part of the problem. Democracy does not have to be a process by which "tyrannical majorities" ignore not only scientific information but also the *facts* that their actions may impinge upon the rights and actions of other entities (both human and nonhuman). Rather, deliberative democracy promises a method of collectively affirming or refuting relevant moral, religious, social, and scientific insights via a discursive model that maximizes openness, equality, noncoercion, and rationality, and minimizes "delusion, deception, power, and strategy."[92] Such deliberation need not be limited to deliberation over policies, but can itself be used to develop a contingent, intersubjective consensus about values, obligations, and priorities that may be necessary for the establishment of public policies.[93] And while not guaranteed, the deliberative process itself becomes a method by which we may more accurately perceive the fundamental relationships that define ourselves and nature.[94] While perhaps a messy and time-consuming process, such discursive practice conceives of the possibility not only of substantive collective deliberation over means and ends, but also *collective action* for those ends.

It has not been my goal in these last few pages to fully detail the dimensions and preconditions of a green deliberative democracy. Rather, it has been my desire to demonstrate the *necessity* of such in the face of the legitimacy crisis facing contemporary environmental ethics and politics. While democracy—and especially deliberative democracy—has its shortcomings and potential for manipulation and abuse,[95] in the twenty-first century we have no other viable choice. As Apel suggests:

> We human beings, as creatures of language, so to speak . . . are condemned to "agreeing" amongst ourselves about the criteria of meaning and validity of our actions and knowledge.[96]

Let us overcome our Enlightenment fears—well grounded though they may be—and use deliberative democracy to debate and challenge our conceptions of the world (our visions of our collective future) and facilitate the combination of our individual wills into a common enterprise.

Notes

1. William Ophuls, *Ecology and the Politics of Scarcity* (San Francisco: Freeman, 1977), 154.

2. Tom Regan, public lecture, University of Wisconsin-Madison, fall 1989.

3. John Locke, *A Letter Concerning Toleration* (1689; reprint Indianapolis, Ind.: Bobbs-Merrill, 1955).

4. James Madison, "Federalist #10," in *The Federalist Papers* (1788; reprint, New York: Penguin, 1987).

5. Daniel Boorstin, *The Genius of American Politics* (Chicago: University of Chicago Press, 1953).

6. J. Baird Callicott, *Beyond the Land Ethic* (Albany, N.Y.: SUNY Press, 1999), 43.

7. Ibid., 33.

8. Ibid., 41.

9. Ibid., 87.

10. J. Baird Callicott, *In Defense of the Land Ethic* (Albany, N.Y.: SUNY Press, 1989), 160.

11. Ibid., 162.

12. Ibid., 65.

13. Callicott, *Beyond the Land Ethic*, 87–88.

14. Callicott, *In Defense of the Land Ethic*, 164. While not using such stark language, Callicott repeats this claim for the standardization of ethics in *Beyond the Land Ethic*, 87–88.

15. Callicott, *In Defense of the Land Ethic*, 65–67, 77–80.

16. See Kristin Shrader-Frechette and Earl D. McCoy, *Method in Ecology* (New York: Cambridge University Press, 1993); Kristin Schrader-Frechette and Earl D. McCoy, "How the Tail Wags the Dog, or How Value Judgements Determine Ecological Science," *Environmental Values* 3 (1994): 107–20; Rob Hengeveld, *Dynamics of Biological Invasions* (New York: Chapman and Hall, 1989); S. L. Pimm, "The Complexity and Stability of Ecosystems," *Nature* 207 (1984): 321–26. Callicott himself recognizes the changes in ecosystem thought but suggests the stability model may be returning as the dominant paradigm. See Callicott, *Beyond the Land Ethic*, 122–6.

17. Callicott, *In Defense of the Land Ethic*, 22.

18. Ibid., 169–72; Callicott, *Beyond the Land Ethic*, 53–54, 83.

19. Callicott, *In Defense of the Land Ethic*, 173.

20. See for instance, John Dryzek, "Green Reason: Communicative Ethics for the Biosphere," *Environmental Ethics* 12 (1990): 195–210; John Dryzek, *The Politics of the Earth* (Oxford, U.K.: Oxford University Press, 1997).

21. Callicott, *Beyond the Land Ethic*, 88.

22. For this effect of sociobiology, see Roger Masters, "Evolutionary Biology and Political Theory," *American Political Science Review* 84, no. 1 (1990): 204–7; Larry Arnhart, *Darwinian Natural Right* (Albany, N.Y.: SUNY Press, 1998). That this is not outside the ken of Callicott's rather sociobiological understanding of social structures, see Callicott, *Beyond the Land Ethic*, 58.

23. Callicott, *In Defense of the Land Ethic*, 27, 23, 57; see also *Beyond the Land Ethic*, 69.

24. Callicott, *In Defense of the Land Ethic*, 72, emphasis added. See also Callicott, "Principal Traditions in American Environmental Ethics: A Survey of Moral Values for Framing an American Ocean Policy," *Ocean and Coastal Management* 17 (1992): 306–7.

25. For critiques of this interpretation of quantum physics, see Dugald Murdoch, *Niels Bohr's Philosophy of Physics* (Cambridge, U.K.: Cambridge University Press, 1987), chapters 7, 10, 11; Evelyn Fox Keller, *Reflections on Gender and Science* (New Haven, Conn.: Yale University Press, 1985), 117; Susan Bordo, *The Flight to Objectivity* (Albany, N.Y.: SUNY Press, 1987), 103.

26. Callicott, *In Defense of the Land Ethic*, 173.

27. Callicott "Rolston on Intrinsic Value: A Deconstruction," *Environmental Ethics* 14 (1992): 140.

28. Callicott, *In Defense of the Land Ethic*, 174.

29. Ibid., 164.

30. See Jim Cheney, "The Neo-Stoicism of Radical Environmentalism," *Environmental Ethics* 11 (1989): 293–325; Cheney, "Callicott's Metaphysics of Morals," *Environmental Ethics* 13 (1991): 311–25. See also Hannah Arendt, *On Revolution* (New York: Viking, 1963); Hannah Arendt, *Life of the Mind Volume II: Willing* (New York: Harcourt Brace Jovanovich, 1977).

31. Callicott, *Beyond the Land Ethic*, 70–76.

32. See Hannah Arendt, *Totalitarianism* (New York: Harvest, 1951), 116, 136ff; Herbert J. Spiro, "Totalitarianism," *Encyclopedia of the Social Sciences* (1968): 106–12.

33. Callicott, *Beyond the Land Ethic*, 46.

34. Ibid., 49.

35. Ibid., 36.

36. Ibid., 49.

37. Ibid., 55–56.

38. Ibid., 56.

39. Ibid., 58.

40. Garrett Hardin, "The Tragedy of the Commons," *Science* 162 (December 13, 1968): 1243–48.

41. Callicott, *Beyond the Land Ethic*, 47, 51.

42. See Peter Wenz, *Environmental Ethics Today* (New York: Oxford University Press, 2001), 21–35.

43. See Beryl Crowe, "The Tragedy of the Commons Revisited," *Science* 166 (November 28, 1969): 1103–7.

44. Callicott, *Beyond the Land Ethic*, 49–51.

45. See, for instance, Andrew Dobson, *Justice and the Environment: Conceptions of Environmental Sustainability and Theories of Distributive Justice* (Oxford, U.K.: Oxford University Press, 1998); Matthew Alan Cahn, *Environmental Deceptions* (Albany, N.Y.: SUNY Press, 1995).

46. See among others, Denise Scheberle, *Federalism and Environmental Policy* (Washington, D.C.: Georgetown University Press, 1997); Michael E. Kraft, *Environmental Policy and Politics* (New York: HarperCollins, 1996); Charles Davis, "Introduction: The Context of Public Lands Policy Change," in *Western Public Lands and Environmental Politics*, ed. Charles Davis (Boulder, Colo.: Westview, 1997).

47. See, for example Susan Buck, "Science as a Substitute for Moral Principle" and "Saving All the Parts: Science and Sustainability," in *The Moral Austerity of Environmental Decisionmaking*, ed. John Martin Gillroy and Joe Bowersox (Durham, N.C.: Duke University Press, forthcoming); Jonathan Baert Wiener, "Sustainable Governance," in *The Moral Austerity of Environmental Decisionmaking*, ed. John Martin Gillroy and Joe Bowersox (Durham, N.C.: Duke University Press, forthcoming).

48. Brookings Institution, *The Promise and Peril of Environmental Justice* (Washington, D.C.: Brookings, 1998).

49. Lois Gibbs and the Citizens' Clearinghouse for Hazardous Waste, *Dying from Dioxin: A Citizen's Guide to Reclaiming Our Health and Rebuilding Democracy* (Boston, Mass.: South End Press, 1995).

50. Robert Bullard, ed., *Unequal Protection: Environmental Justice and Communities of Color* (San Francisco: Sierra Club Books, 1994); Robert Bullard, ed., *Confronting Environmental Racism: Voices from the Grassroots* (Boston, Mass.: South End Press, 1993).

51. See Foreman, *Promise and Peril*, 18, 20.

52. Ibid., 34.

53. Foreman, "Environmental Justice and Risk Assessment: The Uneasy Relationship," *Human and Ecological Risk Assessment* 6, no. 4 (2000): 552.

54. See for instance, Ibid., 553; Foreman, *Promise and Peril*, 17–18, 126.

55. Foreman, "Environmental Justice and Risk Assessment," 553; Foreman, *Promise and Peril*, 92, 28, 133.

56. See, for instance, his statements to this effect in *Promise and Peril*, chapters 4 and 5; "Environmental Justice and Risk Assessment," 553.

57. See his description of Bullard in *Promise and Peril*, 117.

58. Ibid.

59. Ibid.

60. See for example, John Locke, *Letter Concerning Toleration* (1689; reprint, Indianapolis, Ind.: Bobbs-Merrill, 1955); Isaiah Berlin, "Two Concepts of Liberty," in *Four Essays on Liberty* (New York: Oxford University Press, 1970), 118–72, especially at 119, 145–54.

61. See Foreman, *Promise and Peril*, 84–89.

62. See Daniel Boorstin, *The Genius of American Politics* (Chicago: University of Chicago Press, 1953), especially 1–7.

63. Robert A. Dahl, *A Preface to Democratic Theory* (Chicago: University of Chicago Press, 1956), chapters 4 and 5.

64. See Foreman, *Promise and Peril*, chapter 5.

65. See Foreman 1998, 12, 4, 66–67. For a discussion of the rise of the "new politics," see among others, Allan J. Cigler and Burdett A. Loomis, "Introduction: The Changing Nature of Interest Group Politics," in *Interest Group Politics*, 3d ed., ed. Allen J. Cigler and Burdett A. Loomis (Washington, D.C.: CQ Press, 1991), 1–32, especially 10–26. For a discussion of the rise of the "old politics," see John Kenneth Galbraith, *The Affluent Society* (Boston: Houghton Mifflin, 1958); Theodore Lowi, *The End of Liberalism* (New York: Norton, 1979). For examples of nostalgia, see William Lunch, *The Nationalization of American Politics* (Berkeley: University of California Press, 1987); Robert A. Dahl, *The New American Political (Dis)order* (Berkeley: Institute of Governmental Studies Press, 1994).

66. See Robert Booth Fowler, *Believing Skeptics: American Political Intellectuals, 1945–1964* (Westport, Conn.: Greenwood, 1978); James P. Young, *Reconsidering American Liberalism: The Troubled Odyssey of the Liberal Idea* (Boulder, Colo.: Westview, 1996). For the environmental and ethical implications of this phenomenon, see Joe Bowersox, *The Public Space of Environmentalism* (Ph.D. diss., University of Wisconsin Madison, 1995); John Martin Gillroy and Joe Bowersox, "Introduction" to *The Ethical Austerity of Environmental Decisionmaking* (Durham, N.C.: Duke University Press, forthcoming).

67. Foreman, *Promise and Peril*, 64–88; Foreman, "Environmental Justice and Risk Assessment," 550.

68. See Foreman, *Promise and Peril*, 24, 58, 65, 108, 110; "Environmental Justice and Risk Assessment."

69. Stephen Breyer, *Breaking the Vicious Circle: Toward Effective Risk Regulation* (Cambridge, Mass.: Harvard University Press, 1993).

70. Foreman, *Promise and Peril*, 110–11.

71. Ibid., 108.

72. Ibid., 45, 112–13.

73. See generally, Aaron Wildavsky, *But Is It True? A Citizen's Guide to Environmental Health and Safety Issues* (Cambridge, Mass.: Harvard University Press, 1995); John D. Graham and

Jonathan Baert Wiener, eds., *Risk vs. Risk: Tradeoffs in Protecting Health and the Environment* (Cambridge, Mass.: Harvard University Press, 1995); Herman Leonard and Richard Zeckhauser, "Cost-Benefit Analysis Applied to Risks: Its Philosophy and Legitimacy," in *Values at Risk*, ed. Douglas MacLean (Totowa, N.J.: Rowman & Littlefield, 1986), 31–48; Richard Posner, *The Economics of Justice* (Cambridge, Mass.: Harvard University Press, 1983); Richard Posner, "The Ethical and Political Basis of the Efficiency Norm in Common Law Adjudication," *Hofstra Law Review* 8 (1980): 490.

74. For a full discussion of these points see, among others, Steven Kelman, "Cost-Benefit Analysis: An Ethical Critique," in *The Moral Dimensions of Public Policy Choice*, ed. John Martin Gillroy, Maurice Wade (Pittsburgh, Pa.: University of Pittsburgh Press, 1992), 153–64; Mark Sagoff, "Efficiency and Utility," in *The Moral Dimensions of Public Policy Choice*, ed. John Martin Gillroy, Maurice Wade (Pittsburgh, Pa.: University of Pittsburgh Press, 1992), 165–78; Stephen L. Elkin, "Economic and Political Rationality," in *The Moral Dimensions of Public Policy Choice*, ed. John Martin Gillroy, Maurice Wade (Pittsburgh, Pa.: University of Pittsburgh Press, 1992), 353–70; Mary Douglas and Aaron Wildavsky, *Risk and Culture* (Berkeley: University of California Press, 1982), 30, 70.

75. Foreman, *Promise and Peril*, 111, 130–36.

76. Lest I be misunderstood, the point of my argument regarding risk assessment is not its irrelevance, but rather its limitations. Following Kelman, Sagoff, and Elkin (see note 74 above), risk assessment and benefit-cost analysis can provide information to policy makers and the public that is useful for making choices given certain social goals. However, it is not determinative of those goals or the values that give rise to them.

77. Steven Kelman describes a cogent example: during hearings on watering down workplace safety requirements because of the "inordinate" costs associated with the level of risk reduction, U.S. steelworkers pointed out that the Emancipation Proclamation was not subject to benefit-cost analysis. See Kelman, "Cost-Benefit Analysis," 157.

78. Gary A. Abraham, "Book Review: The Promise and Peril of Environmental Justice," *Buffalo Environmental Law Journal* 6, no. 1 (1998), 118.

79. Ibid., 119.

80. See Wildavsky, *But Is It True?*; Murray Weidenbaum, "On Estimating Regulatory Costs," *Regulation* (May–June 1978): 14; Wiener, "Sustainable Governance."

81. J. S. Alper, "Facts, Values, and Biology," *The Philosophical Forum* 13 (1981): 99.

82. In addition to the discussion above, see Karl Popper, *Conjectures and Refutations* (London: Routledge & Kegan Paul, 1969); Peter Galison, *How Experiments End* (Chicago: University of Chicago Press, 1987); P. Duhem, *The Aim and Structure of Physical Theory* (New York: Athenaeum, 1962); W. V. O. Quine, *From a Logical Point of View* (New York: Harper and Row, 1961).

83. Locke, *Letter Concerning Toleration*, 13.

84. John Rawls, "Justice as Fairness: Political, Not Metaphysical," *Philosophy and Public Affairs* 14 (1985): 225.

85. Arendt, *Totalitarianism*.

86. See Hannah Arendt, *Lectures on Kant's Political Philosophy*, ed. Ronald Beiner (Chicago: University of Chicago Press, 1982).

87. Robert Heilbroner, *An Inquiry into the Human Prospect: Updated and Reconsidered for the 1980s* (New York: Norton, 1980).

88. See Charlene Spretnak, *The Spiritual Dimension of Green Politics* (Santa Fe, N.M.: Bear and Co. 1986); Matthew Fox, *Creation Spirituality: Liberating Gifts for the Peoples of the Earth* (San Francisco: Harper, 1991); Anne Primavesi, *From Apocalypse to Genesis* (Minneapolis: Fortress Press, 1991).

89. See Robert Booth Fowler, *The Dance with Community: The Contemporary Debate in American Political Thought* (Lawrence: University Press of Kansas, 1991); Fowler, *The Greening of Protestant Thought* (Chapel Hill, N.C.: University of North Carolina Press, 1995).

90. See John Martin Gillroy, Joe Bowersox, eds., *The Moral Austerity of Environmental Decisionmaking* (Durham, N.C.: Duke University Press, forthcoming), 572–73; Fowler 1995, 159–79.

91. Ironically, in the early twenty-first century we appear to be more philosophically committed to democratic processes at the same time that such philosophical commitments run headlong into the practical demands of competent governance. Today a distrustful yet easily manipulated populace is demanding greater say in all aspects of their lives at the time that social problems like environmental degradation and other arenas of government involvement are increasingly complex, technologically dependent, and with more dire consequences when subjected to incompetent management. The democracies of the late eighteenth and nineteenth centuries—experiencing more mundane tasks of state-building, infrastructure development, and expansion with much smaller populations—were probably more capable of (and practically less threatened by) entertaining broad-based democratic governance.

92. Dryzek, "Green Reason," 202.

93. See Douglas Torgerson, *The Promise of Green Politics* (Durham, N.C.: Duke University Press, 1999), 162ff; Bowersox, *Public Space of Environmentalism*, chapter 8.

94. Bowersox, *Public Space of Environmentalism,* chapter 8.

95. See John Martin Gillroy and Joe Bowersox, "Conclusion," in *The Moral Austerity of Environmental Decision Making*, ed. John Martin Gillroy and Joe Bowersox (Durham, N.C.: Duke University Press, forthcoming).

96. Karl Otto Apel, *Towards a Transformation of Philosophy* (London: Routledge & Kegan Paul, 1980), 158.

CHAPTER 5

Science, Value, and Ethics
A HIERARCHICAL THEORY

J. Baird Callicott

Philosophical Background

The relationship of science, values, and ethics in the formation of democratic environmental policy is a topic of perennial discussion—and perennial confusion. A major source of confusion is a long legacy of Western moral philosophy and the philosophy of science. From David Hume, we have inherited the Is/Ought Dichotomy. Hume pointed out that because something *is* the case, does not—by itself—entail that someone *ought* to behave a certain way.[1] For example, because scientists warn that we human beings are rapidly becoming the agents of only the sixth mass extinction event in the 3.5-billion-year history of the planet, that does not, by itself, entail that we ought to try not to be. This seems contrary to common sense. As Clifford Geertz observed, "The powerfully coercive 'ought' is felt to grow out of the comprehensive factual 'is,' . . . The tendency to synthesize world view and ethos at some level, if not logically necessary, is at least empirically coercive; if it is not philosophically justified, it is at least pragmatically universal."[2] In my opinion, Hume was merely pointing out that there is a missing link in the logic of most ethical arguments moving from *is* to *ought*, but modern analytic philosophers have succeeded in convincing many of us that there is no possible logical relationship whatever that would link scientific facts—or facts of any kind, for that matter—and duties. (I return to this issue and identify the missing link in the concluding section of this chapter.)

In the early twentieth century, another English philosopher, G. E. Moore, coined the phrase, "the Naturalistic Fallacy."[3] To call some natural property good is to commit the Naturalistic Fallacy. The summum bonum or greatest good of the then reigning utilitarian ethic was happiness.[4] Happiness—cashed out as a greater balance of pleasure over pain—was good, the utilitarians declared.[5] But according to Moore, if, by definition, good = happiness, then we cannot intelligibly ask the so-called open question, Is happiness—that is, pleasure—really the good?[6] But we can intelligibly ask, Is it really? After all, other philosophers have seriously proffered other notions about the good—a well-ordered life, a life of service . . . to God, to country, to mankind— all without talking nonsense. And some—Plato for one—have expressly denied that pleasure is good.[7] In the present context of environmental policy, Michael Soulé appears to commit the Naturalistic Fallacy when, in his field-defining paper, "What Is Conservation Biology?" he writes, "diversity of organisms is good."[8] Period. But is it? Is biological integrity good? Is ecosystem health good? To declare that they are, by definition, without argument or debate, according to Moore, is to commit the Naturalistic Fallacy.

As to philosophy of science, the legacy of Logical Positivism is the still general and prevailing belief that science provides "positive" (that is, true or verifiable) statements of fact, while value statements are subjective emotings.[9] To say that happiness, biodiversity, biological integrity, and ecosystem health are good and that misery, murder, genocide, and mass extinction are bad is to say "Hurrah" upon contemplating the former set of things (happiness, biodiversity, biological integrity, and ecosystem health) and "Boo" upon contemplating the latter set (misery, murder, genocide, and mass extinction). Many recent thinkers have ventured into these philosophically roiled waters of science, values, ethics, and policy. Here I take the plunge myself, not confident that I can make them still and clear, but only that I may offer some new directions in which to swim.

Feminist and postmodern critics of science have attempted to deconstruct the Positivist image of science as objective and value free. Science, these critics argue, is a non-privileged social institution in which facts are theory laden, theories are value laden, and values are power laden.[10] In postmodern philosophy of science, even nature itself is alleged to be "socially constructed," and, in the best of all possible worlds, subject to "negotiation" among equally empowered interest groups.[11] Here I assume, rather, a more conventional and conservative "modern" interpretation of science. While postmodern critics of science certainly have a voice in democratic debates about environmental policy, they have not yet succeeded in reorganizing the public discourse. My purpose here is to provide responsible citizens, working scientists, and policy makers—who are not quite ready to embrace postmodernism—with an analysis of values and ethics that may be useful in integrating a coherent consideration of values and ethics with science in forming environmental policy in a democratic context.

Because we have this public legacy of the Is/Ought Dichotomy in moral philosophy and Logical Positivism in the philosophy of science, values are regarded as themselves brute *social* facts, subject to investigation by the social sciences. People just up and adopt values, this legacy leads us to suppose, which are purely subjective, personal, and arbitrary, unconnected to any beliefs about the objective world. People choose their values, we must suppose, like they do their clothes, cars, and coffee—as a kind of political fashion statement. The media reinforce this perception of values holding by sound-bite interviews of potential voters during election cycles who are asked to state their choices about the "issues" of the day. Do you or do you not favor universal health insurance, peace keeping abroad, limiting growth in your community, NAFTA, WTO, tighter controls on immigration, the war on drugs, expanding the national parks and monuments, protecting endangered species at all costs . . . ? Positive knowledge of these subjective, personal, and arbitrary human values may be determined by such research instruments as polls. People are asked, for example, "Do you approve or disapprove of tuition vouchers or excise taxes on fossil fuels?" Politicians then, in democracies, shape their positions or platforms on their assessment, often with the aid of social science research, of the most popular values of those of their constituents who are most likely to vote.

Here I offer an alternative analysis of values that may be useful in three ways for a democratic polity. First, in a democracy, we admire politicians who have the courage to act on "conscience" or "principle" in defiance of the values of the majority of their voting constituents. Such politicians are often called statesmen (or -women). But how are the values of conscience or principle privileged? In the peculiar democratic polity of the United States, where the separation of church and state is a cornerstone, such values cannot be openly grounded in religious dicta. Are there more defensible secular grounds? Here I argue that there are. Second, it may help inform democratic debate to be able convincingly to segregate secularly grounded moral values from personal preferences. And once segregated, we will want a method to prioritize conflicting moral values. One purpose of democratic debate is to persuade one another that some values should prevail over others, so that our politicians/statespersons do not find themselves in the uncomfortable—and politically risky to suicidal—position of having to choose between the seemingly arbitrary political preferences of the majority of their voting constituents and the otherwise mysterious source of conscience or principle. Finally, and most fundamentally, each responsible citizen in a democratic polity must choose among a plethora of value-anchored policies, indirectly by electing executives, legislative representatives, or members of the judiciary, or by voting directly for or against ballot initiatives. How can each responsible citizen sort through his or her suite of values, many of which are mutually contradictory, and make well-reasoned political choices? The greatest utility of my present analysis of values for democratic decision making would be to provide an answer to this question. I begin at the beginning, at the fountainhead of the fact/value distinction and the correlative Is/Ought Dichotomy, specify the difference between preferences and values proper in terms of community membership, establish and illustrate the application of priority principles, and return to the usefulness of this analysis of values for democratic decision making.

Objectivity and Subjectivity

In setting forth the philosophical foundations of modern science, René Descartes drew a fundamental distinction between the *res cogitans* (the realm of the mind) and the *res extensa* (the realm of nature), respectively the subjective and objective domains.[12] The *res extensa* comprises the physical world; the *res cogitans* comprises our emotions and passions, plus both our sensory images of the physical world and our conceptual models of the physical world. Values belong to the *res cogitans*, the realm of the mind; they are subjective. So does science; it too is subjective. A scientific theory exists first as a conjecture or hypothesis in the mind of a single scientist; and then, if confirmed by repeated experimentation, it becomes part of the collective mind, as it were, of the scientific community. While the focus of scientific description is the objective physical world, scientific beliefs about and models of the physical world are subjective constructs. There is no such thing as a false fact, but there is certainly such a thing as a false statement of fact and untenable theoretical organizations of true statements of fact. Thus, as we are all painfully aware, today's science can soon become tomorrow's myth.

Although science is, clearly, not itself objective, scientific statements have a relationship to the objective *res extensa* that values do not have. Consider a geographical scientific statement of fact: "The Wisconsin River is a tributary of the Mississippi River." Such a statement is true if and only if the Wisconsin River *is* a tributary of the Mississippi River and false if it is *not*. In general, scientific statements of fact are true if they correspond element for element (the two rivers in this example) and relationship for relationship (the relationship of being tributary to in this example) to the facts in the *res extensa* that they represent in the *res cogitans*. Some scientific statements are more difficult to verify because some states of the physical world are more difficult to ascertain.[13] The truth of the exobiological scientific statement "Life once existed on Mars" is difficult to verify because the past state of a distant physical system is difficult to ascertain.

Comprehensive cognitive models of the physical world cannot be verified in the same way. We are not able to stand outside a comprehensive cognitive model to see if it corresponds to an independently apprehended reality, as we can detach ourselves from a particular statement of fact and compare it at least with our sensory image of the independently existing physical world.[14] Our most general cognitive models are the conceptual lenses through which we apprehend the *res extensa*, and by means of which we organize and interpret our sensory images of it. We can change lenses—as, for example, in planetary astronomy we discarded the geocentric model and adopted the heliocentric model—but we cannot apprehend reality independently of any and all our cognitive models of it. Rather, our scientific models are provisionally verified by the extent to which they comprehend a wide range of particular facts.[15] Better than any of its competitors, for example, the evolutionary model comprehends the existence of the fossilized remains of long-extinct species and of family resemblances among extant species. Our confidence in scientific models of nature increases when newly discovered facts are easily fit into such models, like missing pieces of a jigsaw puzzle. For example, the similarity of DNA between closely resembling species adds to the credibility of the evolutionary model. Finally, we try to confirm our models by rigorously deriving predictions of fact from them and looking to see if such predictions are borne out by subsequent experience.[16]

As noted, expressions of value do not differ from scientific statements of fact and scientific models of nature in being subjective, while scientific statements of fact and scientific models of nature are objective. Expressions of value, scientific statements of fact, and scientific models of nature are one and all subjective, that is they are human constructs. Unlike scientific statements of fact, however, expressions of value correspond to nothing in the *res extensa*, the objective physical world. Hume noted that the statement, "Murder is bad," cannot be verified by comparison with a state of the physical world—as can the statement, "The Wisconsin River is a tributary of the Mississippi River."[17] Because they correspond to nothing objective, statements of value are incapable of verification. They are *purely* subjective and relative.[18]

Values vis-à-vis Scales in the Social Hierarchy

But relative to what? Because human beings are genotypically and phenotypically highly individuated, some statements of value are relative to the person who expresses them. The statement "Vanilla is good; chocolate is bad" expresses a personal preference. However, because Homo sapiens is not a solitary, but a social and cultural species, a great many other human statements of value are not personal. Rather such statements express values that are relative to various hierarchical levels of social and cultural organization. For example, the statement "Monogamy is good and polygamy is bad" is an expression of value that is relative not to particular persons, but to particular cultures. Monogamy is good and polygamy is bad in the Judeo-Christian family of cultures, but polygamy is good in, among others, the Islamic family of cultures. Finally, some values seem to be transcultural and very nearly universal, perhaps because human beings are a single, universally social species. Murder, for example, is bad in practically every culture and is horrifying to practically every individual.

We can identify hierarchical levels of social and cultural organization in contemporary North American civilization—family, municipality, regional community, nation, international neighborhood, human community—to which we can relate various values.

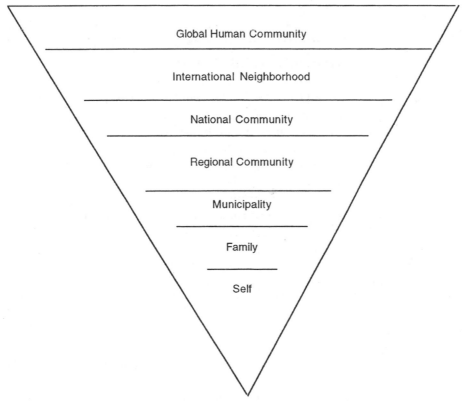

Figure 5.1   Human Social Scales

These are levels of a social hierarchy in a sense analogous to the way biological entities are hierarchically organized: genes within organisms, organisms within populations, populations within biotic communities, biotic communities within land/waterscapes, land/waterscapes within biomes, and biomes within the biosphere. Throughout these remarks "hierarchy" refers to such nested organizational structures, in which the lower level is subsumed by the higher, not to power arrangements in society, such as military and bureaucratic organizations in which some individual persons have more power and privilege than others—those above those below them in the hierarchy. In short, hierarchy here refers to a hierarchy of scale, not to a hierarchy of power.

Hierarchies of social scale are not as rigorously determinate as the hierarchy of biological scale. One could, for example, interpolate neighborhood between family and municipality; and in some social circumstances—in the case of large urban municipalities, such as New York City—it might be useful to do so. In other circumstances—in Texas, for example, where state pride runs high—one might interpolate state, between municipality or regional community or (given the wide variation in the spatial scale of states and provinces in the United States and Canada) between regional community and nation. In non–North American social contexts, still other scales of social organization might be significant as correlates of certain values, such as ethnic group or religious affiliation.

Against the Reduction of Value to Preference in the Social Sciences

Modern science tends toward reduction.[19] The complex behavior of conglomerate entities is often explained, scientifically, in terms of the simpler behaviors of their components. The social sciences are no exception. Individual persons are the components of society. Thus we are tempted to regard the values relative to the several hierarchies of social organization as reducible to the values of the individuals that compose them. In the Judeo-Christian family of cultures the claim that monogamy is good is thus reducible to the claim that monogamy happens to be valued by a large majority of the individuals who have a Jewish or Christian heritage. Accordingly, some reductive social scientists, especially economists, treat all values as "preferences." From this point of view, someone may, for example, prefer vanilla ice cream, monogamy, and organized prayer in the public schools; while someone else may prefer chocolate ice cream, polygamy, and the rigorous separation of church and state. The values institutionalized in a given society will be determined by the numerical strength of the individuals who express those values in the marketplace and in the political arena. For example, if no one prefers vanilla ice cream, there will be no demand for it and therefore no one will make and sell it; and if a majority of voters or their representatives decide that "adult" movie theaters and bookstores should be banned in their municipality, then, in that community, they will be banned.

Two distinct issues are raised by the tendency to reduce values to individual preferences. The first is that such a tendency glosses over an important distinction between values proper and preferences. Preferences are surds. One cannot offer reasons or explanations for or against them. They just exist. For example, if someone likes vanilla but not chocolate ice cream, there is no answer to the question "Why?" than, "They just do." The preference for one brand of cigarettes over another is a surd. To choose to smoke cigarettes, whatever the brand, is also to express a preference, but reasons can be offered to the contrary. In short, cigarette smoking injures your health. One does not merely *prefer* health, however, over its opposite. Rather health is something that one *values*. Here, instead of reducing values to preferences, I suggest we do the opposite. We should treat preferences as a kind of value.

The other issue raised by the tendency to reduce social values to individual preferences is the fact that some values are irreducibly relative to social wholes, not to individuals. Our reductive habits of mind make us reluctant to acknowledge the existence of social wholes, but some social phenomena are simply not reducible to the behavior of the individual constituents of society. Perhaps the most obvious example is language. Although spoken by individuals, language is an irreducibly social phenomenon, as Wittgenstein's droll musing on the impossibility of a private language—a language that an individual speaks only to him- or herself—amply demonstrates.[20] So, I suggest, are some values. Values are held and expressed by individuals but many pertain primarily to social wholes, nor would they be values except in relation to social wholes. Perhaps the most obvious example is the incompletely cataloged collection of values called "family values." Few parents, I would think, *prefer* to spend an evening helping their children do homework, instead of, say, watching a movie on TV, surfing the Internet, or going out for a drink with friends. Nor, like health, is helping children with homework a personal value, something of value, that is, to the parents themselves. So if "emergent properties" such as language and social values exist, then the entities to which they are correlative—that is, of which they are properties—must also exist. Social psychology, sociology, anthropology, and evolutionary psychology are more inclined to acknowledge the irreducibility of hierarchically scaled social wholes as well as the values correlative to them.

The Natural History of Ethical Values

From a modern point of view, ethics seem to be extrascientific, something beyond the pale of science.[21] Charles Darwin, however, attempted to bring ethics into the domain of scientific discourse, rather than exclude it. In Darwin's (1871) own estimation, his was the first account of ethics "exclusively from the side of natural history."[22] Basically, Darwin argued, Homo sapiens inherited social instincts and sympathies from hominid, primate, and mammalian ancestors; then, when the evolving species acquired language, a vivid imagination, and enough intelligence to assess and recall the effects of various behaviors on society, types of behavior that tended to strengthen social integration were deemed "good" and those that tended to weaken it were deemed "bad." As Darwin (1871) puts it with characteristic color, "No tribe could hold together if murder, robbery, treachery, &c., were common; consequently such crimes within the limits of the same tribe 'are branded with everlasting infamy.'"[23]

I suggest a generalization of this Darwinian insight. *An ethical value is one that promotes the holding together, the on-going integration (or integrity), of a social unit*, beginning with and including the individual.

Personal values proper, that is, nonpreference values, such as the value we place on our own health and well-being, are also ethical values—what Darwin called "the self-regarding virtues." Hence to smoke or not to smoke is an ethical question, quite apart from the noxious effects of one's smoking on others. The choice is between satisfying a preference, on the one hand, and realizing a value proper, on the other— the value of personal health in this case. *Family values*, similarly, are codifications of those behaviors—such as parents spending "quality time" with their children— which tend to strengthen the cohesion of family units.

And so we might correlate various values with the several hierarchical scales of social organization identified in figure 5.1.

Participating in "block parties" and "crime watch" associations would be examples of *neighborhood values*, values that foster the integrity of neighborhoods; attending civic events, such as the annual Denton Arts and Jazz Festival, and town meetings to decide, say, zoning regulations, would be examples of *municipal values*. An example of *regional values* might be a cooperative effort on the part of private historical societies and local and state governments to preserve the architecture and other characteristic cultural features of the Southwest, a distinctive region of the United States, by resisting the process of corporate homogenization (viz., Wal-Mart, McDonald's, and other such "chain" stores).

The national scale of social organization has been so important that some of its correlative values even have a name—patriotism, for example. Participation in national democratic self-government (at least by voting in national elections and voluntarily paying taxes) and, beyond that, serving in the armed forces or the Peace Corps are examples of *national values*. The international neighborhood is so newly emerged as a distinct social scale that its correlative values are difficult to identify, but such cooperative structures among nation-states as are presently emerging in Europe are their expression. International responses to famine and natural disasters, such as earthquakes and floods, are expressions of values correlative to the global human community— *global-village values*, we might call them.

Environmental ethics emerged in response to the perception of the natural world in terms of a social metaphor, the biotic community. "A thing is right," wrote Aldo Leopold, the seminal thinker in this newest domain of ethics, "when it tends to pre-

Table 5.1   Correlation of Values with Scales of Social Organization

Social Unit	Sample Value	Sample Ethical Precept
Individual	Health	Do not smoke
Family	"Family values"	Help kids with homework
Neighborhood	Neighborhood values	Join neighborhood "crime watch" association
Bioregion	Bioregionalism	Preserve regional culture
Nation–state	Patriotism	Serve thy country
Global village	Human rights	Stop genocide
Biotic community	Integrity, stability, beauty	Preserve native species

serve the integrity, stability, and beauty of the biotic community."[24] Of course by "when," Leopold did not mean "if and only if." He tacitly recognized that for every scale in the hierarchy of social organization from the individual to the family, the municipality, the region, the nation, the global human community, as well as the biotic community, a thing is right when it tends to preserve the integrity, stability, and beauty of that community.

Cross-Scale Value Conflicts

The problem is, of course, that ethical values correlative to different social scales often conflict with one another, as well as with preferences. What tends to preserve the integrity, stability, and beauty of a particular municipality, say a logging/milling community in the Pacific Northwest, may threaten the integrity, stability, and beauty of the regional biotic community. In Europe, national values sometimes conflict with those of the international neighborhood. A municipal-scale value to rid the community of pornography may come into conflict with the nation-scale value of First Amendment guarantees of free speech.

I am aware of no generally accepted algorithm to resolve such conundrums. One might be tempted to suggest at least that as a general rule, when a mere preference and a value proper conflict, the preference should give way to the value. Thus the personal preference expressed by many North Americans for driving gas-guzzling sports utility vehicles should give way to higher-level community values, such as urban air quality, national energy independence, and the integrity of the global atmosphere. In a democracy, however, freedom to "pursue happiness," by satisfying personal preferences is itself a value proper. Suppose an American politician, in a statesperson frame of mind, decided to sponsor federal legislation to impose a substantial excise tax on vehicles registered to people living in certain smog-prone urban and suburban zip codes that get less than twenty-five miles to the gallon. How could such a popular-preference-defying, principled policy be justified? By appeal to the integrity of the various communities that are variously threatened in various ways by gas-guzzling vehicles. A political ad campaign might be launched to persuade voters to accept making one of their preferences more costly—and thus on average less likely to be exercised—by appealing to the ethical value correlative to their various social identities.

Economists, who tend to reduce all value to personal preferences, employ a familiar algorithm, benefit-cost analysis (BCA). When different things valued by different people compete, BCA awards priority to the highest bidder (Krutilla and Fisher 1975).[25] In my hypothetical example of preserving the unique cultural character of the American Southwest, the economic benefit to the regional community of chain stores—jobs, lower prices, and so forth—is weighed against the benefit of cultural preservation. Since the latter has no readily calculable dollar value, it is "shadow priced." People are polled and asked what they would pay to have the cultural character of the region preserved. This is called "contingent valuation." The "travel-cost" method—calculating the amount of money tourists spend on gasoline, lodging, and such—is another way economists assign a surrogate price to amenities for which there is no market price. BCA has been the subject of much criticism by environmental ethicists, in the final analysis largely because it conflates values proper with preferences.[26]

Ethical values that seem to conflict with one another across scales in the social hierarchy may sometimes be reconciled by creative win-win solutions. For example, a municipality may seem to face a choice between preserving the integrity of its biotic community and preserving the integrity of its economy. Suppose its economy is manufacturing based. A commitment to environmental values might attract business investment in the new information industries, thus helping the municipality effect a transition to a more sustainable and forward-looking knowledge-based economy.

Unfortunately, win-win solutions are not always possible when ethical values conflict across scales in the social hierarchy. One noted environmental philosopher has suggested two complementary priority principles for democratically resolving irreconcilable cross-scale conflicts of value.[27] The first we might call the inverse-scale principle (ISP). Each individual should give priority to the values correlative to the integrity of his or her self, family, municipality, and so forth, in that order. Hence, if, in a time of general scarcity, one faced a choice between sharing one's severely limited resources with family members or with unrelated neighbors, the right thing to do would be to share with family members and refuse neighbors. The second we might call the degree-of-interest principle (DIP). It is intended to counter the first. If the interests at stake are of unequal strength, the lesser interest should give way to the greater. For example, in circumstances not of general scarcity but of unequal distribution of plentiful resources, some are needier than others. If one is relatively wealthy and one's neighbor is desperately poor, then the need (the strong interest in having the wherewithal for survival) of one's neighbor should take priority over the wants (the weaker interest of satisfying preferences) of one's family members.

Applying these priority principles to conflicts of value between the biotic-community scale and the municipality scale, once more, we might conclude that if our choice were between the destruction of a regional biotic community (and the extinction of its endemic species), on the one hand, and the starvation of the citizens of logging/milling communities, then priority should be given to the values correlative to the municipality scale, in accordance with the ISP. In the region mentioned above, the Pacific Northwest, that is not, fortunately, the conundrum we face. Other employment alternatives are available to loggers and mill workers. The biotic-community interests at stake are much greater, the destruction of a unique biome and the extinction of its endemic species. Hence in this case, the DIP countermands the ISP. Unfortunately, in some parts of the world, the ethical conundrum does involve the very livelihood, not just the lifestyles of local peoples. For example, some people face the choice of feeding themselves and their families and by doing so contributing to the destruction of tropical forests and a global mass extinction event or refraining from doing so. For *them* the choice is clear and unambiguous. They must slash and burn. Because, however, they are not my neighbors or fellow nationals, it is not entirely clear what national and international policies, with respect to such practices, I should support.

As plausible as this two-test algorithm may seem, it is not unexceptionable. So much so that one might argue for a principle just the opposite of the ISP, at least in some circumstances. Don't family values take priority in some circumstances over the self-regarding virtues, as when a poor parent works at a health-threatening job to provide a college education for her or his children? Don't national values take priority in some circumstances over family values, as when, for example, a parent and spouse is called on to leave hearth and home and put her- or himself in grave personal danger to defend her or his country? (In this case, of course, one could argue that the DIP overrides the ISP, in accordance with the two-test, ethical value-prioritizing algorithm.)

Further, our most insistent values, those to which we customarily give the greatest weight, seem to be common to all social scales, at least to all those beyond the individual scale. The disvalues highlighted by Darwin—murder, robbery, treachery—are common to all tribes, as he suggests, and to all trans-tribal scales in the social hierarchy. The opposing positive values—security in one's person and property, loyalty, and so on—are good candidates for universal human values, the foundation for which is now investigated by evolutionary psychology. On the other hand, eating certain foods (e.g., kosher) or wearing certain clothes (e.g., the chador) may be highly valued by a particular group of people as essential to their identity as a community. To other people such foods or clothes are of no particular importance. When universal human values conflict with ethnic-scale values, there is a tendency to give priority to what would appear to be the species-scale values. For example, most of us consider the ethnic-scale value of "female circumcision" to be eclipsed by the incompletely cataloged collection of species-scale values called "human rights."

Some persons in society are charged with the special responsibility of preserving the integrity of a particular social entity. For such persons—whom we may think of generally as stewards—the values relative to that hierarchical scale are paramount. For example, the President of the United States has a special responsibility to preserve the integrity of the Union. Hence, when it was threatened by the American Civil War of 1860–1865, President Abraham Lincoln put national values ahead of all others. Those charged with the special responsibility for environmental protection—the U.S. Secretary of the Interior, the head of the U.S. Environmental Protection Agency, the Chief of the U.S. Forest Service, state natural resources managers—are also stewards. They have an obligation, I suggest, to put the integrity of the biotic communities of which they are stewards ahead of all other values—except perhaps the universal human values just mentioned—at least in their professional capacities.[28] Failure to do so, I also suggest, may be regarded as a violation of environmental ethics and dereliction of fiduciary duty.

Conclusion

I return to the shibboleth with which I began, Hume's notorious Is/Ought dichotomy. Contrary to the conventional interpretation—that there is no logical relationship whatever between facts and duties—I am of the opinion that Hume was merely pointing out that there is a missing link in most ethical arguments moving from *is* to *ought*, leaving unanswered the question, What is that link? It is, I suggest, an ethical value, an anthropogenic value proper relative to some scale in the social hierarchies in which we humans live, move, and have our being. Smoking *is* deleterious to your health; therefore, you *ought* not to smoke. The missing link is the value we place on health, the neglect of which threatens the disintegration of the individual. The highest scale in the social hierarchy in which we humans live, move, and have our being is the biosphere. Deforestation of the moist tropics, unrestrained burning of fossil fuels, exponential human population growth *is* deleterious to the health and integrity of the biosphere. Therefore, we *ought* to preserve tropical forests, reduce our consumption of fossil fuels, and stabilize and eventually reduce the human population. Connecting the latter *is* with the latter *ought* is the value we place on the health and integrity of the biosphere, the most encompassing community of which we are members.

But who is "we" here? If such a value is not as universally espoused as family-scale values or ethnic-scale values, that is because such concepts as biotic community, ecosystem, and biosphere are newly formed scientific ideas, while such concepts as family and tribe are primitive. The remedy is universal ecological education. A successful democracy depends on a well-educated and well-informed electorate. Why should we insist less on ecological literacy, on the part of responsible citizens in a democratic polity, than on economic literacy? We expect responsible citizens to cast informed votes on tax cuts, deficit spending, and partial privatization of social security. Why should we expect less of them when they cast votes on curbing global warming or preserving tropical forests?

The ethical conundrum that we face is not that there is no clear connection between *is* and *ought*, but that we are members, simultaneously, of multiple communities, each with its correlative values and therefore correlative duties. We have a duty to preserve tropical forests, reduce our consumption of fossil fuels, and stabilize and reduce the human population. We also have a duty to respect human rights, national sovereignty, regional culture, and all the other values correlative to all the other scales in the social hierarchy. I have suggested here some principles to guide us as we try to make our way through this bewildering maze of often conflicting *oughts*. Unfortunately they cannot be applied mechanically to solve every moral conundrum, unambiguously. So far, no one has, to my knowledge, developed a *perfect* algorithm for resolving conflicts of duty. Until someone does, the best we can do is conscientiously muddle along and try first to reconcile apparently conflicting duties by means of win-win solutions. When that is impossible we may only hope to prioritize wisely and responsibly.

In democratic decision making, each responsible citizen has a voice, minimally at the ballot box, but generally through participation in the political process. As responsible citizens we are often torn between the choices presented to us on the political smorgasbord. In making these choices responsibly, we are not well served by the legacy of the Is/Ought Dichotomy (or Naturalistic Fallacy) in moral philosophy and Logical Positivism in the philosophy of science that together radically subjectivize values and conflate values proper with preferences. Our choices between such mutually inconsistent policies as federal tax cuts and increased federal funding for public education, health care, and welfare or higher domestic wages and free international trade are reduced to something rather like a political fashion statement. If, on the other hand, we distinguish values proper from personal preferences and link ethical values with the integrity of the multiple communities to which we all simultaneously belong, then each of us may have the wherewithal to morally order our values and make more responsible political choices.

Further, when we meet collectively to debate policy options, we may have some means of settling on the proper order of priority among the various values at play—prioritizing, in a word. As things now stand, in the long, dark shadow of the Is/Ought Dichotomy and Logical Positivism, people bring what is regarded as their peculiar set of political preferences to the table and, after patently partisan spinning and special pleading, we count heads and the majority rules. No one expects to persuade others, just to shout louder and longer and outmaneuver others. We leave with the positions we came in with. If, however, we can distinguish values proper from mere preferences and link ethical values with the integrity of the multiple communities to which we all simultaneously belong, then we might expect to genuinely convince one another that one policy is really better than another and that we are duty bound, despite our preferences, to support it. (About this, I have more to say in my "Reply to Bowersox, Minteer, and Norton," at the end of part 1 in this volume.)

Finally, politicians aspiring to statespersonship might be better able to explain and defend their unpopular decisions and give some substance and specificity to the otherwise vague appeal to "conscience" and "principle"—if we can distinguish values proper from mere preferences and link ethical values with the integrity of the multiple communities to which we all simultaneously belong. And those in government who are stewards of some community—be they a head of household, a mayor or city manager of a municipality, a game warden, a forest ranger, an Environmental Protection Agency administrator—may have a clearer understanding of where their overriding responsibility lies and why it lies just there and not somewhere else.

Notes

1. David Hume, *A Treatise of Human Nature* (London: John Noon, 1737).
2. Clifford Geertz, *The Interpretation of Cultures* (New York: Basic, 1973), 126–27.
3. G. E. Moore, *Principia Ethica* (Cambridge, U.K.: Cambridge University Press, 1903).
4. John Stuart Mill, *Utilitarianism* (London: Longmans, 1861).
5. Ibid.
6. Moore, *Principia Ethica*.
7. See Plato's *Republic*.
8. Michael E. Soulé, "What Is Conservation Biology?" *BioScience* 35 (1985): 730.
9. A. J. Ayer, *Language, Truth, and Logic* (London: V. Gollancz, 1936).
10. Helen E. Longino, *Science as Social Knowledge: Values and Objectivity in Scientific Inquiry* (Princeton, N.J.: Princeton University Press, 1990).
11. Sandra G. Harding, *The Science Question in Feminism* (Ithaca, N.Y.: Cornell University Press, 1986).

12. René Descartes, *Meditations de Prima Philosophia* (Paris: Michaelem Soly, 1641); Edwin A. Burtt, *The Metaphysical Foundations of Modern Physical Science* (Garden City, N.Y.: Doubleday, 1954).

13. George Pitcher, ed., *Truth* (Englewood Cliffs, N.J.: Prentice Hall, 1964).

14. Richard Rorty, *Philosophy and the Mirror of Nature* (Princeton, N.J.: Princeton University Press, 1973).

15. Karl Popper, *The Logic of Scientific Discovery* (New York: Harper and Row, 1959).

16. Ernest Nagel, *The Structure of Science: Problems in the Logic of Scientific Explanation* (New York: Harcourt, Brace & World, 1961).

17. David Hume, *An Enquiry Concerning the Principles of Morals* (London: John Noon, 1751).

18. Ayer, *Language, Truth, and Logic.*

19. Nagel, *Structure.*

20. Ludwig Wittgenstein, *Philosophical Investigations*, trans. G. E. M. Anscombe (New York: Macmillan, 1953).

21. Charles L. Stevenson, *Ethics and Language* (New Haven, Conn.: Yale University Press, 1944).

22. C. R. Darwin, *The Descent of Man and Selection in Relation to Sex* (London: John Murray, 1871).

23. Ibid., 93.

24. Aldo Leopold, *A Sand County Almanac and Sketches Here and There* (New York: Oxford University Press, 1949), 224–25.

25. John V. Krutilla and Anthony C. Fisher, *The Economics of Natural Environments* (Baltimore, Md.: Johns Hopkins University Press, 1975).

26. Holmes Rolston III, "Valuing Wildlands," *Environmental Ethics* 7 (1985): 23–48; Mark Sagoff, "Some Problems with Environmental Economics," *Environmental Ethics* 10 (1988): 55–82.

27. Arne Naess, *Ecology, Community, Life Style*, trans. D. Rothenberg (Cambridge, U.K.: Cambridge University Press, 1989).

28. E. P. Pister, "A Pilgrim's Progress from Group A to Group B," in *Companion to a Sand County Almanac*, ed. J. Baird Callocott (Madison: University of Wisconsin Press, 1987), 221–32.

Appendix: Reply to Bowersox, Minteer, and Norton

I thank the editors of this anthology for giving me an opportunity to reply to those authors who have here critically engaged my work. With the limited space allotted me, I want to accomplish three tasks: first, to correct the most egregious misrepresentations of my views by my present critics; second, to respond thoughtfully to their few cogent criticisms of my actual views; and third, to sketch my personal vision of the role that environmental philosophers, philosophy, and ethics can play in a democratic polity, a vision that does not in any way compete with or exclude other visions.

In an earlier article, Minteer held that I "posit the existence of certain basic or privileged beliefs which are supported noninferentially. Such premises are generally claimed to be a priori, self-evident, or directly justified in some manner; they do not depend on any other beliefs for their support."[1] In my response to that article, I point out that although I have certainly tried to provide philosophical foundations for environmental ethics, they were not of the kind that he alleges.[2] In Minteer's chapter in this volume, he levels the same charge in other terms, accusing me of making claims to "*absolute* right reasons and principles . . . *correct* moral justifications for *all* environmental public policies and practices," which I "*deduce* from metaphysical arguments." I have never made such claims, and I shall shortly produce evidence to support this disavowal.

Minteer suggests that I, in tandem with Laura Westra, am skeptical about democracy. I do not agree with Westra's views about democracy; indeed, I am unaware of them except as here discussed by Minteer and Norton. I have never collaborated with Westra, as Norton and Minteer have collaborated or as Rolston and I have collaborated; indeed, I have no intellectual affiliation or affinity with Westra whatsoever. Norton offers evidence of Westra's skepticism about democracy, but Minteer is unable to find any similarly disparaging remarks about democracy in my writing. On the contrary, in my response to Minteer's first critique of my philosophy I wrote, "Personally, I agree with Winston Churchill who once quipped that 'democracy is the worst form of government, except for all the others.'"[3] Writing impassioned defenses of democracy is not my philosophical agenda. (Democracy is, happily, quite robust and needs no philosophical buttressing from me.) But I am no more antidemocratic than I am antigay or antifeminist. My point is that because I have little publicly to say about democracy, gay rights, or feminism, does not imply that I am against any of them or skeptical about any of them.

I am perfectly content for Minteer, Norton, and other environmental pragmatists to go about their business without objection from me. Minteer acknowledges (and for this I am grateful) that there would be no debate between him and me had he not first criticized my work—and, in my opinion, misrepresented it in doing so. Nor would there be any debate between Norton and me had not Norton also first criticized my work—and also, in my opinion, misrepresented it—in an article provocatively subtitled, "Callicott and the Failure of Monistic Inherentism."[4] Norton and Minteer seem to feel that it is necessary for environmental pragmatism to *replace* other kinds of environmental ethics, not just to complement them, as I am inclined to think. From the very beginning of my scholarly career—and more formally as president of the International Society for Environmental Ethics from 1994 to 2000—I have been fostering the vigor of environmental ethics as a legitimate subdiscipline of academic philosophy. The more schools of thought in the field—deep ecology, ecofeminism, social ecology, ecophenomenology, now environmental pragmatism—the more robust it is. I am, in practice, committed to pluralism in environmental philosophy, while, ironically, some who most vociferously advocate pluralism in environmental ethics seem most anxious to squelch well-justified nonanthropocentric environmental philosophies, such as the one I have championed. Minteer, for example, says that he "think[s] that environmental philosophers should stick to" his recommended pragmatic approach, because my approach is somehow a threat to democracy. While he denies that he wishes to silence philosophers, he wants "to make"—*make!*—"philosophical inquiry more democratically accountable and more experimental."

Minteer writes that he would allow environmental philosophers to speak "as politically engaged *citizens*, rather than dogmatic metaphysicians or environmental philosopher kings." Norton, like Minteer, also seems actually to think there is some real threat that we shall be ruled by (environmental) "philosopher kings." In the United States, we do have a government official called the "drug czar," but there is no office of environmental philosopher king (nor, as far as I am aware, is there any such office in any other country where environmental philosophers live and work). Furthermore, democracy is in no more danger of being supplanted by a dictatorship of environmental philosopher kings than by a dictatorship of Martians. Many metaphysicists are *professional* philosophers, but professional philosophers are not licensed or regulated as are some other professional practitioners—doctors and lawyers for example. Philosophers, professional or otherwise, work entirely as private citizens. Thus, one wonders in what other capacity environmental philosophers may speak, now or in any imaginable future, than as politically engaged citizens?

As for the suggestion that I am in some deep or troublesome sense being dogmatic, what could be more dogmatic than Norton's insistence that all philosophers must heed Quine before they proceed—either answer his arguments (which Norton finds so persuasive) or be constrained by the limitations Quine would impose on philosophy? Suppose Norton were advised that he must heed Derrida's deconstruction of scientific claims before he proceeds—to either answer Derrida's arguments or be constrained by the limits Derrida would impose on philosophy? Further, is the dogmatism of the most dogmatic metaphysicist more deserving of censure and sanction than the dogmatism of neoclassical economists or Christian fundamentalists? As politically engaged citizens, metaphysicists do little more than write their academic tracts and vote. Dogmatic neoclassical economists staff the White House, the Treasury Department, and Congress and attempt to privatize everything from education (vouchers) to Social Security (investment in equities). And dogmatic Christian fundamentalists seek, often successfully, elected offices—everything from school board member to state legislator to member of Congress to President—and attempt to impose their beliefs on the rest of us hapless citizens. They seek, by any means necessary, democratic or otherwise, to criminalize abortion and homosexuality, replace the teaching of evolution in public schools with "creation [pseudo]science" or now with "intelligent design," post the Ten Commandments, and establish monotheistic prayer in the public schools.

Something has gone terribly awry here. I should think that philosophers concerned with preserving democracy would spend their limited time and energy exposing democracy's more determined and powerful adversaries—such as transnational corporations, the Republican Party, the regime in China—rather than criticizing a pitiful handful of environmental philosophers. Why aren't Minteer and Norton content to engage in the kind of philosophical activity they believe to be the most worthwhile, without wanting to *make* (as would Minteer) the rest of us conform to their approach and tell us (as does Norton) what we have and have not a *right* to do? (Norton here states that provided I limit myself to the form of philosophical expression he warrants that "pragmatists will . . . *grant him the right* to engage in 'foundational' explications of an emerging worldview.") Indeed, what could be more "democratically objectionable" than Minteer's and Norton's attempt to police and restrict the practice of environmental philosophy to methods they approve?

Still, I wonder: where is this disproportionate and misdirected fear and desire to control coming from? I hazard to guess that it is born of a kind of resentment of what Minteer and Norton perceive to be the assumption of a hubristic vocation. Norton wants us environmental philosophers to limit our activity to "analyzing concepts and clarifying values" at play in "the fray of public discourse." Minteer wants to limit us to "a humbler task," which is more or less the same as Norton envisions. To make an academic analogy, they seem to want to make environmental philosophers chair panel discussions of environmental policy, but not allow us to speak substantively as panelists. They want to reduce environmental philosophy to method and process, without specific content and substance.

Environmental philosophers such as Rolston and I have, however, taken on another very lofty and protracted task. We would like to contribute to the kind of transformation of Western culture and civilization that philosophers in the past—such as Locke, Kant, Bentham, and Mill—have effected. I myself would like to do so, however, without invoking any self-evident or a priori axioms, as some philosophers of the modern Western past have done. That is, I would like to carry forward the *substantive* tradition of Western philosophy in a distinctly postmodern fashion—a "reconstructive postmodern" philosophy, as I have suggested it be called.[5] Norton, to his credit, seems to recognize the importance of this kind of work, but also seems to think that it should be indefinitely postponed in favor of the more humble and immediate task of helping sort out "policy details," "examining fair process and . . . seeking to design fair institutions," and providing "arguments that will convince judges in endangered species cases, arguments that make sense to sympathetic but wavering members of Congress." Would Western civilization be richer or poorer had Plato, Aristotle, Descartes, Spinoza, Leibniz, Locke, Berkeley, Hume, Kant, Bentham, and Mill (some of them, to be sure, dogmatic apriorists) settled for the humbler task of philosophy recommended by Minteer and Norton? Would democracy have been possible in a Western "civilization" devoid of free, substantive philosophical speculation? If substantive, systematic philosophy has indeed enriched Western civilization and contributed to the vigor of Western-style democracy, is it no longer (albeit in the reconstructive postmodern form in which I pursue it) a source of enrichment for the future of Western civilization? And is free thought—even metaphysical thought about such things as the intrinsic value of nature—no longer essential to a free, democratic society?

Democracy, the political practice we know and cherish, owes its existence to substantive, foundational philosophical work of the kind that Rolston and I, as well as many other contemporary environmental philosophers, wish to continue—in my own case, in a reconstructive postmodern way. In response to my challenge (in my reply to his first critique of my work) to justify his apparently a priori assumption that it is a good thing, Minteer here provides a very interesting and compelling foundation for democracy in terms of Dewey's "unified method of inquiry to moral, social, and political life." I have no quarrel whatever with his *apologetica democratia*; it's brilliant. He dismisses, however, another approach to justifying or providing foundations for democracy in terms "of human nature, or the existence of certain . . . rights." But how important has that approach been, historically, to the emergence of democracy in the Western past and, for that matter, the emergence of democracy in developing countries today? Would democracy have emerged or flourished without discourse about human nature (for example that "all men [and women] are created equal") and about human rights (for example, that all human beings are "endowed . . . with unalienable rights . . . [to] life, liberty, and the pursuit of happiness")? Would the Declaration of Independence—a document of incalculable importance to democracy—have been possible without the philosophical groundwork provided by Hobbes and Locke, who directly influenced Thomas Jefferson? In light of the historic and current importance of substantive, foundational philosophy to the development of democracy, Minteer's distrust of this kind of philosophy is simply inexplicable.

What is foundationalism in Western philosophy? And what is the relationship of my work to it? As to the former question, Minteer and Norton appear to agree; as to the latter, they disagree. In their view foundationalism involves (1) self-evident, a priori, axiomatic principles—such as those claimed in the Declaration of Independence—which are the foundations, (2) rigorous deduction of moral precepts (and even policies) from them, (3) which, because they logically follow from the foundations, have the same truth value as the foundations themselves—absolute certainty. As Norton correctly remarks—*pace* Minteer—"those of us who have criticized foundationalism in environmental ethics mean something much narrower, and something with much more epistemological bite than the kind of . . . method that Callicott finds essential." Rather than experientially revisiting the places where I set out the conceptual foundations of the Leopold land ethic to see what is actually going on, Norton, however, is content to construct—as it were, a priori—a severely limited set of methodological options. Besides the pragmatic method and foundationalism proper, there is a third method, which Norton allows, "explicative foundationalism." In Norton's ruminations on this method, such arguments "have validity only within the belief system as it has evolved and been explicated by its midwives." To convince nonbelievers, the only method—the only one Norton can imagine, anyway—is hard-core foundationalism (which, of course, Quine has shown to be futile, in Norton's opinion).

So what actually is the method that I "find essential" to my own reconstructive postmodern project in environmental ethics? In trying to expose the conceptual foundations of the Leopold land ethic, I certainly did not posit self-evident, a priori principles (as in the Declaration of Independence), nor did I attempt to deduce any absolutely certain moral precepts from them (as does Hobbes in the *Leviathan*), Minteer's reading to the contrary notwithstanding. But if not (either rationalistic or empiricistic) foundationalism proper or explicative foundationalism (both sensu Norton), what sort of foundations do I in fact offer for the Leopold land ethic? In "The Conceptual Foundations of the Leopold Land Ethic," I provide a summary:

> The land ethic rests upon three scientific cornerstones: (1) evolutionary and (2) ecological biology set in a background of (3) Copernican astronomy. Evolutionary theory provides the conceptual link between ethics and social organization and development. It provides a sense of "kinship with fellow creatures" as well, "fellow voyagers" with us in the "odyssey of evolution." It establishes a diachronic link between people and nonhuman nature.
>
> Ecological theory provides a synchronic link—the community concept—a sense of social integration between human and nonhuman nature. Human beings, plants, and animals are "all interlocked in one humming community of cooperations and competitions, one biota." The simplest reason, to paraphrase Darwin, should therefore tell each individual that he or she ought to extend his or her social instincts and sympathies to all the members of the biotic community though different from him or her in appearance or habits.
>
> And although Leopold never directly mentions it in *A Sand County Almanac*, the Copernican perspective, the perception of the Earth as a "small planet" in an immense and utterly hostile universe beyond, contributes, perhaps subconsciously, but nevertheless very powerfully, to our sense of kinship, community, and interdependence with fellow denizens of the Earth household. It scales the Earth down to something like a cozy island paradise in a desert ocean.
>
> Here in outline, then, are the conceptual and logical foundations of the land ethic: Its conceptual elements are a Copernican cosmology, a Darwinian protosociobiological natural history of ethics, Darwinian ties of kinship among all forms of life on Earth, an Eltonian model of the structure of biocoenosis all overlaid on a Humean-Smithean moral psychology. Its logic is that natural selection has endowed human beings with an affective moral response to perceived bonds of kinship and community, the biotic community; and that, therefore, an environmental or land ethic is both possible—the biopsychological and cognitive conditions are in place—and necessary, since human beings collectively have acquired the power to destroy the integrity, diversity, and stability of the environing and supporting economy of nature.[6]

I quote myself at length to document my denial that I am the hard-core foundationalist that Minteer accuses me of being, and that Norton here finally acknowledges that I am not. Where in my summary of the conceptual foundations of the land ethic are the assertions of indubitable, self-evident, a priori axioms? Where are the rigorous deductions to absolutely certain and thus coercive (the hard-core foundationalist vainly wishes) moral conclusions? What one finds, instead, is ironically something with a remarkably Quinean structure. We find loose links between large domains—evolutionary biology, ecology, cosmology, philosophical anthropology, moral psychology—of an integrated worldview. The land ethic fits into this worldview, but not—at least not very comfortably—into other worldviews that are at large in our polity. Salient among these are, again, the neoclassical economics worldview and the Christian fundamentalist worldview.

The worldview of Aldo Leopold's *A Sand County Almanac*, moreover, is extremely fallible, ironically another hallmark of pragmatism. Astronomy has not retreated from the Copernican belief that the Earth is a planet (and indeed a small one), but the Eltonian community concept has been seriously criticized and largely rejected in ecology (as, incidentally, Bowersox correctly notes). Far from asserting that the Leopold land ethic is, in Minteer's overwrought phantasm, "valid in all possible worlds," recent developments in ecology compelled me to doubt that, without revision, it is valid in the actual world as now described by ecology. In an article titled "Do Deconstructive Ecology and Sociology Undermine the Leopold Land Ethic?" I tried to revise the land ethic in light of recent developments in ecology.[7] As the long quotation above amply testifies, in any case, the foundations I develop for the Leopold land ethic meet Norton's specifications of post-Quinean philosophy: "Philosophy occupies the abstract end of a continuum of discussions of more or less empirical and contingent claims; philosophy, in a world that countenances only experience and no a priori truths or categories, is continuous with scientific disciplines, not separate from the sciences."

So much for hard-core foundationalism. What about Norton's "justificatory foundationalism"? Is all that I am doing in setting out the philosophical foundations of the Leopold land ethic "preaching to our philosophical choir," to quote Minteer? Hardly. And, here is another irony. Not only are the foundations I provide for the Leopold land ethic Quinean in their cognitive holism and post-Quinean in their continuity with the sciences, not only are they fallible—all hallmarks of contemporary pragmatism—they are recommended and intended to persuade on the basis of what Minteer here calls Dewey's method of unified inquiry or generalized scientific method and what Norton here calls discourse ethics. The Quinean integrated, holistic cognitive complex—that is, the worldview—in which the Leopold land ethic is embedded might fairly be called "the evolutionary-ecological worldview." If we bring this worldview to a democratic forum of ideas in which (as Minteer quotes Dewey) "there is a willingness to question, investigate, and learn, a determination to search for clarity of discourse and evidence in argument" then, in my opinion, it will be more persuasive than its alternatives, such as Christian fundamentalism. Compare what I wrote about a decade ago with the Deweyan method that Minteer recommends and the Habermasean method that Norton recommends:

> The commitment to science and rationality implicit in environmental ethical theory-building is a commitment to agreement through persuasion. It works something like this. I say, here are the facts about nature and human nature afforded by the best efforts of scientific discovery. And here's how they may be integrated with morality. If you do not agree, show me my error and I will come over to your point of view, or if you can find no flaw with my argument, then you come over to my point of view. If both of us remain open-minded, committed to truth and to reason, then we shall eventually come to the same conclusion—and try to act accordingly. If this process is rarely realized in practice, it is nevertheless the ideal against which we measure our failures, either of intelligence or good will.[8]

Meanwhile, Bowersox thinks that I advocate environmental salvation through science. Strangely, that would make me a bedfellow with Minteer and Norton, for Minteer justifies democracy through Dewey's generalized scientific method, while Norton considers pragmatic environmental philosophy to be continuous with the sciences, the "abstract end" of that continuum. And, as I just documented, the philosophical foundations of the Leopold land ethic that I explore are largely elements of fallible sciences. But such reliance on science is a threat to democracy, Bowersox thinks, because we science-oriented environmental philosophers (and now of course that would include Minteer and Norton) use science to "force consensus," instead of allowing "claims about how the world works, what one ought to do, and the good life [to be] contested, amended, and contingently agreed upon." I'll let Minteer and Norton respond to the challenge to their views implicit in Bowersox's challenge to mine. Instead, I'll focus the remainder of my reply on Bowersox's discussion of my use of science in doing environmental philosophy.

First, I thank Bowersox for correctly representing my personal vision of the role that environmental philosophers, philosophy, and ethics can play in a democratic polity. He writes

> Callicott . . . argues that "in thinking, talking, and writing about environmental ethics, environmental philosophers already have their shoulders to the wheel, helping to reconfigure the prevailing cultural worldview." . . . Callicott quite rightly maintains that the world of ideas—of normative claims about the way the world works, of questions of duty and the good life—*does* shape the way we view and act within the world of pocketbooks, mortgages, and video games. Callicott draws attention to two cogent examples of such—the role the Enlightenment conceptions of humanism and rights doctrine, as "articulated by Hobbes, Locke, Bentham, and Kant, among others" played in the abolition of slavery over the last four hundred years.

Unfortunately, however, when Bowersox turns to philosophical substance, he gets me all wrong. He wrongly states that Hume and Smith "provide the basis for a subjectivist axiology . . . based in 'self-love.'" On the contrary, Hume and Smith base their ethics on other-oriented sentiments, such as sympathy. So, although Bowersox *rightly* explains that I attempt to carry forward the general Humean-Smithean theory of moral sentiments as biologized first by Darwin and more recently by Wilson, he *wrongly* attributes to me the same ethics grounded in self-love that he wrongly attributes to Hume and Smith.

More particularly, Bowersox fails to appreciate the contingent or conditional nature of my argument from quantum theory and self-love—which was an afterthought, more or less, to my main argument from quantum theory. He omits from his quotation the following crucial caveat: "The intrinsic value of oneself," I write, "has *for some reason* been taken for granted; how to theoretically account for the intrinsic value of 'others,' rather, has been regarded as problematic."[9] I myself do not assert an unjustified claim of intrinsic value for myself; rather, I simply point out that historically, such a claim has been taken for granted, in, for example, "the two major modern traditions stemming from Kant and Bentham."[10] Then I go on, doing my best to signal to the reader by repeatedly italicizing the word "if," that my argument is purely conditioned by the general historical assumption that oneself has intrinsic value, not my own unjustified assertion of that proposition. If you compare Bowersox's quotations of me (the one that begins with "If we assume" and the one that begins with "If quantum theory") with the published words he is quoting, then you will see that he has omitted the italicization of the "ifs." These omissions facilitate his misrepresentation of my views.

Bowersox concludes that "This allows Callicott to accomplish what other environmental theorists have been unable to do—posit intrinsic value of nature without fundamentally challenging the axiologically privileged position of the self in modern society." This statement is false on two counts. First, the whole argument, as I just insisted, is purely hypothetical or conditional: *If*, **if**, IF, we assume the self is intrinsically valuable—a common assumption in modern Western moral philosophy, but certainly not an assumption that I myself endorse—then . . . Second, other environmental theorists—Deep Ecologists, in general, and Arne Naess and Warwick Fox, in particular—make just this kind of argument the very heart of their theories.[11] They call it "Self- (with a capital 's' or 'S') realization." So it is doubly false to state that I am accomplishing what other theorists have been unable to do. First, I am not attempting to accomplish it. Second, other theorists have.

Basically what Bowersox has done is conflate my philosophy with that of Naess, Fox, and the Deep Ecology theorists and then rehash the standard ecofeminist critique of Deep Ecology as if it were a cogent critique of my philosophy.[12] In his systematic exposition of Deep Ecology and its doctrine of "Self-realization," Fox carefully considers and compares my philosophy to his and Naess's and correctly concludes that I am not a Deep Ecologist.[13] Nevertheless, having made me over into a Deep Ecologist, Bowersox then levels at me the now stock ecofeminist criticism of Deep Ecology: "the problem is that this model of holist ecocentrism is the totalitarian ideal." (Ecofeminists call it "totalizing," not "totalitarian," but the point is roughly the same.) Bowersox goes on to explain that I am liable to the criticism that such totalizing results in "a single organism, unified in purpose and motive and in no need of dialogue and debate, for there can be only one authentic voice from the whole." But it is actually the Deep Ecological Self-realization theorists who are liable to this criticism, not me.

All this is mixed up, in Bowersox's account, with a misrepresentation of my attempt to indicate how Darwin completed Hume's largely naturalistic theory of the moral sentiments. Hume believed that, though subjective, our moral sentiments are universal. Hume attributed this universality to the "Supreme Will, which bestowed on each being its peculiar nature." Darwin explained the peculiar psychological nature of the human species as he did that of other species, by means of natural selection. Normal people all share the same *basic* moral sentiments, which were shaped by natural selection. In "The Intrinsic Value of Nonhuman Species," which Bowersox quotes, I made a physical analogy. Normal people all have the same *basic* body plan—two arms and hands, two legs and feet, five digits on each, a head with the same orifices (mouth, ears, nostrils, ocular orbits) in more or less the same places, and so on. Normal people also all share the same basic psychological plan—we all experience fear, jealousy, love, hate, sympathy, benevolence, and so on. Now, although all normal people share the same basic body plan, there is a very wide range of idiosyncratic variation on this plan—tall people, short people, thin-handed people, stubby-handed people, snub-nosed people, aquiline-nosed people, skinny people, fat people and so on. Similarly, there is a wide range of variation in the normal human psychological plan—brave people, timid people, envious people, empathetic people, and so on.

Further—and this is the point most germane to Bowersox's critique—our basic, shared human sentiments are massively shaped by culture and cognition. As I write in the essay he quotes, "To whom or what these affections are directed, however, is an open matter, a matter of cognitive representation—of 'nurture' not 'nature.'"[14] Even our physical genetic endowment is shaped by culture. Nutrition affects a person's eventual height; diet affects weight and shape; exercise of various kinds can enlarge and sculpt muscles, just as lack of exercise can shrink and wither them. Our psychological genetic endowment is similarly plastic. Culture and cognition can *train* our feelings, much as we train our bodies by means of physical regimes. For example, we can learn to overcome certain fears (of heights, for example).

But, more precisely to the present point, culture and cognition *direct* and *inform*, as well as train, our moral sentiments. Assuming that all normal human beings are genetically endowed with the psychological proclivity to fear, *what* should we fear? In some cultures we *learn* to fear ghosts and witches. In ours we have *learned* to fear germs and viruses. How do we try to redirect fear? Purely by cognitive argument. If we are convinced, for example, that ghosts and witches do not exist, then we will cease to fear them. If we are convinced that germs and viruses do exist and cause disease, then we will fear them instead. And how do we try to convince people to direct their sentiments of sympathy and benevolence toward members of other races or sexual orientations? Again, purely cognitively. We try to minimize differences and stress commonalities. We say things like color is only skin deep; or, more recently, that racial distinctions have little or no scientific basis and are, in fact, mostly a matter of history, culture, and politics. And as to sexual orientation, we try to debunk, cognitively, claims that homosexuality is a morally flawed choice or a curable psychosis with evidence that it is a gift (whether welcome or not), like an aptitude for music or mathematics.

Now the point here is this: I do not anywhere suggest that *environmental ethics* is or ever will become genetically fixed in the human species by natural selection. What I *do* argue, following Hume, is that we are all similarly endowed with very basic, very general, moral sentiments—benevolence, sympathy, loyalty, pride in group identity—which are, following Darwin, indeed genetically inherited, the product of natural selection. But to whom or what they are to be directed is largely a matter of culture and cognition. Should one confine one's inherited capacity for benevolence and sympathy to the members of one's own tribe, race, or nationality, or should one extend them to the whole of one's own species, or beyond one's species, and, if so, how far beyond? Should one confine one's inherited capacity for loyalty and pride in group identity to one's own tribe, race, or country, or should one extend them to the global village, or beyond that to the biotic community? Bowersox's claims that natural selection or the economy of nature settles such questions in my philosophy and that I move them out of the realm of ethical and political discourse into that of science are based on a misrepresentation of my Darwinian account of the natural selection of the universal Humean moral sentiments. The fact that in my philosophy the moral sentiments are informed by culture and cognition actually answers precisely to Bowersox's notion of "deliberative democracy, in which claims about how the world works, what one ought to do, and the nature of the good life are contested, amended, and contingently agreed upon."

As citizens of democratic polities—and only that, not as environmental philosopher kings because in America and other democracies, we don't have any, nor is their any danger we ever will—some philosophers (and I am one of them) are out there pressing claims about the way the world works (ecologically, in my opinion), what one ought to do (adhere to the revised and updated Leopold land ethic, no less than to our inherited social ethics, in my opinion), and the nature of the good life (fostering a healthy and whole environment, first and foremost, in my opinion). Moreover, the claims of environmental philosophers (such as I) who want to contribute more to their democratic polities (than the humbler task of clarifying concepts and values and refereeing policy debates) are vigorously contested—as this book amply demonstrates—and they are amended in light of free and open discussion. Yes, and, in some cases (the Endangered Species Act, for example), they may actually be contingently (too contingently, I fear, for species in harm's way) agreed upon.

Notes

1. Ben A. Minteer, "No Experience Necessary? Foundationalism and the Retreat from Culture," *Environmental Values* 7 (1998): 336.

2. J. Baird Callicott, "Silencing Philosophers: Minteer and the Foundations of Antifoundationalism," *Environmental Values* 8 (1999): 499–516.

3. Ibid., 511.

4. Bryan G. Norton, "Why I Am Not a Nonanthropocentrist: Callicott and the Failure of Monistic Inherentism," *Environmental Ethics* 17 (1995): 341–58.

5. J. Baird Callicott, *Earth's Insights: A Multicultural Survey of Ecological Ethics from the Mediterranean Basin to the Australian Outback* (Berkeley: University of California Press, 1994).

6. J. Baird Callicott, "The Conceptual Foundations of the Land Ethic," in *Companion to A Sand County Almanac: Interpretive and Critical Essays*, ed. J. Baird Callicott (Madison: University of Wisconsin Press, 1987), 194–95.

7. J. Baird Callicott, "Do Deconstructive Ecology and Sociobiology Undermine Leopold's Land Ethic?" *Environmental Ethics* 18 (1996): 353–72.

8. J. Baird Callicott, "The Search for an Environmental Ethic," in *Matters of Life and Death: New Introductory Essays in Moral Philosophy*, 3d ed., ed. Tom Regan (New York: McGraw Hill, 1993), 336–37.

9. J. Baird Callicott, *In Defense of the Land Ethic: Essays in Environmental Philosophy* (Albany, N.Y.: SUNY Press, 1989), 172, emphasis added.

10. Ibid.

11. Arne Naess, "Self-realization: An Approach to Being in the World," *The Trumpeter* 4 (1987): 35–42; Warwick Fox, *Toward a Transpersonal Ecology* (Boston: Shambala, 1990).

12. See, for example, Ariel Salleh, "The Deep Ecology/Ecofeminism Debate," *Environmental Ethics* 14: 195–216.

13. Fox, *Transpersonal Ecology*.

14. Callicott, *In Defense*, 151–52.

Part II

ENVIRONMENTALISM AND DEMOCRATIC CITIZENSHIP

CHAPTER 6

Opinionated Natures

TOWARD A GREEN PUBLIC CULTURE

Catriona Sandilands

> There is no reason to doubt our present ability to destroy all organic life on earth. The question is only whether we wish to use our new scientific and technical knowledge in this direction, and this question cannot be decided by scientific means; it is a political question of the first order and therefore can hardly be left to the decision of professional scientists or professional politicians.[1]

> Reality is different from, and more than, the totality of facts and events, which, anyhow, is unascertainable. Who says what is . . . always tells a story, and in this story the particular facts lose their contingency and acquire some humanly comprehensible meaning.[2]

It is hardly unusual among political commentators to suggest (or more accurately, to mourn) the increasing loss of a democratic "public sphere" in which citizens engage one another in debate over issues of common concern. In Habermasian terms, the past 150 years or so have witnessed a decline in "the institutions that until [the mid-nineteenth century] had ensured the coherence of the public as a critically debating entity."[3] For Habermas, this narrative of demise is premised on the idea that a genuine, critical publicity involves the deployment of a particular kind of formal and deliberative rationality, one in which citizens engage in conversational, noninstrumental reasoning toward generally universalizing goals. With this ideal in mind, the current entertainment-world cacophony of talk shows, radio phone-ins, therapeutic encounter groups, and chat rooms can only appear as a monstrous perversion of a modern democratic ideal, a consumerist veneer of talk masking the absence of any authentic public culture.

By the same token, it is also hardly unusual among political commentators to suggest that new social movements—such as environmental movements—are the primary site of hope for any sort of renewed democratic public sphere. Specifically, thinkers such as Jeffrey Isaac understand particular kinds of movements as democratic "oases in a desert"[4] of late capitalist globalism, consumerism, and "mass" society.[5] In the desert of electoral politics and focus groups, "localist democracy" emerges as an active, critical practice in such oases as the environmental justice movement. For Isaac, environmental justice "began as a series of local responses to the problem of toxic waste disposal and blossomed into a broad-based movement, organized around issues of class, gender, and race, that has heightened public awareness about environmental concerns, raised the cost of corporate negligence, and created an extensive network of organizing and information sharing."[6] In their movement from local reaction to analytic-activist network, Isaac sees both the kind of critical universality and participatory politics that indicate islands of invigorated publicity in a sea of mass apathy.[7]

Dana Villa has a somewhat different (and rather more pessimistic) take on this story. Specifically, he understands that Habermas's emphasis on deliberative rationality as the defining characteristic of the public sphere overlooks other crucial and constitutive dimensions of public life, and thus causes many contemporary analysts to tend to *overestimate* the ability of movements such as environmentalism to generate a truly public culture.[8] Indeed, he argues that "the (currently depleted) energies of social democracy may be occasionally stimulated by such movements as feminism or environmentalism, but 'the return of the political' that so many expect to be generated by the associational life of civil society will be far less transformative than presumed."[9] We need more than deliberative space and participatory politics to approach publicity, even in Habermas's terms of a critical universality; we also need a uniquely "public" orientation to interpersonal interaction, to be juxtaposed to the modes and habits of privacy (as opposed, say, to a talk show publicity that circulates around people's private lives).

Drawing on the works of Richard Sennett and Hannah Arendt, Villa argues that modernity has witnessed an increasing emphasis on the ultimate legitimacy of privacy, inner truth, and intimate experience at the expense of the distinctively public virtues of impersonal interaction, performative greatness, and individual appearance. "The rise of a culture of intimacy," he writes, "means the decline of social theatricality," the specifically performative and agonal quality that is, in Arendt's terms in particular, a hallmark of public life as opposed to the private values of, for example, romantic love and personal morality.[10] Thus, for Villa, "it may be doubted whether single-issue movements or identity politics do anything to transform the interests they articulate into 'a more broadly shared public or common interest' . . . [and may instead foster] an affinity-group culture, one that is inclined to view moral-political issues in terms of 'who one is' in the most rudimentary sense."[11] Although I disagree strongly with Villa's sweeping generalization about the single-issue and identitarian character of social movements, he thus raises a tremendously valid point about the *insufficiency* of deliberative participation (and community) and the *necessity* of a distinctive (and probably performative) orientation to generating and invigorating a truly public culture.

As I have argued elsewhere (and will return to below), some versions of environmental politics—notably, particular moments and strands of environmental justice—are, in fact, strongly oriented to the generation of a distinctively public culture of environmental conversation, even performance.[12] By and large, however, "where environmental issues contain the possibility of constituting and mobilizing diverse publics and [sometimes] do so, as in the case of environmental justice, this potential is seldom fulfilled because 'the political' is not located as a central element in most environmental struggles, as if saving the earth were a task that overrides the importance of democratization."[13] To account for this lack one can, on the one hand, certainly identify within the broad spectrum of environmental politics the sorts of problematic "single issue movements [and] identity politics" that Villa describes as more representative of community affinity than public culture. But on the other hand, I would argue, one can identify within environmental politics another trend that may be universalizing but that also has distinctly depoliticizing effects, namely, its epistemic organization around, and grounding of legitimacy in, scientifically generated *truths* rather than politically negotiated *opinions*.

In this statement, of course, I echo the ancient (and contested) distinction between philosophical and political speech or, as Plato would have it, between dialectics and persuasion. According to Arendt's critical reading of the distinction, in the former the philosopher is oriented to the discovery of the (reflection of the) eternal and converses by exchanging questions with a single other in order to draw out a truth.[14] In the latter, however, the citizen takes part in a theater of rhetorical persuasion circulating around multiple opinions, which Arendt describes as the production in speech of "the world as it opens itself to me . . . not subjective fantasy and arbitrariness, but also not something absolute and valid for all."[15] Crucially, opinion (*doxa*) is something that is revealed, contested, and changed in the company of *multiple* others by way of a performance the persuasiveness of which is judged in the realm of appearances itself (e.g., aesthetics), and not with reference to either inner authenticity or external standard. Arendt understood that political persuasion began from, involved, and engendered forms of knowledge that were qualitatively different from absolute and timeless truths. Moreover—and reversing the Platonic valuation of contemplation over action—she understood that the claim to truth destroys opinion by degrading both the specificity of the world "as it appears to me" (*dokei moi*) and the value of the realm of appearances in which such opinions are judged. To put it differently, the search for the truth that lies below appearance rather than in it degrades the knowledge that is created in appearance itself, that is, opinions created and contested performatively.

To cut a millennia-long story short, the starting-point of this chapter is, in the first place, that most forms of environmentalism, in their reliance on scientific truth for validation (which is different in method but not truth-orientation from philosophy in Plato's absolutist sense), negate the possibility of publicity because they close the spaces in which the world of "nature" potentially appears to individuals as the basis of *opinions*. In the second place, however, most environmental challenges to the dominance of scientific knowledges tend to draw their legitimacy from private "truths," residing in intimate personal experience (e.g., deep ecology) or other private interest (e.g., NIMBY-ism). While there is clearly room in environmentalism for a wide range of knowledges, motivations, and forms of speech, the ability of environmental movements to contribute to invigorating a genuinely public culture (or, for that matter, to *create* a public culture of nature) relies on its ability to cultivate a space of possibility for appearance to multiple others to reveal, and be revealed by, environmental opinion.

Nature: Truth, Interest, and Opinion

In his important book, *Environmentalism and the Future of Progressive Politics*, Robert Paehlke takes up a position shared with many other environmentalists when he argues that the unambiguous first step to making consistently responsible political decisions about environmental issues begins in "developing the connection between environmentalism and scientific knowledge."[16] Further, he notes that the environmental movement has—relatively uniquely among social movements—tended to rely on natural science rather than social science as the foundation of its claims. As Phil Macnaghten and John Urry concur, "roughly speaking, the role of the social scientist [in environmental politics] is seen as that of addressing the social impacts and implications *of* environmental problems, which have been initially and accurately described by the natural scientist—a kind of 'Biology First' model."[17]

The ideal logic of this kind of science-based ecopolitical claim should be familiar: an "expert" delivers (or is asked to deliver) something like a certainty to the movement, the politician, the activist,[18] whose job it is to enter the scrum of politics and emerge, preferably, with some policy or other action that represents the reorientation of the world in accordance with the scientific claim. In fact, writes Paehlke, "environmentalists have tended to use science to extrapolate fearsome futures, assigning to the political process the task of resisting their scientifically demonstrated scenarios."[19] In singling out its natural scientific leanings (even if he also argues for the validity of social scientific insight), Paehlke also reveals that environmentalism is a bit higher up the positivist food chain than, say, feminism. Although the logic in which political action "follows" externally generated truth is similar, in environmental politics we see, I think, the problem more starkly displayed precisely because natural science is, in late capitalism, rather more readily accepted as a reflection of the eternal truths of the world than is, say, social theory (if not, however, economics).[20] There is, thus, also a greater *strategic* reliance on science in environmental than other social and political movements; to the extent that policy makers and private individuals accept any claims about the nature of the world and about environmental issues, science is better placed than philosophy to provide a window into truth, and certainly more than "mere" opinion.

There are many variations on the general theme of environmental politics "following" a truth-speaking science. In some cases, like recent struggles over local water quality in Nova Scotia (fueled, I should add, by the *E. coli* tragedy in Walkerton, Ontario), an environmental issue is not an environmental issue until science can measure a toxin and draw a causal line from the problem to a source, say, nearby industrial livestock production facilities that produce thousands of tons of chemically laced animal feces (read: common sense doesn't matter here). In other cases such as the logging of old growth forests on Vancouver Island, a key political issue is *whose* science will emerge victorious; media campaigns and public meetings pit expert against expert in a contest of industry versus movement science, each side trying to discredit the methods—and, crucially, the biasing *interests*—of the other. In this respect, ecological science has become the bearer of the common environmental good against all other positions, which are framed as inherently limited and self-interested; a key tactic in many environmental struggles is, in fact, to demonstrate this bias by deploying one's own science in the name of a greater and more universal environmental good.

That the critical space of environmental publicity is profoundly withered by this political logic is quite apparent; there is no space between truth and interest, and it is almost impossible to imagine what an environmental *opinion*, in Arendt's sense, might look like. As Arendt pointed out some forty-odd years ago, the increasing complexity of scientific truth is also a barrier to forming an "environmental" opinion about nature; "the 'truths' of the modern scientific world view, though they can be demonstrated in mathematical formulas and proved technologically, will no longer lend themselves to normal expression in speech and thought."[21] The more environmentalists speak the language of chlorofluorocarbons and biodiversity as nature's truth, *which is increasingly its only apparent commonality to all of us*, the less nature can appear to ordinary individuals as anything other than private, intimate experience.[22]

Indeed, the more the truth of nature is understood to lie beyond individual sense-perception (and in the realm of, say, microorganisms and/or geological time), the less nature's commonality can "appear" at all. The truth is something singular, underneath appearance; what *is* known to individuals is understood to be personal, subjective, private, and not in need of discussion. As Arendt wrote, without a world in common "to appear to me" there is no opinion, and without opinion, there is no meaning to be derived from plurality, no "common" sense; scientists' truths about the world should thus not be trusted not because they are more or less "biased" but

> precisely [because] they move in a world where speech has lost its power. And whatever men [*sic*] do or know or experience can make sense only to the extent that it can be spoken about. There may be truths beyond speech, and they may be of great relevance to man in the singular, that is, to man in so far as he as not a political being, whatever else he may be. Men in the plural, that is, men in so far as they live and move and act in this world, can experience meaningfulness only because they can talk with and make sense to each other and to themselves.[23]

The political equation of scientific truth with nature's commonality not only places the essence of nature—and environmental issues—beyond constitutive public discussion, but it also has the effect of forcing those sites and relations in which nature *is* a subject of speech and meaning into the noncommon world of private interest and intimacy. If ecological science has come to dominate the field in which nature is understood as "common," then this "god's eye view," this representation of science in which the ecologist is understood as seeing impartially and for all, not only has the effect of delegitimating the realm of appearances and collective debate about them but pulls the *possibility* of commonness out from under the individual's feet. In a nutshell, in the absence of a public realm in which individual opinions can approach one another and achieve objectivity in common, then in a context like environmentalism in which the truth of nature is understood to lie outside the individual's ken, the only position the individual's view can occupy is that of a private, partial interest.

To be sure, as Sennett's work demonstrates magnificently, the privatization of environmental issues in this sense has more than one cause; it isn't science's "fault," and the process is part of a web of relations by which the worldly realm of commonality and appearance is degraded. Here, the absence of a realm in which appearances are, as part of the "normal" course of things, considered ripe for artful persuasion and spirited debate corresponds to an increasing emphasis on personal authenticity and private interest as sites of primary identification and meaning, and of relativistic rather than relational understanding of the other's perspective. And here also, given both a lack and a growing distrust of precisely the performative aspects of public life, conduct toward multiple others in the realm of "politics" increasingly takes the form of a celebration or defense of private interests against others' interests. Thus it is probably more accurate to say that by and large environmental politics, despite their promise, do very little to create the necessary political space *between* truths and interests.

By way of an example, Julia Butterfly Hill's heroic two-year tree-sit in a giant California redwood demonstrates quite magnificently the ways in which an impassioned environmental campaign was clearly grounded in claims to the authenticity of intimacy rather than appearance. Although it is certainly the case that Hill brought considerable public attention to her cause, the attention was not so much on the forest as it was on the fate of "her" particular tree, Luna. Hill publicly distanced herself from other tree-sitters (and especially from Earth First!) both directly in her statements to the press and indirectly by cultivating a public image of intensely intimate devotion to the tree rather than the more politically infused anticorporate discourses of the sitters whose work preceded (and originally supported) hers. Thus, Hill actively *refused* the politicization of Pacific Coast forestry by transforming a public protest (tree-sitting is an excellent example of ecopolitical theater) into a personal quest to save Luna. Because of her charismatic and repeated insistence on her intimate relationship to the tree as the ground of legitimacy for her cause, members of the public were able to admire her personal courage and commitment without ever considering the political movement or forest activists who had, both conceptually and physically, enabled that relationship.[24]

One can list a litany of examples in which environmental issues, in their emergence into popular awareness and political contest, take the shape of private interests rather than common concerns. The "Not in My Back Yard" character of many local struggles to refuse particular environmental hazards (landfills, incinerators, etc.), while often striving to push a particular environmental concern into public life and common debate, just as often circulates around the defense of private property or other values of a particular community. The defense of a particular wilderness area is as often propelled by the desires of recreational users and local small business owners as it is by an overarching concern for the health of the nonhuman world in the face of global capitalism. In fact, as Macnaghten and Urry (among others) point out, much of the identity of contemporary environmentalism derives from a sense of *consumer* entitlement, in which individuals not only understand environmentalism as a lifestyle question (ranging from the three R's to organics to voluntary simplicity) but consider "uncontaminated" water, air, soil, and food as a consumer right rather than an ecological or social good.

"Politically," Arendt writes, "interests are relevant only as group interests, and for the purification of such group interests it seems to suffice that they are represented in such a way that their partial character is safeguarded under all conditions."[25] To put it another way, Arendt is arguing that the point of claiming an interest is to defend and solidify, against other claims, precisely the particularity of that interest. This is in contrast to opinions, which "will rise wherever men [*sic*] communicate freely with one another and have the right to make their views public," views not only oriented to the scrutiny of multiple others but "formed and tested in a process of exchange of opinion against opinion."[26] While interests are clearly important, especially in a context where basic questions of equity, access, and justice are not close to being met in environmental or other terms, it remains important to distinguish acts of community defense and empowerment from the acts of political reflection and imagination that cultivate a common world. They may coexist, but they are not the same.

Public Natures: From Rationality to Performativity

Given what would seem to be the large political and ecological significance of something like a green public culture—meaning here a cultivated practice of reflection and imagination by which individuals' opinions about nature might be debated and refined in public—I find it surprising that so very little attention has been paid to questions of these broadly *performative* dimensions of environmental politics. By and large, while there are many ecopolitical thinkers who address questions of democracy and citizenship, who argue for community access to scientific resources for ecological measurement and grassroots activism, and who address questions of representation and justice in their formulation of environmental issues,[27] there is a widespread assumption that environmental politics are always already "political" and that there are no particular conflicts between a "Biology First" political logic and democratic political or epistemic goals. By and large also, few ecopolitical thinkers consider the intrinsic value of political practice as a mode of knowing nature in which environmental opinions might take prominence over scientific or philosophic truths; most environmental politics tend toward an instrumental conception of politics, in which "what is to be done" takes immediate prominence over the generative qualities of the doing.

Unlike most ecopolitical thinkers, Douglas Torgerson in his book *The Promise of Green Politics* argues strongly for the importance of a noninstrumental green politics, specifically, for "sustaining a process of ecologically informed discourse that through its agenda, presuppositions, and cultural images challenges the monological administrative mind and the prevailing discourse of industrialism."[28] Using Arendtian thinking, he argues that green politics can be roughly divided into three parts that correspond to Arendt's tripartite division of the qualities of the *vita activa*.[29] Functional green politics, meaning those struggles oriented to the maintenance of basic survival within current institutions, correspond to Arendt's realm of labor, those activities oriented to the biological maintenance of the species. Constitutive green politics, struggles oriented to the development of entirely new institutions that reflect genuinely ecological values, correspond to Arendt's realm of work, associated with the construction of artificial things that outlast the lives of their creators. Most importantly, however, Torgerson argues for the importance of a performative green politics, for noninstrumental political theater oriented to the presentation of self in persuasive argument and debate. This is the kind of green politics that, for Torgerson, corresponds most closely to Arendt's precious realm of action, of speaking and acting in concert on issues of the world, of revealing and debating opinion, and of performing and constituting oneself as an individual in the company of multiple and plural others.

It is precisely the noninstrumental character of such a performative politics—political debate for its own sake, theater as intersubjective creation—that marks its radical necessity for green politics and that orients Torgerson's argument in favor of a green public sphere as distinct from the green movement more generally (which he generally associates with more instrumental political forms). If one considers politics as an end in itself, a realm of activity on the self and in the world the value of which is not always overdetermined by other interests and goals, then the cultivation of a green public sphere necessarily includes such noninstrumental dimensions: "keep[ing] the conversation going and maintain[ing] the relationships that constitute it."[30] Which means, for Torgerson, that performativity is necessarily separate from both functional and constitutive green politics, forms that are, perhaps more familiarly, precisely oriented to the institution of forms of green rationality (e.g., ecocentrism) derived from modes of analysis (biological/ecological science, philosophy, etc.) that lie outside the political realm itself and are "applied" toward either maintenance or transformation. Performative green politics are thus, for Torgerson, purely formal; acts of carnival, persuasion, argument, and public theater serve no particular "green" purpose outside their own enactment and outside the relationships that are created as a result of political action itself.

A tension arises, however, when Torgerson tries to conceive of the relationships among these three political forms. If (as he suggests) some notion of ecological rationality or ecocentrism, however broadly conceived, is the thread linking environmental politics, then how can one think of genuinely *open* public environmental debate when "environmental" is apparently already established (and in a rather particular way) as a term of reference? How can we think about a noninstrumental *green* performativity when the boundaries of "green" are formulated according to a language that derives largely from instrumental environmental concerns, and especially from notions of ecological rationality that would have us draw much firmer lines around understandings of the common environmental good than Torgerson, I think, would like? His resolution is to argue in favor of a very minimal conception of green rationality in order to keep the concept of debate as central as possible in the green public sphere:

> Green politics serves to enhance and expand the public sphere by promoting debate conducted on the terms of green discourse. Though these terms themselves often remain vigorously contested, the emergence of a language of the environment offers enough commonality for meaningful discussion.[31]

To be sure, this tension is part and parcel of the green political world that Torgerson attempts to describe and, by virtue of his obvious commitment to "the fragile promise . . . of the intrinsic value of politics,"[32] that he also seeks to challenge. But I think that his challenge does not go far enough. Specifically, despite Torgerson's defense of the plurality of green political forms, he fails to stress that the performative does not so much build on the prior existence of the instrumental (i.e., a green public sphere as a space in which to debate an established green language formed from the constitutive legacies of the environmental movement) as it *challenges the very foundational legitimacy of such instrumentalism as a mode of knowing the issues around and through which green politics are defined.* The tension between rationality and performativity is thus a *tension*. Where green rationality at the very least creates a very particular common language from which to begin an environmental discussion (and generally operates much more teleologically than that, often closing down other forms of expression as neither green nor rational), green performativity challenges precisely the commonality of that language by grounding its knowledge claims in, and creating them from, different realms of experience. Simply, political performance is about the realm of appearances, opinions, and public life.

Thus performativity is not purely formal; it is *alternatively constitutive*. Indeed performance, for Arendt, does not just involve debate even if speech is a form of action. Rather, it involves bringing new events into being *through* public performative speech and deed as a result of the creative abilities inherent in individuals (natality, the ability to begin anew), enacted when they appear to one another to influence the world beyond their own selves and interests. In fact, one of the key elements in Arendt's understanding of action, of political performance in the company of others, is "the burden of irreversibility and unpredictability, from which action draws its strength."[33] The outcome of action cannot be predicted in advance; its conclusion is not determined by prior process. But neither is the impact of action self-contained or negligible; its stake is the *world*. And this combination is the risk, what I would argue is the crucial politicality of action, its unique creativity, its challenge to other forms of human activity that rely on sameness, continuance, function, and institutionalization. Action involves appearance and speech whose character is not guaranteed outside of itself instrumentally; only in the company of others, out of the plurality of congregated human experiences, can the world be made anew, and newness can only come into being in the company of others equally committed to exercising their freedom to act.

I emphasize my differences from Torgerson in order to underscore the unique importance of performativity as a creative act for environmental politics and not just as an add-on (however intrinsically valuable) to a politics of survival or even radical institutionalization. A green public culture that includes and fosters individual performance in the company of others enacts the importance of appearance, in other words, demands the creation—and the opinionated iterative expression—of a self in relation to the multiple others of public life. It opens up a world of debate and persuasion in which the object of discussion is not to arrive at truth but to reveal one's distinctiveness in relation to others, and thus also to witness of the revelation of others' distinctiveness. It shifts the substance of environmental discussion from nature's truth to its appearance-to-me, an appearance that is necessarily partial and only achieves meaning and force in the company of others. Thus, the knowledge that arises from performative politics is qualitatively different from the truths upon which ideas of environmental rationality almost inevitably instrumentally rest. Simply, a green performative politics is about developing a different set of knowledge practices, a different set of relations to the world and the others with whom we inhabit it, and a different set of understandings of nature and environment as a result.

Giovanna Di Chiro, for example, has documented some of the ways in which community understandings of environmental issues are deployed, within environmental justice (which she abbreviates to EJ) politics, as a way of destabilizing the truth-claims of epidemiological and other research and opening doors to the presentation and legitimation of alternative forms of knowledge.[34] Although this is only one moment of environmental justice politics, it is very important to note that this EJ strategy of grounding claims to environmental knowledge in commonsense perception is a way to return nature to the realm of appearance and thus indicates some of the tensions between opinion and truth, performative and instrumental action. Di Chiro describes one situation in which an environmental chemist, once firmly attached to the standard single-chemical testing models for environmental contamination, changed his mind when he looked out of an activist's kitchen window to *see* three different factories spewing out three different, and obviously interacting, sets of airborne pollutants. Or another in which a community activist insisted on defining the effects of an environmental disaster as including the integrity of her daily experience of African American cultural community, again something that appears to her and that can be rhetorically produced in public debate without recourse to a necessary rationality existing outside the political sphere itself. Or a third, clearly performative moment, in which a distinctly theatrical approach effectively undermines the oppressive uses toward which rationality is put in ecological politics:

> So when I started this stuff on toxic waste and nuclear waste, I went back to the [North Carolina] General Assembly . . . and I said, "You're exactly right, We're hysterical, and when it comes to matters of life and death, especially mine, I get hysterical." . . . If men don't get hysterical there's something wrong with them.[35]

As Di Chiro notes, EJ politics often include at the same time an active strategy of developing community scientific expertise, a practice tinged with a clear understanding of the political dimensions of scientific study itself (especially risk science). Combined with its ongoing insistence on linking environmental issues with broader questions of social and political justice, this has the effect of situating scientific practice *within* political relations rather than placing science prior *to* political enactment, thus disrupting "Biology First" logic by a different means. Of course, neither of these strategies rejects science out of hand and neither explicitly prioritizes the development of environmental performativity; while I would still argue that additional elements are necessary for a more robust green publicity, I think it's also interesting to note that there are places where a realm of environmental appearance and performance is *already* the terrain of significant developments toward a green public culture, precisely by displacing the political logic by which science directs environmental politics in the main.

Green Public Culture: Plurality and Representation

For Arendt, political action is a mode of heroic appearance in which an actor demonstrates her or his distinct individuality by artistically fashioning a performance to others. Two crucial dynamics are at work here. In the first place, the actor becomes an individual (or "who" she is) by appearing to others, by bringing herself anew into the realm of appearances aside from the categorical and biological categories (or "what" she is) that organize her private life of labor and work. Political appearance, for Arendt, is thus not about the expression of private interest; it is about coming to be an individual connected to multiple other individuals through the cultivation of a distinct appearance, a distinct relationship to the public world that is the common creation of political actors. In the second place, of course, the individual's appearance is only meaningful in the company of multiple and equal other individuals. Thus, for Arendt, performative action is about the creation of an individuality-in-commonality through the performance and witnessing of opinions, and the public sphere is thus the realm in which the inherent human condition of plurality is able to be expressed.

Although many have criticized Arendt's emphasis on individuality (and pointed out that women and slaves were, in the original Greek formulation of this agonal polis, not individuals),[36] the fact is that for Arendt, the key value of action, of political life as opposed to any other activity, was that it necessarily occurred in the company of multiple others. Opinions, then, are not thoughts generated in private and defended against others; they are the *product* of appearance, of risking one's ideas in public and, through argument and critical interchange, of refinement from the perspectives of multiple others.[37]

The validity of an opinion is not judged against truth; it is a product of plurality, its quality developed according to its ability to incorporate the perspectives—the "world-as-it-appears-to-me"—of multiple others. Arendt explains it this way:

> I form an opinion by considering a given issue from different viewpoints, by making present to my mind the standpoints of those who are absent; that is, I represent them. This process of representation does not blindly adopt the actual views of those who stand somewhere else, and hence look upon the world from a different perspective; this is a question neither of empathy, as though I tried to be or to feel like somebody else, nor of counting noses and joining a majority but of being and thinking in my own identity where actually I am not. The more people's standpoints I have present in my mind, the better I can imagine how I would feel and think if I were in their place.[38]

This quality of "representative thinking" is, for Arendt, a form of activity unique to public life. Thinking in the place of the other requires abstraction from detail, not intimacy,[39] but it also requires active participation in the realm in which the other appears, not disconnected reasoning about the other's potential based on "what" she is. Representation also suggests a process by which opinion is multiply challenged and filtered, so that thinking actively includes the mark of the other as part of its dynamic. Representative thinking is thus a mode of knowing that derives from iterative and critical appearance; it is constitutionally public, multiple, and reflexive.

Of course, representative thinking is a quality sorely atrophied in modernity both as a result of the predominance of contemplation over action and as a result of the incursion of "social" issues into the public domain,[40] both of which place truth and authenticity outside the realm of collectivity, plurality, and publicity. Common sense, although the basis for the revelation of the world-as-it-appears-to-me, all too often resorts to privately generated ideas of the good (e.g., personal authenticity) or external standards of truth (e.g., reasoning based on probability). Without a desire for public argument and political theater, without a forum in which to practice representation, and without an appearing and critically engaged plurality, is representative thinking even possible?

In my view, it is precisely this possibility that has been one of the greatest strengths of environmental politics, and here especially of environmental justice politics. Common sense is precisely the basis of everyday claims to know and speak nature. But to transform a problem of everyday nature (as it appears to me) into a subject for political conversation requires its rethinking according to some understanding of "commonality." As I have argued, mainstream environmentalism *tends* to accept that the "common" is best represented by environmental science, and tends to avoid the messy business of agreeing upon the nature of the common, so to speak, as a result. But environmental justice, at least in its origins, has taken a different logic.[41] In resistance to environmental politics that claimed nature (e.g., wilderness) as a distinct and scientifically knowable subject apart from human relations, environmental justice politics have publicly produced nature as an open term around which to organize multiple and everyday claims to justice, freedom, and expression; these are centered around but expressly not limited to antiracist and civil rights struggles. This production of environmentalism leaves the subject of "the environment" open and legitimates the realm of appearance, making the process of contestation by which environmental issues appear a political rather than a scientific one.

The political logic of environmental justice is also not about imposing a singular definition of justice on the broad network of struggles that are connected under its umbrella of affinities. Justice itself is the subject of grassroots political debate. I would suggest that the logic is, broadly, to take NIMBY to "Not in Anyone's Back Yard," thus performatively forcing the particular community issue to appear as a common good but without a preexisting understanding of how that "good" will work in any other situation, in other words, without a prepolitical claim to the nature of the issue and without a definite idea of the shape of its resolution. Environmental justice politics thus invite the appearance of a variety of different claims to know nature and to know justice; without a clear sense of what an ecological rationality will look like before the process of debate and politicization itself, environmental justice thus suggests the necessary but critically interacting multiplicity of views on nature. And this strikes me as similar to the green public sphere I suggest above. If we don't know in advance of the conversation what environmental justice will look like, then we have to pay very close attention indeed to how the world appears to the others with whom we share responsibility for its construction.

Conclusion

The typical response to the argument I make in this chapter is one of critical incredulity. Surely I'm not advocating an environmentalism without science? Surely science is more complex than the political logic I describe? Surely some of the most articulate speakers of environmental opinion have been, precisely, scientists? Surely we can't trust opinion? Surely there are ecological truths that extend beyond individual awareness and that cannot be adequately addressed, especially given the severity of the problems and the complexity of the causes, by ordinary individuals with knowledges derived from appearances?

Like all of the ecopolitical thinkers whose work I cite in this text, I am actually advocating a strategy of healthy multiplicity for environmental politics. The political logic by which environmental scientists are able to "speak" for nature in ways that ordinary citizens cannot is not likely to disappear any time soon, and I make this argument secure in the knowledge that there are many who will argue with me about the continued relevance of this logic. But other relations suggest a more complex discussion as well. Current robust debates within science and science studies, for example, indicate to me a promising awareness that ecological science is a particular and socially located set of truth-making practices, and that the reified logic by which environmentalists claim "truth" from scientific work misrepresents the richness and complexity of scientific work itself.[42] In addition, as Raymond Murphy notes, environmentalism has many elements of a paradoxical relationship to science.[43] On the one hand, individuals are increasingly aware—perhaps especially in the context of widely publicized biotechnological developments—of the risks of an unaccountable scientific practice and are thus deeply critical of science's ability to act independently in the common good; on the other hand, we remain reliant on science to develop the arguments with which to make science accountable.

In this context, the point of the chapter is not so much to argue for the displacement of science as it is to advocate for the vital importance of something *else*. In fact, to continue the Arendtian turn, an environmental politics holding the display, cultivation, and spirited debate of opinion at its center would seem to suggest a new role—or perhaps a very old one—for science. For Arendt, the Platonic rift between politics and philosophy was based on a very particular reading of Socrates' trial, one that she would claim is extremely anti-Socratic. To Socrates, the philosopher is not a disembodied recluse contemplating eternal truths, but an actively engaged citizen whose pedagogical role is not to tell other citizens a singular truth but, through careful and dialogical questioning, to help them clarify, refine, and develop precisely the truthfulness *of* their multiple opinions.[44]

This maieutic practice, I think, could be actively embraced by environmental scientists and ecopolitical theorists alike to great effect. As a way of encouraging respect for the multiplicity of opinions through which environmental relations are expressed, as a way of returning appearances to politics, as a way of learning to appear, to listen, to distinguish and be distinguished and, crucially, as a way of developing the precious faculty of representative thinking in the place of multiple others, environmental "experts" can and should take on the role of midwife rather than oracle. Ultimately, a green public culture should be neither a realm in which environmental truths, created elsewhere, are simply "played out" in political strategy, nor a realm in which expressive and carnivalesque performances have no effect on the world that is their subject and creation. Performance constitutes a world on alternative grounds, and those grounds are inherently multiple and imaginative. Ultimately, then, a green public culture is a realm in which the world can *appear* and be made meaningful in light of the opinions of multiple others thinking, reflecting, and imagining in each other's company.[45]

As Villa indicates, however, this potential is not broadly realized within environmental politics, and I have attempted to demonstrate that the absence of a space "between" science and interests in mainstream environmentalism is a contributing factor in this failure. As I have alluded throughout, environmental justice politics certainly represent a promising terrain in which glimpses of a performative, opinionated green public culture can already be viewed. In addition to its important socialization of environmental issues—and its clear challenge to the idea of a "common" nature, the truth of which lies outside the realm of human influence and activity—environmental justice begins its claims to justice by pulling nature back into the *political* realm: of appearances, of everyday experiences, of recognizable and discussable problems. Thus, perhaps paradoxically, I firmly believe that the seeds of a green public culture in the way I have described it, if they are going to take root, will do so in articulation with environmental justice politics that begin in the realm of particular and discussable appearance and opinion. But I also think that the hegemonic logic of science "preceding" environmental claims combined with the compelling strategy of using the legal system to formulate, argue, and defend measurable group interests, makes the job of holding onto the realm of opinion a particularly difficult one for environmental justice politics. Interests can be overwhelming; the promising performative logic I described above is crucial, but it is also very fragile when communities are at risk. Thus I think there is also a need within environmentalism more generally to focus on developing a challenge to the relations through which the common world of nature is increasingly understood as a collection of private interests working within a set of natural truths that only ecological science can see. The world, in Arendt's sense, depends on it.

Notes

1. Hannah Arendt, *The Human Condition* (Chicago: University of Chicago Press, 1958), 3.
2. Hannah Arendt, *Between Past and Future* (Harmondsworth, Middlesex: Penguin, 1963), 261–62.
3. Jürgen Habermas, *The Structural Transformation of the Public Realm* (Cambridge, Mass.: MIT Press, 1989), 162.
4. The phrase is originally Arendt's. "If we equate these spaces of freedom . . . with the political realm itself, we shall be inclined to think of them as islands in a sea or oases in a desert." Hannah Arendt, *On Revolution* (London: Penguin, 1963), 275.
5. Jeffrey C. Isaac, *Democracy in Dark Times* (Ithaca, N.Y.: Cornell University Press, 1998), 148.
6. Ibid.
7. Isaac is not claiming a Habermasian rationality for environmental justice; his ideas on publicity differ significantly from Habermas's, even if both emphasize association, participation, and critical commonality.
8. Dana R. Villa, *Politics, Philosophy, Terror: Essays on the Thought of Hannah Arendt* (Princeton, N.J.: Princeton University Press, 1999).
9. Ibid., 153.
10. Ibid., 147–52. See also Hannah Arendt, *The Human Condition*; and Richard Sennett, *The Fall of Public Man* (New York: Norton, 1976).
11. Villa, *Politics, Philosophy, Terror*, 153. Note that he does not mean "who one is" in the Arendtian sense; she would use the phrase "*what* one is" to make Villa's point.

12. Catriona Sandilands, *The Good-Natured Feminist: Ecofeminism and the Quest for Democracy* (Minneapolis: University of Minnesota Press, 1999), especially chapter 7.

13. Ibid., 154.

14. Hannah Arendt, "Philosophy and Politics," *Social Research* 57, no. 1 (spring 1990): 73–103.

15. Ibid., 80.

16. Robert Paehlke, *Environmentalism and the Future of Progressive Politics* (New Haven, Conn.: Yale University Press, 1989), 114.

17. Phil Macnaghten and John Urry, "Towards a Sociology of Nature," *Sociology* 29, no. 2 (May 1995): 204.

18. Paehlke actually notes that "environmentalists . . . have generally seen [the roles of scientist and citizen] as irretrievably linked." Paehlke, *Environmentalism*, 114.

19. Ibid., 114–15.

20. Of course, many ecological scientists (and Ulrich Beck along with them) would argue that science is *not* considered, in late capitalism, a source of absolute truths and that its legitimacy (and research funding) has been seriously called into question. While I agree with this analysis in a broad sense, I see in environmental politics (and political theory) a continued reliance on scientifically generated scenarios as if science *should* be the most legitimate source of nature knowledge rather than a willingness to make more democratic use of any skepticism with scientific authority. The logic remains: one must have scientific certainty to make environmental political decisions. And of course, such certainty is seldom possible. But environmental politics tend to proceed as if it were not only possible but necessary.

21. Arendt, *The Human Condition*, 3.

22. Indeed, when Paehlke argues that environmentalism also requires "that we must construct and use an appropriate, consistent, and humanly meaningful set of values," (Paehlke, *Environmentalism*, 114) he is able to produce a coherent list of thirteen "central value assertions" that derive not from political discussion but from the writings of naturalists, philosophers, economists, and political theorists. Although his inclusion of values clearly points to the political quality of environmental discussion—even of opinion—his reliance on another set of experts to tell us what environmental values *are* would seem to close the political space that the question of values might open up.

23. Arendt, *The Human Condition*, 4.

24. I am indebted to Audrey Vanderford for this analysis. See "Can't See the Forest for Her Tree: Activism, Celebrity and Julia 'Butterfly' Hill," presentation at the University of Oregon, "Taking Nature Seriously: Citizens, Science and the Environment," February 2001. It should be noted that Hill "saved" Luna by shelling out a cash fine, that much of the rest of the forest was still cut, and that Hill's actions and celebrity are the subject of considerable criticism by the larger movement of forest activists on whom Hill so clearly turned her back.

25. Arendt, *On Revolution*, 227.

26. Ibid.

27. One collection that includes many of these dimensions is Daniel Faber, ed., *The Struggle for Ecological Democracy: Environmental Justice Movements in the United States* (New York: Guilford Press, 1998).

28. Douglas Torgerson, *The Promise of Green Politics: Environmentalism and the Public Sphere* (Durham, N.C.: Duke University Press, 1999), 20.

29. Arendt's description of the *vita activa* is, famously, located in *The Human Condition*. Although it is clear that she did not reject the *vita contemplativa* (it was the topic of her unfinished, final book), she wanted to refocus attention and value on the activities of the world, and especially on the neglected realm of action.

30. Torgerson, *The Promise of Green Politics*, 156.

31. Ibid., 160. Although one can certainly argue that there is a need for basic agreement on some terms of reference so that a meaningful conversation can take place, the term "environment" has, at

least since the rise of feminist, antiracist, and postcolonial challenges to more mainstream conceptions, seen more dissent than consent: hence the need to append the term "justice" to the "environmental" of the movement to which many justice advocates respond. Thus, it is not simply a basic term from which dissent can proceed; it is itself a subject of contest, and must remain open. Torgerson's broad definition of "environmental" would seem to gesture in the direction of such contestational diversity—which is to be applauded—but his underlying reliance on a very particular debate between environmental rationality and ecocentrism (combined with a very superficial reading of ecofeminism and environmental justice) suggests that he is not really interested in contesting "green" boundaries beyond this rather circumscribed field. Hence my point that performative green politics are not just a layer on top of other green forms—they constitute it precisely through challenging the terms of reference of the others. Many feminists have made similar points about the definition of "the political"; contesting this boundary is a vital part of politics itself. See Judith Butler and Joan Scott, eds., *Feminists Theorize the Political* (London: Routledge, 1991).

32. Torgerson, *The Promise of Green Politics*, 168.

33. Arendt, *The Human Condition*, 233.

34. Giovanna Di Chiro, "Environmental Justice from the Grassroots: Reflections on History, Gender, and Expertise," in Faber, *The Struggle for Ecological Democracy*, 104–36.

35. Cora Tucker, cited in Faber, *The Struggle for Ecological Democracy*, 121. Originally in *Empowering Ourselves: Women and Toxics Organizing*, ed. Robbin Lee Zeff, Marsha Love, and Karen Stults (Falls Church, Va.: Citizens Clearinghouse for Hazardous Waste, 1989), 5.

36. For a review of these arguments (notably from feminists) in addition to a more sustained discussion of the specificity of action for an *ecofeminist* politics, see Sandilands, *The Good-Natured Feminist*, chapter 7.

37. For Arendt, the opinion itself is already a product of having thought with and against oneself, the two-in-one conversation of thinking. So the key question of politics as opposed to contemplation is not conversation as opposed to solitude, but multiplicity as opposed to duality.

38. Arendt, *Between Past and Future*, 241.

39. Friendship is generally the metaphor used to describe the nature of political relationships in this sense. It is based on both particularity and equality.

40. See Sandilands, *The Good-Natured Feminist*, chapter 7.

41. The more institutionalized EJ politics have become, however, the less they seem willing to contest many aspects of this political logic. There is a growing trend in EJ, for example, toward a legal rather than political contestation of environmental rights.

42. Thanks to Peter Andree for pointing out to me that one can think of the practice of peer review as a specific practice through which science itself can be rethought as a realm of opinion.

43. Raymond Murphy, *Rationality and Nature: A Sociological Inquiry into a Changing Relationship* (Boulder, Colo.: Westview, 1994), 216–17.

44. Arendt, "Philosophy and Politics," 81.

45. I have argued elsewhere that thinking in the company of others can include nonhuman others, and that a performative public realm does not exclude, on the traditional bases of language and rationality, the appearances of nonhuman individuals as active agents. My example was orcas, who *do* speak, appear, and perform, both to one another and also to human beings of their own free will (I don't mean Sealand, here). See "Whalewatching: Political Speech, Political Appearance and Multi-Species Citizenship," presentation at the University of Oregon, "Taking Nature Seriously: Citizens, Science and the Environment," February 2001.

CHAPTER 7

Vulnerability and Virtue

DEMOCRACY, DEPENDENCY, AND ECOLOGICAL STEWARDSHIP

John Barry

That we depend on the earth is something that cannot be denied and upon reflection is something that most rational people would recognize and acknowledge. However, for "modern humans," that is, those who do not live close to nature (either as hunter-gatherers or farmers), this dependence is something likely to go unrecognized and unacknowledged in their everyday lives. Dependency is something that modern society and the modern mentality finds hard to deal with, except in the sense of seeing dependency as a "problem" to be eliminated or solved, a weakness within the "human condition" to be overcome. Human dependency on nature and related ideas of vulnerability, neediness, frailty, limits, precaution, which the global environmental movement has done so much to put on the public agenda, also raises unsettling questions (from the modern worldview) about humanity's essentially dependent and vulnerable character. That is, human dependency on external nature is related to claims about the dependent and vulnerable character of "internal" human nature.

Making this connection about the relations of vulnerability and dependency that exist between humans and nature has of course been a central feature and aim of the green movement. The green movement and the ecological perspective also develops this connection between dependency and vulnerability, by making the point that that upon which we are dependent and are vulnerable to (as well as reciprocally it being vulnerable to our actions) ought (for human, prudential, and self-interested as well as various ethical reasons) to be cared for. That is, the appropriate disposition toward that which we have not made (or can remake) and cannot control, and to which we stand in a relation of dependence and co-vulnerability, is one of care. Thus, the motivation behind the green movement's aim of highlighting this dependent, vulnerable nature of the human relationship to and with the environment is not (or ought not) to somehow wallow or take some perverse pleasure in unmasking the "great lie" of modern society's supposed and much vaunted "superiority" to and "domination" or "mastery" of nature (though this is an important issue), but rather to turn attention to the urgent need to move and persuade people to care about the environment.

We are also dependent upon each other, something equally obvious, yet often overlooked, downplayed, or denied.[1] Indeed, increasingly as societies across the globe become more intensively linked through networks of trade, transport, communications, and the other processes of "globalization," and an ever more complex division of labor proceeds both within and between countries, the dependence of our species on itself becomes more and more apparent. As we enter the third millennium we are not just social animals, we are rapidly becoming a more interconnected, interrelated, and codependent species, coevolving with human institutions and practices of power, economics, politics, and culture. And with this interdependence (itself unevenly spread across and within countries) comes an increasing vulnerability of humans to each other. Examples of this range from how a financial crisis in one part of the world, or a decision by the head office of a large multinational corporation, can have rapid and devastating effects on the economies, livelihoods, and well-being of people (and environments) in other parts of the world, to how the excessive consumption of fossil fuel by a minority of the world's population can affect the global climate system with serious consequences for people and the environment in other vulnerable parts of the world. In short, as a species we are becoming more and more interconnected and interdependent and with that comes increased vulnerability to the actions and decisions of people, institutions, and socioenvironmental changes located in distant parts of the world.

Part of the problem with both types of dependence and their associated vulnerabilities is that while when we reflect on them we recognize and acknowledge them, in the normal course of events, the networks, processes, institutions, and relations of cause and effect are such that these relations of human and environmental dependence and vulnerability are, to say the least, opaque, complex, and complicated and thus for most of the time "invisible" or "nonexistent." Yet it is the case that increasingly these processes of dependence and vulnerability are causing serious and long-term damage to people and planet. As many critics of globalization and economic modernization have pointed out, the continuation, maintenance, and intensification of these processes are carried out behind people's backs (yet often in their name or in the name of "progress" or "modernization" itself), that is, undemocratically.[2] It is thus no coincidence that the broad coalition of the antiglobalization movement (combining groups and movements representing environmental, labor, women, the developing world, and indigenous peoples' interests) shares a common commitment to:

- revealing these relations of vulnerability, and the real-world effects they have on people and planet;
- identifying relations of power and responsibility and thus raising important issues of global, social, and environmental justice;
- highlighting the extremely undemocratic, hidden, and often secret manner in which these relations of vulnerability are established, extended, and organized, and finally,
- proposing democratic procedures, elected institutions, and transparent processes as essential elements of both dealing with the "democratic deficit" that they have identified and that is absolutely central to coping and addressing their many related social and environmental problems, both locally and globally.

Thus, democratic norms, habits, and procedures between citizens and the state, between citizens both within and between/beyond/beneath states, together with social, global, and environmental justice, are intrinsically related to the human and environmental dimensions of the modern vulnerability of life on planet earth. Democracy makes relations of interdependence more transparent and makes processes and agents of decision making more open, public, and (in theory at least) accountable to the demos, the political community. Democracy is thus linked to green/environmental politics as a way to allow people to both see the often invisible (mostly economic) groups, institutions, and processes (such as the World Trade Organization), and also the more mundane and often complex causal network of relations among people, planet, practices, and goods (mediated by institutions), which result in the increasing environmental and social degradation we witness around the planet today. In other words, democracy is presented as an antidote to the damaging social and environmental consequences of the way human societies organize themselves in relation to other societies and the environment. Democracy promises to trace, monitor, and make accountable (and hopefully ultimately regulate) relations of power, and in that process identify relations of responsibility, and thus begin the process of making reparations for social and environmental injustices. In short, while not naïve or idealistic enough to think that democracy is the solution to all the environmental and political problems of the world, I am convinced that the claims of nature and people, especially where these are relations of vulnerability, require democracy both in order to recognize these claims and as a method of resolving the conflicts and problems these claims raise. My sense is that Benjamin Barber's view that democracy and democratic citizenship is "the only legitimate form our natural dependency can take,"[3] is something that can, a fortiori, be applied to human dependence upon and vulnerability in respect to the natural world. In short, the claims of democracy and democratic citizenship (understood ecologically as a form of "ecological stewardship") are the only legitimate form our mutual vulnerability to and collective dependence upon each other and the earth can take.

Overview

The paper is divided into two main parts, the first, moral, and the second, political. In the first part I argue that "ecological stewardship" constitutes an appropriate and in some respects "ideal" ethical idiom and practice guiding human relations with the natural world. In part, this is because ecological stewardship is sensitive to the dependence, contingency, and vulnerability that characterizes human relations with the natural world, yet explicitly recognizes human use and productive interests in the environment. I then proceed to develop ecological stewardship as a form of ecological virtue ethics, which has practical political advantages over other ethical approaches—such as deep ecology and intrinsic value theory—in that by not rejecting anthropocentrism, it has a better chance of being accepted by and intelligible within modern liberal-democratic societies. Ecological stewardship, I suggest, expresses an anthropocentric "ethic of use" for the environment (as opposed to some putative "environmental ethic"), the principal aim of which is to distinguish legitimate human use of the environment from illegitimate abuse. At the same time, the idea of ecological stewardship is something that can be supported by and accords with many of the cultural and ethical worldviews that characterize modern multicultural and morally pluralistic societies. In Rawlsian terms, "ecological stewardship" can be part of an "overlapping consensus." The two main reasons for this are that, first, stewardship is a moral tradition which can already be found in many cultural and substantive ethical worldviews, and second, stewardship articulates a commitment to intergenerational justice, which again is something that can find overlapping support across many different moral views.

The second part links ecological stewardship to democracy via the notions of the "greening of citizenship" and "collective ecological management." Here the main claims are that ecological stewardship requires and is based upon the "greening of citizenship," which is understood as a widening of the rights and responsibilities of citizenship to encompass both "political" and "nonpolitical" dimensions of individual and collective behavior that affect the environment. That is, while the greening of citizenship is politically based, it is not exclusively politically centered in that it encompasses other modes of human action and identities, such as those associated with the "private sphere" of consumption, production, and parenting. The greening of citizenship I suggest aims to encourage individuals to become "citizens in community in environment," that is, it represents the double re-embedding of individuals, first, within their communities, second, within their environments. Collective ecological management is then outlined as a form of democratic ecological stewardship, which explicitly recognizes and acknowledges the ineliminable productive character of the fundamental relationship between human society and the environment.

Thinking of ourselves (individually and collectively) as ecological stewards not only reconnects us to the environment and reminds us of our dependence upon it (and our responsibility for it), but at the same time connects us to future generations (and our responsibility to them). As such, ecological stewardship is, I suggest, a powerful political-ethical idea that should form the basis of the transition to a more sustainable society.

Part I: Ecological Stewardship and Virtue Ethics

ECOLOGICAL STEWARDSHIP

Before outlining how I understand ecological stewardship, there are (at least) two potential criticisms that can be made of making a stewardship ethic the main ethical basis for creating a more sustainable society and articulating how we ought to treat and use the natural world. The first has to do with its religious origins and overtones, the second, its agricultural context and direct, unmediated experience of the environment.

An apparent problem with the stewardship tradition is its theological/religious legacy and origins. The idea of humans as "stewards" of "God's creation" is something that can be found in various religious worldviews. An early expression can be found in Plato, who in the *Phaedrus* wrote that, "'It is everywhere the responsibility of the animate to look after the inanimate.' Man . . . is sent to earth by God 'to administer earthly things,' to care for them in God's name."[4] Later Judeo-Christianity articulated its own stewardship ethic (a minority tradition in comparison to the "domination of nature" tradition it bequeathed to modern society), and one can find similar stewardship traditions in most of the great "agricultural" religions, such as Buddhism, Hinduism, and Islam.[5] Within the stewardship tradition, rather than the nonhuman world being made for humans (a position that did eventually come to dominate Western views of the environment in particular), as stewards of God's creation, humans were in a sense made for the nonhuman world, or rather they were God's "managers" or stewards holding responsibility for God's property.

Now, a religiously based idea of the environment as "God's creation" and humans as "God's stewards," is something that is obviously not shared by everyone and cannot be the basis of an ethical agreement of how a multicultural, pluralist society can or ought to treat, value, use, and interact with nature. However, there are two things worth considering here. First, there are large numbers of people in Western societies who believe in religions that express and/or are consistent with a stewardship ethic. As such, from a political point of view a stewardship ethic and policies based on it can (at least in principle) be supported by those subscribing to these religious worldviews. Second, it is not too difficult to secularize the stewardship ethic, if instead of conceiving the earth/environment as "God's creation," we replace this with a view of the earth/environment as something passed down from one human generation to the next. What I am getting at here is something close to the Native Amerindian saying that, "We do not inherit the earth from our parents, but borrow it from our children." The stewardship ethic is something that can be articulated by, translated into, or compatible and intelligible within both religious and secular ethical commitments. Thus the fact that a stewardship ethic can be supported by both religious and secular ethical worldviews is actually an advantage rather than a disadvantage.[6]

Even though the agricultural context and origins of stewardship are no longer the background against which individuals in contemporary Western, urban, and industrialized societies experience and relate to the natural world, the notion of stewardship as a particular morally informed mode of social-environmental interaction is something that is worth retaining. One of the reasons for this is that the idea of stewardship carries with it a view of the relation between humanity and nature as informed and governed by both productive and ethical concerns.

The task facing us is how to translate a stewardship ethic to a mode of life that, on the face of it, could not be more removed from an agricultural and rural setting. The practical issue for stewardship in the modern age is not about direct, unmediated experience and management of the environment through ownership and use, but rather stewardship qua environmental management or regulation, based on nondirect, mediated, and institutionalized social-environmental interaction. Given this, what is required is a shift from "agricultural" stewardship based around daily, direct, and individual productive interaction with the land/environment to "ecological" stewardship based around mediated, distant, and inherently collective modes of interaction with the environment. Thus, ecological stewardship is a form of stewardship appropriate to urban-based societies in which our productive (and often other nonproductive) relations to the environment are necessarily mediated by political and other institutions (such as those we find in the market economy, or the media), individual and collective practices, such as consumption, and forms of knowledge not necessarily based on direct experience of (private or other) ownership of the land. Democracy is thus appropriate to apply to ecological stewardship insomuch as it is, in large part, an institutionally mediated mode of organizing our economic-productive relations to and overall environmental impact upon the natural world.[7] That is, democratic procedures and institutions through which societies debate, argue about, and ultimately organize and regulate their relations (or what I have called elsewhere their "metabolism"[8]) to the environment are the modern substitute for direct experience of the "land" that characterizes agricultural stewardship. The issue is not that a democratic mode of ecological stewardship means that each and every aspect of a society's metabolism with the environment has to be voted upon. Rather, the overall macro-level organization of a society's metabolism should be open, democratic, and accountable ultimately to the demos, "the people," rather than organized in "private," behind peoples' backs, by undemocratic and nondemocratic unelected institutions, agencies, and groups.

Of particular importance here is that the type of knowledge necessary for ecological stewardship is largely, but by no means exclusively, of a scientific character. Again, the reason for this is that a scientific view of the environment and our productive relation to it is a form of knowledge that can be consistent with different ethical commitments and different substantive ethical worldviews. While, of course, there are still people who work the land, and farming still constitutes an important form of "ecological management," in Western societies the numbers within agriculture have been and continue to decline.[9] The vast majority of people in Western societies live in cities and other urban areas and indeed the movement of people from rural to urban areas is something that is and will continue to increase globally.[10] Thus, ecological stewardship is presented as an appropriate way of reconnecting people to the environment in a manner that does not abstract from the fundamental productive and mediated character that must always inform any realistic discussion of human-environment relations.

I understand the productive-ethical character of ecological stewardship as orientated toward avoiding unsustainable uses of and material interaction with the environment, and establishing what I call "ethically symbiotic" and avoiding "ethically parasitic" or illegitimate (ab)uses of the environment. In brief, ecological stewardship is about the following:

1. Ecological sustainability for humans (that is, maintaining long-term, productive social-environmental metabolisms). I take it that ecological sustainability is premised on human interests (which does not necessarily "rule out" the interests of the nonhuman world).
2. Distinguishing moral symbiosis and parasitism in terms of relation to, valuation, treatment, and use of the natural environment (how to distinguish "use" from "abuse," but also raising the question of when "nonuse" of the environment is the ethically proper course of action).
3. The issue of repairing ecological damage and ecological restoration (in part, this is explained by recognizing that while humans depend on and are vulnerable to the environment, some parts of the environment also depend on and are vulnerable to human activity and choices).

Hence, in large part, the aim of ecological stewardship is to reconnect and remind us of our dependence upon nature (and its dependence upon us), and to premise a responsibility toward our use of nature on establishing this reconnection.

While we can collectively choose the form and content this dependency takes (in the sense of choosing particular modes of interaction with and use of the environment, as mediated by human technology, political and economic institutions and practices, and cultural and ethical considerations), that is *how* we structure our dependent relation, we cannot choose *whether* to depend on the environment or not. As such these various mediating institutions are and will be central in effecting urban forms of environmental management. At the same time, parts of the natural world are increasingly dependent upon human collective action, so that the social-environmental relation can described as one of mutual dependency.

ECOLOGICAL STEWARDSHIP AND VIRTUE

Virtues are qualities of character enabling their possessor to be responsive to the inherently contingent and changing character of human experience. That is, virtues, such as courage, for example, are dispositions which humans need or find useful in order to live because of the type of beings they are and the type of world(s) they inhabit. It is important to point out that virtues are commonly held to help human beings *cope* with rather than to *eliminate* the problems and contingencies of the "human condition," such as death, luck, conflict between competing goods, human plurality, and unpredictability, among others. Thus, ecological stewardship as a form of ecological virtue does not seek to definitively answer or solve the existential riddle of human existence, or discover some permanent solution to social-environmental relations.

That is, one of the reasons why I think that the idiom of virtue ethics is appropriate to discussions of environmental issues is that I do not think we can ever reach a "final" and lasting "harmonious" coexistence with the environment. This is not to mean that I think humans are somehow condemned to stand to the environment in a state of permanent conflict. What I mean is that I believe that any harmony, balance, stability, sustainability, and so on that can possibly exist between humans and the environment will always be provisional, dynamic rather than static, and something that has to be actively established, monitored, and maintained rather than "automatic." Even in a less unsustainable context than we can presently witness between particular societies and their environments as well as globally between the human species and the planet, "harmony" between humans and their (local and global) environments is better thought of in terms of "coping" with or successfully negotiating environmental problems rather than somehow "solving" or eradicating them in principle. Virtues are useful precisely because they help us cope with contingency, unexpected change, unforeseen difficulties, challenges, and so on, terms that convey the overarching character of any realistic view of human–nature relations now or in the future. To assume otherwise is not only naïve but positively dangerous. Ecological stewardship, as befits a virtue ethics approach, can be regarded as a mean between "struggling" against nature in the attempt to "master" or "dominate" it, the ecological vice of an ignorant, instrumental, and arrogant anthropocentrism,[11] and a well-meaning but equally ignorant and foolish desire for human societies to "submerge" themselves within and "return" to the natural order, the ecological vice of a sentimental, unrealistic, and submissive ecocentrism.[12] Ecological stewardship therefore concerns "coping" with rather than either "struggling" against or "submitting" to the natural environment.

Following classical moral thought, we can distinguish between the "intellectual virtues" (knowledge, wisdom) and those associated with character (such as humility, prudence, generosity, friendship), what Aristotle called the "moral virtues." Ignorance of our dependent relation on the natural world and its processes, entities, and products, as given by ecological and other sciences, which tells us that we are, for example, social animals evolved from primates, and that we are a part of the natural order, is a vice, and a fortiori an ecological vice. Thus, knowledge (both scientific and other forms) of and acknowledgement of the ecological "facts of life" is an extremely important ecological virtue that needs to be cultivated. This is especially important given that it is ignorance rather than a willful and conscious desire to destroy or harm the environment that is often a cause of environmental damage, or at least a central factor in not reversing destructive ecological practices. Evidence for the positive effects of ecological knowledge and awareness should go without saying. Proposals for "environmental education,"[13] and the integration of ecological aspects to the educational curriculum (as is the case in the United Kingdom and elsewhere for example) are important developments. However, it also needs to be said that environmental education, knowledge, and awareness by themselves are not sufficient conditions for changing individual and collective behavior in a more sustainable direction. Merely making people aware about the environment impact of human consumption practices, for example, will not automatically make them alter their consumption. On top of knowledge of their effects on the environment and their dependence upon it, people also need to be given reasons to change their ways of thinking and acting. And one of the aims of ecological stewardship is to provide people with sufficient moral and practical reasons why they ought to change their behavior in a manner which (a) does not seek to persuade them in a language and with reasons that are very far removed from their own or (b) does not deny the reality and legitimacy of human productive use of and such human productive interests in the natural world.

SOME ADVANTAGES OF THE ECOLOGICAL STEWARDSHIP IDEA

There are a number of advantages of ecological stewardship that for reasons of space I will simply state.

1. Human Interests and the Ecocentric/Anthropocentric Debate
Stewardship can be viewed as conveying a sense of responsibility toward nature, which does not necessarily depend on ecocentric ethical claims, and which strives to harmonize the sometimes conflicting human interests in the environment, as well as reconciling these interests with those of the nonhuman world as much as possible. Yet, it has to be said that it is resolutely an anthropocentric position, but not an arrogant one. Ecological stewardship is based on and for humans and their interests but not solely centered on these. Thus, it is not a disinterested or impartial mode of thinking and acting in relation to the nonhuman world, but an interested and partial one that seeks to

harmonize long-term human productive interests while being respectful of the interests of the nonhuman world.

2. Planning, the State, and Stewardship

Ecological stewardship is a form of intentional use and management of the environment, and is thus particularly suited as an ethical framework compatible for the democratically legitimated planning and regulation by the state (both national and local) and public authorities that the achievement of sustainability will require. As Meadowcroft and Kenny put it,

> One of the principle implications of "planning" in liberal democratic contexts concerns the setting of "meta-social objectives" by the state, or the "steering" of economic life to meet pre-determined social goals. The state thus looks like one of the most likely candidates for an agency which may oversee the shift to a (more) sustainable society. In this sense the objective of environmental sustainability, contestable and changing as this is, may well logically entail "planning" in this "meta-level" sense.[14]

And there is plenty of real-world evidence of this planning dimension to dealing with environmental problems, as can be seen in the various "environmental plans" one finds in European countries and elsewhere,[15] going from the international level (such as those initiated at the Rio "Earth Summit"), right down through the European Union's "Environment Action Programs," to national plans (such as the Dutch National Environment Policy Plan), to local government plans (such as the Local Agenda 21 process). All of these various forms of planning, steering, and regulation, if they are to be both normatively justified and indeed effective, need to engage not just state and other public agencies but democratic citizens as ecological stewards.

3. Stewardship, Knowledge, and Precaution

By explicitly relating to scientific knowledge as well as ethical considerations, ecological stewardship can be said to express an "integrated" mode of relating to the natural world, in which scientific assessment is not somehow separate to the outcome of political and moral judgment. While scientific knowledge is accepted as a legitimate and important part of the stewardship mode, nonscientific and/or local forms of knowledge concerning respectful and sustainable use of the environment are not ruled out. Equally, an ecological stewardship position recognizes that there are limits to what we know and can know about the natural world. Thus, ecological stewardship recognizes limits to our capacity to accurately and fully know the environmental effects of our environmental practices.

As a result of this, ecological stewardship in integrating scientific, productive, and ethical considerations about human uses of the environment is able to include considerations relating to the increasingly central precautionary principle for regulating human productive relations to the environment. The issue of responsibility arises as a result of the fact that we can never predict or know the environmental effects of our actions in advance. For Hans Jonas, "The gap between the ability to foretell and the power to act creates a novel moral problem," one that he describes as leading to an "imperative of responsibility."[16] This is in sharp contrast to the confident assertions often associated with science (and its technological application) about its existing (or more often predicted future) capacity to fully explain, predict, control, and manipulate the natural world.

The precautionary principle has come to be seen as an appropriate principle governing environmental policy making under conditions of uncertainty and against a background of heightened public sensitivity to "risk."[17] In adopting a precautionary approach to the planning and regulation of social-environmental interaction, ecological stewardship may be said to express the old-fashioned virtue of prudence, and in reference to planning has more to do with avoiding negative outcomes (avoiding unsustainability) rather than producing positive ones, that is, establishing a particular "greenprint" for sustainability.[18] As noted earlier, the issue is not the establishment of some permanent "harmony" between society and environment but to establish a process by which socioenvironmental problems can be negotiated, dealt with, and some provisional degree of balance be maintained.

4. Stewardship and Intergenerational Justice: Connecting Past, Present, and Future
What I mean by this is that ecological stewardship "taps into" and incorporates the idea that one of the most politically and ethically robust grounds upon which to defend the preservation of nature, and many other policy objectives of environmental politics, is an appeal to the obligations we owe to future generations.[19] As indicated earlier, this idea of obligations to future generations is integral to the stewardship ethic. Stewardship does not see the earth as belonging to any one particular human generation, but rather as a patrimony passed down the generations. Given that this sense of obligations to future generations is widespread across different ethical perspectives it can thus serve as a useful form of "overlapping consensus" mentioned earlier to give normative political backing to environmental protection and the shift toward sustainability.

Part II: Ecological Stewardship and Democracy: Collective Ecological Management and the Greening of Citizenship

COLLECTIVE ECOLOGICAL MANAGEMENT: ECOLOGICAL STEWARDSHIP AND DEMOCRACY

That the achievement of sustainability and the respectful treatment of the nonhuman world, which are the main aims of ecological stewardship, should be done via democratic political means is something that goes without saying. Indeed, given the reality (and I would add desirability) of moral pluralism in contemporary societies and thus the inability and illegitimacy of any one substantive ethical view (such as ecocentrism) as the moral basis for social agreement around how we ought to treat and use nature, any democratic and just approach to creating a less unsustainable society must seek ethical and practical reasons that can be understood, accepted, and acted upon by people with a variety of substantive ethical worldviews. To use Rawls's terminology, what we need to find is an "overlapping consensus"[20] for the achievement of ecological sustainability. It is my view that ecological stewardship can do this.

A recognition that we are responsible for managing our (material and nonmaterial) relationships with the nonhuman world is not to be confused with the attempt to manage the nonhuman world, as in the "global ecology" discourse and practice criticized by Sachs and others.[21] Their concern is that any talk of "managing" the environment in the sense of dominating, pacifying, and exploiting the environment motivated by exclusively anthropocentric, instrumental valuations, and interests, utilizing scientific knowledge and technology, is not only "arrogant," false, and dangerous but ultimately based on exploiting and distributing the benefits of this domination in an undemocratic, unequal, unjust, and unsustainable manner. The problem here is that the legacy of "management" in general and environmental management is not a particularly positive one in the sense that the same language of management has been and continues to be used to justify (in the name of progress, GNP growth, industrialization, globalization, free trade, state building, socialism, capitalism, or whatever) the "management" of people and environments that were and are exploitative, unjust, and undemocratic.[22] So, we have reason to be wary of "management speak," as it were. However, the fact that management has this legacy and can be used in organizing and continuing unjust, exploitative practices against people or planet should not blind us to its positive connotations and political advantages. The idea of "managing the/our environment" contained within collective ecological management does explicitly place human intentionality and use at the center of its concerns. If we accept that current patterns of environmental degradation and unsustainable socioeconomic practices are the result of human, aggregated action, often unintentional, unplanned, and mediated by institutional networks that occlude our individual responsibility for or knowledge of the environmental consequences of our decisions, then it may be that more open, transparent, explicitly political and collective, planned, and ultimately democratic modes of managing or regulating human practices offer a better alternative.[23] Since we are already interfering and damaging the environment at an increasing rate, the suggestion is that an open, political, and democratic mode of overseeing our interaction with the environment offers a much better chance of recognizing, coping, and perhaps alleviating what Carter has called the "environmentally hazardous dynamic" of the dominant liberal democratic political and capitalist economic system.[24] An open, planned, political mode of managing and organizing our collective dependence upon the environment is suggested as better able to cope with environmental and human dimensions of vulnerability and dependence. Essentially, what is "managed" in collective ecological management is primarily our relations to the environment rather than the environment per se.

A proper understanding of stewardship as collective ecological management actually begins from and explicitly acknowledges our dependence and vulnerability on and to nature, rather than somehow authoritatively "managing" and controlling the environment. Collective ecological management as a mode of stewardship is one characterized by an acknowledgement of the limits of human knowledge about the natural world. Thus, the nonhuman world from the perspective of collective ecological management is one which we neither have made or fully know. However, that we have not made or fully know the natural world does not do away with the need for conscious, collective planning and regulation of our metabolism with the natural environment. Just as it was mentioned earlier that while we can choose the form our dependency on nature can take, but not the brute fact of our dependency, likewise it seems that we can choose the form of planning and management, but not that we need to plan and manage. This is only dimly beginning to be perceived as central to the achievement of a less unsustainable relation to the environment, through the less politically loaded language of "regulation," "steering," and "restructuring." As Jacobs puts it, "Understood as a process of ecological restructuring, therefore, sustainability will require detailed government involvement: in setting environmental-economic objectives, in choosing techniques, and in the use of instruments. This must be described as a form of planning."[25]

Equally, collective ecological management, though related to, should not be confused with the discipline and discourses of "environmental management" and "resource management," that is, with forms of knowledge and associated practices oriented toward training and educating a designated minority of "experts" and institutions to manage particular ecosystems, national parks, natural resources, and so on. While many of the debates and developments within environmental management are important, where collective ecological management differs is in making the task of society regulating, intentionally managing the metabolism with the environment an object of explicit, public, nonspecialist, nonelite, collective debate and discussion. Whereas environmental management discourse is aimed primarily at actual or apprentice "environmental managers," collective ecological management begins from the premise that we are all environmental managers in the sense that we all effect and are affected by the environment. The most appropriate way to develop this idea of everyone being environmental managers is through a discussion of the greening of citizenship as a way to realize ecological stewardship as an integral part of collective ecological management, which I turn to next.

ECOLOGICAL STEWARDSHIP AND THE GREENING OF CITIZENSHIP

The greening of citizenship is proposed as a way in which ecological stewardship can be best understood and practiced as denoting the integration of ecological stewardship concerns within the discourses, identities, and practices commonly associated with democratic "citizenship." Citizenship within the context of collective ecological management becomes a way of transforming urban dwellers into "ecological stewards," giving those who may have no direct experience of nature some responsibility for, and democratic input into, managing the metabolism between society and the environment. In its strongest sense, it involves a fundamental rethinking of identity, seeing oneself as a "citizen-in-society-in-environment," reflecting on one's sense of identity as both part of as well as apart from the order of nature. The greening of citizenship as a mode of character thus transcends the purely "political" or formal status and legal standing of citizenship, and comes to denote a way of acting which tends toward ecologically rational/sustainable and morally symbiotic forms of social-environmental action. Essentially the greening of citizenship is an attempt to encourage and create an identity and mode of thinking and acting, and ultimately character traits and dispositions that accord with the standards and aims of ecological stewardship. Strong green citizenship therefore requires the cultivation of ecological habits and dispositions and the internalization of ecological norms of thinking and acting. That is, strong green citizenship as ecological stewardship requires that one self-consciously act in an ecologically responsible manner, that is one not only "acts" green but "thinks" green.[26] While strong green citizenship sets a good example to aim for, it is impossible to think that everyone, or even a majority of citizens, will reach this level of, for want of a better word, "ecological enlightenment."[27] Far more realistic is a view of a more sustainable society in which while some are so "enlightened," what is important is the degree of the "greening of citizenship." That is, the greening of citizenship is a continuum rather than a dichotomy between "ungreen" and "green" citizens.[28]

Andrew Dobson has recently written about the emergence of "ecological citizenship" as a distinctive (and potentially disruptive) contribution that green/ecological politics brings to debates about citizenship, and raises some interesting issues that are pertinent about the ideas of ecological stewardship and collective ecological management as outlined above.[29] Ecological citizenship, as Dobson understands it, shares many features of ecological stewardship in the sense that both stress the centrality of care and compassion, are oriented toward the future and future generations, and have human-environment interaction at their center. There is much in Dobson's argument that accords with, complements, or otherwise can be incorporated into the idea of ecological stewardship. However, in this section I wish to develop the suggestion that "ecological citizenship," like environmental management discussed above, while undoubtedly an important step in connecting democracy and sustainability, needs to be seen as a stepping stone toward ecological stewardship.

As I have written elsewhere, what is distinctive about "green citizenship" is that it represents a mode of thinking and acting that concerns the establishment and maintenance of ecologically virtuous ("symbiotic," or morally justified/legitimate) and sustainable forms of use and interaction between societies and environments.[30] This mode of action is one that transgresses the "public"/"private" boundary since it ranges across those spheres of human action that have the most environmental impact, that can be found in both public and private realms. Primary among these spheres are those of production, consumption, investment, politics, and parenthood. Associated with each sphere are important identities individuals and groups may have—that is, as workers/producers, consumers, investors, citizens, and parents. "Green citizenship" represents the integration of all these modes in accordance with the standards of ecological stewardship.

One of the features Dobson identifies as important to "ecological citizenship" is its nonreciprocal character, the fact that, as he puts it, "The source of the ecological citizen's obligations does not lie in reciprocity or mutual advantage, but in a non-reciprocal sense of justice, or of compassion. The obligations that the ecological citizen has to future generations and to other species . . . cannot be based on reciprocity by definition."[31] While this nonreciprocal sense of compassion is doubtless commendable, Dobson's ecological citizens are more akin to ecological angels in their selfless concern for future generations, the nonhuman world, and strangers in other parts of the world. Dobson's notion of ecological citizenship demands too much, especially in the absence of any discussion of the balance to be struck between legitimate "self-interest" and concern for others. This is not to say that I disagree with the motivation behind his laudable attempt to introduce notions of care, compassion, and nonreciprocity into debates about citizenship. However, the degree of disinterested, impartial care possessed by ecological citizens gives rise to serious concerns about its applicability and practicability within modern societies. Dobson does not specify the reasons why ecological citizens care; rather it is assumed that by definition they care. Now, to use a phrase of Rousseau's, "taking men as they are" is my starting point rather than positing what theoretical duties of nonreciprocal care and compassion theoretical ecological citizenship may demand. Advocating such a nonreciprocal notion of care for the natural world, divorced from any sense of the need and legitimacy of humans to use, consume, kill, eat, transform, and develop parts of it, is a serious flaw in Dobson's otherwise powerful idea of ecological citizenship. The advantage of casting the greening of citizenship as ecological stewardship in this respect is that the relationship it posits between humans and nature is partial, interested, reciprocal, and ultimately based on the "reality of the human situation" in having to interact with nature as phenomenal rather than noumenal beings.[32] It is for this reason that ecological stewardship explicitly embodies an "ethic of use for the environment," rather than a putative "environmental ethic."

The idea that "stewardship" as ecological/green citizenship is not confined to ostensibly political and/or public activities is of particular note. For example, recycling is a classic example of the type of activity associated with ecological stewardship and citizenship that on first gloss seems to be just a private act of getting rid of waste. Yet it is quite clear that the act of recycling is not either performed or perceived by others as a purely "private" act, rather it is seen as paradigmatically an example of someone being a responsible "ecological citizen."

My suggestion is that ecological stewardship traces and is related to those webs of dependence and vulnerability, those relations among people, planet, and the two together, creating a community of dependence and vulnerability, the most appropriate attitude toward which is a disposition of responsibility, care, and mindfulness. This allows us to explain why recycling is paradigmatically an example of ecological stewardship and citizenship—it acknowledges the fact that private acts (and omissions) do have public effects on others. Ultimately this leads, I think, to the centrality of an ecologized notion of the harm principle that can be used in both manners John Stuart Mill indicated (that is, as demarcating the boundary between legitimate state/social interference in, or regulation of, behavior in the private sphere).[33] At the same time, the harm principle's transformation and internalization along ecological lines helps explain why ostensibly private acts such as recycling, ethical investment, green consumption, and so on are acts of good green citizenship or ecological stewardship. It is relations of harm and vulnerability that underpin the community or network within which ecological stewardship and citizenship operate.

Rather than the individual being concerned with her own interests, she is encouraged to consider the interests of all those potentially affected by human actions. As

Goodin suggests, "It might be empirically more realistic, as well as being morally and politically preferable, to think . . . of democracy as a process in which we all come to internalize the interests of each other and indeed of the larger world around us."[34] This view of democracy as a process within which we recognize that we are, to a greater or lesser extent, each other's keeper, as well as being responsible for the nonhuman world, is clearly compatible with the ecological view that holds that environmental consequences transcend various boundaries—between societies, between generations now living and those in the future, and between species.

Voting in elections is often used as an example of citizen public spiritedness and civic virtue in action, but it is not connected to vulnerability in the same way as other actions, such as recycling, composting organic waste, reusing and repairing durable and other goods, cycling, walking, or using public transport instead of the car, and other "environmental" actions, which all cut across the public/private division. The fact that most of these activities aimed at limiting one's impact on the planet are regarded as "virtuous," praiseworthy, or examples of "good citizenship," acknowledges that that individual is doing something for others (fellow citizens, future generations, nonhumans perhaps) and for the planet, doing his or her bit for sustainability, and thus doing something that is good for everyone—a real generalizable interest.

Green Democracy, Citizenship, and Stewardship

One powerful argument for linking democracy and environmental aims is that changes in people's behavior motivated by the internalization of norms is more effective and longer lasting than behavioral changes based on external or coercive imposition. This suggests a critique of the eco-authoritarian position on the grounds of effectiveness, premised on the assumption that change motivated by an acceptance of its moral rightness is more effective in sustaining that change than if that change is grounded in fear or coercion. The state cannot do everything. As Cairns and Williams suggest in another context, "What the state needs from the citizenry cannot be secured by coercion, but only by co-operation and restraint in the exercise of private power."[35] Responsible citizenship, in other words.

The centrality of citizenship to green arguments for democracy comes from the belief that the achievement of sustainability will require more than institutional restructuring of contemporary Western liberal democracies.[36] Such institutional changes are necessary, but not sufficient, from a green point of view. The green contention is that macro level reorganization needs to be supplemented with changes in general behavior (weak green citizenship) and values and practices (strong green citizenship).

Although green citizenship is politically based (which also means a continued role for the state), the activities, values, and principles it embodies are not confined to the political sphere, as conventionally understood. The virtues one would expect to be embodied in this green form of responsible citizenship, as a form of moral character, would be operative in other spheres of human action and roles, including the "nonpolitical" private sphere. The point about ecological stewardship is that the private sphere, when considered from an ecological point of view, moves from being a "nonpolitical" to a political site of activity, and thus a legitimate site for the types of political obligation and rights that characterize relationship between and among individual citizens, and the state. That is, given that activities within the domestic sphere can and do affect other people (including those in other countries and the future), the environment, and morally significant nonhuman entities, those activities cannot be insulated from ecologically motivated political regulation, monitoring, and encouragement in the sense of seeing the private sphere as a site of "ecological virtues" (and also its opposite, "ecological vices"). In part, because the private/domestic sphere is ecological (in the sense of being a site of ecologically significant behavior and action), it is by the same token, from a green/ecological point of view, political (in being a site for "green citizenship" and legitimate state regulation). In this way, the extension of political, democratic regulation over the domestic sphere is in keeping with how from an ecological point of view it is not only legitimate but absolutely essential that there be democratic control/regulation over the "private" sphere of business and the corporate world. And while I do not have time to develop the argument here, the full development of collective ecological management (as a mode of democratic "green political economy") requires the extension of democratic political power, public accountability, and (where necessary) state/public regulation of both the domestic and especially the economic dimensions of the "private" sphere, in particular the "private economic" power of corporations.[37]

To be a good green citizen does not entail an obligation to actively promote the interests of nonhumans or others over one's own, but rather to justify and assess one's interests in the light of the interests of others. In practice this implies that a virtue of responsible green citizenship is a willingness to accommodate the interests of others within an expanded conception of the "ecological common good," a common good within which one's own good is located. When faced with social-environmental problems, good ecological citizens are motivated to seek solutions in which human and nonhuman interests are rendered as compatible as possible. In order to satisfy as many interests as possible, of course, requires that there be a willingness to compromise as well as an openness to persuasion through public debate. Ceteris paribus, the good of satisfying as many interests as possible, is a key goal of green politics and ecological stewardship.

Conclusion

Taking democracy as, in part, a public, political process by which citizens of a particular political community place themselves into each others hands in deciding how the community should be governed, what laws and principles should regulate their collective lives, and so on, brings home the idea of democracy as a way of both acknowledging and coping with human dependency on and vulnerability to fellow humans. Democracy on this account is, in part, about how members of a community care for each other.[38] Ecological stewardship extends this notion of vulnerability and dependency to include our dependency upon and responsibility to and for the natural world. While the notion of the "greening of citizenship" (and associated ideas of "strong" and "weak" green citizenship) convey the political core of stewardship, given that these relations of vulnerability and dependency encompass "nonpolitical" spheres or modes of human action, ecological stewardship extends beyond what is normally considered the scope of democracy, politics, and "democratic citizenship." Ultimately ecological stewardship is an attempt (of course imperfect and incomplete) to (re)introduce the "human" back into politics through an examination and acknowledgment of the "prepolitical" (one is tempted to say existential or indeed "natural") relations of dependency, vulnerability, care, and responsibility that characterize the "human condition." Our (shared) frailty, mortality, limitations, and vulnerability with and dependence upon fellow humans and the nonhuman world is not something that can be or should be denied, nor should it be naively taken as somehow fixing human development and progress. These features of both the human and nonhuman worlds and relations between the former and the latter are to be negotiated, coped with, though not amenable to any "final solution." Democracy, the greening of citizenship, and ecological stewardship are, in the end, suggestive of legitimate and practical ways of collectively negotiating these aspects of life (both human and nonhuman) on earth.

Notes

1. Although I do not have the space to enter into it here, I would go so far as to say that dependence and vulnerability are constitutive of what it means to be human. As Richard Sennet has recently put it, "if you think dependence is bad, what you produce is a damaged human being." Michael Benn, "Inner-City Scholar: A Profile of Richard Sennett," *The Guardian*, February 3, 2001.

2. As Ulrich Beck revealingly puts it, progress is basically "legitimate social change without democratic political legitimation." Ulrich Beck, *Risk Society: Towards a New Modernity* (London: Sage, 1992), 214.

3. Benjamin Barber, *Strong Democracy: Participatory Democracy for a New Age* (Berkeley: University of California Press, 1984), 104.

4. In John Passmore, *Man's Responsibility for Nature* (London: Duckworth, 1980), 28.

5. Peggy Morgan, "Religions and the Environment," in *International Encyclopedia of Environmental Politics*, ed. John Barry and E. Gene Frankland (London: Routledge, 2001). Perhaps the definitive version of the Christian view of stewardship can be found in Genesis. According to Passmore, "Genesis . . . makes this duty [of 'man' toward all nature and all life] clear when it tells us that God put Adam into the Garden of Eden 'to dress and to keep it,' i.e. to manage and protect it." Passmore, *Man's Responsibility*, 29. The Jewish position has been outlined by Swartz, "And though their efforts to tame the land, to make it more productive and more dependable, were often marvels of ingenuity, they understood, as well, the limits to their mastery—for they knew God as Sovereign of the Land, and . . . they acknowledged God's ownership." Daniel Swartz, "Jews, Jewish Texts, and Nature: A Brief History," in *This Sacred Earth: Religion, Nature, Environment*, ed. Robert Gottlieb (London: Routledge, 1996), 88.

6. A third advantage is that most green/ecological moral arguments are compatible, in broad terms, with a stewardship ethic (at least at the level of applied/practical ethics, if not in principle).

7. That our relation to the environment is mediated by various institutions also indicates a prima facie case for democracy and democratic accountability of those institutions.

8. John Barry, *Rethinking Green Politics: Nature, Virtue, and Progress* (London: Sage, 1999).

9. It is interesting to note how in many Western societies, farmers are no longer thought to be or trusted by the majority of people as "stewards of the land." In part this has to do with the shift within agriculture toward more intensive, agribusiness forms of food production and land management, which results in agricultural practices that are markedly at odds with the stewardship ideal of ethically informed, sustainable uses of the land. Equally, in places like Britain, the fall of the farmer as a wise steward of the countryside has to do with urban-based perceptions and misperceptions of the reality of rural life, itself part and parcel of the increasing conflict between "town" and "country." See John Barry, *Environment and Social Theory* (London: Routledge, 1999), chapter 3. If farmers are no longer the designated stewards of a nation's countryside, the question is, who is or ought to be? And the answer seems to be "all of us."

10. Nicholas Low and Brendan Gleeson, "Urbanization/Urban Planning," in Barry and Frankland, *International Encyclopedia of Environmental Politics*.

11. Adopting a virtue-ethics perspective thus recasts the critique of anthropocentrism. From this perspective the arrogance, hubris, and inflated self-importance that can characterize the latter are vices, that is, unworthy (and ultimately damaging) attributes or dispositions of individual character (and culture). Thus, a virtue ethics approach can enable us to find the correct target: the "arrogance" rather than the "humanism."

12. This submissiveness, according to Frasz, is typical of "someone who has lost all sense of individuality when confronted with the vastness and sublimity of nature." Gary Frasz, "Environmental Virtue Ethics: A New Direction for Environmental Ethics," *Environmental Ethics* 15, no. 3 (1993): 274. This opposite extreme of "arrogant anthropocentrism" typifies many unreflective sentimental or romantic views of human–nature relations that pepper green moral and political discourse, sometimes expressing itself as "quietism." Marcel Wissenburg, "The Idea of Nature and the Nature of Distributive Justice," in *The Politics of Nature: Explorations in Green Political Theory*, ed. Andrew Dobson and Paul Lucardie (London: Routledge, 1993), 9. And as an extreme this moral disposition is thus not an environmental virtue, but rather an environmental vice. Sentimentality with regard to human–nature relations does not give nature or humans their proper regard since it often occludes "negative" aspects of this relationship, such as predation, use, consumption, labor, and death, but which are, in reality, inescapable "facts of life," ineliminable aspects of the "human condition."

13. Joy Palmer, *Environmental Education in the 21st Century* (London: Routledge, 1998); Edmund O'Sullivan, *Transformative Learning: Educational Vision for the 21st Century* (London: Zed Books, 1999).

14. James Meadowcroft and Michael Kenny, "Introduction," in *Planning Sustainability*, ed. James Meadowcroft and Michael Kenny (London: Routledge, 1999), 4.

15. Barry, *Rethinking Green Politics*, 129–35.

16. Hans Jonas, *The Imperative Responsibility* (Chicago: University of Chicago Press, 1984), 7–8.

17. Beck, *Risk Society*.

18. See James Meadowcroft, "Planning, Democracy and the Challenge of Sustainable Development," *International Political Science Review* 18, no. 1.

19. Avner de-Shalit, *Why Posterity Matters* (London: Routledge, 1995); Bryan Norton, *Toward Unity among Environmentalists* (Oxford, U.K.: Oxford University Press, 1991).

20. John Rawls, "Justice as Fairness: Political not Metaphysical," *Philosophy and Public Affairs* 14, no. 2 (1985).

21. Wolfgang Sachs, ed., *Global Ecology* (London: Zed Books, 1993).

22. For example, the idea of "carrying capacity,' which is a central concept in both environmental management and ecological science, has a colonial, exploitative origin. According to Bandarage, "The concept of 'carrying capacity,' for instance, was first put into use by French and British colonial scientists and administrators seeking to estimate the minimum amount of land and labor needed by local people to meet their subsistence needs so that what was deemed

in excess of that could be taxed by the colonial state and appropriated for export production." Asoka Bandarage, *Woman, Population and Global Crisis: A Political Economic Analysis* (London: Zed Books, 1997), 127–28.

23. Other ways of enhancing transparency are decentralizing decision making and making the decision at the lowest level appropriate, thus improving prospects for citizen participation. On this issue of decentralization both those in favor of improving democracy and achieving environmental goals converge.

24. Alan Carter, "Towards a Green Political Theory," in *The Politics of Nature*, ed. Andrew Dobson and Paul Lucardie (London: Routledge, 1993).

25. Michael Jacobs, "Sustainability and Markets: On the Neo-Classical Model of Environmental Economics," in Meadowcroft and Kenny, *Planning Sustainability*, 94.

26. The reason for distinguishing strong from weak green citizenship lies in the fact that one does not necessarily have to care about the environment or the achievement of sustainability in order for one's behavior to have environmentally positive effects. For example, adherence to laws, rules, or codes which result in ecologically positive results is not dependent on one internalizing ecological norms or indeed even being conscious of the positive impact of one's behavior. See John Barry and John Proops, *Citizenship, Sustainability, and Environmental Research* (Cheltenham, U.K.: Edward Elgar, 2000).

27. An example of strong green citizenship is the sentiment of care for the environment in Onora O'Neill's view that, "Universal indifference to the care and preservation of natural and man-made environments undermines and withers human life and capacities and capabilities for action . . . lives and cultures will remain vulnerable if they depend on environments which, although not damaged, are also not cherished." Onora O'Neill, *Towards Justice and Virtue* (Cambridge, U.K.: Cambridge University Press, 1996), 203.

28. In terms of connecting green citizenship to ecological virtues and the avoidance of ecological vices, an important part to be played in the greening of citizenship is hypocrisy (the "tribute vice pays to virtue," according to Voltaire)—in terms of saying one thing but doing another, and weakness of will in terms of knowing what one should do, but failing to do so.

29. Andrew Dobson, "Green Citizenship: A Disruptive Influence?" Unpublished manuscript, cited with permission from the author.

30. Barry, *Rethinking Green Politics*.

31. Dobson, "Green Citizenship," 6.

32. It may be that Dobson has gone too far in his "ecological Kantianism," ending up with a vision of ecological world citizens, universally and impartially compassionate and caring but living in the Kantian rather than the real world.

33. John Barry, "Greening Liberal Democracy: Practice, Theory and Political Economy," in *Sustaining Liberal Democracy*, ed. John Barry and Marcel Wissenburg (Basingstoke, U.K.: Palgrave, 2001).

34. Robert Goodin, "Enfranchising the Earth and Its Alternatives," *Political Studies* 44, no. 3 (1993): 18.

35. Alan Cairns and Cynthia Williams, *Constitutionalism, Citizenship, and Society in Canada* (Toronto: University of Toronto Press, 1985), 43.

36. Wouter Achterberg, "Sustainability, Community, and Democracy," in *Democracy and Green Political Theory*, ed. Brian Doherty and Marius de Geus (London: Routledge, 1996).

37. A good example of how taking an ecological view of economic activity opens it as an area of legitimate political, democratic accountability is the notion of private property in land, and also suggests that private land ownership is, from an ecological point of view, more akin to stewardship than exclusive ownership. According to Varner, "Increasingly, taking an ecological view of land forces us to treat it as a public resource that individuals hold only in stewardship (or trust) capacity . . . in this age of ecological literacy we have discovered that land uses depend so heavily on ecological infrastructure—on processes that, if they are property at all, are inherently

public property—that it hardly makes sense to conceive of land as private property." Gary Varner, "Environmental Law and the Eclipse of Land as Private Property," in *Ethics and Environmental Policy: Theory Meets Practice*, ed. Frederick Ferre and Peter Hartel (Athens: University of Georgia Press, 1994), 158.

38. This "vulnerability" view of democracy can also be linked to a view of progress or development in that we measure the advancement of a society by how well it looks after the most vulnerable.

CHAPTER 8

Restoring Ecological Citizenship

Andrew Light

The Argument So Far

Restoration ecology is the practice of restoring damaged ecosystems, most typically ecosystems that have been harmed by anthropogenic causes. Such projects can range from small-scale urban park reclamations, such as the ongoing restorations in Central Park and Prospect Park in New York City, to huge wetland mitigation projects. On two indicators of the importance of environmental activities—number of voluntary person hours logged and amount of dollars spent—restoration ecology is one of the most pressing and important environmental priorities on the environmental agenda in the United States, as well as in many other industrialized countries and increasingly in developing areas. For example, the cluster of restorations known collectively as the "Chicago Wilderness" project, in the forest preserves surrounding Chicago (to be discussed more below), would attract at their height thousands of volunteers to help restore 17,000 acres of arguably native Oak Savannah that have become lost in the area.[1] The final plan for the project is to restore upward of one hundred thousand acres.

Also, in the United States, government and corporate funding for restoration initiatives is rapidly rising. In an attempt to remedy damage done through extensive channelization of the Kissimmee River in Florida, various government agencies have spent hundreds of millions of dollars on returning the river closer to its earlier meandering condition.[2] Work on the Kissimmee and other watersheds in Florida has revealed that even more extensive restoration is needed to fully address the threats caused by channelization to water reserves, endangered species, and the Everglades ecosystem itself. A plan submitted by the Clinton administration and approved by the then Republican Congress has appropriated $7.8 billion of funding over the next twenty years making it one of the largest single pieces of environmental legislation in history.[3]

Ecological restorations can be produced in a variety of ways. While the Chicago restorations have involved a high degree of public participation others have not. Partly the differences in these various projects have been a result of their differing scale and complexity. Dechannelizing a river will be a task for an outfit like the Army Corps of Engineers and not a local community group. But many restorations that could conceivably involve community participation often enough do not, and some that already involve community participation do not utilize that participation as much as they could.

The alternative to community participation is to hire a private firm or use a government service to complete the restoration. One need only scan the back pages of a journal such as *Ecological Restoration* (formerly *Restoration and Management Notes*, one of the main journals in the field) to see the myriad of businesses (mostly landscape design firms) that have either grown up around or now increasingly rely on restoration as the bread and butter of their operations. Given the alternatives, the question becomes which method to use to complete a restoration. One answer is that we should simply indulge our Aristotelian intuitions and concentrate on the ends of the practice in determining the means. What do we hope to achieve in any particular restoration? As most restorations are justified through some appeal to either increasing the ecosystemic health or integrity of a landscape or other biome, an appropriate answer is simply that the biological or ecological ends of the practice should drive the means. Therefore, we should use the most efficient and proficient scientific means for achieving this end. Without more careful scrutiny, one can imagine that the best option that comes to mind in any case given such reasoning would be to use either a private professional firm or a government agency specializing in such work. So, where a town decides to restore a wetland as part of a municipal park in order to secure a habitat for migratory waterfowl, a request for proposals (RFP) should be issued. The process will not differ substantially from any other public works project such as building public housing or bringing investment to a new business district. No doubt one of the firms advertising in the back of *Ecological Restoration* would apply.

But such a response to the question of what means to utilize in a restoration assumes that the only relevant criteria for what counts as a good restoration are scientific, technological, and indeed economic factors. In my previous work I have argued that another important dimension to what counts as a good restoration is the degree of public participation involved in the project.[4] The defense of this view has been in both ethical and political terms, involving a set of arguments about the unique values that are at stake in restorations that involve public participation (as opposed to the values produced or protected in acts of preservation of nature). Taking into account these values warrants the conclusion in most cases that a good restoration must maximize the degree of public participation allowable for a project where scale and complexity of the project permit public participation. The value of such participation should be understood as making possible stronger and better relationships of stewardship or care between human communities and the nature around them. The kind of participation required is hands-on participation, with volunteers engaged in all aspects of the project, including planning, clearing, planting, maintenance, and so on. This does not meant that expertise should be abandoned in restorations; it just means that experts should help to guide voluntary restorationists and eventually expect to be able to turn over large components of such projects to volunteers in order to count a restoration as, in the end, successful.

Based on such arguments I have claimed that the practice of restoration ecology is as much about restoring the human relationship with nature as it is about restoring natural processes themselves. To fail to attempt to achieve both of these ends in restorations that are amenable to public participation is to fail to have as good a restoration as is possible. Therefore, the degree of public participation in a project becomes one basis, among others, for its evaluation. As such, a community planning a restoration of a wetland on public property would not turn first to a landscape design firm, but instead, where feasible, hire a consultant to plan the project and then engage volunteers to carry it out, or else turn over the project to a local volunteer environmental organization proficient at planning and completing such projects. While such a process would not be as efficient as hiring a private landscape design firm it would nonetheless approximate a better restoration, all other things being equal.

While I will say something in the next section about the importance of participation in restoration, I will not here revisit the more detailed ethical arguments I have made previously (see note 4). Those skeptical of such a case should consult my previous publications on this matter. Instead, in this chapter, I want to press harder on what kind of participation is best for a restoration, assuming we think participatory restorations are to be preferred. My claim will be that a democratic model of participation, which aims at understanding participation in restoration as a form of "ecological citizenship," is the best model for achieving the full potential of restoration in moral and political terms. Those interested in bolstering the claims for a democratic basis for environmental practices and policies should find this argument of some importance. I will argue that our choices of how we shape practices and policies involving restoration are a critical test for how deep a commitment to encouraging democratic values we have in publicly accessible environmental practices.

I will begin with an overview of the general arguments for why participation in restoration is important and try to show how the value of participating in a community project emerges as an important part of the experience of voluntary restorationists. I will then describe two possible models for framing this participation—the "ecological identity" and the "ecological citizenship" models—giving reasons why the latter of these models is to be preferred over the former. Finally, I will point toward some possible implications for public policy that follow from this investigation.[5]

Restoration and Democratic Participation

Arguments for the importance of democratic participation in environmental decision making have, by now, a distinguished history. Such a view can be seen in Mark Sagoff's arguments that a tradition already exists in the United States for encouraging a citizenship model of environmental decision making over a consumer model.[6] This argument was given perhaps its strongest empirical defense in Adolf Gundersen's study of the positive environmental consequences of democratic decision making.[7] More recently, Avner de-Shalit has articulated a methodology of public reflective equilibrium to better enable environmental philosophers to respond to the need for a more open and democratic approach to environmental policy making.[8]

My own view on this topic stems from my commitment to a methodological form of environmental pragmatism.[9] This view attempts to provide a specific framework for a robust moral pluralism for environmental ethicists of all stripes (pragmatist or not) toward the end of better serving the converged upon ends of the broader environmental community. This view has evolved significantly from my earlier allusion to a "metaphilosophical" pragmatism that Robyn Eckersely criticizes in this volume.[10]

Those interested in the details of this argument can look elsewhere to get a better picture of it. What is more important to realize here is that my view, as well as those of Sagoff, Gundersen, and de-Shalit (who I will refer to collectively as "democratic environmental theorists"), rely on a set of crucial common premises. First, that environmental ethicists and political theorists must accept the democratic context of environmental decision making in which we in the developed world (and largely in international institutions) find ourselves, and second, that we must go further and actively endorse and expand the democratic context of environmental decision making.

The first premise stems from a variety of politically realist positions taken by all of these authors; the second is committed to a position that only a democratic environmentalism can actually achieve long-term sustainability. Such a position commits democratic environmental theorists to taking human-centered forms of valuation of nature seriously as those are the forms of value, which are most often debated in a democratic context. While many will find investigation of such forms of valuation uncontroversial, those familiar with the development of contemporary ethics will understand that the foil for this position is one that sees the role of environmental ethics and political theory more properly as the defense of some claim for the noninstrumental (sometimes intrinsic) value of nature itself. This view is supposed to make possible the direct moral consideration of nonhumans and ecosystems from a nonanthropocentric perspective regardless of the anthropocentric forms of valuation applied to those entities. Such a view resists appeals to human interests as a basis for valuing some bit of nature because such appeals cannot guarantee that nature will be protected against competing claims for a human interest in exploiting or developing nature. Development of such nonanthropocentric views are the predominant focus of most work in environmental ethics.

One problem, however, is that such views often wind up degenerating into a bizarre form of ethical externalism whereby we assume that compliance with a moral principle will follow if the principle can be shown to be justified in a rigorous and defensible moral theory. If traditional environmental ethicists can provide the rationale for the direct nonanthropocentric moral consideration of nature then it is assumed that people will eventually follow that rationale and act accordingly. In contrast, a more internalist approach assumes that theoretical justifications do not necessarily motivate agents to act contrary to whatever other interests they may hold. Internalists, such as David Hume, argue that an adequate moral theory must entail a robust moral psychology that helps to explain how and why compliance with a moral principle can be expected, which in turn helps justify the theory.[11] While externalism in and of itself is not a priori a bad assumption, it is very odd to assume that a position justifying the direct moral consideration of nature would have any hope of succeeding given the obvious fact that most humans begin with an assumption that nature is not directly morally considerable, but most likely indirectly considerable for reasons they perceive in their own interest, or for reasons that fit more traditional notions of altruism, such as obligations to future human generations.[12]

Democratic environmental theorists of all kinds, assuming an internalist moral framework, are not uncomfortable appealing to human interests to help justify a particular theoretical position concerning environmental value. Thus, Tim Hayward argues that part of the problem with intrinsic value approaches to environmental ethics and political philosophy is both their lack of a coherent sense of intrinsic value and their failure to generate reasons for agents to defer their immediate self-interests for longer-term environmental goals.[13] Because democratic arenas give voice to human interests, they are not a place for an environmental theory committed to a naïve externalism. The question then becomes how to morally motivate people to differ their interests, or see their self-interests, as inclusive of environmental concerns. Here, I would argue that we need to go beyond abstract discussions of moral psychology and democratic theory and pay attention to which practices actually create changes in behavior. Encouragement of such practices, I would argue, becomes crucial for maintaining the long-term sustainability of the environment. This point however requires further elaboration.

A direct participatory relationship between local human communities and the nature they inhabit or are adjacent to is at least a necessary condition for encouraging people to protect natural systems and landscapes around them rather than trade off these environments for short-term monetary interests from development. Such relationships encourage communities to develop a sense of stewardship, or if one prefers, care for the ecosystems around them. Communities in a normative and participatory relationship with the land around them are less likely to allow it to be harmed. The reason is that environmental protection, as is the case with other laws governing common resources, often admit to free rider problems. If environmental legislation is mandated from above, and local populations have no reason to take an interest in environmental protection, then little would motivate citizens from abstaining from free rides, or even out and out violation of environmental regulations. This point has been demonstrated through several well-publicized examples in the developing world. Using a Western model and drawing lines around an area and declaring it a park, without consent from local populations (let alone encouraging active participation in protection of the park), has often done little to ensure environmental protection.[14] For reasons such as these I am tempted to gauge the relative importance of different environmental practices in terms of their ability to engender a more participatory relationship between humans and the nature around them. Those practices that encourage such relationships of stewardship or care are more resistant to free rider problems and satisfy the internalism sought by democratic environmental theorists.

My argument concerning restoration ecology is that when restorations are performed by volunteers they create the sorts of relationships more conducive to environmental responsibility. Social science research to date on the Chicago restorations confirms these intuitions. In a recent study of 306 volunteers in the Chicago projects, intended to ascertain the results of their involvement in restoration, the highest sources of satisfaction reported were in terms of "Meaningful Action," and "Fascination with Nature."[15] "Meaningful Action" was gauged, for example, in the sense in which restorationists felt that they were "making life better for coming generations," or "feeling that they were doing the right thing." "Fascination with Nature" was correlated with reports by volunteers that restoration helped them to "learn how nature works."[16] But following a very close third was a category that the surveyors called "Participation," understood as the sense in which participation in restoration activities helped people to feel that they were "part of a community," or that restoration helped them to see themselves as "accomplishing something in a group." Additionally, participation in restorations gives volunteers a strong sense of connection with the natural processes around them and a larger appreciation of environmental problems in other parts of the world. Said one volunteer, "The more you know, the more you realize there is to learn," not just in terms of understanding the peculiarities of a particular restoration site, but also generating a greater appreciation for the fragility of nature in other places in the face of anthropogenic distress.

One of the most striking and encouraging findings of this particular report however was the strong evidence that length of tenure in restoration activities was not a discriminating factor in helping people to come to understand lessons like these. According to the authors of this report, while the range of period of involvement among the 306 respondents was from two months to twenty-seven years, "the benefits an individual derived from restoration were the same whether the individual was a relatively recent recruit or an 'old hand.'"[17] This was a finding that was not expected in the survey but was in part explained because the benefits of participation in restoration were in some sense immediate. While a fully functioning ecosystem is not created in a day, several hours' work does nonetheless produce tangible results in terms of development of a commitment to environmental renewal in conjunction with the work of others.

Participation in restorations should count as at least one practice that can help promote attempts at achieving long-term sustainability within a context that assumes that such sustainability will best be achieved by appeal to human interests as they evolve in democratic processes. One is tempted to say that participatory restorations, through their emphasis on community building inclusive of environmental priorities, will produce better ecological citizens. But arguing that participation in restoration projects produces people interested in a connection with nature as a community and in a general culture of connection with nature is not sufficient to get us such a conclusion. "Citizenship" is a technical term in moral and political philosophy that entails a particular set of democratic relationships. Restorations, even those including a high degree of public participation, need not follow a model of democratic participation along the lines of conceiving of volunteers as good ecological citizens. Such a model must be explained and justified further. I turn now to this set of issues.

Ecological Identity Versus Ecological Citizenship

In previous work I have characterized the goal of encouraging public participation in restorations as one where we seek to encourage the development of a new and more expansive "culture of nature."[18] By this I meant that beyond the advantage of producing a bond of interest between local communities and the nature around them, restorations also aim at creating a set of culturally based moral norms that is more supportive of environmental sustainability overall. In these terms, my concluding point from the last section could be put like this: if the advantage of restoration is that it helps to produce a culture of nature, what kind of culture will that be? Twentieth-century fascists arguably also had a culture of nature that helped feed the antidemocratic policies that justified some of their most extreme and deplorable practices. What will be the culture of nature of twenty-first century environmentalism? Using restoration as an example, I want to argue that the culture of nature to be preferred is a democratic culture of nature, which in turn means that the practices that will serve as a foundation for that culture should also be democratic. Members of this culture of nature must understand themselves as ecological citizens working simultaneously to restore nature and to restore the participatory and strong democratic elements of their local communities. To better evaluate this claim it may help to provide a contrast.

We need not look to fascism to provide the contrast case for an ecological citizenship. Such a comparison would be too prejudiced against the contrast case to be very informative. I propose that in addition to the citizenship model we consider what I will call the "ecological identity" model as an alternative framework in which to conceive of the possibility of shaping the relationships between agents to each other and to other communities in a culture of nature. While my argument will be aimed at endorsing the citizenship model, the comparison with an ecological identity will serve as a useful foil for helping to better understand the advantages of the citizenship model. This is also not a haphazard comparison: as I will show below, there are some criticisms of restoration that may have been generated by the appearance of an identity model among some restorationists, and some practices in restoration that may be best expressed in the identity model.

What are these two models? I will spend more time on the notion of ecological citizenship below. For now, let us define it as the description of some set of moral and political rights and responsibilities of agents in a democratic community, defined in terms of their obligations to other humans taking into account those forms of human engagement and interaction that best preserve the long-term sustainability of nature. Such a view need not consider nature as a direct object of moral concern or as a moral subject in its own right (though there is nothing in principle that would prohibit ecological citizens from holding such views). The point is only that one's duties to nature, as an ecological citizen perceives them, cannot be abstracted away from one's duties to one's larger human community as well. The goal of an ecological citizenship is to bring together the interests of a human community to be fair and open and conducive to allowing each member of a community to pursue his or her own private interests while also tempering these pursuits with attention to the environment. A strengthened relationship with nature is to be found in forming open-ended organizational bonds that entail specific moral, and possibly legal, responsibilities to care for the nature around one's community and respect the environmental connections between communities.

In contrast, an ecological identity conceives of the right relationship between agent and nature as more a matter of one where nature shapes the subjectivity of the agent, which in turn creates a political framework whereby agents feel that they have individual and collective duties to nature and to those humans who share that same subjectivity. Ecological identity would count as a form of identity politics, usually defined in terms of those forms of politics at the heart of the new social movements emerging since the 1960s: feminism, race-based politics, the politics of sexual identity, and so on. The question of whether environmentalism should be counted as a form of identity politics is a tricky one even though it is largely assumed to be the case that it should be included in a complete description of the new social movements. The problem is articulating what sort of identity is constituted by an ecological identity, understanding which character trait justifies an embrace of that identity, and explaining how the political content of that identity stems from some character trait of those who embrace it.

In other work I have called these general parameters for the content of an identity politics its "constitutive profile."[19] The constitutive profile of other forms of identity politics is relatively straightforward (setting aside issues involving mixed identities). For example, with race-based identity politics, the politics of such identities stem from one's identification with a range of interpretations of the distinct political issues associated with one's race in relation to the larger racial politics of one's society. On the surface though, environmentalism in general does not seem to have a clear constitutive profile outside of strong claims, such as are found in some versions of deep ecology, that environmentalists should identify themselves as coextensive with nature, that is, as a self-conscious part of the natural whole. While this view or something like it will ground some versions of an ecological identity, I have argued that most ecological identities are best expressed as a political position generated out of an agent's sense of empathy for nature as a subject of mistreatment. The only difference with other forms of identity politics is that what is being internalized as one's politics is not a trait one already has, such as one's race or gender. Thus, ecological identities are expressed over a range of subjectivities, some that see a direct connection with nature (such as deep ecology) and others (most others) that see an ecological identity as a more indirect form of empathy with nature.

Despite such conceptual difficulties, many authors have embraced an identity model of environmentalism. Catriona Sandilands, for example, has explicitly argued for an environmental identity politics in order to join environmentalism to the broader call for "radical democracy," as the basis for a unified politics of the new social movements.[20] Shaping a culture of nature on the identity model would most likely entail strengthening our relationship with nature by creating intentional communities of environmentalists who conceive of their identities as constituted through their relationship with nature. We can imagine that such a community would in part be formed around environmental practices like restoration.

Both the ecological citizenship and the ecological identity models have several advantages over an externalist claim that we only need to generate a moral theory about the value of nature itself and then wait for the rest to follow. For example, both accounts allow for and encourage a strong attachment to place. On the citizenship model, a culture of nature can be formed by a local public around the environmental issues that are native to that place. Clearly the Chicago restorations would be supported by such a model as they encourage people to become connected to their local environment, their place, and then come to see their duties to that place as coextensive with their duties to their fellow citizens. Because such practices also encourage a broader understanding of larger environmental questions it is not the case that this attachment to place degenerates into some form of insularity. So too with an identity model. If the subjectivity of environmentalists is formed by making nature the object of their empathetic concern, it is most likely the case that such a subjectivity will be place specific. It is no surprise to see that interests in forming ecological identities also connect to one or another form of bioregionalism.[21]

Nonetheless, I have several worries about the identity model. The recent resurgence of work in political philosophy on citizenship, it is important to remember, has been in part spurred by the search for an answer to identity politics as the dominant framework of progressive political theory. The distinction between the two, as historian Thomas Bender notes, has often been lost: "Many scholars today do not even make a distinction between identity and citizenship, not realizing how much is being given up."[22] What is being given up in failing to make this distinction is in part an attempt to orient the ends of political theory around a model of inclusivity as opposed to exclusivity. The rise of identity politics was justifiably driven by the exclusion of the interests of disenfranchised groups from the political arena as well as arguably from representing their interests as disenfranchised groups in political theory. But in the quest to articulate the needs of these groups and to justify their ends they have created forms of politics that are often resistant to inclusion from the outside. In order to create a coherent identity formation, these views often define those outside of their identity as incapable of fully participating in the normative community created by that identity. Following such intuitions I have four objections with using the identity model as a foundation for grounding a culture of nature. The first two objections are more general and the last two, while general, can be more specifically applied to questions involving restoration.[23]

First, if environmentalism is best described as a form of identity politics, then it may serve the interests of those who would want to claim that concern for the environment is merely a "special interest," as other forms of single-issue identity politics have been described. The goals of the environmental movement after all should not be to marginalize environmental interests as something that people should have only if they have a particular view of the world (here a subjective empathy with nature as constitutive of their identities). Instead, the goals of environmentalists should be to form broader reasons that justify a variety of practices whereby as many people as possible can see the ends of environmental sustainability as part and parcel of their own personal interests or with their broader communal interests. After all, we do not want only committed environmentalists to recycle and the like, we want everyone to, preferably without having to coerce them to do so.

Such an objection is a bit tricky as it would be difficult to claim that other identity groups do not want those outside of their group to care about their interests. Surely they do, so we would expect that feminists (where we understand feminism as a form of identity politics) would want nonfeminists to acknowledge the equal status of woman such that they do not, for example, unfairly discriminate against women in the workplace. But an identity-based feminism may not require that men who do not count themselves as feminists actually see the necessity of such antidiscrimination from the point of view of feminists, but only that they comply with laws or customs that would prohibit such discrimination. Indeed, some forms of feminist-identity politics may argue that men, insofar as they do not share the subject position of gender oppression occupied by women, cannot fully appreciate the gendered rationale that determines, from an identity standpoint, the necessity of respect for the equal status of women. Again, we can imagine that the best and broadest form of environmentalism would not want to risk such exclusivity of interests if it could be avoided.

Second, nothing procedurally (or at least internal to the logic of an identity formation) prohibits identity groups from becoming excessively hierarchical. In fact, I would argue that identity formations are prone to hierarchies because of the ontological structure of what I have called their constitutive profiles. If I count myself as an environmentalist because I feel that my subjectivity as a person is grounded in some claim about my connection to nature and that this stance makes me an environmentalist, then I will probably be tempted to compare my environmentally grounded subjectivity with that of others. Because, as I said before, an ecological identity can either be grounded in a subjectivity whereby one empathizes with nature or where one sees oneself as an indistinguishable part of nature, then there is a very broad range of subject positions that could count as an ecological identity and some subjects in these positions may claim to be greener than others. Anyone spending much time in those parts of the environmental movement where ecological identities are dominant has no doubt experienced this phenomenon. There are environmentalists who claim to be more tuned in, to be "closer to the Earth" than others, and who, as a consequence, tend to claim to be able to speak for nature in a way that others cannot. Such identity positions become very difficult to reconcile when honest disagreements arise between environmentalists. To claim to be closer to nature than others is to claim a privileged position that can degenerate into a nondemocratic hierarchy of "closeness." Such a view often also winds up overly romanticizing traditional cultures that are claimed to have a privileged position with respect to their relation to nature.[24] In contrast, a citizenship model, though certainly not immune to problems of hierarchy, would at least mitigate this problem by conceiving of connection to nature as something mediated by connection to one's local community, and the broader human community as well. The emphasis is not on who can best claim to understand and then speak for nature (which, after all, can never confirm or disconfirm whether one or another person is really closer to it than another), but who can claim to best serve the environmental and civic interests of one's larger human community that can report on who better serves those interests.

Third, while earlier I indicated the need to distance identity formations from fascism or nativism, it is unfortunately true that many people are unable to make such distinctions. As such, an ecological identity risks what can mildly be put as a kind of public relations problem. In particular, restoration ecology has drawn much criticism in this regard already, and the fact that many restorationists do overtly embrace what amounts to an ecological identity has only strengthened such criticisms. The focus of this critique has come mainly from the common practice in restoration ecology of aiming many projects, for sound ecological reasons, at elimination of exotic species that threaten the viability of native flora and fauna.

For example, in 1995 the subject of restoration came up at a pubic discussion on nature and culture at an American Association of Geographers meeting featuring David Harvey and Donna Haraway. A question arose (by me) concerning the practice of ecological restoration as involving questions of both natural and cultural value.

Surprisingly, Haraway answered the question by first implicating restorationists as na-tivists:

> A student at UCSC [University of California at Santa Cruz] has been study-ing contemporary restoration ecology projects, writing forcefully about comparisons between some of the Nazi-period commitments to getting rid of xenophytes, extricating foreign plants and re-establishing the native ones. From his work, the only addendum to what you said that I want to throw in is that my own suspicious hackles are raised by restoration ecology's po-tentials for deepening nativism and xenophobia in what is still a white su-premacist country. And I think it's working that way ideologically.[25]

Such worries over the neo-fascist and nativist potential of environmentalism be-come much more serious if environmentalism is conceived as a form of identity poli-tics. The reason is that such objections, when directed at a political identity, rather than aimed at a simple preference for environmental protection, are easily generaliz-able from the critique of a particular environmental act to the entire culture of an iden-tity with nature. Fully expressed, Haraway's claim could become that by identifying with nature through the performance of restorations, weeding out exotics, and so on, restorationists are symbolically embodying the sort of action that they believe should be generalizable to all of society. While restorationists most likely do not believe this, it is not enough to just say that those who identify with nature really don't believe that human society should also be weeded of its exotics since an identity model could in principle support such a deplorable view. There have been, after all, plenty of misan-thropes in the environmental world, and some, like Edward Abbey, were very vocal about such views. In contrast, however, a citizenship model would have an easier time avoiding such criticisms as it would not represent environmental priorities as isolated from other, larger democratic ends. Ecological citizens are not only ecological, they also owe obligations to their larger human communities, which are inclusive of other issues, such as equal protection of all humans against undue coercion or persecution.

Fourth, identity formations, as suggested above, are less critical of elements of practices that tend to promote exclusivity favoring a kind of clannish behavior that may be off-putting to those trying to enter such practices from the outside. It is also the case that an identity model may favor practices that evidence exclusivity in order to create a stronger sense of cohesion, as suggested above. We can see this in the case of restoration in controversies over whether such practices should include a ritualistic component. Here we have an issue where the identity and citizenship models would diverge, with at least clear reasons existing for why a citizenship model would reject this aspect of restoration.

Because restorations often involve ongoing maintenance, such as the need to reg-ularly burn restored prairies in order to ensure their further propagation, a number of events have arisen to motivate people to annually engage in such practices. Fall prairie burnings are often accompanied by celebrations of local communities as prairie festi-vals. In and of themselves, such celebrations are wonderful: helping to keep a com-munity of restorationists together as well as bringing new people into such communi-ties in the form of a joyous event. As such, these occasions only continue and extend the positive benefits mentioned in the previous section, encouraging the development of a community of care for nature. There are, however, problems when such festivals and other similar events evolve into more exclusive ritualistic practices.

The literature on ritual and restoration is growing and I only have space here to comment on it briefly. Essentially though, work on such practices tends to swing somewhat hyperbolically from enthusiastic, unhesitant embrace to strong condemnation. Issues are muddled by the fact that it is often not clear what counts as a ritual. While some would include the prairie festivals just mentioned as rituals, others would not. There is also a question whether to include artistic projects attached to restoration as rituals that otherwise have no intrinsic ritualistic role. Some would include fairly mundane activities such as the morning "workday circle" at the North Branch Prairie Project (part of the Chicago Wilderness restorations) that amounts simply to a short social gathering among volunteers to share stories and receive instructions preceding their day's work.[26] Many however would reject any of these as proper examples of ritual in restoration (at least the kind of rituals that are generating controversies). Here, by "ritual" I will reserve my criticisms to the overt, more religious-oriented practices such as prayers to the Earth prior to a restoration, asking restorationists to apologize to the plants they are removing, or organizing meditations to help restorationists feel a connection with the stones and soil around them. These are all practices we would fairly associate with an environmentally oriented new-age spiritualism.

Lisa Meekison and Eric Higgs argue that ritual in restoration is an attempt to more fully flesh out the full range of human endeavors (beyond mere scientific and technological practice) involved in restoration.[27] If restorations are about building community, then rituals should help to highlight these community-building elements of restoration. Some commentators, however, appear to want to build only a certain kind of community through ritual in restoration. These rituals often involve a more explicit and potentially alienating spiritual component. For example, Beatrice Briggs argues that humans have a "primordial instinct for rituals" that restorationists should use. These will provide a "heightened sense of meaning and identity" to restorations. She suggests experimentation by restorationists: "Only invite colleagues and neighbors to join you. Keep it simple, biocentric and place-based, and you have the makings of an eco-ritual."[28] Such practices, however, are not supported by all. Responding to similar sorts of pronouncements by Bill Jordan (an enthusiastic supporter of ritual in restoration and one of the leading theorists in the field), Jack Kirby comments that "the restoration ecologist's aim is to do nothing less than save neo-Europeans' souls" on the North American continent. "Salvation is accomplished by ritual, which reconnects humans with nature." The religious overtones of these rituals lead Kirby to balk, claiming, "no need for such redemption."[29]

A puzzling fact about these disagreements is that they often involve a kind of can/ought confusion. While it is certainly the case that rituals can be part of a restoration, and be very meaningful as a full expression of the range of endeavors possible in restoration, it is unclear whether many promoting the more spiritual rituals in restoration consider the broader question of whether they really ought to be promoting such practices all or even most of the time. As with any kind of practice, we can imagine the beneficial elements of ritualizing it and conclude that rituals are good for a practice because they enrich an activity that we have already decided is a good idea. Rit-ualizing restoration, as Meekison and Higgs put it, is just a way of seeing it flower to its full potential. We should not be surprised then to find proponents of ritual who take seriously objections such as Kirby's, arguing in response that restorationists should therefore make a self-conscious effort to not be exclusive and alienating with their rituals (to be "pluralistic" as Meekison and Higgs put it). But it is highly unlikely that any human practice can be so theoretically prescribed. Absent some sort of rules and policies over rituals (which would entail the need for an overarching guiding gov-ernance of restoration that would in and of itself be oppressive and objectionable) there is really no way to ensure that such rituals are not alienating except in our the-oretical and stipulative imaginations.

The easier fact to digest is that, like it or not, ritualized behavior is a way of mark-ing a community distinct from others and will inevitably be alienating for those sub-jects (such as Kirby) who simply do not like feeling like an outsider in such events. Ab-sent some kind of governing principle—some supernatural deity or force that wants us to ritualize this practice—this issue should then be resolved in a consequentialist framework, guided by some end like the need to promote full participation, citizen-ship, or democracy in restoration practices. If rituals are not absolutely necessary for keeping volunteers from participating then the risk of alienating newcomers to these practices should give us a reason to minimize these practices. This is not to silence those who want restoration rituals, akin to violating their freedom of religion, as Meek-ison and Higgs caustically suggest, but simply to downplay one part of a practice be-cause the overall goal of participation in restoration is aimed at something broader and richer than building an exclusive community.

Considered in this way, I do not think that much is lost if we downplay ritual in restoration in a model of ecological citizenship. Every environmental practice that we engage in need not be ritualistic in order to be more complete and to fully express the range of human endeavors connected to the practice. We can imagine a community of environmentalists constituted as citizens that would still hold prairie festivals, encour-age artistic expressions and the like without resorting to alienating rituals that would, as suggested in the first point above, mark environmentalists as a special interest, a closed community that one had to gain access to through some ritualized process. Restoration does not need functional high priests and priestesses if it is to achieve its democratic potential.

One may object that an ecological identity would not be required to favor ritual-ization in restoration. But the question would be on what grounds such a position would reject ritual in restoration, or at least downplay it? From an ecological identity view, where a culture of nature is defined in terms of the subjective identification of agents with nature, there would seem to be no good answer to those who would wish to ritualize restoration. The reason is that the subjective ontology of an identity view makes it difficult, if not impossible, to form a sound basis for critique of the subjectiv-ity of an agent, with respect to some political identity, by another. While some person A who embraced an ecological identity might disagree with B's basis for embracing an ecological identity—A might reject the claim by B that nature is a subject deserving of equal moral status or a claim by some other person C that he is an indistinguishable part of a larger natural whole—there is no basis by which A could claim that B or C does not have an ecological identity. One has an ecological identity, subjectively construed, insofar as one can defend this position to one's self. So if B or C find it necessary to engage in rituals in order to build their community of restorationists, A can object for strategic reasons (such as alienating outsiders) but cannot claim that somehow engaging in such rituals is inconsistent with the identity basis of their connection to nature. An ecological citizenship, in contrast, could make a stronger claim against fellow ecocitizens who would want to include ritual in an environmental practice by appeal to the argument that a citizenship model must be open unless there is some principled reason to dissuade others from engaging in these same practices.

Some of the reasons why I prefer a citizenship over an identity model for creating a democratic culture of nature should be clear by now. But following the rejection of the identity model for forming a culture of nature, how then do we begin the process of formalizing an ecological citizenship? In addition to the short description of the citizenship model mentioned above, two general points. First, we need to articulate a notion of citizenship that is, as much as possible, intrinsically ecological. Such a conception of citizenship should not be too far off for us, especially if we stick to a classically republican idea of citizenship that conceives it in thick rather than thin terms (or, if you prefer the more technical language of political philosophy, as a "constitutive" community rather than an "instrumentalist" community).[30] Contemporary republican theorists such as Richard Dagger and Philip Pettit have already written much that helps us to conceive of citizenship as inclusive of environmental concerns. Following Dagger, citizenship, as more than simply a procedural or juridical notion (e.g., as something other than formal voting rights), more accurately describes a way of life for persons that privileges a "required commitment to the common good and active participation in public affairs."[31] This conception of citizenship has a long history in political thought, back to Aristotle. But the question is begged concerning what unit of day-to-day life (which scale of experience with our fellows) we wish to find morally significant as a ground for republican citizenship. Aristotle's polis of the past is gone as a meaningful and indeed realistic object of our project of building a thick conception of citizenship. A ground for citizenship must be found at a smaller scale where citizens can know and interact with each other. One reason is that it is only at such a scale, as Dewey put it so well, that engagement and access to authority is possible by citizens. Reading Dewey's *The Public and Its Problems*, and bemoaning the decent into particularism in much of contemporary urban studies, Bender puts the point this way:

> A larger public, what [Dewey] called "the Great Community," is built upon the habits and accomplishments of local publics. Urban critics tend to focus on the diversity of public space and publics. Diversity is important; but so too are access to political institutions and the opportunity to give voice to public concerns. . . . I am proposing a public that is a public not because of mere propinquity, however important that is, but *because they propose to do something together*. The essential quality of what I call the "local" public is not, as we are inclined to think, sameness; it is accessibility to networks of informal power and to institutions of formal politics.[32]

So, second, a conception of ecological citizenship must be grounded in practices where local publics can, as Bender suggests, "do something together." Local public spaces should provide access to others as having shared lives, rather than only serving as symbolic representations of bonds of community. From all that has been argued so far, restorations can be one of those projects that we do together.

Realizing this second point brings us to a very interesting, and possibly unexpected conclusion. It is not simply the case that democratic public participation in restoration ecology should best be conceived in a citizenship model but that the larger project of encouraging an ecological citizenry is bound up in projects such as encouraging participatory restorations. Further, if, following Dagger and Pettit, the ecological part of a renewed push for citizenship is critical to revitalizing the language and practice of citizenship, then public participation in restoration is an important part of the broader project of revitalizing a more substantive notion of republican citizen obligations over and above any narrowly construed ecological concern. Participation in restoration promotes an ecological citizenship that in itself promotes a more constitutive, republican model of citizenship. Admittedly, this set of arguments has now become a bit circular—the framework for public participation in ecological restoration should be one of democratic ecological citizenship because the project of promoting an ecological citizenship in part relies on the success of encouraging democratic participation in practices like restoration. This is not however a vicious circle. The democratic participation of citizens in restoration at bottom is about building a democratic culture of nature, or more prosaically a stronger human community that not only takes into account, but is actively inclusive of, concerns over the health, maintenance, and sustainability of larger natural systems. Such concerns will be important for the goal of encouraging the evolution of a more responsible citizenry overall given the role such healthy environments empirically play in making human communities themselves sustainable. We ought to expect that such a project of community building would involve such reciprocal relationships.

Conclusion: Citizenship and the New Problem of Dirty Hands

What more explicit directions would the citizenship framework take us for the actual practice of restoration other than rejecting exclusive practices such as new-age rituals in restorations? While I will shortly conclude with a more explicit policy suggestion, we can initially build on the first two problems with ecological identities to get three general recommendations for orienting a culture of nature around restoration on the citizenship model.

1. In answer to the questions I started out with, citizenship is necessarily and not contingently attached to a more robust notion of participation as democratic participation. Mere participation in an environmental project is not enough but must be accompanied on this model (or at least we must aim at) an attunement to a democratic decision-making process for such participation. Such a framework is more likely to capture the advantages of participation raised by Sagoff and Gundersen, as well as create

the framework for stewardship or care by a community of agents for the nature around them, which I argued in section two were necessary for achieving sustainability.

2. The ideal of citizenship is one of universal inclusivity rather than exclusivity, even though the history of citizenship has involved a debate between the two. Conceiving of participation in restoration on the citizenship model therefore directly puts on the table the question of the breadth of environmentalism. Environmentalism as embodied in the practice of restoration, and in other practices on this model, must be as inclusive as possible and must not engage in practices that work against broadening the scope of environmentalism unless there is a strong reason to do so.

3. The expectation on the citizenship model would be to institutionalize the obligations and rights of agents in an environmental community as the obligations and rights of citizens. This will entail coming up with formal proposals for getting more participation in restoration as part of the larger goal of encouraging an ecologically minded citizenry and in turn a more robust model of citizenship over all. I will close with a more specific proposal following this recommendation.

Compared with acts of preservation, which often involve minimal public participation, and which are restricted to areas deemed worthy of preservation (such as wilderness areas), restorations can be initiated in a wide range of areas and can involve, as I mentioned at the start, maximal participation from planning to implementation to follow through. But the participatory benefits of restoration are most palpable, as evidenced from the sociological studies available from Chicago, when participation is literally at the ground level. My conclusion above that restorations help to produce ecological citizens as much as they benefit from a citizenship model of democratic participation is arguably only possible if volunteers in restorations actually get their hands dirty. We might call the challenge to get more people involved in direct participation in environmental practices the "new problem of dirty hands." While I do not have the full argument to make the claim here, I think that other environmental practices that afford the opportunity of people to get their hands dirty will also get the same sorts of advantages of stewardship and care as is found with restoration.[33]

But we should not forget the other side of the circle mentioned at the end of the previous section: participation in dirty-hands activities, as a way of encouraging the development of ecological citizenship, should also favor projects that not only produce good outcomes for nature but also good outcomes for forming stronger bonds between citizens at the level of what Bender called the "local public." One example is New York City's Bronx River Alliance, a project of the City of New York Parks and Recreation Department and the nonprofit City Parks Foundation. The alliance is organized by paid city employees who have brought together and coordinate sixty voluntary community groups, schools, and businesses in dirty-hands projects along the twenty-three miles of the Bronx River. The focus is not only on the environmental priorities of the area, but also the opportunities afforded by it to create concrete links between the communities along the river by giving them a common project on which to focus their civic priorities. In the words of the alliance, the project is to "restore the Bronx River to a Healthy Community, Ecological, Economic and Recreational Resource." The activities of the alliance are thus jointly civic and environmental and the scale of the environmental problem, crossing several distinct communities, helps to create a common interest between them. The environment becomes the civic glue between various local publics.

The Bronx River Alliance did not emerge fully formed out of the good will of citizenry groups but was shaped by the New York City Parks Department attempting to follow other successful models such as the Central Park Conservancy, which has dramatically improved the ecological viability of Central Park, at least as a species habit for migratory birds, as well as increased the level of citizen involvement in the maintenance of the park. Where such successful projects point the way, the citizenship model, as indicated in Recommendation 3, should try to formalize and institutionalize these models through legislation and policy. But what is happening in New York City is somewhat haphazard. While the encouragement of the alliance is favored by the current parks department leadership (and was in part a response to financial exigencies which made it impossible for the department to maintain these parks solely through public expenditure) we can imagine that a different leadership or a different set of conditions would have produced a different outcome. As I said at the start, we always have a choice of how to restore once we decide to restore. If public participation in restoration gets the stewardship advantages mentioned in section two of this chapter, and if in turn public participation helps to ready the ground for the growth of an ecological citizenry mentioned at the end of section three, then it is appropriate to pursue legislation that would, where possible, encourage more developments such as the Bronx River Alliance.

This sort of reasoning gets us at least one clear goal if restoration is understood now to be an important facet of a larger mosaic of ecological citizenship. We must promote and encourage laws that would mandate local participation in restoration projects that are publicly funded on the assumption that local participation in restoration is part of the overall criteria for what counts as a good restoration because of its potential benefits to encouraging citizenship and grounding connections between local citizens and their local environments. Because restorations become opportunities for forming bonds of citizenship they therefore take on the mantle of a state interest.

One approach to achieving this interest would be to follow the Bronx River model and institutionalize in city, state, and federal parks agencies a requirement to pursue, where possible, such pubic-government alliances. Another approach (which would not be limited to designated park land) would be to propose a set of laws that would mandate that democratically organized local citizen groups have a "right of first refusal" to participate in government-funded restoration programs. So, when federal, state, or municipal money is allocated for a restoration, and certain other conditions are met (such as that scale and complexity of the project admit to what I am calling dirty-hands participation), the RFP announced by the government body would stipulate that priority for license of the project will be given to voluntary organizations that either must provide approved scientific direction themselves or accept outside advisors paid for with public money. In the United States there are ample precedents for such riders on RFPs, to be found in laws mandating use of local, minority contracting firms in government-funded housing projects. These regulations not only create local jobs but are intended to build local interest in such projects (legislative history is clear on this point even if it is not always true in practice).

In addition to the reasons for encouraging such participation offered above, such a set of laws could be justified on the grounds that when states have an interest in promoting a healthy citizenry or environment (for whatever reason) they also have an interest in achieving these goals at the lowest cost. Using volunteer labor will in most cases cost less than armies of paid restorationists and will also create a community of interest around a restored site that may produce a bank of volunteers to maintain the site later rather than relying on paid government employees to do the job. If the state does not take such an activist role in creating links such as the Bronx River Alliance, or if legislation is not forthcoming to mandate participation where possible, then environmentalists must take an activist role in encouraging such participation. In the case of the Chicago Wilderness this has involved the leadership of the Nature Conservancy, which has purchased land for restoration as well as coordinated volunteer restorationists on public lands.

To help orient this legislative goal we will want to focus our attention as ethicists and environmentalists on those areas most likely to generate such foundations for ecological citizenship, namely those geographical areas that are most amenable to public participation through projects like restoration. Larger restorations, such as the multi-million-dollar projects undertaken by the U.S. Army Corps of Engineers to dechannelize rivers, are too unwieldy for significant voluntary efforts, at least in terms of "dirty-hands" participation. But smaller-scale restorations, such as the Chicago projects and Bronx River restorations, are perfect for serving this purpose. While such a conclusion may seem uncontroversial, we need to remember that much of the environmental community tends to put a much higher priority on larger, "wilderness"-oriented projects of preservation or restoration over such smaller-scale municipal projects.[34] To fully plough the democratic depths of the potential of restoration we must broaden our horizons as environmentalists and, ironically, look closer to home to smaller-scale initiatives. This is not a naïve call to think globally and act locally, but a mandate to act locally in order to make more ambitious global transformations possible.

Notes

1. William K. Stevens, *Miracle under the Oaks* (New York: Pocket Books, 1995).

2. L. A. Toth, "The Ecological Basis of the Kissimmee River Restoration Plan," *Biological Sciences* 1 (1993): 25–51.

3. Michael Wald, "White House to Present $7.8 Billion Plan for Everglades," *New York Times*, July 1, 1999, 14A.

4. See Andrew Light and Eric Higgs, "The Politics of Ecological Restoration," *Environmental Ethics* 18, no. 3 (fall 1996): 227–47; and Andrew Light, "Restoration, the Value of Participation, and the Risks of Professionalization," in *Restoring Nature*, ed. Paul Gobster and Bruce Hull (Washington D.C.: Island Press, 2000), 163–81.

5. There are many questions in the philosophical literature about whether restorations are beneficial or not, which many believe should be answered prior to an investigation such as this one (such as the arguments levied by Eric Katz and Robert Elliot against restoration). There are also controversial issues involving what we choose to restore to and why (whether pre-Columbian is the appropriate choice for restorations or not, etc.). For my position on the first

set of worries see my "Ecological Restoration and the Culture of Nature: A Pragmatic Perspective," in *Restoring Nature*, ed. Paul Gobster and Bruce Hull (Washington D.C.: Island Press, 2000), 49–70. I strongly believe that this set of concerns can be resolved so as to proceed with more productive debates about restoration. As to the second set of issues on what we should restore to, I will leave that to a later inquiry. I will say, however, that the relative flexibility of what we can restore an ecosystem to should make it easier to open up new possibilities for public participation in restoration.

6. Mark Sagoff, *The Economy of the Earth* (Cambridge, U.K.: Cambridge University Press, 1988).

7. Adolf Gundersen, *The Environmental Promise of Democratic Deliberation* (Madison: University of Wisconsin Press, 1995).

8. Avner de-Shalit, *The Environment between Theory and Practice* (Oxford, U.K.: Oxford University Press, 2000).

9. See Andrew Light, "Callicott and Naess on Pluralism," *Inquiry* 39, no. 2 (June 1996): 273–94; and Andrew Light, "Taking Environmental Ethics Public," in *Environmental Ethics: What Really Matters? What Really Works?* ed. David Schmidtz and Elizabeth Willott (Oxford, U.K.: Oxford University Press, 2001).

10. Eckersley's references in her chapter in this volume are to my coauthored introduction to *Environmental Pragmatism*, ed. Andrew Light and Eric Katz (London: Routledge, 1996). While I am in some sympathy with her worries about the conservative tendencies of a more proceduralist approach to pragmatism, I do not think that these worries apply to a charitable reading of my current views, or what I earlier called a "metaphilosophical" environmental pragmatism. It is curious to me that when Eckersely characterizes this view she only makes reference to the introduction to the *Environmental Pragmatism* volume rather than my two substantive chapters in the book where I give a more explicit account of the implications of the view even though it is an account that does not fully reflect my presently evolved state of these views. Eckersley's criticisms may apply more appropriately to others who she considers methodological pragmatists, though I would argue that very few other people explicitly embrace this view. Eckersley's examples of the chapters by Paul Thompson and Kelly Parker in the *Environmental Pragmatism* book seem wrong to me as examples of methodological pragmatism since both of these authors embrace an explicit *philosophical* pragmatism, grounded in the work of the classic pragmatist authors.

11. I give more detail on the critique of environmental ethics as externalist, especially in its approach to applying ethics to matters of public policy, in "Contemporary Environmental Ethics: From Metaethics to Public Philosophy," forthcoming in *Metaphilosophy* 33, no. 3 (2002).

12. I outline the empirical case for this conclusion, which is quite strong, in "Taking Environmental Ethics Public."

13. Tim Hayward, *Political Theory and Ecological Values* (New York: St. Martin's, 1998).

14. Deane Curtin's work on development ethics provides a thorough account of some of these cases, including the failing attempt by the Nepali government to create the Chitwan National Park over the needs of local communities to collect firewood. See Deane Curtin, *Chinnagounder's Challenge: The Question of Ecological Citizenship* (Bloomington: Indiana University Press, 1999).

15. See Irene Miles et al., "Psychological Benefits of Volunteering for Restoration Projects," *Ecological Restoration* 18, no. 4 (2000): 218–27. For more social science research on the environmental benefits of participation in restoration, see *Restoring Nature*.

16. Ibid., 222.

17. Ibid., 223.

18. Light, "Ecological Restoration."

19. See Andrew Light, "What Is an Ecological Identity?" *Environmental Politics* 9, no. 4 (2000): 59–81.

20. See Catriona Sandilands, *The Good-Natured Feminist: Ecofeminism and the Quest for Democracy* (Minneapolis: University of Minnesota Press, 1999).

21. See Mitchell Thomashow, *Ecological Identity* (Cambridge, Mass.: MIT Press, 1992).

22. Thomas Bender, "Describing the World at the End of the Millennium," *Harvard Design Magazine* (winter/spring 2000): 70.

23. The following arguments may appear to depart from my apparent endorsement of an ecological identity in my previously published "What Is an Ecological Identity?" referenced above. But as I tried to make clear in that earlier effort, I was not trying to make an ecological identity coherent in order to endorse it, but simply to make it available in the toolbox of theoretical frameworks available to environmentalists and to point out some ways of resolving the political problems entailed by such a form of environmentalism. If it is possible to create one kind of culture of nature around one set of practices and another kind of culture around another, then my pluralism would entail that I can endorse a citizenship model for the cultural practices of restoration and reserve the right to endorse an identity framework for some other set of practices, such as questions of environmental justice where an identity model may better serve the need of linking environmental claims to claims of social justice. I am not certain that pluralism at this level is really possible though I do not wish to rule it out at this time.

24. I believe such a view is expressed in David Abram's *The Spell of the Sensuous* (New York: Pantheon, 1996).

25. Donna Haraway, "Nature, Politics, and Possibilities: A Debate and Discussion with David Harvey and Donna Haraway," *Society and Space* 13, no. 5 (1995): 524.

26. Karen M. Holland, "Restoration Rituals: Transforming Workday Tasks into Inspirational Rites," *Restoration and Management Notes* 12, no. 1 (1994): 122.

27. Lisa Meekison and Eric Higgs, "The Rise of Spring (and Other Seasons): The Ritualizing of Restoration," *Restoration and Management Notes* 16, no. 1 (1998): 73–81.

28. Beatrice Briggs, "Help Wanted: Scientists-Shamans and Eco-Rituals," *Restoration and Management Notes* 12, no. 1 (1994): 24.

29. Jack Kirby, "Gardening with J. Crew: The Political Economy of Restoration Ecology," in *Beyond Preservation: Restoring and Inventing Landscape*, ed. A. Dwight Baldwin, J. De Luce, and C. Pletsch (Minneapolis: University of Minnesota Press, 1994), 238–39.

30. Richard Dagger, *Civic Virtues: Rights, Citizenship, and Republican Liberalism* (Oxford, U.K.: Oxford University Press, 1997), 49.

31. Dagger, *Civic Virtues*, 99.

32. Thomas Bender, "The New Metropolitanism and a Pluralized Public," *Harvard Design Magazine* (winter/spring 2001), 73, emphasis added.

33. I have just begun to make this sort of argument with respect to the practice of community gardening. See Andrew Light, "Elegy for a Garden: Thoughts on an Urban Environmental Ethic," *Philosophical Writings* 14 (2000): 41–47. I have tried to expand this analysis to the general approach to forming environmental grounds for a renewal of urban citizenship in "Urban Ecological Citizenship," currently under review.

34. I have made this argument at much greater length in "The Urban Blind Spot in Environmental Ethics," *Environmental Politics* 10, no. 1 (2001): 7–35.

CHAPTER 9

Aldo Leopold's Civic Education

Bob Pepperman Taylor

I.

Aldo Leopold begins his master work, *A Sand County Almanac*, with a brief account of a walk during a January thaw. Following the trail of a skunk through the snow, he startles a meadow mouse. Leopold notes that the thaw that has roused the skunk is a disaster for the mouse: the tunnel system so laboriously built is wrecked by the warmth. "Indeed the thawing sun has mocked the basic premises of the microtine economic system!"[1] The mouse's work is not only wrecked; his life is endangered as a result. Exposed above the snow, he becomes vulnerable to the rough-legged hawk.

Leopold tells us that the mouse "is a sober citizen." He "knows that grass grows in order that mice may store it as underground haystacks, and that snow falls in order that mice may build subways from stack to stack."[2] The hawk that threatens him, however, "has no opinion why grass grows, but he is well aware that snow melts in order that hawks may again catch mice."[3] The skunk, meanwhile, wanders along with "no concern over the rompings or retributions of his neighbors."[4] Leopold speculates about what has brought the skunk abroad, wondering if one can "impute romantic motives to this corpulent fellow."[5] Leopold's walk comes to an end when he finds the skunk tracks entering, but not emerging from, a jumble of driftwood. Reckoning that the skunk hears the trickling of water among the logs just as he does, Leopold heads home.

In this light, charming, and poetical three pages, Leopold has subtly introduced the work of the *Almanac*. First, we are taken into nature to have a good look around. Second, we are shown the narrowness of any perspective that takes individual wants and desires as the whole of the world. Third, there is a hint in the structure of the story of the idea that looking at the natural world will help us to transcend such narrowness—the narrowness of the skunk, the mouse, and the hawk—in our own perceptions.

If there is only a hint of the third task in this opening story, any question is quickly removed in the next chapter, "February," which famously begins with Leopold's comment that the two "spiritual dangers" of not owning a farm are "supposing that breakfast comes from the grocery" and thinking that "heat comes from the furnace."[6] Having a farm disabuses us of these mistakes, so common to people who don't spend time observing and working in the natural world. The bulk of this chapter is devoted to an account of the production of firewood from an old oak struck by lightning. Leopold not only explains the process of producing heat; he also weaves the cutting of the oak into the human history of the periods represented by the rings of growth. We are reminded of the message of "January" when Leopold observes that "Man brings all things to the test of himself,"[7] and two pages later when he says that "An oak is no respecter of persons."[8] We have learned not only that heat comes from more than the furnace; Leopold has also gently pointed out that we aren't as different from the animals in the narrowness of our own inclinations as we might like to think, but that our recognition of and contact with the reality of natural objects like the oak promises to help us overcome these limitations.

The lessons of *Sand County* continue thus throughout the cycle of the year. Observing nature shows us beauty beyond a narrow utility (such as we learn when we observe the "sky dance" of the woodcock)[9]; that the world of nature is a unity greater than the nation-state (birds understand "hemispheric solidarity")[10]; that nature offers adventure aplenty ("Almost anything may happen between one red lantern [red oak leaf] and another.")[11]; and that to reap these rewards requires a humility in our approach to nature ("And if you have come quietly and humbly, as you should to any spot that can be beautiful only once, you may surprise a fox-red deer, standing knee-high in the garden of delight").[12] A life in nature is one that takes risk, is not timorous or overly prudent; "How utterly dull would be a wholly prudent man, or trout, or world!"[13] Noting that people grieve only for what they know,[14] this walk through the annual cycle is a first step in knowing nature, or at least in aspiring to know it. Leopold is preparing us to love the natural world and grieve for harms we do it. He even hopes that this education will lead us to associate with nature more closely, to view our activities as bringing us closer to and implicated in the lives of nonhuman creatures. In the final passage of the *Almanac*, Leopold relates the story of Chickadee 65290 (the number on the band Leopold placed on his leg). After this (relatively) long-lived little bird dies, Leopold wishes him all the best in his "new woods," and, in the final sentence of the book, he hopes that the chickadee continues to wear Leopold's band in bird heaven.[15]

"November" is Leopold's climactic month in the *Almanac*, the month in which he makes explicit a number of claims that are only implied or less developed elsewhere. First, there is no avoiding the reality that to own land is not only to learn the facts of life about breakfast and heat; it is also to become a creator and destroyer. "Whoever owns land has thus assumed, whether he knows it or not, the divine functions of creating and destroying plants."[16] If owning land is a good tool for developing our education, it also thrusts upon us, regardless of our intention, the godlike responsibility of making life and death decisions about the natural world that is giving us and teaching us so much. Second, Leopold lets us know that in reality, it is not only the farm owner who bears this responsibility. Indeed, since we all are responsible, to greater or lesser degrees, for decisions that shape and control the natural world, the problems we face become explicitly philosophical concerning the ends with which we wield our tools.

> We classify ourselves into vocations, each of which either wields some particular tool, or sells it, or repairs it, or sharpens it, or dispenses advice on

how to do so; by such division of labors we avoid responsibility for the mis-use of any tool save our own. But there is one vocation—philosophy—which knows that all men, by what they think about and wish for, in effect wield all tools. It knows that men thus determine, by their manner of think-ing and wishing, whether it is worth while to wield any.[17]

And this leads us to the third crucial claim in this chapter: that the philosophical in-clination of the contemporary world—the "modern dogma" of "comfort at any cost"[18]—is out of line with the philosophical lessons that lead to conservationism, or becoming aware that "with each stroke" we are writing our "signature on the land."[19] Prior to our education in nature, we are like the skunk, mouse, and hawk; we think of the resources of nature as no more than the means to our own material needs and plea-sures. To become a conservationist is to reject this dogma, to expand our vision about the nature of what is good beyond the demands of a too-narrow utility. What the farm teaches, either by ownership, but even more through the lessons of a teacher like Leopold (after all, not all farmers have learned to look at their land as Leopold has, which is why he taught courses for farmers at the University of Wisconsin), is a richer and broader human life than is possible without such an education.

In fact, we might think of the overall message of *Sand County* in the following terms. Leopold presents us with a conception of the good life that includes these ele-ments (my list is not intended to be exhaustive):

(a) Moderation. This concerns our approach to the use of nature, and is by no means to be confused with *not* using nature (just as Leopold's nature is not to be confused with wilderness). Consider, again, Leopold's discussion of the woodcock. Having dis-covered and followed the "sky dance," he does not stop hunting the bird, but he finds himself "calling one or two birds enough." He still loves to hunt the woodcock as much as anybody, but "I must be sure that, come April, there be no dearth of dancers in the sunset sky."[20] We must use nature for both our economic and recreational needs, but we must also be moderate in this use and know when a humane life requires us to leave the natural world alone.

(b) Adventure. The world Leopold presents is not only entertaining (although it is cer-tainly that); it is engaging (consider the distractions that continually draw him away from his lunch in "October"[21]), dramatic (consider "The Alder Fork—A Fishing Idyl" from "June"), mysterious and magical ("What a dull world if we know all about geese!"[22]), and risky (remember the comment disparaging prudent men and trout re-ferred to above). This is a world beyond pleasure, comfort, and safety; these are known, of course, but in moderation only, as modestly necessary but insufficient elements of a vigorous and exciting physical and intellectual experience.

(c) Beauty. Concerning the seductions of "August," Leopold writes, "I know a paint-ing so evanescent that it is seldom viewed at all, except by some wandering deer. It is a river who wields the brush."[23] We are drawn to nature in the hope of experiencing beauty. This beauty is all around us, but requires our attention to be consistently and fully uncovered.

(d) Humility. The full definition of a conservationist, only partially referred to above, is "one who is humbly aware that with each stroke he is writing his signature on the face of the land."[24] We become disciplined by the love of the land itself.

The enemy of these qualities is what Leopold calls the modern dogma of comfort, the shortsighted economics of consumer satisfaction. The only weapon that can possibly combat this powerful dogma is an education in a world of experience beyond these constricted boundaries. An ecological education can accomplish this task, since it shows that the utilities and disutilities of individual organisms cannot begin to capture the whole character and wonder of life. For example, the first great lesson of the liberal education Leopold gained from owning his farm was his discovery that he owned almost as many tree diseases as trees. "I began to wish that Noah, when he loaded up the Ark, had left the tree diseases behind." But he soon learned "that these same diseases made my woodlot a mighty fortress, unequaled in the whole county."[25] His own education, that is, revealed a natural world in which death worked with life to provide for the health of the land as a whole, and that without this partnership there would be no habitat for the raccoons, roughed grouse, bees, and other creatures of these woods. When we begin to see this, we become open to the various goods beyond our own comforts and pains, beyond the lives of individual trees or other organisms. Without this education, we are in danger of becoming like the farmer and his wife who cannot appreciate the beauty of the cottonwood tree "because in June the female tree clogs the screens with cotton."[26] As Leopold writes in the "Foreword," now that our breakfasts have been secured, and science has disclosed the drama of ecology,[27] "nothing could be more salutary at this stage than a little healthy contempt for a plethora of material blessings."[28]

II.

No one familiar with the body of Leopold's writings will be surprised by these teachings in *A Sand County Almanac*, for they are found throughout his life's work. Underlying Leopold's consistent promotion of moderation,[29] adventure,[30] appreciation of natural beauty,[31] and humility before the natural world,[32] is Leopold's lifelong criticism of the excessive American preoccupation with material wealth and economic development. In 1923 he is as disgusted by this preoccupation ("In past and more outspoken days conservation was put in terms of decency rather than dollars"[33]) as he is in the essays published with *A Sand County Almanac* ("What do economists know about lupines?"[34]). His symbols for the excesses of American society are economists, "Boosters," and "Babbitts," and he fears the degree to which we are being overwhelmed by the spirit of a false progress.[35] He never underestimated the power of the economic forces currently dominating the country, as when he criticized the "good roads mania" in the 1920s: "Do not forget that the good roads mania, and all forms of unthinking Boosterism that go with it, constitute a steam roller the like of which has seldom been seen in the history of mankind."[36] Throughout his career, Leopold consistently attacked the crude utilitarianism of contemporary economic calculation. His fear was that this economic perspective threatened to silence all other moral commitments and values. In "The River of the Mother of God," Leopold explicitly contends that "wilderness and economics are, in every ordinary sense, mutually exclusive."[37] If we are to value wilderness, and other parts of life that the market has a difficult time accounting for, we will need to challenge, contain, limit, and control the economic impulse and perspective.[38]

There are two essential elements of Leopold's critique of modern economics that are found in much of his writing. The first is a vision of *recovery* that informs his criticism. In the passage quoted above, Leopold suggests that we can find, in our history, "past and more outspoken days" in which moral values were greater than the sum total of economic values. The language of conservation itself, of course, is the language of preserving, saving, preventing certain kinds of change, so it is not surprising that much of Leopold's moral language reflects a fear of loss and a longing for return to an earlier historical moment. In this spirit, Leopold promotes what he calls "split-rail Americanism,"[39] the sensibilities promoted by pioneer and traditional rural life. He lambastes all modern political ideologies as "competitive apostles of a single creed: *salvation by machinery.*"[40] Early in his career he offered the biblical teachings of Ezekiel as an alternative to these modern views, insofar as the ancient prophet understood better than we seem to the need to preserve to earth into the unforeseeable future: "We might even draw from his words a broader concept—that the privilege of possessing the earth entails the responsibility of passing it on, the better for our use, not only to immediate posterity, but to the Unknown Future, the nature of which is not given to us to know."[41] In "Wildlife in American Culture," published with *A Sand County Almanac,* Leopold writes that "Mechanization offers no cultural substitute for the split-rail values it destroys; at least none visible to me."[42] In many passages like this scattered throughout Leopold's writings, something very akin to Frederick Jackson Turner's view of the relationship between American culture and the frontier informs his perspective. In fact, in an essay written at the time when Turner had just become Leopold's neighbor in Madison, Leopold writes along lines very similar to Turner's: "For three centuries the environment has determined the character of our development; it may, in fact, be said that, coupled with the character of our racial stocks, it is the very stuff America is made of. Shall we now exterminate this thing that made us American?"[43] The mechanized world has produced a moral transformation, destroying "split-rail values" of self-sufficiency and the ethical restraints of an earlier time, replacing these with a crude utilitarianism and the worship of material progress.[44]

The second of these elements is the essentially *political* nature of Leopold's critique. Leopold, it is true, was not a conventional political activist or ideologue even though he was deeply involved in public affairs throughout his career; Susan Flader has commented that "Leopold was himself about as apolitical as a man in public life could be."[45] It is also true that Leopold's respect for private property led him to think of conservation more as a matter of the education of private landowners than the exercise of the command power of the state. If the majority of land is to be held in private hands, after all, the project of conserving the land must be voluntarily assumed by those who own and work it. "This face-about in land philosophy cannot, in a democracy, be imposed on landowners from without, either by authority or by pressure groups. It can develop only from within, by self-persuasion, and by disillusionment with previous concepts."[46] For this reason, the project of conservation education is the fundamental goal of the bulk of Leopold's writings, and we could be led by this fact to think of his work as primarily ethical rather than political.

This would be a mistake. Leopold thought of the educational task he set himself as fundamentally civic in nature. As suggested above, his goal was to promote a particular form of American character. And this character, he believed, was essential to the restoration of civic health in the American polity. Our current biological education, he tells us in "Natural History," is insufficient to the task of "building" good citizens.[47] The implication, of course, is that a proper biological or ecological education is necessary for such civic education. Wild game is a "source of democratic recreation . . . a social asset,"[48] and therefore wildlife education is a part of "social philosophy."[49] So, too, is wilderness a "cultural inheritance" that must be preserved because of its cultural influence.[50] When Leopold addresses farmers, he is engaged in an act of civic persuasion, an attempt to convince them to think of their land in a way that is different than the view taught by market society: "The landscape of any farm is the owner's portrait of himself. Conservation implies self-expression in that landscape, rather than blind compliance with economic dogma."[51]

So Leopold assumed the role of an educator because of his commitment to democracy and private property.[52] But he is also clear that this role is not only about teaching individuals to live ethical private lives. On the contrary, it is about winning the contest for the spirit of American democracy itself. Conservation education aims to remind us, a people "many of whom have forgotten there is any such thing as land, among whom education and culture have become almost synonymous with landlessness," that we must strive for harmony with nature.[53] Unless we can do this, our very culture will lose its value and "ethical restraints."[54] American society will become increasingly comfortable and decreasingly serious, richer but with fewer meaningful goods and pleasures, utilitarian yet ethically shallow. Curt Meine points out that even in his early career in New Mexico, Leopold "was out to reform civic affairs just as he was out to reform attitudes toward game."[55] His ambition was to educate and shape the very structure of American political culture.

These two qualities, together, suggest the degree to which Leopold can be thought of as an exemplar of a civic or political educator in a democratic society. His common rhetorical strategy was to recall the country to its deeper values, what he took to be its earlier and foundational commitments. Although it is impossible to recreate the pioneer world that originally generated these values, Leopold's desire was to keep them alive in the new social contexts within which we currently live. The thrust of his appeal was to a recognizable, if dim and largely forgotten, moral sensibility. His hope was that this appeal would resonate as shared values, as an inheritance we could recognize and respect as a common good. As an act of democratic persuasion, his attack on the political economy of the twentieth century combined a respect for our political institutions and private property with an appeal to what he was afraid were disappearing ideals of self-sufficiency and personal independence, moderation and self-restraint, and a strong sense of the duties we owe to others, located in our cultural and political inheritance. The emphasis throughout is on the way the land can remind us of this earlier political culture, and the need to keep the land before us for the sake of this reminder.

III.

On the basis of this reading of Leopold's project, there are three observations I would like to make. First, this overall project is in noticeable tension with the thrust of Leopold's most famous essay, "The Land Ethic." Second, it is also in noticeable tension with the thrust of the secondary literature on Leopold. Third, Leopold's appeal to nature as a grounding for his normative persuasion, in "The Land Ethic" and throughout his work, reflects a traditional and distinguished strategy in Western political philosophy, but does so in ways that raise peculiarly modern difficulties.

The first observation begins by noticing that Leopold argues in "The Land Ethic" that we need an expansion of our ethical perspective. Our conventional moral languages have been unable to capture our proper relationship with nonhuman life, as they have been based upon an incomplete understanding of the nature of the ethical community. In fact, he claims that "philosophy and religion" have yet to hear about conservation, the ethical concern for the land as a whole.[56] The contrast between conventional ethical obligations and the new "land ethic" could therefore not be greater: "a land ethic changes the role of *Homo sapiens* from conquerer of the land-community to plain member and citizen of it."[57] Luckily, the growth of a proper conservation or land ethic "is actually a process in ecological evolution,"[58] and such evolution is now both a possibility and a necessity given our modern ecological knowledge. "An ethic to supplement and guide the economic relation to land presupposes the existence of some mental image of land as a biotic mechanism."[59] Such an image of the biotic mechanism is now available as a result of our modern science, and is hampered from becoming the foundation of a generally recognized land ethic only because of economic corruption (shortsightedness, at the very least) and inadequate education.[60]

The similarities in this argument with the rest of Leopold's writings are obvious: he is as concerned as always that modern economic calculation is undermining our ethics; he is also, as always, assuming the role of the conservation educator. But the difference in perspective between this argument and much of the rest of his work is equally obvious: rather than looking for moral guidance from a shared tradition of values and principles, here he is looking ahead to the development of an entirely new way of thinking about and experiencing ethical life; and while he most commonly bases his moral appeals on a shared history and culture and political tradition, his argument in this essay grows out of purely scientific claims about the nature of the biotic community. Rather than engaging in an act of moral retrieval and reinterpretation, Leopold here views our ethical inheritance as radically incomplete and imperfect. As such, the past has little to offer by way of guidance for a more satisfactory moral perspective, so science (Darwinian evolutionism) must point the way instead. To this degree, the argument Leopold presents has lost its political character (its appeal to community standards) and attempts to discover new values by scientific fiat.

There are other moments in Leopold's writings when he appears to be making moves similar to these in "The Land Ethic." In a public talk in 1934, he claims that "For twenty centuries and longer, all civilized thought has rested on one basic premise; that it is the destiny of man to exploit and enslave the earth."[61] The following year he wrote that "All science can do is to safeguard the environment in which ethical mutations might take place."[62] In these comments, and a few rare others scattered through his work, we find both the hostility to our moral inheritance and the ethical hope for science we see in "The Land Ethic." But these comments are few and far between. And even in "The Land Ethic" it appears as though Leopold is unsure of this move. At the end of the essay, the perspective at least hints at Leopold's more conventional way of thinking about things. In the concluding passage, "The Outlook," Leopold explains that "Your true modern is separated from the land by many middlemen, and by innumerable physical gadgets. He has no vital relation to it. . . . In short, land is something he has 'outgrown.'"[63] The problem is that our practical life has taken us farther from, rather than closer to, our "evolutionary" possibilities. As such, "The case for a land ethic would appear hopeless but for the minority which is in obvious revolt against these 'modern' trends."[64] Now it isn't clear *why* the minority is in revolt against these modern trends; is it because of an ecological education, or because of experiences in "vital relation" to the land, or because of an appreciation for an earlier epoch in American history, or some other reason? What *is* clear is that this minority rebels against the way we reduce our ethical life to economic calculation. Here is the old Leopold, the social and political critic, shining through even in an essay that had taken him in a different direction.

It seems that the moments when Leopold is most critical of our moral traditions, and thus relies most heavily on hopes for science, are moments of deep frustration that are more the exception than the rule in his writings and character. This brings us to my second observation: ironically, these elements have become the primary components in the most influential contemporary interpretations of Leopold's "land ethic." Despite their deep and significant differences, for example, J. Baird Callicott and Bryan Norton (perhaps the two most distinguished of these contemporary interpreters) agree that Leopold is primarily a Darwinian ethicist, building a new ethical perspective out of his scientific understanding of nature.[65] This view is also held by thinkers as otherwise different as Lewis Hinchman and Larry Arnhart.[66] If I am right, however, in my claim that "The Land Ethic" is the exception rather than the rule in Leopold's thought, and that the project of *A Sand County Almanac* is much more representative of his general sensibility and concerns, then contemporary readings of Leopold have failed to capture the primary purpose of his writings: the attack on utilitarian economic thinking and behavior in the name of an older set of political and ethical values. Leopold's conservation aims at more than teaching us to respect and live in harmony with nature. It aims for this in the name of restoring and reinvigorating American political culture by appealing to a cultural inheritance deeply at odds with contemporary social and political life. As Leopold tells us in the foreword to *A Sand County Almanac*, it is at the sand farm that he and his family "try to rebuild, with shovel and axe, what we are losing elsewhere. It is here that we seek—and still find— our meat from God."[67] His foremost aim is to inspire other citizens, as he himself has been inspired, to resist "too much modernity."[68] When he suggests that such a "shift in values" can be best achieved by "reappraising things unnatural, tame, and confined in terms of things natural, wild, and free,"[69] he is indicating that conservation is less an end in itself than a means to his broader political project.[70]

And this brings us to my third observation: that Leopold defends a conception of the good, and thus his social and political criticism, by appealing to nature. As mentioned above, this is a time-honored tradition in political theory and not at all surprising in and of itself. But there are two different strategies that Leopold takes when making this appeal. In *A Sand County Almanac* nature is used as a cultural reference, a "cultural inheritance" that he hopes will resonate with his readers. The shack on the sand farm is a reminder to him and his readers of a different moment in American history, a time prior to the triumph of uncontrolled utilitarianism and gadgetry. The power of Leopold's experience of the sand farm, and the images he presents from this experience, grow from the possibility of a collective recognition of the historical moments it represents.[71] In "The Land Ethic," in contrast, Darwinian nature has become the only (or at least primary) hope for the generation of moral commitments. The education that Leopold provides is no longer a cultural education but an ecological one. Rather than appealing to "split-rail Americanism," he appeals to the "biotic mechanism" that modern ecology has taught us to imagine. Rather than appealing to the historical American community and its best potential, the land "community" replaces the political community as the fundamental moral referent.

I've already suggested that this second approach is one Leopold seems to have turned to only in moments of great frustration, and that even then he appears to not be fully comfortable with it. It is also clear, however, that this turn is itself the result of Leopold's occasional loss of confidence in the success of the first approach. Neither strategy offers Leopold a knockdown defense of his political agenda. On the one hand, he knows that "split-rail Americanism" produced individuals whose very characters may destroy the environment that produces them: "It must be admitted that the split-rail flavor and free-for-all exploitation are historically associated."[72] The success of the pioneer spirit can transform the environment that generates such a spirit in the first place. On the other hand, modern science is clearly as much a player in the march of "progress" as anything else: "Professors serve science and science serves progress. It serves progress so well that many of the more intricate instruments are stepped upon and broken in the rush to spread progress to all backward lands."[73] Leopold is in a very tough position, and one can see him throwing up his hands in despair of the whole project in "Wilderness" when he writes, "I suppose some will wish to debate whether it is important to keep these primitive arts [of wilderness travel] alive. I shall not debate it. Either you know it in your bones, or you are very, very old."[74]

Before we also throw up our hands in despair, however, it should be noted that there is reason to think that the historical strategy is more promising both conceptually and strategically than the Darwinian strategy Leopold is most famously praised for. Late in his life, Leopold observed that our modern science was "false" for failing to capture aesthetic values. To the degree that science fails in this task, it simply reinforces the view that "the human relation to land is only economic."[75] The problem is to develop a science that speaks to the heart and our aesthetic sense, and not just to a cold, opportunistic, and calculating reason. "The ecological conscience, then, is an affair of the mind as well as the heart. It implies a capacity to study and learn, as well as to emote about the problems of conservation."[76] It is not at all obvious, however, that the heart is prepared to receive these aesthetic values by scientific theory and learning alone; it is more likely, one would think, that the heart be prepared by philosophy or religion. Indeed, to claim that the love of nature is a necessary and natural part of Darwinian evolution begs rather than answers the question. Leopold writes in "Goose Music" that the man who does not want to see, hunt, photograph, "or otherwise outwit birds or animals is hardly normal. He is supercivilized, and I for one do not know how to deal with him. Babes do not tremble when they are shown a golf ball, but I should not like to own a boy whose hair does not lift his hat when he sees his first deer."[77] This appeal to "normal instincts"[78] is clearly unpersuasive; boys' hair can lift their hats when they see their first bulldozer too, or even their first bouncing ball. And why is the "supercivilized" individual that so exasperates Leopold not the "natural" product of our evolution? Leopold himself admits that the love of wilderness and outdoor recreations are "primitive" and "atavistic."[79] If anything, the task of conservation seems to be to preserve activities and values that are not *useful* in the evolutionary sense at all— activities, resources, and values that are a part of a good life unconstrained by evolutionary or economic necessity.[80] Leopold's Darwinian rhetoric fails to solve the problem he has set for himself.

Which brings us back to Leopold's primary strategy, of appealing to concrete American experience as an inspirational alternative to "Boosterism" and the world of "Babbits." To promote an alternative tradition, and support the material conditions (i.e., wilderness) under which it might flourish, is a political project of uncertain future, since there is no guarantee that American citizens will show the wisdom of actually choosing it over current values and priorities. But this approach has the advantages of respecting democratic society by appealing directly to democratic choice, and assuming the burden of proof for persuading others that this choice represents the best in our political tradition and possibilities. The appeal to nature as a cultural inheritance, representing the highest American values and potentials, is not an appeal that is subject to the kind of proofs aspired to by Darwinian science. It has the practical advantage, however, of speaking to a real and widely recognized public good and aiming to persuade fellow citizens on the grounds of the character of these shared goods.

IV.

Moral appeals to nature by political theorists and critics have classically been built on teleological claims about the nature of the best human life (or lives).[81] This philosophical approach is not available to Leopold, who rejects both religion[82] and any philosophical system committed to such a human teleology.[83] This leaves him with only the two options for promoting his political project that I have discussed above: claims about the science of nature, or an appeal to our cultural understandings and experience of nature. I am obviously more sympathetic to the second strategy, as I think it is more conceptually defensible *and* democratically respectful. As Avner de-Shalit writes, "If one suggests that the public seeks guidance for its politics in nature, one might see many people adopting Social Darwinian and other anti-liberal and a-democratic positions."[84] Darwinism, that is, has no inevitable or single moral consequence, no unambiguous telos, and thus fails to settle our moral problems and concerns.[85] To attempt to determine the political good from such a science is to fool ourselves about what science can tell us. It also fails to build a persuasive political argument on grounds that can appeal broadly throughout democratic society, to shared traditions and discourses and experiences, which are the stuff of democratic debate. Such are true debates, insofar as there is no final truth to discover that can put an end to the conversation once and for all. The attractiveness for environmental ethics of building on science rather than moral and political traditions grows out of the seduction of scientific certainty, a certainty that would put an end to the very need for democratic politics.

Leopold concludes one essay by arguing that the "Ability to see the cultural value of wilderness boils down, in the last analysis, to a question of intellectual humility."[86] The power of Leopold's work is a result of the eloquence with which he speaks of and promotes a humility at odds with the egocentrism of modern day *Homo economicus*. The political problem Leopold addresses is the problem of the arrogance of human wants, the self-preoccupied hostility toward any boundaries and limitations that drives market society. This not only threatens the health of our environment; it threatens the quality of our human experience even if we are able to contend with the environmental consequences of our behavior. Leopold reminds us that a purely artificial environment, even if it were entirely successful from the perspective of economic utility, would be a kind of inhuman hell. While economic comforts and pleasures might be multiplied and satisfied infinitely, such a world would lose much beauty, mystery, excitement, satisfaction, and the development of a deep, human sensibility and character. Such a sensibility and character requires the discipline of humility, the recognition of things greater than our own wants and desires. We are drawn to Leopold because he speaks so beautifully and sensitively to this need.[87]

Perhaps religion or a morality built upon a classical teleology would be best poised to promote the kind of intellectual humility Leopold seeks.[88] For better or worse, these are not feasible options in modern political debate, which leaves us with the types of options presented in Leopold's writings. The very popularity of readings of Leopold that have drawn on the Darwinian arguments from "The Land Ethic" suggests the degree to which modern environmentalism hopes for the science of ecology to put an end to the need for political argument and persuasion. The broader political spirit of *A Sand County Almanac*, however, leads us to a more modest, and potentially more widely acceptable, environmentalism, built upon the invocation of shared democratic experience and traditions.[89]

Notes

1. Aldo Leopold, *A Sand County Almanac* (New York: Ballantine, 1988), 4.
2. Ibid.
3. Ibid., 5.

4. Ibid.

5. Ibid.

6. Ibid., 6.

7. Ibid., 8.

8. Ibid., 10.

9. Ibid., 36.

10. Ibid., 38.

11. Ibid., 69.

12. Ibid., 56.

13. Ibid., 42.

14. Ibid., 52.

15. Ibid., 96.

16. Ibid., 72.

17. Ibid.

18. Ibid., 76.

19. Ibid., 73.

20. Ibid., 36.

21. Ibid., 62.

22. Ibid., 22.

23. Ibid., 54.

24. Ibid., 73.

25. Ibid., 78.

26. Ibid., 76.

27. Ibid., xvii.

28. Ibid., xix.

29. See, for example, his comments about our enslavement to a "ruthless utilitarianism" in "The Farmer as a Conservationist," Aldo Leopold, *The River of the Mother of God and Other Essays* (Madison: University of Wisconsin Press, 1991), 259.

30. See his discussion of the need for wilderness sport as a form of adventure in "The River of the Mother of God," in Aldo Leopold, *The River of the Mother of God and Other Essays* (Madison: University of Wisconsin Press, 1991), 124–25.

31. One of the values of conservation, Leopold writes in 1934, is to provide the "opportunity of personal contact with natural beauty." Leopold, "River of the Mother of God," 193.

32. See his beautiful discussion of the need for "Unknown Places in Our National Life," in "River of the Mother of God," 125.

33. Leopold, "Some Fundamentals of Conservation in the Southwest," in Aldo Leopold, *The River of Mother of God and Other Essays* (Madison: University of Wisconsin Press, 1991), 94.

34. Leopold, "Wisconsin," in Aldo Leopold, *A Sand County Almanac* (New York: Ballantine, 1988), 109.

35. See Leopold, "A Criticism of the Booster Spirit," in Aldo Leopold, *The River of Mother of God and Other Essays* (Madison: University of Wisconsin Press, 1991), 98–105; Leopold, "Wisconsin," 119.

36. Leopold, "Conserving the Covered Wagon," in Aldo Leopold, *The River of Mother of God and Other Essays* (Madison: University of Wisconsin Press, 1991), 131.

37. Leopold, "River of the Mother of God," 125.

38. See Philip Cafaro, "Thoreau, Leopold, and Carson: Toward an Environmental Virtue Ethics," *Environmental Ethics* 23 (spring 2001): 3–17, for a discussion of Leopold's (and Thoreau's and Carson's) conception of the good life.

39. Aldo Leopold, *For the Health of the Land: Previously Unpublished Essays and Other Writings*, ed. J. Baird Callicott and Eric T. Freyfogle (Washington, D.C.: Island Press, 1999), 148.

40. Leopold, "The Conservation Ethic," in Aldo Leopold, *The River of Mother of God and Other Essays* (Madison: University of Wisconsin Press, 1991), 188.

41. Leopold, "Some Fundamentals of Conservation in the Southwest," 94.

42. Leopold, *Sand County*, 219.

43. Leopold, "Wilderness as a Form of Land Use," in Aldo Leopold, *The River of Mother of God and Other Essays* (Madison: University of Wisconsin Press, 1991), 137.

44. See Leopold, "Wildlife in American Culture," in Aldo Leopold, *A Sand County Almanac* (New York: Ballantine, 1988), 216.

45. Susan L. Flader, *Thinking like a Mountain* (Columbia: University of Missouri Press, 1974), 194.

46. Leopold, "Planning for Wildlife," in Aldo Leopold, *For the Health of the Land: Previously Unpublished Essays and Other Writings*, ed. J. Baird Callicott and Eric T. Freyfogle (Washington, D.C.: Island Press, 1999), 198.

47. Leopold, *Sand County*, 208.

48. Leopold, "Wild Lifers vs. Game Farmers: A Plea for Democracy in Sport," in Aldo Leopold, *The River of Mother of God and Other Essays* (Madison: University of Wisconsin Press, 1991), 63.

49. Leopold, "Planning for Wildlife," in Aldo Leopold, *For the Health of the Land: Previously Unpublished Essays and Other Writings*, ed. J. Baird Callicott and Eric T. Freyfogle (Washington, D.C.: Island Press, 1999), 197.

50. Leopold, "Wilderness," in Aldo Leopold, *A Sand County Almanac* (New York: Ballantine, 1988), 265.

51. "The Farmer as a Conservationist," 263.

52. "I assume that it is not necessary to argue that the development of any undemocratic system in this country is to be avoided at all costs." Leopold, "Wild Lifers vs. Game Farmers," 63.

53. Leopold, "Natural History," in Aldo Leopold, *A Sand County Almanac* (New York: Ballantine, 1988), 210.

54. Leopold, "Wildlife in American Culture," 216.

55. Curt Meine, *Aldo Leopold: His Life and Work* (Madison: University of Wisconsin Press, 1988), 167.

56. Leopold, "The Land Ethic," in Aldo Leopold, *A Sand County Almanac* (New York: Ballantine, 1988), 246.

57. Ibid., 240.

58. Ibid., 238.

59. Ibid., 251.

60. Ibid., 262–63.

61. Leopold, "The Arboretum and the University," in Aldo Leopold, *The River of Mother of God and Other Essays* (Madison: University of Wisconsin Press, 1991), 209.

62. Leopold, "Land Pathology," in Aldo Leopold, *The River of Mother of God and Other Essays* (Madison: University of Wisconsin Press, 1991), 215.

63. Leopold, *Sand County*, 261–62.

64. Ibid., 262.

65. See J. Baird Callicott, *In Defense of the Land Ethic* (New York: SUNY Press, 1989) and *Beyond the Land Ethic* (New York: SUNY Press, 1999); Bryan G. Norton, "Conservation and Preservation: A Conceptual Rehabilitation," *Environmental Ethics* 9 (1986): 195–220, "The Constancy of Leopold's Land Ethic," *Conservation Biology* 2 (March 1988): 93–102, and "Epistemology and Environmental Values," *The Monist* 75 (1992): 208–26.

66. See Lewis P. Hinchman, "Aldo Leopold's Hermeneutic of Nature," *Review of Politics* (spring 1995): 225–49; and Larry Arnhart, "Aldo Leopold's Human Ecology," in *Conservation Reconsidered*, ed. Charles Rubin (Lanham, Md.: Rowman & Littlefield, 2000), 103–32.

67. *Sand County*, xviii.

68. Ibid.

69. Ibid., xix.

70. "Here I want . . . to reclaim Aldo Leopold from the theorists. Bryan Norton reminds us, for example, that Leopold's widely cited appeal to the 'integrity, stability, and beauty of the biotic community' occurs in the midst of a discussion of purely economic constructions of the land. It is best read, Norton says, as a kind of counterbalance and challenge to the excesses of pure commercialism, rather than as a criterion for moral action all by itself." Anthony Weston, "Before Environmental Ethics," in *Environmental Pragmatism*, ed. Andrew Light and Eric Katz (New York: Routledge, 1996), 150.

71. In one of the best essays written about Leopold, John Tallmadge argues that "*A Sand County Almanac* is a subversive book. It questions the deepest values of our civilization and challenges us personally on every page. In doing so, it allies itself more closely with Thoreau's method of social criticism based on the standard of nature." John Tallmadge, "Anatomy of a Classic," in *Companion to A Sand County Almanac*, ed. J. Baird Callicott (Madison: University of Wisconsin Press, 1987), 115.

72. Leopold, "Wildlife in American Culture," 218.

73. Leopold, "Chihuahua and Sonora," in Aldo Leopold, *A Sand County Almanac* (New York: Ballantine, 1988), 162.

74. Ibid., 271.

75. Leopold, "Wherefore Wildlife Ecology," in Aldo Leopold, *The River of Mother of God and Other Essays* (Madison: University of Wisconsin Press, 1991), 337.

76. "The Ecological Conscience," in Aldo Leopold, *The River of Mother of God and Other Essays* (Madison: University of Wisconsin Press, 1991), 343.

77. Leopold, *Sand County*, 227.

78. Ibid.

79. Leopold, "Wildlife in American Culture," 216.

80. Remember that Leopold has "no hope for conservation born of fear." "The Farmer as Conservationist," 258. His strongest claims for conservation were claims about proper and ethical ways of living, not about necessity and survival.

81. See Alasdair MacIntyre, *After Virtue* (Notre Dame, Ind.: University of Notre Dame Press, 1984).

82. Leopold's daughter reports that in his final illness, she asked him about his religious views. "He replied that he believed there was a mystical supreme power that guided the Universe. . . . But to him this power was not a personalized God. It was more akin to the laws of nature. He thought organized religion was all right for many people, but he did not partake of it himself, having left that behind a long time ago." See Meine, *Aldo Leopold*, 506. Meine comments earlier that "Aldo remained absolutely mum on the subject of religion." Ibid., 376.

83. Leopold's pragmatism has been well investigated by Bryan Norton in the articles referred to in note 65 above. A number of times in his written work, Leopold refers to the pragmatic axiom that "The truth is that which prevails in the long run." See, for example, Leopold, "The Wilderness and Its Place in Forest Recreational Policy," in Aldo Leopold, *The River of Mother of God and Other Essays* (Madison: University of Wisconsin Press, 1991), 79.

84. Avner de-Shalit, *The Environment: Between Theory and Practice* (New York: Oxford University Press, 2000), 103.

85. When Roderick Nash claims that "Darwinism took the conceit out of man," he unwittingly illustrates this point. Although it is obviously true that such a deflation of conceit is a possible outcome of Darwinism, the history of Social Darwinism in the twentieth century would counsel prudence in claiming that this is the *only* possible consequence of Darwinism. Darwinism, in short, is necessarily and inevitably morally ambiguous. See Roderick Nash, "Aldo Leopold and the Limits of American Liberalism," in *Aldo Leopold: The Man and His Legacy*, ed. Thomas Tanner (Ankeny, Iowa: Soil Conservation Society of America, 1987), 58.

86. Leopold, "Wilderness," 279.

87. Lewis Hinchman is just one example of an interpreter who is drawn to this element of Leopold's work. He concludes his study of Leopold like this: "Nature, of course, cannot offer guidance in every moral choice we must make. But it does suggest criteria for making *some* of those choices, and it helps develop the sort of character that will enable us to make *all* of them in a spirit of self-restraint and humility." Hinchman, "Aldo Leopold's Hermeneutic of Nature," 249.

88. Alasdair MacIntyre argues that only such a teleology can allow for the development and cultivation of true human virtues. See MacIntyre, *After Virtue*.

89. De-Shalit writes, "I believe that, if environmental ethics is approached modestly, as opposed to pretentiously, if it does not claim to solve meta-ethical questions, if it is more accurate (e.g. acknowledging that intrinsic value can apply to individuals only), and if it does not seek to replace political theory, then it will be regarded as reasonable." De-Shalit, *The Environment*, 58.

Part III

ENVIRONMENTALISM AND THE BOUNDARIES OF DEMOCRATIC DISCOURSE

CHAPTER 10

Justice, Democracy, and Global Warming

Peter S. Wenz

In all probability, global temperatures are rising due to human activities, such as burning fossil fuels, reducing forests, and maintaining large livestock herds. These activities increase atmospheric concentrations of greenhouse gases, such as carbon dioxide and methane, that trap heat and cause Earth's atmosphere to warm.

The present chapter focuses on possible conflicts between democracy and justice, especially in the United States, related to this warming. In democracies, key government decision makers attain and retain their positions by competing successfully for votes in elections. Gaining and retaining voter support is key to political success. U.S. voters and their elected representatives seem to disfavor treaties and regulations designed to reduce the amount of greenhouse gas the United States is allowed to pass. A common view is that American voters tend to favor policies that improve their narrow economic interests. On this view, citizens resist the 1997 Kyoto Protocol requiring U.S. emissions to fall 7 percent below their 1990 levels in the years 2008–2012 because, it is feared, such requirements will stifle economic growth. Thus, at this time, American-style democracy seems to call for laissez-faire government policies that allow increased emissions, which rose 14 percent between 1990 and 1997, and continue to rise.[1]

Justice generally requires us to refrain from harming others without good cause. Focusing on issues of international justice, the present paper argues that justice requires the United States to curtail greenhouse gas emissions. Global warming is likely to gravely harm many poor people in the Third World who cannot protect themselves and who benefit least from industrial processes that generate the gases. The United States is the single greatest emitter of these gases. Justice requires that we curtail emissions to avoid further harm to innocent others. Yet, as we have seen, many doubt that American-style democracy can result in government policies that meet this demand of justice.

I argue that American interest-group democracy can approach, if not achieve, justice in this area. I argue also that the two main rivals to such democracy, decentralized bioregionalism and centralized authoritarianism, are less promising in this regard.

The Dangers of Global Warming

Global warming is dangerous to human beings. Sea levels rise as the world warms, threatening island nations, coastal agriculture, and coastal cities where millions of people live. Environmental journalist Grover Foley summarizes the work of scientists at the United Kingdom's Met (meteorological) Office:

> A one-meter rise in sea-level, easily on the cards, . . . would affect up to 5 million square kilometres, therefore three per cent of the total land area of the planet, including many of the world's major cities, such as New York, London, Bangkok. It would also affect as much as 30 per cent of the total cropland in the world.[2]

People living in poor countries would suffer most because they can least afford massive projects of coastal protection, and because any decrease in world food supply threatens them with starvation. Lester Brown, director of the Worldwatch Institute, writes, "Since the mid-twentieth century, grainland area per person has fallen in half, from 0.24 hectares to 0.12 hectares," and during the 1990s, grain yields per hectare began to level off. Third World populations are expected to increase in the next fifty years, and already, the World Health Organization reports, "6 million [children] worldwide . . . die each year from hunger and malnutrition."[3]

Global warming has not produced current food insecurity, but would likely aggravate it by reducing available cropland and moisture.

> According to the U.S. Geophysical Fluid Dynamics Laboratory, warmer, drier summers over the U.S. Great Plains, Western Europe, Northern Canada and Siberia because of a doubling of effective carbon dioxide concentrations from pre-industrial times, would lead to soil drying out by at least 20 percent during the crucial growing season.[4]

The resulting reduction of grain available on the world market would lead to prices increasing beyond the means of many poor people.

Rising global temperatures jeopardize human health. Environmental journalist Paul Kingsnorth summarizes a 1996 report of the London School of Hygiene and Tropical Medicine: "Many disease-carrying insects—most obviously the malarial mosquito—thrive in warm conditions; as the world warms, they will begin to find more places in which they can breed." Already, "two million people die from [malaria] every year." The Intergovernmental Panel on Climate Change (IPCC) "predicts that malaria will spread from affecting 45 percent of the [world's] population to affecting 60 per cent." It seems that this is happening now. "Malaria has already begun to affect the previously mosquito-free African highlands, and upland rural areas of Papua New Guinea," according to the IPCC's Second Assessment Report (1995). Increased ranges are expected for other dangerous vector-borne diseases.[5] Again, the world's poor will suffer most, as they have least access to health care.

Justice and Global Warming

Justice requires massive reductions in greenhouse gas emissions from the United States. A Chinese government official told a reporter for *The New York Times*: "Two hundred years after the Industrial Revolution the world economy has greatly advanced and the developed countries are the main beneficiary. About 80 percent of the world's pollution is caused by the developed countries and they should be responsible for those problems."[6] This is particularly true of the United States. "With only 4 percent of the world's population," environmental researcher Simon Retallack reports, "the U.S. is responsible for nearly a quarter of total greenhouse gas emissions."[7] Jane Holtz Kay, architecture critic for *The Nation*, highlights the role of automobiles. Americans "own half the cars, produce half the automobile's carbon dioxide emissions in the world, and manufacture one-quarter of the vehicles."[8]

It is a common moral principle that people should refrain from harming others without just cause. Many consider this principle intuitively obvious. Others ground it in the view that all human beings are of equal moral worth. Either way, this perspective justifies, for example, restrictions on cigarette smokers exposing unconsenting others to the harmful effects of secondhand smoke. Our energy habits foul the atmosphere in a different way, but also threaten unconsenting others with grave harm for the relatively trivial reasons of pleasure and convenience. The equal consideration of all human interests, a fundamental principle of justice, requires that we mend our ways.

I now consider several objections to this reasoning:

FIRST OBJECTION

One objection, noted by Henry Shue, is that people currently alive in the United States did not create the problem.[9] Fundamental decisions about industrialization and the use of fossil fuels in manufacture and transportation that have resulted in global warming were taken by previous generations. We have inherited a highly polluting country. It would be unfair, someone might claim, for current people to suffer economic dislocation to rectify poor decisions made in the past.

This objection is weak. Just as people who inherited the institution of slavery were unjust to resist its abolition, the current generation of Americans is unjust if it resists reducing greenhouse gases now that their harmful effects are known.

SECOND OBJECTION

A related objection is that immediate reductions of harmful emissions threaten average Americans with grave hardships, such as the loss of jobs. Manufacturing jobs in industries that emit CO_2 may be lost in efforts to reduce total U.S. emissions.

There are three replies to this objection. First, abolishing slavery did impose great hardships on slave owners, but was still morally required. Second, the United States is so much richer than nations harmed most by global warming that the United States on a strict CO_2 allowance deserves about as much sympathy as real estate magnate Donald Trump in 1990, in the hands of his creditors, "on an allowance (of $450,000 a month)."[10] In other words, if some Americans experience grave hardships, it is only because more affluent Americans have not shared resources adequately with them. Finally, as we shall see below, reduced emissions through the use of emission-efficient technologies can aid, rather than harm, the American economy.

THIRD OBJECTION

Another objection claims that poor countries, too, benefit from industrial processes that produce greenhouse gas emissions. At the very least, objectors maintain, the justice-based duty of the United States to reduce emissions, a duty predicated on harm to poor countries, is mitigated by benefits that industrialization brings to those countries.

Unfortunately, most people in the Third World do not enjoy such benefits. Typically, Third World elites benefit while life for most people gets worse. *New York Times* correspondent Thomas L. Friedman notes in *The Lexus and the Olive Tree*:

> According to the 1998 United Nations Human Development Report, in 1960 the 20 percent of the world's people who live in the richest countries had 30 times the income of the poorest 20 percent. By 1995 [they] had 82 times as much income. . . . Today the wealthiest one-fifth of the world's people consume 58 percent of total energy, while the poorest fifth consume less than 4 percent.[11]

One might think that even if industrialization increases the *relative* poverty of poor people, it alleviates their *absolute* poverty, thereby improving their quality of life. But this is mostly wishful thinking. Industrialization often contributes to the further material impoverishment of the already poor. Development economist David Korten discusses an example of Japan furthering industrialization in the Philippines by financing the Philippine Associated Smelting and Refining Corporation (PASAR):

> The plant occupies 400 acres of land expropriated by the Philippine government from local residents at give-away prices. Gas and wastewater emissions from the plant contain high concentrations of boron, arsenic, heavy metals, and sulfur compounds that have contaminated local water supplies, reduced fishing and rice yields, damaged the forests, and increased the occurrence of upper-respiratory diseases among local residents. Local people . . . are now largely dependent on the occasional part-time or contractual employment they are offered to do the plant's most dangerous jobs.[12]

In sum, the relatively healthful bases of a local, nonindustrial economy, fishing and rice, were undermined to make way for an industrial plant that benefits local elites and industrialized foreigners. This is typical, according to Korten:

> Rapid economic growth in low-income countries brings modern airports, television, express highways, and air-conditioned shopping malls . . . for the fortunate few. It rarely improves living conditions for the many. This kind

of growth requires gearing the economy toward exports to earn the foreign exchange to buy the things that wealthy people desire. Thus, the lands of the poor are appropriated for export crops. The former tillers of these lands find themselves subsisting in urban slums on starvation wages paid by sweatshops producing for export. Families are broken up, the social fabric is strained to the breaking point, and violence becomes endemic.[13]

Optimists may think that such horrid outcomes for the world's poor are only temporary, like the horrid outcomes of the Industrial Revolution in Charles Dickens's England. In time, optimists assume, industrialization will benefit almost everyone. Such thinking ignores environmental limits. Industrialization as we now know it cannot possibly yield First World benefits to most Third World people. Korten considers it "a physical impossibility . . . for the world to consume at levels even approximating those in North America, Europe, and Japan."[14]

FOURTH OBJECTION

The Kyoto Protocol has no provisions to inhibit Third World countries from increasing emissions, but it requires the United States to cut back. Some people argue that this puts American businesses and workers at an unfair disadvantage. The issue is not just hardships imposed on Americans, but hardship imposed unfairly. Consider the reaction of my colleague, Management Professor Joe Wilkins, to the Kyoto Protocol. He wrote in my newspaper's "Local Opinion" column:

> The economic impact on Illinois is crippling. Shoes, computers, automobiles—all can be manufactured to the same precise standards anywhere in the world. . . . It is important to understand that the United States is being asked to play by an entirely more restrictive set of rules than many other nations. While we would be required to reduce greenhouse gas emissions by 7 percent, China, Mexico, India and 126 other nations would not. . . . Estimates are that Illinois would lose as many as 180,000 jobs by the year 2010. Illinois hosts auto manufacturing plants [which] could very likely shift overseas, where industrial air standards would be much more liberal.[16]

Wilkin's claim of unfairness is illogical. He predicates his case on the belief, which I argue below is mistaken, that permission to emit greenhouse gases confers economic advantage in manufacturing. Otherwise, restrictions would not be a disadvantage. Given that belief, it is hard to see how the United States could be unfairly disadvantaged during the time period governed by the Kyoto Protocol (2008–2012). Americans are still expected, even with required reductions, to emit greenhouse gases at several to many times the per capita rate in China, India, Mexico, and other Third World countries that compete with us in manufacturing.

FIFTH OBJECTION

A final objection to the United States curtailing greenhouse gas emissions also relates to projected increases of emissions from the Third World. If poor countries were to increase emissions as projected, catastrophic global warming will result no matter what Americans do. The Worldwatch Institute's Christopher Flavin and Nicholas Lenssen point out that if Third World countries follow current plans and "raise per capita energy use in developing countries to even one fourth the current industrial-country level by 2025, this by itself would increase world energy use by 60 percent."[15] Justice does not require futile gestures, so it does not require the United States to curtail greenhouse gas emissions until there is a credible plan to avert enormous increases in emissions from Third World counties.

Strictly speaking, this consideration does not affect the justice of adhering to limits imposed by the Kyoto Protocol, because those limits apply only to the years 2008–2012, when poor countries will not yet emit enough to make our reductions futile. However, the more general point is a good one. *Eventually* poor countries will have to develop their economies in ways that do not imitate our heavy reliance on fossil fuels. This matter is addressed below.

In sum, the harm inflicted by the United States on unconsenting poor people around the world through high per capita emissions of greenhouse gases is unjust. The injustice is not lessened by the fact that high emissions result from using an industrial infrastructure created by previous generations. It is not lessened by any hardships Americans may experience while lowering emissions, because those hardships are not imposed unfairly. And it is not lessened by the benefits of industrialization to the world's poor. The issue now is whether American-style democracy can serve justice, or whether pork-barrel politics shackles Americans to the energy trough.

Democracy in (a Warming) America

In democracies major decision makers depend on voter approval, either directly or indirectly, to attain, and in most cases to retain, their posts. In the United States, perhaps more than in some other democracies, voters are believed to respond most reliably to economic (so-called bread and butter) issues, such as those affecting the supply of good jobs and affordable consumer items. Wealthy corporate interests can influence public (voter) opinion on these matters through the public relations industry.[17] They can influence candidate success also through contributions to political campaigns. Thus, American democracy tends to favor policies acceptable to wealthy corporations.

In July, 1996, the heads of more than one hundred major U.S. corporations, including Exxon, Occidental Petroleum, Chevron, Texaco, Union Pacific, Chrysler, Motorola, Ford, Caterpillar, Boeing, and Goodyear, presented the following perspective to President Clinton before global warming negotiations in Kyoto, Japan. They wrote

> The U.S. must take care to avoid commitments that will cost U.S. jobs, retard economic growth or damage U.S. competitiveness. . . . We urge you to ensure that the U.S. negotiating team recognizes that the unique needs of the U.S. economy are of the utmost priority and to adopt a negotiating position that protects U.S. interests.[18]

In 1997 Mobil Corporation ran an additional ad on the eve of negotiations:

> We are concerned that policy makers are not considering the implications
> of controlling CO_2 emissions. Studies have examined some of the emission-
> control plans tabled to date and concluded that they will impose painful
> burdens on developed economies, particularly if timetables are short and
> targets unrealistic. For Americans, such solutions mean jobs will disappear
> and lifestyles will be pinched as industrial infrastructure shrinks.
>
> The cost of limiting emissions could [add] . . . costs to consumers of 50
> cents to $1.50 per gallon of gasoline in today's dollars.[19]

Negative public reaction caused the Clinton administration to withdraw quickly its idea of combating global warming with a carbon tax amounting to fifty cents per gallon of gas.

Journalist Ross Gelbspan details some of the public relations activities of corporate interests opposed to changes required for major reductions in American greenhouse gas emissions. In 1992 and 1993 the National Coal Association "spent more than $700,000 on global climate efforts. Similarly, the American Automobile Manufacturers' Association in 1993 spent nearly $100,000 on 'global climate change representation.'"[20] More important, these associations and others formed the Global Climate Coalition that spent more than a million dollars in 1994 and 1995 to

> downplay the threat of climate change. The GCC projected it would spend
> nearly another million on the issue in 1996. . . . In 1993 alone, the Ameri-
> can Petroleum Institute (API), just one of the fifty-four industry members
> of the GCC, paid $1.8 million to the public relations firm of Burson-
> Marsteller—a firm credited by former Treasury Secretary Lloyd Bentsen
> with spearheading the defeat of a proposed tax on fossil fuels.[21]

In 1997 the fossil fuel lobby spent $13 million on TV ads opposing CO_2 limits.

And then there is the issue of hardships imposed on Americans. Even if these are consistent with justice, hardship is a hard sell outside of monasteries. It is easy to imagine voters worried about pocketbook issues hesitating to back the Protocol when it appears to threaten the country with financial decline. Little wonder, then, that the Clinton administration did not bring the Protocol before the U.S. Senate for ratification; it faced certain defeat. Before the Kyoto meeting, the Senate passed a resolution 95 to 0 against U.S. participation in any climate treaty.[22] Within months of taking office in 2001, President Bush renounced all U.S. participation in the Protocol.

The news gets worse. The Kyoto Protocol would require only a 7 percent reduction of U.S. greenhouse gas emissions from their 1990 level. However, this is not nearly enough to satisfy the demands of justice, which require reductions sufficient to protect poor countries from additional harm caused by our emissions. Michael Grubb writes in his analysis of the Kyoto Protocol

> Even if global emissions of carbon dioxide were stabilized at current levels,
> its atmospheric concentration would still continue to grow; stabilization of
> concentrations would require emissions ultimately to drop well below cur-
> rent levels. . . . Notably, global CO_2 emissions would have to be more than

halved from current levels . . . compared with projected doubling of global emissions over the next few decades in the absence of controls.[23]

Worse yet, Worldwatch Institute researchers Flavin and Lenssen write, "Third World energy use . . . is generally projected to double . . . in the next 15 years and expand sixfold by 2050." Over the next fifty years, they conclude, "To avoid the risk of potentially catastrophic climate shifts . . . the world needs to achieve a rate of carbon emissions per dollar of gross world product that is roughly one tenth the current level. This essentially means an end to the fossil-fuel-based energy economy as we know it."[24]

Exxon-Mobile Corporation objects to ending the fossil-fuel-based energy economy as we know it. So might Americans who love their cars. If the U.S. Senate resists the relatively mild Kyoto Protocol, and President Bush rejects it completely, is there any chance that American democracy will accept the much greater restrictions that justice demands? The prospects look grim.

Trading Schemes

American negotiators in Kyoto were aware of the difficulty of gaining popular and congressional support for policies that require even mild reductions of greenhouse gases emitted from the United States. Recognizing that the issue is really global, not national, they advocated various ways within the Kyoto framework to allow countries to trade emission permits. The United States could potentially meet its targets of reduced emissions not by reducing emissions, but by paying people in some other country either to reduce their emissions, or to increase their CO_2 sinks, such as by expanding forest reserves. The effects on climate are the same whether required changes take place in the United States or elsewhere, and whether greenhouse gases are kept from the atmosphere by curtailing emissions, or by expanding the earth's capacity to absorb them.

For example, before the Kyoto Protocol was drafted, three Midwestern utilities engaged in a project in the Czech Republic city of Decin. According to Wisconsin Energy Company Chief Executive Officer (CEO) Richard Abdoo, the project

> replaced inefficient, highly polluting coal-fired district heating boilers with new, state-of-the-art, natural gas-fired internal combustion engines. In addition to emissions reductions and improvement of local air quality, this technology produces both electrical power and warm water, through cogeneration, for building heat and has improved the efficiency of the warm water distribution system.[25]

Patrick Mulchay, chief operating officer (COO) of Northern Indiana Public Service Company (NIPSCO), also part of the Decin project, cites the cost advantages of reducing CO_2 emissions this way:

> Assuming a twenty-year life, the cost to NIPSCO of carbon dioxide emissions reductions at the [new] plant is approximately $0.20 per ton. In com-

parison, NIPSCO's rural tree plantings sequester carbon dioxide at a cost of $58.50 per ton, and biomass cofiring (assuming a fuel cost of $1.20 per ton) would offset carbon dioxide emissions at a cost of $1.70 per ton.[26]

So what's not to like?

Costs of creating carbon sinks are generally lower in many Third World countries than in the industrial north. The price of land is cheaper, and the climate often favors rapid growth. Thus, the Wisconsin Energy Company is reducing atmospheric CO_2 through its "Rio Bravo Carbon Sequestration Pilot Project, in Belize, [which] seeks an optimal balance between carbon sequestration, forest yield, and environmental protection while providing sustainable development opportunities for the local community."[27]

The American public and their political representatives may welcome ventures like these. If the United States and its corporations can reach emission reduction targets this way, there appears to be no conflict between American democracy and justice.

Unfortunately, this appearance is largely deceptive. There is nothing wrong with emission permit trading among developed countries, such as Japan, the United States, and the European Union. Such trading may reduce emissions at the least cost, which is good. However, the two examples above concern, in the case of the Czech Republic, what is called an "economy in transition" (EIT), and, in the case of Belize, a Third World country. Problems attend emission trading with countries of both sorts.

Some background is needed to see the problems of trading with EITs. The Kyoto Protocol sets emission limits for industrial countries (which the Protocol calls "Annex I"), but not for developing countries. EITs are Annex I countries with emissions limits. The limits are a percentage of what the countries emitted in 1990. Since 1990, however, the former Soviet bloc nations, here called EITs because their economies are in transition toward greater market orientation, have experienced great economic losses. Production is way down, especially in Russia. So their emissions of greenhouse gases are way down. They have emission permits that they cannot use except as assets to sell to countries such as the United States that are loath to reduce their own emissions. Grubb explains that this may be good. "Russia would be given an incentive to restructure its staggeringly inefficient and polluting economy in more efficient and sustainable ways, so as to enhance the allowances it could sell."[28]

But then, again, it may be bad. "The EU [European Union] concern [was] that emissions trading would undermine any success in imposing more stringent U.S. emission targets. . . . The United States might not even have to take significant action elsewhere. . . . it might simply buy a surplus of what the EU termed 'hot air' from Russia."[29] In other words, trading permits with EITs could enable Americans to increase CO_2 emissions through purchase of rights to emit that are currently allocated to, but not used by, EITs. Since the EITs currently are not emitting these gases, when the United States buys and then uses the rights to these emissions, total emissions increase. This may please American voters, but creative accounting does not combat global warming.

The second example of pollution trading given above concerns Belize. As noted already, 129 developing countries are not subject to emission limits, according to the

Kyoto Protocol; Belize is one of these. Projects designed to curtail greenhouse gas emissions or enhance greenhouse gas sinks in these countries are generally called projects of "joint implementation" (JI). JI can involve payments from a rich country to a poor one to save a rain forest, for example. The payment boosts the host country's economy and the money can be used to develop the forest as a tourist attraction, which many would consider sustainable economic development.

However, there are problems of justice here. Grubb notes that at the Kyoto negotiation:

> Perhaps the most fundamental and principled criticism of JI was that it could allow developed countries—those with the highest emissions and an acknowledged responsibility to lead—to achieve their emission targets without taking adequate action at home. JI was seen as enabling developed countries to escape their prime responsibility to put their own house in order.[30]

This escape from responsibility is unjust. If all human beings have an equal right to use Earth's ability to absorb CO_2 then justice requires that we move toward equalizing per capita emissions from people around the world.

Another potential injustice is that JI projects may "focus on and 'use up' the cheapest reduction options in developing countries, so that if and when developing countries came to adopt emission commitments, they would only have more expensive options left."[31]

Additionally, many JI projects, such as those that protect forests or develop hydro dams for electricity, consume large tracts of land in poor countries. Populations are increasing in many of these countries and arable land is scarce. Thus, many JI projects may deprive poor people in Third World countries of the land they need to feed themselves. This explains a heated exchange at a meeting in the early 1990s that Grubb recounts. An American economist

> expounded the virtues of JI and explained how much cheaper it could be to absorb CO_2 in Africa than to limit emissions in the United States. Shaking with anger, an African present rose and asked "why should African governments let their land be used as a toilet for absorbing emissions from Americans' second cars?"[32]

The answer is cost. It is cheaper this way.

The issue of cost raises the most fundamental objection to JI based on matters of justice. It is economically advantageous for Americans, through JI, to purchase rights to use land that poor people in the Third World need for bare survival, because by economic calculations, the monetary worth of a human life is less in the Third World than in the United States. Indeed, Grubb reports, "Ambassador Estrada echoed common fears about the supposed economic efficiency of [JI] when he remarked after Kyoto that 'of course everything is cheaper in developing countries—including life.'"[33] Why is this?

Economists claim that "the observed value of statistical life does unquestionably differ enormously between countries: it would . . . be absurd for India to try to put the same resources into modern medical services as the United States, when its people suffer many more basic threats to life and health." To this reasoning the Indian Environment Minister, Kamal Nath, responded as a Kantian. "We unequivocally reject the theory that the monetary value of people's lives around the world is different because the value imputed should be proportional to the disparate income levels of the potential victims. . . . It is impossible for us to accept that which is not ethically justifiable."[34]

In sum, JI highlights, but offers no solution to, problems of justice regarding global warming. First, there is the injustice of some people creating grave problems for innocent others. Second, JI addresses this injustice with an accounting system that places more value on some lives than on others, contravening the principle of equal respect for all human beings. Third, JI would allow those who have created the problem of global warming to address that problem without major lifestyle changes.

Many in the Third World believe that the ultimate goal of efforts to ameliorate global warming must be what they call "contraction and convergence." Rich countries must reduce their emissions of greenhouse gases (contraction) while poorer countries increase emissions in the process of industrialization. The eventual result will be equal per capita emissions around the world (convergence). This is the only just solution if all human beings are of equal worth and have equal rights to Earth's atmosphere.

Technological Possibilities

We saw earlier that many industry leaders object to CO_2 limits because, they believe, growing economies must use increasing amounts of fossil fuel. However, they are wrong. Currently available technology allows the United States to reduce greenhouse gas emissions while the economy grows. History suggests, in fact, that industries are often wrong about these matters. They tend to exaggerate problems associated with changes needed for environmental protection. For example, Flavin and Lenssen point out, "in the past the auto industry . . . claimed that catalytic converters and airbags—now standard equipment—would be impossibly expensive."[35]

Jonathan Lash, president of the World Resources Institute, gives another example. In the 1980s "industry could not imagine giving up chlorofluorocarbons (CFCs), the chemicals that scientists discovered were depleting the earth's protective ozone layer. Firms warned that adopting substitutes would be technically impossible and disastrous for the economy." Then, however,

> Manufacturers of large building air conditioning systems, like the Trane Company, introduced alternative systems that were more than 20 percent more energy efficient than 1990 CFC-based models. Such technology advances increased sales and saved building owners money. Electronics manufacturers, such as Nortel, redesigned production processes to eliminate the need for CFC solvents, saving millions of dollars along the way.[36]

The control of acid rain during the Clinton administration was similar. Grubb reports, "major emission reductions were implemented at far lower cost than originally predicted."[37] Political scientist Andrew Hoffman quotes a 1997 *New York Times* editorial by Bob Herbert: "Industry groups . . . lack credibility. They *always* claim that taking steps to improve air quality will lead to economic catastrophe."[38]

Actually, Flavin and Lenssen point out, energy efficiency saves money and improves the economy:

> The Ford Foundation projected in 1973 that the country would use 140 exajoules of energy in 1993, and [conservationist Amory] Lovins said that the figure would be 100, but the actual figure turned out to be 91. During those 20 years, energy use rose only 15 percent while the economy as a whole expanded 57 percent.[39]

The U.S. auto industry, spurred by government mandates, was part of this success. "After decades of stagnant fuel economy, average new-car efficiency doubled from 14 miles per gallon in 1974 to 28 in 1985."[40] This makes Flavin and Lenssen optimistic about "new car designs [that] may be three to five times as efficient as today's, and reduce emissions . . . of carbon dioxide by 75–90 percent."[41] More generally, "In North America, Europe, and Japan, the best overall measure of energy productivity—the amount of GNP produced per unit of energy used—has risen by 40–45 percent since the early seventies."[42]

These savings only scratch the surface. Enormous energy savings are possible in the production of electricity from fossil fuels, writes Thomas Casten, cofounder, president, and CEO of Trigen Energy Corporation. "Today's best turbines convert as much as 38 percent of the energy in the fuel to electricity. . . . The remaining 62 percent of the fuel energy remains as heat, which is usually dumped into a nearby river or lake, or is vented into the atmosphere."[43] This heat energy need not be wasted, however:

> Instead of one large electric-only plant, a series of smaller "local" plants [can be] built near thermal users—factories, universities, medical centers, and city centers. The same 100 units of fuel now produce three products: heat, cooling, and electricity. Up to 90 percent of the energy in the fuel can be converted to useful energy in these trigeneration plants and waste can be reduced to 10 percent.[44]

Currently, only 9 percent of America's electricity is produced in this way, whereas 60 percent is produced in ways that waste over 60 percent of the fuel's energy.

Saving energy is cost effective. Casten notes that "most of Europe has long had policies to encourage energy efficiency. . . . Europeans use far less energy. Yet, they do not seem to be at an economic disadvantage to the rest of the world."[45]

Amory Lovins claims that much energy saving occurs when engineers question old assumptions and rules of thumb. Lovins gives the example of

> a Dutch engineer designing a pumping system for a carpet factory in Shanghai. He adopted a practice . . . imported from Singapore of using big pipes and small pumps instead of small pipes and big pumps and of laying out the pipes first and then the equipment. This is not rocket science, but it saved 92 percent of pumping energy, cost a lot less to build, and worked better in all other respects.[46]

Lovins argues also that energy saving would improve with more realistic and consistent methods of evaluating capital expenditures. Most companies expect "energy-saving engineers to meet about a two-year payback horizon. . . . That's demanding a 64 percent real return, which is an awful lot more than you pay for capital. This means you're misallocating capital. You should be buying a lot more efficiency."[47]

Transportation is another area where Americans can improve efficiency, reduce greenhouse gas emissions, and save money (and human lives). About one-third of U.S. fossil fuel consumption occurs in the transportation sector, most of it for individual transportation in cars and light trucks. About 43,000 people die in crashes each year in the United States, reports Jane Holtz Kay.[48] (The unsentimental may translate this into billions of dollars of lost wages, lost tax revenues, and increased life insurance premiums.) Millions are injured in auto accidents (with concomitant lost wages and increased health insurance premiums). Auto exhausts foul the air. Kay claims that "the car's airborne toxins . . . are . . . implicated in some 120,000 premature deaths" per year.[49]

It would be wrong to think that Americans simply love their cars so much that they are willing to foot the bill as consumers. Automotive transport receives much more government subsidy than rail. This makes car travel seem cheaper and more efficient than it really is. Kay quotes Elmer Johnson's report for the Urban Transportation Project. "The suburban commuter pays only 25 percent of the costs of travel to the central district by car." Kay adds: "Private industry's trucks . . . pay only 40 percent of their way."[50] How could this be? Kay explains:

> Things we rarely consider bear a dollar sign: from parking facilities to police protection, from land consumed in sprawl to registry operations, environmental damage to uncompensated accidents. . . . According to one estimate, exactions from U.S. cars and trucks carry three-quarters of a trillion dollars in hidden costs each year.[51]

Consider the loss of time from being stuck in traffic. "The costs of our 8 billion hours a year stuck in traffic range from $43 billion, according to the Federal Highway Administration, to $168 billion in lost productivity estimated by other economists."[52]

In sum, Americans could save time, money, and lives with better public transportation, especially light rail and interurban fast trains. This would help the country economically due to cost savings (why consider the efficiency of labor on the job but not the efficiency of getting labor to the job?), strengthen the country strategically (through less dependence on foreign oil), and reduce America's contribution to global warming. Flavin and Lenssen conclude, the United States "could continue to expand [economically] while reducing energy use by roughly 50 percent over the next 35 years."[53]

Some people may be skeptical that there is money to be made from technological innovations that improve energy efficiency. After all, such people reason, technological innovation to improve efficiency is common in the United States, especially in competitive contexts, such as the marketplace. It seems unlikely, therefore, that there really are available, but unused, technologies that can aid both the economy and the environment.

Such skeptics remind me of the joke about the economist and the $10 bill lying on the sidewalk. She won't bend over to pick it up because if it really were a $10 bill, she reasons, someone else would have picked it up already.

Human affairs are not so logical as the skeptic assumes. Sometimes the profit motive of entrenched interests frustrates, rather than fosters, efficiency in many areas. Communications Professor Everett Rogers gives this example in *Diffusion of Innovations*. About 1930, when prototypes of electric refrigerators were developed, a superior alternative was developed as well. This was "the gas refrigerator, in which the ammonia refrigerant is vaporized by heating with a gas flame, and dissolves in water, thus cooling the refrigerator box. The gas refrigerator has no moving parts, and hence is unlikely to break down, or to make any noise." The gas refrigerator did not succeed commercially, according to Rogers, simply because

> General Electric, General Motors, Kelvinator, and Westinghouse . . . decided that larger profits could be made from the electric refrigerator, and poured huge amounts of funding into . . . aggressive promotion. . . . Several companies who marketed the gas refrigerator could not compete with these larger opponents.[54]

Another example of corporate profits over efficiency is the promotion of bottle feeding in the Third World. Multinational corporations used "ads, carried mainly on radio and in newspapers, [that] portrayed bottle-feeding as essential to raising healthy babies; the infants depicted in the print ads are fat and happy." In reality, however,

> most Third World families cannot afford to buy sufficient amounts of powdered milk products, so they water down their baby's formula. They lack pure water, or the resources to boil polluted water, for preparing the powered milk formula. Often these poor families are unable to clean the bottles and other bottle-feeding equipment properly . . . [so] germ-ridden baby bottles become a lethal threat.[55]

In short, commercial interests promoted replacing an efficient with a dangerously inefficient method of feeding babies. International protests eventually convinced these companies that bad publicity in the First World would cost them so much that they owed it to their stockholders to cease harming Third World children.

In the light of such cases as these, is it any wonder that major automobile companies portray CO_2 reduction as unrealistic? These are the folks who maintained the economic unfeasibility of catalytic converters, airbags, and government-mandated increases in automotive fuel efficiency, all of which have since been implemented with success. Now they oppose public transportation, such as light rail within cities and fast trains between cities, pretending in the face of successes in Western Europe and Japan, that these more efficient modes of transportation will not work. The issue for car companies is really corporate profit. They resist investment uncertainties associated with diversification and new product lines.

The same concerns explain global warming denial among oil companies, coal companies, electric utilities, earthmoving companies, makers of concrete and other highway construction material, and so on. These are among the largest and richest corporations in the United States. It is the profit motive, not the entrepreneurial search for efficiency, that accounts for such companies creating the Global Climate Coalition to block government moves to mandate reduced CO_2 emissions. It accounts also for much of the energy policy released by the Bush administration in May 2001. The policy even states that automotive regulations should "increase efficiency without negatively impacting the U.S. automotive industry."[56]

In sum, the profit motive sometimes sparks innovations that improve efficiency, but it sometimes delays or blocks such innovations.

A second reason for failure to adopt helpful innovations is the human resistance to change. I know if I could place a five-year moratorium on changes from the computer services unit at my university, I would do so in a minute. The computers work fine now. Leave me alone. I don't want to learn anything new. Benjamin Franklin noted more than two hundred years ago that the metric system is superior to the English system of measurement, but we still do not use it. The keyboard I am using to enter this material into my computer is of the traditional QWERTY variety. A keyboard that is more efficient for this purpose was invented in 1932 by August Dvorak.[57] I don't want to learn to use it, do you? In all these years, neither profit motive nor competition has pushed companies to require their employees to learn and use the more efficient keyboard. The office efficiency of using the newer keyboard is one among many $10 bills just waiting to be picked up.

Opportunities in American Democracy

Overall, but not for companies that prefer obfuscation to innovation, the U.S. economy can thrive by developing and using energy-saving technologies that are *cost effective*. All other things being equal, the use of such technologies will improve U.S. competitiveness with the rest of the world, by lowering costs, and so will foster job growth and profit. What is more, *if they are cost effective*, other countries will want to adopt these technologies to remain competitive with us.[58] That is the meaning of "cost effective." Cost effectiveness produces a price advantage in competitive markets.

Many Third World countries, too poor to buy and deploy these technologies, may be tempted to develop economies based on fossil fuels. This could nullify our efforts to lessen global warming and lead eventually to increased misery for us as well as for them. We, too, stand to suffer from global warming, which is expected to damage American agriculture, for example. Under these conditions it is in the interest of the United States to subsidize the export of new energy-saving technologies, much as the government supported the export of the Green Revolution and nuclear energy. International loan agencies, such as the World Bank, would aid this effort as part of their mission to promote Third World development. The result would be enormously increased job opportunities in the United States as well as accelerated development in the Third World, all compatible with reduced greenhouse gas emissions. Energy savings in the United States would far exceeding Kyoto's requirements while our economy prospers, partly through competitive success and partly through government subsidies of technology exports.

But how can we get such programs started? Considerations of justice and economic prosperity suggest retooling the economy for energy efficiency, but most people resist. American-style democracy seems stuck in the status quo.

The traditional answer is education. People must be made aware of the benefits, both economic and moral, of energy efficiency and reductions in greenhouse gas emissions. However, the power of recalcitrant special interests in public discourse makes the path of education difficult. Education is important, but hard to effect.

Alternatives to American-Style Democracy: Centralization and Decentralization

Considerations such as these inspire some thinkers to reject American-style democracy. Among these, some favor authoritarian central control over environmental decision making (centralists), whereas others favor democratic environmental decision making at the local or bioregional level (decentralists).

DECENTRALISM: BIOREGIONALISM AND LOCALISM

According to political scientist Lester Milbrath, the kernel of the bioregionalist idea is that "economic, social, and political life should be organized by regions that are defined by natural phenomena."[59] An example would be a watershed that includes a river and its valley. Today, rivers often form borders between two different political units, as the Delaware River separates Pennsylvania and New Jersey, and the Mississippi separates Illinois from Iowa and Missouri. Such political separation could hinder the cooperation necessary to manage the river system well if separate political units were allowed to make unilateral decisions. Missouri might regulate factory effluents in a way that would not damage the river appreciably if those were the only point sources of pollution. However, Missouri's Environmental Protection Agency may not consider sufficiently the volume of effluents from Illinois, Iowa, and other states. Upstream states might not consider adequately the water quality of downstream states, such as Mississippi and Louisiana. Including the entire Mississippi Valley in a single political unit would encourage more responsible environmental management, bioregionalists believe.

Theologian Thomas Berry writes, "The solution [to environmental degradation] is simply for us as humans to join the earth community as participating members, to foster the progress and prosperity of the bioregional communities to which we belong. . . . Such a bioregional community is self-propagating, self-nourishing, self-educating, self-governing, self-healing, and self-fulfilling."[60] People will act responsibly, on this view, only when they can appreciate the effects of their actions on the entire system. When political units are not based on ecosystems, people do not appreciate the effects of their actions on others and tend to act irresponsibly.

A related view stresses localism more than natural biological units because, as the case of the Mississippi River Valley illustrates, bioregions may be too vast for people truly to appreciate the effects of their actions on the whole system. David Orr writes, "The transfer of power, authority, resources, talent, and capital from the countryside, towns, neighborhoods, and communities to the city, corporations, and national government has undermined in varying degrees responsibility, care, thrift, and social cohesion—qualities essential to sustainability."[61] Orr believes that when political control is at the local, rather than state or national, level, people become more interested and informed. Interested and informed citizens empowered to chart their own environmental futures are likely to choose sustainable paths.

As a psychological generalization, localism makes sense. However, political scientist Daniel Press points out

> Orr jumps from civic virtue and participation to sustainability and does not fill the gap with testable propositions. . . . Does social cohesion change a community's long-term discount rate, thereby encouraging it to value the future more? Is self-reliance somehow linked to greater participation and consensus building in natural resource management?[62]

Another problem is that the trend in the world today is toward more globalization. Milbrath writes concerning bioregionalism:

> Economies interpenetrate so inexorably that it would require the most draconian measures to force economic actors to think and act regionally. (My wife just purchased a bottle of California sherry because it was cheaper than New York State sherry; should she have been forced to buy the more expensive local product?)[63]

Finally, decentralization, whether of the bioregional or the local variety, is particularly unpromising where global warming is concerned because the problem is truly global and its solution requires global coordination and cooperation. People who identify only with their local area are likely to ignore the effects of their actions on climate change, resulting in the very problems of justice confronted here. Bioregionalism is unpromising because the region of global warming is the entire earth, so any localizing features distinctive of bioregionalism disappear.

AUTHORITARIANISM

Robert Heilbroner articulates the other major alternative to American-style democracy, authoritarian centralization. Heilbroner questions the ability of democracies to foster the changes needed during times of environmental deterioration. He writes

> The passage through the gauntlet ahead may be possible only under governments capable of rallying obedience far more effectively than would be possible in a democratic setting. If the issue for mankind is survival, such governments may be unavoidable, even necessary.[64]

Consider in this context what seem to be the most promising approaches to problems associated with global warming. Technologies already exist to combat global warming effectively. In addition to ones mentioned already, we know how to use sunlight to make electricity through photovoltaics. Such electricity can be used to isolate hydrogen from oxygen. The hydrogen so isolated can be transported with little waste of energy and then turned back into electricity in fuel cells wherever electricity is needed. When the dollar value of pollution avoided is considered, such a system not only has less environmental impact than burning fossil fuels, but is more cost effective as well.[65] This system would end the fossil-fuel economy as we know it, which, as we have seen, is what combating global warming requires.

Today's electric utility companies are not enthusiastic about this technology because it requires an entire overhaul of the industry. Where there is great change, there is great uncertainty, and most companies would like to continue to pretend that the life of inefficient power plants will never end. So far, American-style democracy has enabled this delusion and forestalled change that should have begun in the 1980s. An authoritarian regime could simply require installation of a new electricity infrastructure.

Special interests and lobbying groups oppose less fundamental and visionary pollution-reducing changes as well, such as light rail within cities and fast trains between them. An authoritarian government would have the power and legitimacy to institute these changes and others related to global warming, regardless of opposition.

Nevertheless, the authoritarian alternative to American-style democracy is not promising. In the first place, authoritarian centralization in the United States requires a political revolution. Such a revolution does not seem likely in the near future, so this alternative does not address the problem of urgency. From the perspective of justice, we need to work effectively on the problem of global warming right away, because we are harming innocent people already.

The second problem with the authoritarian solution is that even if there were a revolution resulting in an authoritarian regime, the greens may not gain power. (Few football teams are called "the Greens." You have to wonder why.) The revolution may yield authoritarian leaders who are environmentally challenged. Like President Bush, their political family trees may be so old that they have turned to oil.

Third, centralizing regimes, whether of the left or right, had poor environmental records in the twentieth century. This may be due to problems endemic to authoritarian regimes. To the extent that they are truly authoritarian, leaders of such regimes can distance themselves from problems they create for others and are not vulnerable to negative public opinion or protest. People in charge who do not have to deal personally with environmental problems, and who can ignore others who care about or suffer from those problems, are unlikely consistently to act in environmentally responsible ways unless environmental protection was one of their major interests to begin with. And, again, it may not be.

Possible Futures

Can American-style democracy do better? I think it can. In this system, when government officials favor a policy, they often create a constituency to lobby for it. For example, the car culture and auto lobby in the United States thrive on government subsidies. The government started the nuclear power industry, which then became a powerful lobbying group. The government supports the Internet and other aspects of "the information superhighway," resulting in an e-commerce lobby. Similarly, with modest financial support, the government could create an energy-efficiency lobby.

Imagine a president of the United States who wants to address the problem of global warming. There are many things that could be done under the current political system, even with an initially hostile Congress. The president could use the threat of veto to gain federal subsidies for energy research (at many state universities), for the production of energy efficient appliances (ever-popular corporate welfare), for the purchase of such appliances (voters like tax rebates), and for installation of energy-efficient heating and cooling systems. The president could get more money for public transportation by appending its funding to bills supporting big oil and the automotive infrastructure. Also, through executive order, the president could make the federal government a major consumer of renewable energy.

Such actions build a business constituency that can eventually lobby, offer public service ads, and make campaign contributions to friendly candidates. Increasing numbers of people in Congress will have constituents whose jobs depend on energy efficiency or renewable energy. Green businesses will join others on the government run gravy train.

Of course, we do not currently have such a president, although Al Gore might have been one had he been elected. The May 2001 energy proposals of the Bush administration contain more help for fossil fuel industries and large corporations than for the environment.[66] But events could scare even Bush into environmentalism. For example, if global warming precipitates extreme weather events, New Orleans, or Miami, or Galveston could be flooded in some hurricane as never before. Like the discovery of the ozone hole over the Antarctic, such a flooding would change the climate of opinion much faster than greenhouse gases change the climate.

A diehard fossil-fuel lobby will probably still oppose change. But supportive corporations exist already, including some in the oil industry. Ross Gelbspan reports:

> In a speech to the World Energy Congress in late 1995, John S. Jennings, chairman of a Shell subsidiary, said, "we have to start to prepare for the orderly transition to new, renewable forms of energy at the lowest possible economic and environmental cost."
>
> In October 1996, the U.S. subsidiary of British Petroleum withdrew from the Global Climate Coalition [a powerful fossil fuel lobby]. In May 1997, John Browne, the CEO of BP, acknowledged the destructive potentials of climate change. . . . Shortly thereafter, BP announced a $1 billion investment in solar energy, while Shell announced it was investing $500 million in renewable energy technology. Shell also quit the GCC in 1998.[67]

At Kyoto the insurance industry aligned itself with a coalition of island nations that called for the most aggressive actions against global warming. Gelbspan writes, "In the 1980s insurance payouts for weather-related (nonearthquake) losses had averaged less than $2 billion a year. . . . But from 1990 to 1995 that number skyrocketed to over $10 billion a year." On the chance that extreme weather is due to global warming (insurance is all about odds) insurance companies want to fight global warming.

Changes in insurance practices will affect other industries that require insurance. For example, Employers Reinsurance Corporation, the fourth largest reinsurer in the United States, is extending the areas where it will not write insurance along storm-prone coasts. Whereas previously they did not write insurance for property within ten miles of the coast, in the future they may refuse to insure property up to fifty miles from the coast.[68]

Energy efficiency is gaining momentum. Here is a commentary dated December 11, 2000 in *Business Week* (yes, *Business Week*) by senior writer Paul Raeburn:

> The U.S. Energy Dept. released a report that concluded the nation can "significantly reduce inefficiencies, oil dependence, air pollution, and green-house gas emissions at essentially no net cost to the U.S. economy." The U.S. could cut its predicted energy consumption in 2020 by 20%. . . . That would cut the nation's energy bill by $124 billion. Carbon dioxide emissions would fall by one-third.[69]

Raeburn clearly endorses this approach. He takes this position, as do corporations cited above, not to further democracy or justice, but on traditional grounds of profitability.

Conclusion

American-style democracy can be used to move climate change policies toward what justice demands. In fact, all things considered, I believe that we not only can, but probably will, more than meet the requirements of the Kyoto Protocol, even if the U.S. Senate never ratifies it. Energy efficiency is generally profitable, and our economic and political systems are flexible enough to recognize and take advantage of this.

Projects of joint implementation will do some environmental good, by saving some forests, for example, but will often be unjust due to impositions on the poorest of the poor, who will be denied access to resources they need to live, or lead decent lives.

As companies making and using clean and renewable energy technologies gather wealth and political backing, resulting in subsidized exports, the world will move toward the goal of contraction and convergence. U.S. energy consumption per capita will decrease while it increases in the world's poorest countries, reducing total emissions worldwide, as well as the ratio of emissions per unit of gross world product. Those who think that justice requires merely movement in this direction will be satisfied, whereas those who insist on actually *reaching* worldwide convergence will probably be disappointed, at least in the foreseeable future.

Additionally, some people think that justice requires Americans to relinquish their lavish lifestyles. I believe that American-style democracy can result in policies that reduce greenhouse gas emissions, but not in policies that reduce material comforts.

Finally, the requirements of the Kyoto Protocol do not approach what justice demands, which is, over the next fifty years, a tenfold increase of gross world product for each input of fossil-fuel energy, in other words, an end to the fossil-fuel energy economy as we know it. As noted already, such a change became technologically feasible by the 1980s. Although I believe we will make this change eventually, I doubt we will do so *in time* to avert disasters for people in the Third World.

In sum, American-style democracy may not result in ratification of the Kyoto Protocol, but is likely to result in emission reductions greater than the Protocol requires, even if less than justice demands.

Notes

1. Thomas R. Casten, *Turning Off the Heat* (Amherst, N.Y.: Prometheus, 1998), 16.

2. Grover Foley, "The Threat of Rising Seas," *The Ecologist* 29, no. 2 (March/April 1999): 76–78, at 77.

3. Lester R. Brown, "Challenges of the New Century," in *State of the World 2000*, ed. Lester R. Brown (New York: Norton, 2000), 3–21, at 5 and 7–8.

4. Peter Bunyard, "A Hungrier World," *The Ecologist* 29, no. 2 (March/April 1999): 86–91, at 87.

5. Paul Kingsnorth, "Human Health on the Line," *The Ecologist* 29, no. 2 (March/April 1999): 92–94, at 93.

6. Quoted in Ross Gelbspan, *The Heat Is On: The Climate Crisis, the Cover-up, the Prescription*, updated ed. (Reading, Mass.: Perseus, 1998) 112–13.

7. Simon Retallack, "How U.S. Politics is Letting the World Down," *The Ecologist* 29, no. 2 (March/April 1999): 111–18, at 111.

8. Jane Holtz Kay, *Asphalt Nation: How the Automobile Took Over America and How We Can Take It Back* (Berkeley: University of California Press, 1997), 98.

9. Henry Shue, "Global Environment and International Inequity," *International Affairs* 75, no. 3 (July 1999): 531–45, at 536.

10. James Traub, "Golden Boy," *New York Review of Books* 47, no. 20 (December 21, 2000): 31–34, at 33.

11. Thomas L. Friedman, *The Lexus and the Olive Tree* (New York: Farrar, Straus and Giroux, 1999), 259.

12. David C. Korten, *When Corporations Rule the World* (West Hartford, Conn.: Kumarian Press, 1995), 31–32.

13. Ibid., 42.

14. Ibid., 35.

15. Christopher Flavin and Nicholas Lenssen, *Power Surge: Guide to the Coming Energy Revolution* (New York: Norton, 1994), 25.

16. Joe Wilkins, "Kyoto Accord Bad for Illinois," *State Journal-Register*, Springfield, Ill., Sunday, December 20, 1998, 16.

17. See John C. Stauber and Sheldon Rampton, *Toxic Sludge Is Good for You: Lies, Damn Lies and the Public Relations Industry* (Monroe, Maine: Common Courage Press, 1995).

18. Found in Simon Retallack, "Kyoto: Our Last Chance," *The Ecologist* 27, no. 6 (November/December 1997): 229–36, at 232.

19. Andrew J. Hoffman, ed., *Global Climate Change* (San Francisco: New Lexington Press, 1998) 4.

20. Gelbspan, *The Heat Is On*, 6.

21. Ibid., 56.

22. Ibid., 102.

23. Michael Grubb, *The Kyoto Protocol: A Guide and Assessment* (London: Royal Institute of International Affairs, 1999), 10–11.

24. Flavin and Lenssen, *Power Surge,* 24–25.

25. Richard Abdoo, "An Electric Utility Perspective on Climate Change," in *Global Climate Change*, Andrew J. Hoffman, ed. (San Francisco: New Lexington Press, 1998), 63–71, at 69.

26. Patrick J. Mulchay, "The Importance of Flexibility Implemented through Voluntary Commitments to Reduce Greenhouse Gas Emissions," in *Global Climate Change*, Andrew J. Hoffman, ed. (San Francisco: New Lexington Press, 1998), 85–91, at 86.

27. Abdoo, "An Electric Utility Perspective," 69.

28. Grubb, *Kyoto Protocol*, 93.

29. Ibid.

30. Ibid., 97.

31. Ibid.

32. Ibid., 99.

33. Ibid., 219.

34. Ibid., 306.

35. Flavin and Lenssen, *Power Surge*, 196.

36. Jonathan Lash, "The Safe Climate, Sound Business Challenge," in *Global Climate Change*, Andrew J. Hoffman, ed. (San Francisco: New Lexington Press, 1998), 41–48, at 46.

37. Grubb, *Kyoto Protocol*, 53.

38. Found in Andrew J. Hoffman, "Introduction," *Global Climate Change*, 3.

39. Flavin and Lenssen, *Power Surge*, 75.

40. Ibid., 42.

41. Ibid., 197.

42. Ibid., 42.

43. Casten, *Turning Off the Heat*, 46–47.

44. Ibid., 48.

45. Ibid., 128.

46. Amory Lovins, "Dialogue: Economic Implications of Climate Change Policy," in *Global Climate Change*, Andrew J. Hoffman, ed. (San Francisco: New Lexington Press, 1998), 125–63, at 145.

47. Ibid., 149.

48. Kay, *Asphalt Nation*, 110.

49. Ibid., 111.

50. Ibid., 119–20.

51. Ibid., 120–21.

52. Ibid., 121.

53. Flavin and Lenssen, *Power Surge*, 86.

54. Everett M. Rogers, *Diffusion of Innovations*, 4th ed. (New York: Free Press, 1995), 138.

55. Ibid., 112–13.

56. Quoted by Joseph Kahn, "Excessive Regulation Is Blamed for Energy Woes," *New York Times*, May 18, 2001, A15.

57. Rogers, *Diffusion of Innovations*, 9.

58. See Grubb, *Kyoto Protocol*, 219.

59. Lester W. Milbrath, *Envisioning a Sustainable Society: Learning Our Way Out* (Albany, N.Y.: SUNY Press, 1989), 211.

60. Thomas Berry, *The Dream of the Earth*, "Bioregions: The Context for Reinhabiting the Earth" (San Francisco: Sierra Club Books, 1988), 163–70, at 166.

61. D. W. Orr, *Ecological Literacy: Education and the Transition to a Postmodern World* (Albany, N.Y.: SUNY Press, 1992), 71.

62. Daniel Press, *Democratic Dilemmas in the Age of Ecology* (Durham, N.C.: Duke University Press, 1994), 16.

63. Milbrath, *Envisioning a Sustainable Society*, 214.

64. See Robert L. Heilbroner, *An Inquiry into the Human Prospect* (New York: Norton, 1974), 110.

65. See Luther W. Skelton, *The Solar-Hydrogen Energy Economy: Beyond the Age of Fire* (New York: Van Nostrand, 1984), 12–13.

66. See *New York Times*, May 18, 2001, A1, and A14–A16.

67. Gelbspan, *The Heat Is On*, 86.

68. Ibid., 99.

69. Paul Raeburn, "It's Perfect Weather to Fight Global Warming," *Business Week* (December 11, 2000): 52.

CHAPTER 11

Environmentalism, Democracy, and the Cultural Politics of Nature in Monte Verde, Costa Rica

Luis A. Vivanco

> Their proximity to the forest makes them easy targets for blame, and their lack of political capital makes it difficult to refute this charge. . . . The problem for forest peoples is that they inhabit a resource which is coveted by groups that are more powerful than they are.[1]

When I met him during the mid-1990s, José Castellanos had just begun a joint venture with a friend of his to grow vegetables on a small plot of land on the outskirts of Santa Elena, a village in the Monte Verde region of Costa Rica. Their plan was to sell the vegetables to recently built hotels that lodge visiting ecotourists, since Monte Verde had become a world-famous biodiversity hotspot and tropical cloud forest destination. José no longer owned any land where he could undertake such a venture, so the land belonged to his friend. The reason he did not own land, José often told me regretfully, is that he sold his land to an environmental nongovernmental organization several years before. Until 1992, he owned seventy-five hectares of rain forest wilderness with his brother six kilometers north of Santa Elena, in an area called San Gerardo. Even now, but especially when he was a boy growing up there, San Gerardo is known as a remote area of difficult access and even more difficult possibilities for agricultural production due to its high precipitation. He never had any illusions about the difficulty of living there and making the land productive, but he had great passion for the landscape and its intricacies. José was known to some as a *baqueano*, a rural Costa Rican term for someone adept at traveling through forests and highly knowledgeable of their flora and fauna, and he had often been called upon to guide people (including environmental organization officials) who needed to map property boundaries, or to help find a lost forest traveler.

José told me bitterly that since he sold his land, he had not returned to the forests of San Gerardo, but not because he had become disinterested in them. Indeed, on our walks to and from the plot of land he worked near Santa Elena, he often delighted in identifying specific plant and animal species and describing their interactions. He was still profoundly resentful that he had to sell his land, telling me he was forced into it for several reasons, the immediate cause being that the brother with whom he owned the land was in debt. Nonetheless, he often explained, this is not as important as the broader conditions under which they sold their land, including the fact that San Gerardo falls within a national hydroelectric reserve established in 1977 where cutting trees is prohibited. Until the early 1990s, there were few or no buyers for the land, leaving José and other landowners in a difficult position since they could not work their lands in accustomed ways, including subsistence farming and small-scale agriculture and cattle ranching for regional food markets. He told me that he was especially frustrated that no one ever told landowners that their land would be legally frozen until one day when government forest guards showed up and started making arrests, or when one of them went to the bank for a loan and was told that he could no longer use land as collateral. Adding to the frustration was that several politically connected landowners were able to negotiate government expropriation of their lands. So when environmental activists showed up fifteen years later with substantial amounts of money from international sources, many felt they had no choice but to sell, debt or no debt. Yet, when he sold his land, José knew he would not be welcome there again. He told me, "There will always be national parks and protected areas, but we the people who lived there before are no longer welcome there. Conservation closed the forests, so I don't go there anymore. Plenty of tourists see it because they have the money. I don't have any contact with the tourists, but I see that they come with a lot of money. Many people are making business on these forests right now. Where does that leave me?"

The conditions that led to what José considered the coerced sale of his land were the result of several trends, some geographically diffuse and others very localized and place specific, that converged between the early 1970s and 1990s that situated San Gerardo, and the Monte Verde region more generally, as a key site in battles to save the world's remaining tropical forests. Situated along the Continental Divide in Costa Rica's northwestern central Tilarán highlands, Monte Verde's identity has long been related to a settlement of North American Quakers who arrived in 1951 to escape U.S. militarism.[2] Following the establishment of the Monteverde Cloud Forest Reserve during the early 1970s by a North American ecologist, the Quakers, and a Costa Rican scientific nongovernmental organization, Monte Verde's visibility in environmentalist and scientific imaginaries grew discontinuously until the late 1980s and early 1990s, when activists succeeded in placing Monte Verde on the agenda of an acephalous transnational "Save the Rainforest" movement whose focus was largely on land purchases and "adopting acres." With the financial aid of organizations like World Wildlife Fund (WWF), The Nature Conservancy, and an astonishing array of grassroots activists around the world, Monte Verde environmental organizations established Central America's largest private nature reserve (17,500 hectares) and more than doubled the Monteverde Cloud Forest Reserve (to 10,500 hectares). Consequently, many have described Monte Verde as a conservation success story, a key site in a country that provides a model for other poor countries struggling with 'sustainable development.'[3]

But in our conversations, José did not find much satisfaction in this reputation of success, and tended to express his discontent in a language of socioeconomic and political justice. The initial injustice, José pointed out, was that after generations of official incitements and legal inducements to colonize the agricultural frontier, the Costa Rican government unilaterally imposed restrictions on San Gerardo land without residents' knowledge or consultation.[4] Like many others who sold their land, José also claimed that he was not fairly compensated, although he was paid market value. José pointed out that because the state did not expropriate lands in San Gerardo, the door was opened for opportunistic nongovernmental environmental groups to buy a substantial amount of land in a region once distinguished for its many small and medium-sized landholdings. He added that the resulting situation is not dissimilar to the long-term concentration of lands and resources as *latifundios* (large cattle ranches) in the Guanacaste lowlands that he and other landless *campesinos* had invaded in the past.[5] In fact, he speculated that, along with some other people who were unhappy about the sale of their lands, he might someday return to San Gerardo, most likely as an illegal invader. José was not alone in holding the view that the concentration of lands as protected reserves controlled by private organizations presented a long-term problem of access to land, local economic autonomy, and even national sovereignty. Tapping into that widespread frustration, a study of conservation land purchases in Monte Verde by a team of Costa Rican scholars concluded that land purchase processes were "extremist" and that so-called sustainable development as practiced in Monte Verde is as vertical and antidemocratic as traditional forms of economic development.[6]

Only once in our relationship did José explicitly invoke "democracy" to refer to his situation, describing a local environmental group as "*anti-democrático*," precisely for its commitment to accumulating and enclosing land and redefining its use as a protected nature reserve, which José viewed as complicit in the economic and geographic displacement of people like him. But the fact that other rural Costa Ricans I encountered also referred to environmentalism as antidemocratic suggests that it is worth exploring the relation between "democracy," viewed as a process by which social decisions are made, and environmental activism and management, viewed as a substantive outcome. As Lafferty and Meadowcroft have pointed out, the relationship is by no means clear.[7] It is relatively common for nature protectionists and environmental activists to identify and vilify multinational corporations and development agencies as enemies of nature and fairness in the exploitation of resources.[8] In spite of the potential risks (lawsuits over libel), these processes gain an aura of heroism because of their David and Goliath quality and "grassroots" tinge. They also reflect a politically progressive agenda for environmentalism that many Northerners find comfortable, based on a critique of the potentially antidemocratic or centralizing tendencies of capitalism and development, and an assumption that social control of the environment should rest on foundations of social and political equality.[9] But, as Sachs correctly points out, in the discourses of sustainable development and the apparatus of Northern environmentalism, "justice" and "nature" often collide, and when they do, Northern elites promoting "nature" often succeed over Southern majorities desiring "justice."[10] The epigraph to this chapter points to this insight, one that José often told me in his own way: transformations like those in Monte Verde are implicated in and reflect unequal material and ideological relationships, and rural people find themselves inhabiting landscapes desired by more powerful interests than themselves, including states, national elites, and transnational environmental movements and organizations.[11]

One of the central purposes of this chapter is to explore how a particular matrix of events and processes converged in Monte Verde that allowed environmental organizations to gain significant landholdings and why some people, including not only

José, expressed their discontent with this situation in a language of justice and democracy. Why, in other words, have certain people in rural Costa Rica described environmental groups, and environmentalism more generally, as "antidemocratic?" This happened even though environmentalists for the most part bought lands that were already formally protected by state action. What conditions, and who (if anybody) "coerced" José and others to sell their land? It would be too simplistic to see local critics as scapegoating environmentalism for their own long-term material poverty, landlessness, or lack of access to formal political processes and institutions. There are several reasons for this, including the fact that José and others commonly distinguished the actions of environmental groups from the politics of the state, viewing them as qualitatively different, though sometimes strategically connected, realms. Furthermore, the same environmental group José called antidemocratic has worked hard to incorporate *campesinos* as members, and José and other *campesinos* often rhetorically asserted their own identities as environmentalists, or as José once told me, "*yo tambien soy conservacionista*" ("I too am conservationist"). We need to identify who is making claims of environmentalism as antidemocratic, what that might mean (and by implication, what democracy signifies locally), and how it connects to the processes through which the formal protection of Monte Verde's landscapes has been achieved. Indeed, this last process raises comparative and critical concerns about the transnational organization of environmental activism itself, specifically the differentially power-laden roles of mediating organizations and the difficulty of maintaining local authority and determination over the geographically diffuse and socioeconomically unequal relationships that characterize efforts to "save" rain forests.

A central aspect of this story is that the authority of environmentalist claims for control over the stewardship of tropical landscapes depends upon the assumption that the inhabitants of a region do not properly manage a natural resource or ecosystem, and that more appropriate forms of management exist. This is an aspect of what Escobar calls the "irruption of the biological," or the very survival of biological life itself, and its transnational emergence as a central concern for politics, capital, and science.[12] Tropical forests in particular represent key sites of concern and conflict, related to their status as symbols of biological profusion and fragility and their increasing value as reservoirs of biodiversity, biotechnology, and tourism. But as nature has become problematized in places like Monte Verde, it has collided with ongoing struggles over access to land and public goods. While it is a highly contested category, the category "nature" does represent and justify new forms of intervention in and authority over Monte Verde's landscapes and social processes. Characteristic of these forms of authority, however, is a fundamental contradiction: while management perspectives increasingly stress that "local people" like José represent essential *resources for* protection,[13] those people are also often characterized and treated as *obstacles to* proper management of rain forests. As I will show in this chapter, this ambivalence is both a product and determinate of powerful stereotypes of rural Costa Ricans as destroyers of nature, and plays a motivating role in the construction, justification, and extension of environmentalist agendas and practices.

The emphasis on land purchases and preserve establishment as a central strategy to save nature is neither predetermined nor the only strategy of nature protection environmentalists have employed in Monte Verde. It is, however, a highly tangible and appealing form of environmental activism. It is also the product of specific ideologies about what nature is and how it works, the logistics and legitimacy of raising money to protect it through private associations, ideas about the role of rural Costa Ricans in the landscape and the crises of environmental degradation they provoked, and the local contingencies of real estate markets and ideas of property ownership. The point is not to discredit the significant achievements of environmental activists in formally protecting Costa Rican forests, for land purchases do indeed represent one important possibility and method among others to achieve goals of positive social and natural change. Instead, the purpose is to analyze the sociocultural processes whereby certain normative and intellectual definitions of nature, with their potential to redefine existing social relations and knowledge production, become prominent in places like Monte Verde, and what the implications are for local discourses and practices of democracy. What is at stake here—and by implication in comparative contexts—is not simply who lives in and interacts with tropical forest landscapes, but who has the social authority to define those relationships in the first place, over the claims of others who also interact with those forests. In this sense, enclosing nature as unpeopled wilderness preserves is not simply a technical activity, but a profoundly moral and political act with significant consequences for the conceptual and practical relevance of environmentalism in rural Costa Rica and beyond.

Environmentalism and Democracy in Costa Rica

Along with other touted political and cultural attributes, especially stable liberal democracy and peace ("the Switzerland of Central America"), Costa Rican public discourse has recently incorporated the attribute of ecological appreciation as a positive national characteristic. One prominent perspective states, "Conservation is congruent with the political and social values of the country . . . It can be argued that Costa Rica, with its natural resources and traditional values supported by international academic and conservation organizations, has established a model system for the preservation of tropical diversity."[14] Proponents also contend that Costa Rica's identity as the "Green Republic" is the result of an educated and literate populace that understands the practical importance of ecology, and the "stability of an unarmed democracy and its satisfactory attention to the basic socioeconomic needs" of its people.[15] Recent social scientific treatments of Costa Rican (and Latin American) environmentalism and ecology movements, however, have challenged such oversimplifications and critically focused on the political and economic implications of environmental crises and nature protection campaigns for the nation-state. In particular, they have been productive in historicizing the national policy and civil society contexts though which environmentalist agendas have been defined, struggled over, implemented, and imposed.[16] In Costa Rica, it is by no means clear what the relationship is between formal democracy, widely conceived there as being based on electoral integrity and egalitarian civilian rule, and the emergence and relative normalization of environmentalism as a sociopolitical movement and public policy concern. As a case study, Costa

Rica raises key questions about how transformations in traditionally defined political arenas open possibilities for the formulation and advancement of environmentalist agendas of nature protection.

Significantly, the emergence of environmental and ecology movements throughout Latin America coincided with the restoration of civilian governments during the 1980s and the rise of neoliberal policies advocating the retraction of state involvement in markets and the provision of public services.[17] While initial conservation efforts in Costa Rica began as early as the 1960s, and Costa Rica never underwent a shift from authoritarian to democratic rule as did other Latin American countries in the 1980s, it has been argued that a commonality of Latin American social and environmental movements is their challenge to the very boundaries of what is properly defined as the political arena: its participants, institutions, processes, agenda, and scope.[18] In translating their critiques of existing social and developmental processes that degrade ecosystems into concrete activist and public policy agendas, environmental social movements challenge received meanings of citizenship, political representation and participation, and democracy itself.

These insights raise several key questions, especially about the nature of the relationship between broad cultural forces and traditional political processes, perhaps posing the former as a motivational factor for the transformation of the latter. But it also raises questions about the organizational ability of environmental groups to position themselves to redefine social power, and the sociopolitical conditions under which such possibilities become realities. A key aspect of beginning to answer this question is the realization that as a program of political and social reform, environmentalism is distinctive in that individuals and organizations far removed in space collaborate and sometimes compete in ways that transcend national boundaries and cultures, yet act on highly specific physical and social places.[19] From a cultural perspective, environmentalism also draws on and itself represents a diverse and internally conflicted arena of social debate and knowledge production.[20] Viewed in these terms, of environmentalism as unsettled battleground where normative definitions of nature and society compete and collaborate in the process of constructing social, natural, and political alternatives, however, intensifies the questions raised above. Specifically, how can shifting and sometimes loose alliances of individuals and social groups gain transformative access to processes of governance and public authority?

The Costa Rican case offers a particular answer to this question, for the success of environmental activists and organizations in gaining visibility and influence within public policy arenas and civil society agendas is related to two key factors that have gone unrecognized in the claims of Costa Rican environmental boosterism: the transformation of Costa Rican formal democracy itself, from welfare state to neoliberal experiment, and the state's resulting contradictory position with respect to the environment from the late 1970s to the 1990s.[21] Throughout much of the twentieth century, the Costa Rican state had pursued welfare and reformist policies in social and economic arenas, to the extent that state agencies and regulations eventually permeated virtually every aspect of economic production and development.[22] Particularly after the 1948 civil war, state interventionism satisfied several demands, including social stabilization and the legitimation of the new post–civil war political order.[23] But the economic crisis of the early 1980s that brought high inflation, stagnation, and exposed large public sector deficits forced the acceptance of several rounds of IMF structural adjustment measures and the aggressive pursuit of free market economic policies. Structural adjustment marked the rupture of previous forms of social consensus achieved and maintained through mediating state institutions, and the introduction of new forms of economic development and insertion in international markets.[24] In ecological terms, the result was the expansion of nontraditional agroexport sector of ornamental plants and tropical fruits, that coincided with and intensified ongoing ecologically degrading processes in rural areas already undergoing transformation related to cattle ranching, bananas, palm oil, and timber extraction.[25]

At the same time, however, the Costa Rican state had already begun vigorously pursuing the creation and expansion of national parks and formally protected wilderness areas, as well as the establishment of a ministry-level natural resources agency to manage these areas and oversee regulatory processes. By the early 1990s as much as 21 percent of the national territory came under some category of formal public protection, with an additional estimated 5 percent of national territory under private protection regimes.[26] During this period, the national legislature also passed progressive laws governing forestry, wildlife conservation, biodiversity, and a constitutional reform guaranteeing all citizens "the right to a healthy and ecologically-balanced environment."[27] Preserving, packaging, and selling tropical habitats have become central concerns in national socioeconomic development strategies and rhetoric, and recent governments have promoted Costa Rica as a "laboratory of sustainable development" and a leader in global efforts to unite economic growth and environmental conservation.[28]

This situation has led some to describe the central characteristic of this period of Costa Rican history as "the Grand Contradiction," emphasizing the fact that while successive Costa Rican governments in the 1980s and 1990s promoted their country as a laboratory of nature conservation, ecotourism, and sustainable development to Costa Rican and international audiences, these governments also oversaw one of the highest rates of deforestation in Central America.[29] The nongovernmental sector, that had responded to the neoliberal dynamic by providing social, technical, and financial services to buffer the negative social impacts of IMF structural adjustments, found itself in an advantageous position to assume some of the social and technical duties previously controlled by the state.[30] The number of environmental groups grew significantly during this period because the inconsistencies in and lack of public funding often required government agencies responsible for environmental concerns to pursue and rely on strategic alliances with civil society groups, international development and environmental organizations, and debt-for-nature swaps to achieve regulatory goals and park expansion.[31]

The functional decentralization of environmental politics at the national level has meant that no single entity (state or otherwise) has maintained uncontested or hegemonic control over the definition and implementation of environmental projects. Does this functional decentralization suggest that through environmentalism "associative" forms of democracy have been strengthened in Costa Rica? According to O'Neill and Achterberg, the establishment and maturation of professional and voluntary associations, or "communities of choice" in the language of Hirst, offer great promise in the construction and regulation of environmental policy and the movement toward an eco-logically sustainable society.[32] A multitude of overlapping and mutually related environmental associations, coordinated through processes of negotiation and alliance building, provides the foundation for pluralistic politics and is therefore reflective of greater democratic potential.[33] Such arguments, of course, assume that civil society is a (relatively) even playing field and that associations have more or less equal access to knowledge, financial resources, and formal political institutions or processes (or can, through alliance, enhance their access). Nevertheless, Achterberg himself recognizes that associative democracy can be complicated by factionalism and particularism within and between associations, and offers that "regional inequalities" within a nation-state also present difficulties for associative democracy.[34]

In the Costa Rican system of functional representation, "regional inequalities" are not simply characteristic of dynamics within the nation–state, for wider systems of "regional inequality" beyond the nation-state—of markets and geopolitical relationships—represent other levels of political and economic contingency, further undermining any notion of civil society as an even playing field.[35] In fact, critics have asserted that Costa Rican liberal democracy is an overstated myth, diverting attention from the structural inequalities and hierarchies of wealth and power that characterize the country's social, political, and economic histories.[36] Similarly, "associative democracy" may be problematic in diverting attention from the structural inequalities of wealth, power, and access that characterize the uneven operations of international, national, and local associations. In other words, some associations have comparatively more ability to define and implement projects than others. This is due to their access to financial resources, forms of privileged knowledge, and/or convergence with strategic geopolitical agendas of powerful nation-states, development agencies, or social movements.[37] Furthermore, as I will show in the case of Monte Verde, where the state has played an inconsistent role in environmentalism, politically or economically weaker associations find themselves in the position of having to seek out and supplicate the programs of more powerful associations or donors.[38] Similarly, we should not assume that associations themselves represent stable social or political entities, for associations at all scales can be internally conflicted over the realms and mechanisms of action, engaging in relationships with other associations precisely to enable processes of institutional expansion or stabilization. We now turn to Monte Verde, to examine in more detail how these latter two processes (the uneven relationship between international donors and local associations, and the institutionalization of small-scale associations) created the conditions under which land purchase campaigns took place.

The Scope and Criteria of Land Purchase Campaigns

Monte Verde's encounter with environmentalism since the early 1970s has profoundly transformed the lives of many residents, not simply people like José who sold their land. The encounter has contributed to the widespread redefinition of concepts of property ownership, land use, and forest management; created new economic, social, educational, and work opportunities for residents; provoked an ongoing realignment of political hierarchies and alliances; generated new forms of economic development; attracted more than 70,000 visitors and ecotourists a year to a region with a population of several thousand, and hundreds of Costa Rican and Nicaraguan workers who serve them; and coordinated the involvement of powerful transnational nongovernmental organizations. Perhaps most important, it has generated a "culture of nature" that has prompted significant transformations in how residents and visitors alike think about and experience the boundaries between nature and culture.[39]

At the center of these ongoing transformations is the concentration of lands as nature preserves. Nature preserves were the product of land purchase and adopt-an-acre campaigns that involved many international nongovernmental environmental institutions and literally hundreds of thousands of adults and children from mainly Northern industrialized countries. The mediation of these campaigns by local environmental activists enabled the formation and consolidation of several nongovernmental institutions in Monte Verde itself, situating these groups as new public authorities in a historical context of minor and inconsistent state involvement in environmental politics but also social and economic programs. It is possible to divide Monte Verde's history of preserve establishment into two general phases, both of which share characteristics and themes. Perhaps what differentiates the first efforts in the 1970s and later efforts in the late 1980s and early 1990s is scale and the pluralization of environmentalist strategies, since the second phase was much more elaborate, differentiated, and far-reaching in its international connections and local consequences. These characteristics include skepticism over the inconsistency of state and public forms of tenure and management, the inconsistent status of scientific knowledge and expertise, real estate market opportunism, and powerful stereotypes about rural Costa Rican culpability for environmental degradation.

When it was established in 1973, the Monteverde Cloud Forest Preserve (MCFP) became Costa Rica's first formally protected cloud forest and would eventually become a premier worldwide destination for the ecological study of cloud forest ecosystems and species. The story of its founding is now well known in the environmentalist and ecotourist literature: when a group of Quakers from Alabama and Iowa settled their village, Monteverde, on the Pacific slope of the remote Tilarán Highlands in 1951, they agreed to set aside several hundred acres of forest as a watershed, recognizing that the long-term sustainability of their agricultural and dairy cattle activities required it.[40] In the early 1970s, a North American ecology graduate student studying mixed-feeding bird flocks in the area, concerned over the threat of colonization in and near the watershed, purchased several adjacent homesteads and land claims to preserve the ecosystems and their unique species in perpetuity. He was also able to convince a small San José–based scientific and forestry research organization, the Tropical Science Center (TSC), to collaborate with him to acquire and manage more land. The TSC had previously undertaken a land use capacity study of the area for the Costa Rican government's National Planning Office (OFIPLAN), supporting OFIPLAN's intention to declare 35,000 hectares in the area off-limits to further colonization and development, which formally occurred in 1977.

Both institutions considered this action necessary to ensure the long-term viability of the watershed for the Arenal hydroelectric dam being planned nearby, although under political pressure from prominent landowners, OFIPLAN later reduced the area to 18,000 hectares.

From the beginnings of the Monteverde Cloud Forest Preserve, the ecologists, Quakers, and TSC administrators in San José promoted the private ownership, management, and patrolling of the forest. They were concerned that the political situation of preserving lands in Costa Rica was too volatile and uncertain, believing that lumber and cattle interests or land colonization programs of the state's Institute of Lands and Colonization (ITCO) might threaten the government's resolve to maintain the forests in the Tilarán Highlands. They were also concerned that the government's new environmental agency, the National Park Service (SPN), could not attend effectively to Monte Verde because it was struggling to consolidate itself bureaucratically while at the same time trying to create and manage new national parks. Indeed, during its first years, Costa Rican government support for the preserve was inconsistent, reflecting the conflicting agendas of different state agencies. For example, in the first year of the preserve, ITCO sided with the TSC to overturn the claims of a group of settlers who sought to clear forest in the protected area and establish homesteads.[41] In 1975, however, a new threat emerged when the Santa Elena Integral Development Association, a municipal economic development agency, obtained government funds to build a road through the MCFP into lands in the Peñas Blancas Valley. Similarly, in 1978 Ministry of Public Works and Transportation (MOPT) workers arrived to build a road into the preserve to build television repeating towers, proposing to expropriate Quaker landholdings without remuneration.[42] In both cases, TSC and MCFP engaged in legal battles to maintain the protected areas, succeeding with the support of various state agencies. By 1979, the president of the republic, Rodrigo Carazo, inaugurated the new visitor's center at the MCFP, symbolically marking high-placed support for the MCFP and TSC. Throughout this period, even into the present, the National Park Service has expressed its moral (not financial) support for the MCFP, as well as its desire to someday incorporate the preserve into its national system of parks.

Founders and managers of the MCFP considered land purchases to be a direct method to combat the settlement and further conversion of forest by land speculators and homesteaders working near the boundaries of the preserve. In their communications to environmentalists in the United States and Europe they tended to emphasize the threats without describing them in detail, focusing instead on endemic and charismatic species such as the golden toad, tapirs, and the resplendent quetzal.[43] By 1975, they had successfully obtained an $80,000 donation from the WWF's "Tropical Rain Forests Campaign" to assist land purchases and support administrative costs for three years. A 1978 BBC documentary on the cloud forests that aired in Europe and the United States spread knowledge and images of the MCFP as a pristine and unique wilderness. By the early 1980s, as a result of donations from Northern environmentalist sources, the MCFP had expanded to approximately 5,000 hectares and received just under 6,500 visitors annually.

By the mid-1980s, however, some North American residents of Monteverde village were concerned that the TSC was not doing enough to expand the protected area.

Indeed, many residents (including some Quakers) had grown dissatisfied with the TSC's management of the MCFP, viewing the institution as an absentee landlord interested in mining the increasingly touristed preserve for profits to fund its other endeavors. In 1985, several resident and visiting biologists and others interested in conservation met to discuss the protection of the Pacific slope forest habitat threatened by encroaching agricultural production. As a result of these meetings, the group formed the Monteverde Conservation League (MCL) in 1986, and defined one of its central goals to be the purchase of land for formal protection, precisely because the TSC had discontinued land purchases. That these people decided to establish a new organization rather than work through the TSC reflects important shifts in Monteverde village demographics and economy, including a shift from a primarily dairy farming economy dominated by the Quakers to an increasingly tourist economy in which the Quakers shared social and institutional power with more recent immigrants from North America and Europe, including biologists, retirees, artists, and tourism entrepreneurs. Members of the MCL considered their efforts to be a self-consciously "grassroots" organization, and described the group as the central organizer of environmental initiatives in the region: "As the local conservation group in the Monteverde zone, the Monteverde Conservation League has the responsibility of communicating the local, regional, national and global conservation perspectives to the surrounding communities. . . . In addition, we identify the socio-economic obstacles that are blocking sustainable land use, and look for ways to remove those obstacles."[44]

Through an arrangement with the TSC, the MCL embarked in 1986 on an international fund-raising campaign to raise money to expand the MCFP into the nearby Peñas Blancas Valley, on the Atlantic slope of the Monte Verde region. In exchange, the MCL would turn the land they purchased over to TSC administration. Following the international connections of the mainly North American volunteers involved in the MCL, the fund-raising campaign spread throughout U.S., Canadian, and European university, Quaker, and environmentalist contexts. Central to the campaigns were slide shows consisting of images of pristine tropical wilderness, and the message that the destruction of the valley was inevitable and in progress at the hands of Costa Rican settlers and speculators. As a 1986 MCL proposal to the WWF explained, pressures on the valley included "squatters, forest clearing, and lobbying local authorities to put in a road that would open up the area to rapid lumbering and colonization. . . . If this movement is not stopped immediately or if pressure mounts to put through a road, the entire watershed may be lost and the present Reserve jeopardized. THIS YEAR IS IT! . . . If the MCL is unable to accommodate these people, their only option will be to push for the destruction of the Peñas Blancas habitat."[45] The proposal adds that the WWF grant would "immediately stop the cutting by buying out the two or three individuals responsible for 90% of the pressure."[46]

The imagery of the destructive settler or speculator is a culturally loaded one designed to provoke a response, even though by the proposal's own admission, only two or three individuals (out of sixty landowners) were responsible for most of the pressure to convert forest. The imagery, which does not draw on the historical specificities of Monte Verde but on an isomorphism of Monte Verde's situation with crises of forest loss in other parts of the world, was not limited to MCL proposals: a Canadian magazine article on Monte Verde describes "poverty-stricken migrant farmers [who] have cleared [once lush and verdant woodland] to provide land and fuel."[47] In fact, in more than forty years of settlement and speculation, the area the MCL proposed to buy was 92 percent "pristine virgin forest" (the proposal's description) reflecting perhaps the *non-inevitability* of widespread forest destruction at the hands of local settlers, and the bias of environmental groups toward static, closed canopy forest, and unpeopled landscapes.[48] The point is not to romanticize rural Costa Ricans as innocent of forest conversion; rather, it is to ask why several landowners threatened to cut or did cut trees while most others did not, and why imagery of poverty-stricken and avaricious peasants does not apply in this case. Part of an answer lies in the fact that the Peñas Blancas Valley remained mostly forested precisely because most landowners in the valley were not subsistence farmers who needed this land to survive (only nine actually lived on their lands), but considered their landholdings to be long-term investments or alternative cattle pasturing for times when the Pacific slope of Monte Verde was in dry season or drought. Aside from the dairy industry the Quakers had established, there were no strong economic forces driving the conversion of the forests. Furthermore, even during the 1980s, landowners' intentions were not necessarily the immediate and inflexible destruction of the forests, for as soon as negotiations over land purchase began, cutting stopped. The threat to cut forests was in fact a symbolic political action for landowners to provoke either government or environmental groups to force a resolution to their problem of frozen lands stemming from the 1977 declaration of the area for hydrological protection. As a result, one criteria the MCL used to know which lands to purchase was based not on technical or scientific criteria, but on which landowners had threatened to cut trees.

Indeed, in considering which landowners to approach and lands to purchase, MCL land purchase strategies and criteria varied, depending on institutional priorities, opportunism, clarity of land ownership records, and the desire to control access and use of the forests. Aside from some interest in conserving habitat of the migratory quetzal, scientific and technical criteria tended to be minimal in preserve creation. The contingencies of negotiating land purchases were sometimes related to the opportunism of landowners and speculators themselves, who often claimed to sell land to which they had no legal claim, or who argued their land claims overlapped with the claims of others. To some extent, this stemmed from the ambiguities inherent in rural Costa Rican traditions of land settlement and ownership: in areas where people did not commonly hold title to their lands, as in much of the Monte Verde region, forested lands were considered *tierras baldías* (common lands), while deforested areas (*mejoras* or improvements) were considered private property, and it was common for claims to *tierras baldías* to be contested and subject to negotiation among neighbors. But, as one MCL land purchase agent pointed out, "there will always be conflict and overlapping, but we were willing to pay people twice for an overlap. The point was to close the deal and get the people out of there so they don't do anymore damage." Once "obstacles" (people) were removed, other criteria came into play, including consolidating areas already purchased by encouraging recalcitrant landowners to sell by suggesting that their access would thereafter be restricted.

During its first fund-raising campaign to purchase the Peñas Blancas Valley (1986 to 1989), the MCL won its initial proposal to WWF, generated hundreds of thousands of dollars from U.S., Canadian, and European sources for land purchases, and met its target number of hectares (6,200), most of which it turned over to TSC administration.[49] Most importantly, the success of this campaign placed the MCL as a legitimate "grassroots" effort on the maps of international rain forest fund-raising groups and transnational environmental institutions interested in extending Costa Rica's formally protected wildlands, and opened the door to the MCL's participation as one of Costa Rica's first beneficiaries of a "debt-for-nature swap" coordinated by the WWF. Although one MCL director asserted "Buying tropical forest is our first and most important purpose," these processes also enabled the MCL to assert its independence from the TSC and begin to manage land itself, professionalize its personnel, and scale up its activities to include environmental education, sustainable economic development, reforestation, biological corridors, and patrolling forests.[50] This differentiation also brought new populations into contact with the MCL, and brought a new cultural diversity to the organization as farmers sought membership, mainly because of their involvement as participants in the reforestation program.

The MCL's internal social differentiation also generated meaningful institutional tensions as newer employees and members (especially some Costa Ricans) criticized land purchases as problematic symbols of increasing foreign control over Costa Rican lands. By the early 1990s, in the midst of the MCL's highly successful International Children's Rainforest campaign (1988–93), which generated several million dollars of donations from children in mainly industrialized countries, even members and employees committed to land purchases began to be concerned that the institution could not effectively patrol and manage the lands it was purchasing. Part of the issue stemmed from the MCL's practice that it would spend money in whatever manner the donor specified. For many of these donors, "adopting an acre" was the specified priority, for which they received a symbolic "deed." Following the desires of the donor gave moral weight to the MCL's land purchase campaigns (especially if the money came from children), and ensured its reliability and legitimacy to continue receiving donations. In fact, the MCL did lose some credibility with donors when, because of accounting problems, it could not clearly show that the money was spent on land. This also meant that MCL officials confronted limitations in how they could spend donations, bound to the interests and priorities of donors and their mediators like the WWF.

Recognizing this problem, the MCL began a new fund-raising campaign in 1992 focused on generating money for projects other than land purchases (such as support for patrolling its now vast territory), but had little success generating donor interest even though it approached the same donor and organizational networks that brought it millions of dollars during the Children's Rainforest campaign. This may be a product of a dynamic Dahl has observed in his analysis of the relationship between democracy and international organizations: it is hard for citizens in one place to perceive or understand the conditions, situations, needs, wants, aims, and ends of other citizens who are distant and different from themselves.[51] A good example of this is reflected in the words of a Swedish schoolteacher who, along with her students and thousands of

Swedish children, raised several million dollars for rain forest preservation and land purchases, much of it for the MCL: "The favorite television programs of these children were films about nature that always ended: 'We do not know how long this animal will survive on this planet because its habitat is disappearing.' The kids wanted to do something about it."[52] In such circumstances, subtleties and local particularities, such as local practices of land management or the impacts of land purchases in places like Monte Verde, go unrecognized, especially when these documentaries often frame the loss of habitat with powerful images of "locals" with chainsaws and torches, as they often do.

Land Purchases and Local Democracy

In spite of growing discontent among some MCL employees and members during the late 1980s, donations marked for acreage adoption continued to pour in from children's groups and transnational environmental associations like the WWF and TNC. By the early 1990s, however, donations began to decline, reflecting decreasing interest in Monte Verde as a target of international environmentalist investments. As one representative of a U.S. fraternal order observed in 1996 during his visit to Monte Verde, "We aren't interested in giving here anymore, because they've been successful. We're trying to find other places to give money." Consequently the MCL experienced considerable downsizing and institutional redefinition during the mid- and late 1990s. Still, for some members of the MCL, the concern for land purchases persists, although the high cost of land has so far been prohibitive for any large-scale land purchase campaigns. For example, during its first campaign in the late 1980s, the average price of land was $35, and by a decade later it was as high as $1,000 per hectare in certain areas. There is no doubt locally that the inflation of land prices was caused by the previous land purchase campaigns.

In the Monte Verde region, land purchases have been the single most controversial environmentalist practice, sparking the most public debate and rancor. Even while landowners literally lined up at the MCL office to sell their lands, some happy to have a chance to sell their lands frozen by the establishment of the hydrological reserve, there was considerable concern throughout the region that the MCL and its international funders were aggressively displacing landowners. In 1990, those tensions came to a head when the local Catholic priest, Santa Elena high school teachers and students, and several Costa Rican entrepreneurs organized a march on the MCL office. One participant described the march as a response to rumors that the land-hungry MCL was secretly lobbying to buy a government property under the control of the high school. A publicity flyer for the event, though it did not name the MCL, announced: "Friends, it is the hour to defend our rights and demonstrate that this is our community, and that neither opportunists nor foreigners without conscience that not only ignore but abuse us can detach us from what belongs to us and that which we inherited from our parents and grandparents. It is the hour to take out these black hands that dirty the dignity of this town." MCL officials denied such rumors, but the local response was vigorous, reflecting a concern that land purchases threatened local Costa Rican control over natural resources in the long term.

At the height of its land purchase campaigns in the late 1980s, the MCL became involved in San Gerardo, the area where José owned land. Since the declaration of the hydrological reserve, landowners sought to negotiate with the Ministry of Natural Resources and Mines (MIRENEM) and the Ministry of Agriculture and Livestock (MAG) to resolve their situation. Because of financial limitations, both ministries claimed they could not help landowners. In 1988, MIRENEM asked the MCL to participate in these discussions, inviting the MCL to draw on its international fundraising connections to buy land. Some landowners were furious at the prospect of MCL involvement, partly because they considered the government more accountable to them than a private nongovernmental organization with a local reputation for adopting acres for foreigners. In addition, some landowners had decided not to pursue the sale of their lands, in order to develop a "sustainable community" project that would allow them to continue living within the protected area. With the government's blessing, the MCL agreed to help those who wanted to stay to develop the project, called the San Gerardo Socio-Biotic Community Project, that initially included more than twenty families and was organized around organic production and ecotourism. The dynamic shifted when the MCL received money to begin buying land in San Gerardo, from its participation in the WWF coordinated debt-for-nature swap in the early 1990s. The combination of MCL pressure to use the money quickly (lest it lose access to those funds) and landowner discontent with the slowness by which their project was being developed led the majority to sell, and only five families stayed in the project. By the mid-1990s, all but three of the families had left, and the MCL owned virtually all of the land in San Gerardo. Although there are many reasons for the dissolution of this project, some ex–San Gerardo residents consider the MCL's concentration of lands to have shifted the balance so that remaining project participants lost equanimity in dealings with the organization.

Tensions over land purchases are still often barely under the surface of some peoples' attitudes toward environmentalism, even though some initiatives of environmental activists, especially the MCL's reforestation program, have been widely regarded as successful. For example, in 1996 the TSC was greeted with profound skepticism and rejection when it proposed a biological corridor through a village in the Monte Verde region that borders the MCFP. Some of the residents had once lived in San Gerardo, and argued to neighbors that the TSC's ulterior motive was to control and eventually buy their lands, as the MCL did in San Gerardo. Commenting on the TSC plan, one former San Gerardo landowner argued: "They destroy communities. I don't need their help. Call it a biological corridor, call it a reserve, call it what you want. It simply means more controls on the *campesino*." Whether or not the TSC had ulterior motives is more or less irrelevant since some people believed it did and the belief had a life of its own. As a result, its efforts were significantly complicated and indefinitely delayed, because it could not prove to its donors that it had secured community support and participation.

Underlying these concerns is a conviction that land purchase campaigns have tended to consider landowners and farmers to be obstacles to biodiversity preservation, which is a question of the relationship between environmentalism and democracy. It is significant that in their commentaries on environmentalism and democracy, people like José were not necessarily referring to the Costa Rican system of formal representative and institutional democracy. Rural Costa Ricans may in the abstract be quite proud of their country's tradition of formal electoral democracy, especially when compared to neighbors like Nicaragua or Panama.[53] But for people whose land becomes a formally protected hydroelectric reserve without their knowledge, and then who see more politically connected and wealthy landowners gain favorable treatment through expropriation, the formal institutions of Costa Rican democracy may exist to serve the privileged rather than themselves. In fact, cultural meanings and expectations of "democracy" and "justice" have quotidian realities that may be quite distant from processes and institutions of centralized governance, reflecting vernacular meanings and connotations through "common sense."[54] In this sense, polemical accusations of environmentalism and environmentalists as "antidemocratic" have less to do with formal institutions of national governance and abstract rights, and more to do with the processes of social life and conventions of morality and conviviality that characterize rural life, and how environmental activists and organizations did or did not fit those specific discourses and practices of social custom.

International environmentalists and Costa Ricans alike recognize that environmentalism is a movement with highly political goals and methods. What environmentalists have not necessarily appreciated or accepted, though, is that some of the rural Costa Ricans with whom they have dealt maintain distinctive ideas about political processes and public interactions, ideas that are embedded in local social relations. One Costa Rican who worked in the MCL as a reforestation officer explained that land purchases sparked significant controversy precisely because of these differing concepts of negotiability that he and other Costa Ricans take for granted:

> It is becoming more clear that these mountains no longer belong to the national community. They belong to the environmental organizations, their biologists, their foreign funders, students, the tourists, the tourism entrepreneurs. Because there was no negotiation, a space in which to search for agreement, we could find ourselves living a situation that is neither magic nor imaginary, but concrete and real. I do not mean to be so apocalyptic, but sadly, all this hard work to protect forests could be undermined by people who do not care about these forests and are willing to invade them, simply because conservation did not care to establish a communication and a sharing of information, participation, and shared interests. And this is not because people are ignorant or do not know the value of forests. Culturally, we are close to the concept of the pact. What is a pact? It is an assembly of dissimilar interests, with diverse necessities, but that are disposed to meet on the grounds they share, and together find ways to further their common interests. This is also not magic. Negotiation, a pact, communication are not a gift of divine providence. It is something to construct with intention or a true practical sense of opening, of learning to listen.

Central to this polemic is the perception that environmental groups and their funders have been primarily concerned with outcomes, such as formally protecting a certain number of hectares of rain forest or building infrastructure to attract tourists, and they never came to recognize the conflicting political, social, and economic interests of rural people. The tendency throughout land purchase campaigns, in fact, had been to reject the claims and interests of rural people, representing them in generalizing terms and thereby delegitimizing their specific claims and histories. This has posed a fundamental challenge to local concepts of democracy as being based on values of recognizing and airing differences and of openness to negotiation, thereby affirming common bonds instead of undermining them. Furthermore, this commentator raised a provocative challenge for environmentalism, asserting that rural Costa Ricans have been thought of primarily as passive subjects to be acted upon, only collaborated with insofar as it helps achieve certain institutional, strategic, or ideological goals. In this sense, the practices of environmentalism ensure the centralized control of large territories by international elites through local institutions. The point is that if processes are not based on an attitude of openness and willingness to listen to diverse visions of the people who also have a long-term stake in the landscape, the grounds for a richer, more inclusive, and ultimately stronger environmentalism remain elusive. This is also perhaps why the reforestation project had greater popular success than land purchases, because it enrolled landowners as participants, not obstacles, and provided concrete benefits for them in terms of enhanced agricultural production in a working landscape.

Perhaps this is a strong and polemical indictment of land purchase campaigns, and environmentalism more generally, and many (especially environmentalists) would vigorously disagree. However, there is no doubt that land purchases have had a significant effect on local concepts and practices of property ownership: specifically, the reification of property boundaries and clarification of title in a region where concepts of ownership and rights of passage have been relatively fluid and flexible. Reflecting on this, one Costa Rican man described a walk he took with his young son. When he suggested to his son that they take a shortcut through a forest to get home more quickly, the boy's reaction was that forests belonged to environmentalists and were off-limits. Interpreting his story, the man explained that this is a negative reflection of the absolutist policing policies that environmentalists have assumed, in an area where conventions of property ownership were never absolutist, and where neighbors certainly could walk through each other's lands. Under the surface is a concern that people who once had a stake in the landscape no longer do, or as another man who was present at the telling explained, "Growing up here we were always told that these forests were our patrimony. But now they are not." Central to this are new forms of control over peoples' movements throughout the countryside and their use of natural resources. Because those decisions are made in the context of centralized institutions (not in the flow of everyday interactions), and with an absolutism backed by legal authority and conviction, environmentalism represents a new and potentially antidemocratic force in the region.

Returning to José's assertion that he has considered returning to his lands in San Gerardo, some residents have pointed out that Monte Verde has never had a culture of aggressive takeovers of land, as in other parts of the country. This is not to say that conflicts over land never happened, for they often did as landowners worked out both their boundaries and animosities. However, such skepticism toward environmental groups and their control over the landscape leaves many questions unanswered, including whether or not these efforts to preserve landscapes represent a "stopgap" measure that may be jeopardized in the long term precisely because of local ambivalence or hostility toward environmental groups. Furthermore, no matter how much potential "associative" forms of democracy have for sustainability, the centralization of authority over large territories by several private organizations leads to a paradoxical effect: if those institutions are not themselves organized democratically and relate democratically to local populations, there is a concomitant decrease in local sustainability. If local people are viewed by organizations and their supporters in generic terms and as obstacles to be removed, and attention is not paid to the culturally relevant definitions of relationship and negotiation, the sustainability of environmentalism itself is at stake.

Notes

Acknowledgements: This chapter is based on one and a half years of ethnographic research conducted for my Ph.D. thesis. This research would not have been possible without the generous support of the Wenner-Gren Foundation for Anthropological Research, MacArthur Foundation, Mellon Foundation, and the following Princeton University entities: Center of International Studies, Council of Regional Studies, Program on Latin American Studies, and Department of Anthropology. The writing phase was supported by the New England Board of Higher Education and the University of Vermont. Special thanks to Bob Pepperman Taylor and Ben Minteer for their interest in this work and their constructive comments.

1. Michael Dove, "A Revisionist View of Tropical Deforestation and Development," *Environmental Conservation* 20, no. 3 (1993): 17–24, 56, 23.

2. After four young Quaker men in Fairhope, Alabama, were jailed in 1949 because they did not register for the peacetime draft, they decided with a group of forty other Quakers (twelve families, some of whom were from Iowa), to search for a nonmilitarized country in which they could live and pursue ideals of personal spiritual development and create a community based on processes of consensus building. They chose Costa Rica because two members of their party had visited it on an agricultural tour of Central and South America and had been impressed by the recent abolition of the army after its 1948 civil war. See Marion Pack Howard, "An Alternative Way of Being: The Ethnographic Study of a Quaker Community in the Cloud Forest of Costa Rica—1987" (Ph.D. diss., Teachers College, Columbia University, N.Y., 1989); Catherine Caufield, *In the Rainforest: Report from a Strange, Beautiful, Imperiled World* (Chicago: University of Chicago Press, 1991); and Luis Vivanco, "Green Mountains, Greening People: Encountering Environmentalism in Monte Verde, Costa Rica" (Ph.D. diss., Princeton University, N.J., 1999).

The astute reader may have noticed that I refer to Monte Verde (two words) and Monteverde (one word). Within the Costa Rican governmental system of administrative partitioning, "Monte Verde" (two words) is District 10 of the Central Canton, Puntarenas province. Under these terms it includes the villages of Santa Elena (its political and economic center) and several other villages, which have a population of several thousand. In popular imagination, "Monte Verde" can include as many as fifteen villages and neighborhoods. Monteverde (one word) refers to the Quaker settlement.

3. See A. Forsyth, "The Lessons of Monteverde," *Equinox* (March/April 1988): 56–61; Tamara Budowski, "Ecotourism Costa Rican Style," in *Toward a Green Central America: Integrating Conservation and Development*, ed. V. Barzetti and Y. Rovinski (West Hartford, Conn.: Kumarian Press, 1992), 48–62; Bruce Aylward et al., "Sustainable Ecotourism in Costa Rica: The Monteverde Cloud Forest Preserve," *Biodiversity and Conservation* 5 (1996): 315–43; A. Baez, "Learning from Experience in the Monteverde Cloud Forest, Costa Rica," in *People and*

Tourism in Fragile Environments, ed. M. F. Price (Chichester, N.Y.: Wiley, 1996), 109–22; Sterling Evans, *The Green Republic: A Conservation History of Costa Rica* (Austin: University of Texas Press, 1999); M. Honey, *Ecotourism and Sustainable Development: Who Owns Paradise?* (Washington, D.C.: Island Press, 1999); and Vivanco, "Green Mountains."

4. Official incitements to colonize the agricultural frontier are discussed in John Augelli, "Costa Rica's Frontier Legacy," *The Geographical Review* 77, no. 1 (1987): 1–16.

5. On the relationships among rural poverty, landlessness, and land invasions in rural Costa Rica, see Mitchell Seligson, *Peasants of Costa Rica and the Development of Agrarian Capitalism* (Madison: University of Wisconsin Press, 1980); and Marc Edelman, *The Logic of the Latifundio: The Large Estates of Northwestern Costa Rica since the Late Nineteenth Century* (Stanford, Calif.: Stanford University Press, 1992).

6. R. Vieto and Jaime Valverde, "Efectos de la Compra de Tierras con fines de Conservación," unpublished manuscript (San José, Costa Rica: Recursos Naturales Tropicales, S.A., 1996).

7. William M. Lafferty and James Meadowcroft, eds. *Democracy and the Environment: Problems and Prospects* (Cheltenham, U.K.: Edward Elgar, 1996).

8. Andrew Rowell, *Green Backlash: Global Subversion of the Environment Movement* (London: Routledge, 1996).

9. Lafferty and Meadowcroft, *Democracy and the Environment*.

10. Wolfgang Sachs, "The Need for the Home Perspective," *Interculture* 2, no. 1 (winter 1996).

11. By using Dove's insight from the extract here, I do not mean to suggest that José is a "forest person" in the same sense as the indigenous rain forest dwellers to whom Dove refers in his work. Rather, José is more properly described as a *campesino*, which connotes an agrarian affiliation. It is important to recognize, however, that many *campesinos* have had extensive involvement in and use of the forests. See Anja Nygren, *El Bosque y la Naturaleza en la Percepción del Campesino Costarricense: Un Estudio de Caso* (Turriabla, Costa Rica: CATIE, Programa Manejo de Recursos Naturales, 1993).

12. Arturo Escobar, "Cultural Politics and Biological Diversity: State, Capital, and Social Movements in the Pacific Coast of Colombia," in *Between Resistance and Revolution: Cultural Politics and Social Protest*, ed. Richard Fox and Orin Starn (New Brunswick, N.J.: Rutgers University Press, 1997), 40–64.

13. One representative perspective states, "Conservationists, economists, and tourists have awakened to the realization that you can't save nature at the expense of local people. As custodians of the land, and those most likely to lose from conservation, locals should be given a fair share. Sound politics and economics argue for making local people partners and beneficiaries in conservation, as opposed to implacable enemies of it." K. Lindberg and D. Hawkins, *Ecotourism: A Guide for Planners and Managers* (North Bennington, Vt.: The Ecotourism Society, 1993), 8.

14. Rodrigo Gámez and Alvaro Ugalde, "Costa Rica's National Park System and the Preservation of Biodiversity: Linking Conservation with Socio-Economic Development," in *Tropical Rainforests: Diversity and Conservation*, ed. Frank Almeda and Catherine M. Pringle (San Francisco: California Academy of Sciences, 1988), 134.

15. Luis Fournier, *Ecología y Desarollo en Costa Rica* (San José, Costa Rica: EUNED, 1981), 33; and Rodrigo Gámez, "Biodiversity Conservation through Facilitation of Its Sustainable Use: Costa Rica's National Biodiversity Institute," *Tree* 6, no. 12 (December 1991): 377–78.

16. Arturo Bonilla, *Crisis Ecológica en América Central* (San José, Costa Rica: Ediciones Guayacán, 1988); David Rains Wallace, *The Quetzal and the Macaw: The Story of Costa Rica's National Parks* (San Francisco: Sierra Club Books, 1992); Eduardo Mora Castellanos, *Claves del Discurso Ambientalista* (Heredia, Costa Rica: Editorial UNA, 1993); Roxana Salazar, *El Derecho a un Ambiente Sano: Ecología y Desarrollo Sostenible* (San José, Costa Rica: Asociación Libro Libre, 1993);

H. Collinson, ed., *Green Guerillas: Environmental Conflicts and Initiatives in Latin America and the Caribbean* (London: Latin American Bureau, 1996); and Evans, *Green Republic*.

17. Kathryn Hochstettler and Stephen Mumme, "Democracy and the Environment in Latin America," in *Assessing Democracy in Latin America: A Tribute to Russell H. Fitzgibbon*, ed. Philip Kelley (Boulder, Colo.: Westview, 1998), 37–53.

18. Arturo Escobar and Sonia Alvarez, *The Making of Social Movements in Latin America: Identity, Strategy and Democracy* (Boulder, Colo.: Westview, 1992); and Sonia Alvarez, E. Dagnino, and Arturo Escobar, "Introduction: The Cultural and Political in Latin American Social Movements," in *Cultures of Politics/Politics of Cultures: Re-Visioning Latin American Social Movements*, ed. Sonia Alvarez, E. Dagnino, and Arturo Escobar (Boulder, Colo.: Westview, 1998), 1–29.

19. Ramachandra Guha, *Environmentalism: A Global History* (New York: Longmans, 2000).

20. Steven Yearly, *The Green Case: A Sociology of Environmental Issues, Arguments, and Politics* (London: Routledge, 1991); and Kay Milton, *Environmentalism and Cultural Theory: Exploring the Role of Anthropology in Environmental Discourse* (New York: Routledge, 1996).

21. Sylvia Rodriguez, "Conservación, Contradicción y Erosión de la Soberanía: El Estado Costarricense y las Areas Naturales Protegidas (1970–1992)" (Ph.D. diss., University of Wisconsin, Madison, Spanish translation, 1994).

22. Jorge Rovira Mas, *Costa Rica en los Años 80* (San José, Costa Rica: Editorial Porvenir, 1989); and Marc Edelman, *Peasants against Globalization: Rural Social Movements in Costa Rica* (Stanford, Calif.: Stanford University Press, 1999).

23. Manuel Rojas Bolaños, "La Democracia Costarricense: Mitos y Realidades," in *Mitos y Realidades de la Democracia en Costa Rica* (San José, Costa Rica: DEI, 1990), 25–30.

24. María Eugenia Trejos, "Nuevas Fórmulas de Consenso Social: El Ajuste Estructural en Costa Rica," in *Mitos y Realidades de la Democracia en Costa Rica* (San José, Costa Rica: DEI, 1990), 47–54.

25. Edelman, *Logic of the Latifundio*; and John Vandermeer and Ivette Perfecto, *Breakfast of Biodiversity: The Truth about Rain Forest Destruction* (Oakland, Calif.: Food First, 1995).

26. Luis Fournier, *Desarrollo y Perspectiva del Movimiento Conservacionista Costarricense* (San José, Costa Rica: Editorial UCR, 1991); and Johnny Rosales, "Reservas Naturales Privadas en Costa Rica y un Estudio de Caso: Asociación Conservacionista de Monteverde y el Bosque Eterno de los Niños." Paper presented to First Latin American Congress on National Parks and Other Protected Areas, Santa Marta, Colombia, May 1997.

27. Salazar, *El Derecho a un Ambiente Sano*.

28. UNED/INBio, ed., *Del Bosque a la Sociedad/From Forest to Society* (San José, Costa Rica: UNED, 1994); and Mario Boza et al., "Costa Rica Is a Laboratory, Not Ecotopia," *Conservation Biology* 9, no. 3 (1995): 684–85.

29. See Evans, *Green Republic*. The rate of deforestation fluctuated between the 1950s and the 1980s, and has generally been put at anywhere between 30,000 and 60,000 hectares per year, or rates of 2.5 to 3.9 percent of the national territory.

30. Laura Macdonald, "NGOs and the Problematic Discourse of Participation: Cases from Costa Rica," in *Debating Development Discourse: Institutional and Popular Perspectives*, ed. D. Moore and G. Schmit (London: MacMillan, 1995), 201–29.

31. Luis Fournier, *Desarrollo y Perspectiva del Movimiento Conservacionista Costarricense*, and Evans, *Green Republic*. A key example of the tendency of state agencies to rely heavily on international nongovernmental fund-raising organizations and expertise is in the birth and growth of the Guanacaste National Park, with North American biologist Daniel Janzen as a major proponent, mediator, and fund-raiser for the park's expansion. Daniel Janzen, *Guanacaste National Park: Tropical Ecological and Cultural Restoration* (San José, Costa Rica: UNED, 1986); and W. H. Allen, "Biocultural Restoration of a Tropical Forest," *BioScience* 38, no. 3 (1988): 156–61.

32. J. O. O'Neill, *Ecology, Policy, and Politics: Human Well-Being and the Natural World* (London: Routledge, 1993); Walter Achterberg, "Sustainability and Associative Democracy," in *De-*

mocracy and the Environment: Problems and Prospects, ed. William M. Lafferty and James Meadowcroft (Cheltenham, U.K.: Edward Elgar, 1996); and P. Hirst, *Associative Democracy* (Cambridge, U.K.: Polity Press, 1994).

33. Achterberg, "Sustainability and Associative Democracy,"168.

34. Ibid., 170.

35. Marc Edelman and Joanne Kenen, eds., *The Costa Rica Reader* (New York: Grove Weidenfeld, 1989); Vandermeer and Perfecto, *Breakfast of Biodiversity*; Edelman, *Logic of the Latifundio*; Alvarez et al., *Cultures of Politics*.

36. Samuel Stone, "Aspects of Power Distribution in Costa Rica," in *The Costa Rica Reader*, ed. Marc Edelman and Joanne Kenen (New York: Grove Weidenfeld, 1989); John A. Booth, "Costa Rica: The Roots of Democratic Stability," in *Democracy in Developing Countries: Latin America*, vol. 4, ed. Larry Diamond et al. (Boulder, Colo.: Reiner, 1989); Yadira Calvo et al., *Mitos y Realidades de la Democracia en Costa Rica* (San José: DEI, 1990).

37. A good example of this is CINDE (Coalition of Development Initiatives), a USAID-funded initiative in the 1980s that sought to promote entrepreneurialism and market-oriented production systems, ease social tensions that resulted from the debt crisis and structural adjustment, and diminish the reliance of lower-class groups on the state and thereby weaken state paternalism. See Macdonald, "NGOs," 210.

38. M. Edwards and D. Hulme, "Too Close for Comfort? The Impact of Official Aid on Nongovernmental Organizations," *World Development* 24, no. 6 (1996): 961–73.

39. Andrew Wilson, *The Culture of Nature: North American Landscape from Disney to the Exxon Valdez* (Cambridge, Mass.: Blackwell, 1992).

40. L. Burlingame, "Conservation in the Monteverde Zone: Contributions of Conservation Organizations," in *Monteverde: Ecology and Conservation of a Tropical Cloud Forest*, ed. Nalini Nadkarni and Nathaniel Wheelwright (Oxford, U.K.: Oxford University Press, 2000), 351–88.

41. George Powell, "To Save a Forest: The Monteverde Preserve's First Year," *Tapir Tracks: The Newsletter of the Monteverde Conservation League* (July/October 1989): 5.

42. Joseph Tosi, "Una Historia Breve de la Reserva Bosque Nuboso de Monteverde del Centro Científico Tropical—1972–1992," unpublished manuscript (San José, Costa Rica: Tropical Science Center, 1992), 7.

43. George Powell, Application to World Wildlife Fund for "Monteverde Project" (Washington, D.C.: WWF Files #6080, 1974).

44. Monteverde Conservation League, *Tapir Tracks: A Newsletter of the Monteverde Conservation League* 5, no. 1 (January/April 1990): 2.

45. Monteverde Conservation League, "Saving the Monteverde Cloud Forest." Proposal to the World Wildlife Fund (Washington, D.C.: WWF Files, 1986), 3.

46. Ibid., p. 4.

47. V. Dwyer, "Cheap Conservation at $25 an Acre," *MacLean's* 101 (1988): 52.

48. William Cronon, ed., *Uncommon Ground: Rethinking the Human Place in Nature* (New York: Norton, 1996).

49. The agreement to turn over land ownership has never been formalized, although the TSC has been de facto administrator of the lands. This unresolved transaction has led to tensions between the two organizations, and the TSC has taken the MCL to court in recent years.

50. Monteverde Conservation League, *Tapir Tracks: A Newsletter of the Monteverde Conservation League* 3, no. 1 (August 1988): 1.

51. Robert A. Dahl, "Can International Organizations Be Democratic? A Skeptic's View," in *Democracy's Edges*, ed. Ian Shapiro and Cadiano Hacker-Cordón (Cambridge, U.K.: Cambridge University Press, 1999), 26.

52. Monteverde Conservation League, "Barnens Regnskog, Suecia," *Tapir Tracks: A Newsletter of the Monteverde Conservation League* 6, no. 2 (Mayo–Julio 1991): 6.

53. This reflects an exceptionalism for which Costa Ricans are well known. See Edelman and Kenen, *Costa Rica Reader*; and Bruce M. Wilson, *Costa Rica: Politics, Economics, and Democracy* (Boulder, Colo.: Reiner, 1998).

54. C. Douglas Lummis, *Radical Democracy* (Ithaca, N.Y.: Cornell University Press, 1996).

CHAPTER 12

Environmental Rights as Democratic Rights

Tim Hayward

> All human beings have the fundamental right to an environment
> adequate for their health and well-being.
>
> World Commission on Environment and Development[1]

The fundamental right proposed in 1987 by the Brundtland Report as the first legal principle for environmental protection and sustainable development has since, increasingly, been taken up into states' constitutions. There are many questions about how effective constitutional environmental rights may be, and answers to them depend on specificities of particular states' constitutional and political organization and culture.[2] However, there are certain general questions that must, in some form, be addressed in any constitutional context at all, and that have in fact been addressed even from within states that have resisted constitutionalizing environmental rights. The focus of this chapter is on one issue of principle that has been appealed to, both by politicians and by theorists, as a reason for not constitutionalizing environmental rights, namely, that to do so would be undemocratic.

On the one hand is the issue of the democratic legitimacy of environmental values. While virtually no constitution in the world that has been drafted or amended in the past ten years omits reference to principles of environmental protection, even if not in the form of a rights provision, such principles, it seems, cannot be directly justified by reference to principles of democracy. As Robert Goodin observes: "[t]o advocate democracy is to advocate procedures, to advocate environmentalism is to advocate substantive outcomes";[3] there is no necessary connection between them such as to guarantee that the former procedures will yield the latter sorts of outcome. Hence a commitment to environmentalism does not entail a commitment to democracy, or vice versa. Of course, it also does not follow that there is any necessary conflict between environmental and democratic principles, provided, at least, that a state's constitutional commitments to environmental protection are presented in terms of general policy statements allowing latitude of interpretation and political negotiation of their practical implications. However, when a constitutional provision is entrenched in the form of a right, this can mean that it is presumed to have a "trumping" force with respect to other social values and policies if these conflict with it. Thus, on the other hand, there is the question of the democratic legitimacy of constitutional rights that thereby set certain substantive values beyond the reach of routine political revision and have the effect of preempting decisions that might otherwise be arrived at through democratic procedures. To the extent that environmental rights can be taken to embody substantive value commitments, therefore, they would appear to be vulnerable to the criticism that the constitutional entrenchment of them is undemocratic. It is to this criticism that the present chapter seeks to develop an answer.

In the first section I address arguments for the view that the constitutionalizing of any right at all is undemocratic; I show why these arguments are hyperbolic in that they cannot apply with the requisite force to *all* rights, and that they ultimately depend on assumptions about the meaning of democracy that are so problematic that it remains an open question whether they would necessarily apply to *any* rights. The critical arguments certainly seem unsustainable in relation to certain procedural rights that are necessary for the very functioning of democracy as such, and in the second section the scope of these "democratic rights" is considered, and it is shown how procedural environmental rights can be counted among them. The question then, though, is whether environmental rights have any democratic legitimacy over and above that conferred by neutral procedures: this leads us to ask whether and how substantive environmental rights might be defended. In section 3, I investigate whether arguments for the democratic legitimacy of social rights can be applied to environmental rights. However, I suggest, because such arguments are somewhat problematic in their own terms, and because there are also important differences between environmental and social rights, a separate line of defense could be more appropriate. What I argue in sections 4 and 5 is that a distinct defense, which is actually more robust than that available for social rights, can be developed on the basis of considering environmental rights as "negative" rights more similar to established protective rights than to "positive" social rights. I suggest that substantive environmental rights, in common with some existing and far less controversial rights, can in fact be justified not indirectly, by reference to the material preconditions of democracy, but on the very grounds that democracy itself is justified. Such rights would have a very strong democratic legitimation that could undercut the main criticism altogether.

Are Constitutional Rights Inherently Undemocratic?

If an aim of constitutionalizing rights, in general, is to set them beyond the scope of ordinary political revision, this may be considered fundamentally undemocratic for a number of reasons as set out by Jeremy Waldron in his article "A Rights-Based Critique of Constitutional Rights."[4]

UNDEMOCRATIC TRANSFER OF POWERS FROM LEGISLATURE TO JUDICIARY

A major concern of Waldron's is that any proposal for entrenching a constitutional right is in effect a proposal to transfer power from an elected legislature to an unelected judiciary. Since courts do not simply enforce rights, but unavoidably also have to interpret them, "the courts will inevitably become the main forum for the revision and adaptation of basic rights in the case of changing circumstances and social controversies."[5] We should have grave misgivings about this prospect: "our respect for . . . democratic rights is called seriously into question when proposals are made to shift decisions about the conception and revision of basic rights from the legislature to the courtroom."[6]

Waldron's view is that courts should not have powers to make decisions about the scope and applications of constitutional rights because such decisions can have politically controversial content, and political controversies should be settled in political fora. A democratically illegitimate erosion of legislative power can follow from the entrenchment of constitutional rights. "When a principle is entrenched in a constitutional document," he writes, this is, in effect, "a disabling of the legislature from its normal functions of revision, reform and innovation in the law. To think that a constitutional immunity is called for is to think oneself justified in disabling legislators in this respect (and thus, indirectly, in disabling the citizens whom they represent)."[7]

However, while a degree of caution is certainly appropriate, it seems that the genuine worry here can be overstated. A justified concern about *too much* power being transferred to the judiciary—or even being arrogated to themselves by activist judges—should not lead to a disregard of the democratic importance of the judiciary's *legitimate* powers. Nor should the legitimacy of constraints on legislators' powers be disregarded. Constitutional rights have the effect of placing certain constraints on the exercise of law-making powers, which are also conferred by the constitution, of the legislature. To be *constrained* in the exercise of a power with regard to certain specific matters, however, is not the same as being *disabled* from using a general power; and so Waldron's claim, as stated, appears somewhat hyperbolic.

It also has to be recognized that the legislature's supposed monopoly of legitimate law making is not qualified only by constitutional law. A good deal of law may be made, altered, and interpreted at "lower" levels too—for example, secondary legislation, regulation, and so on, as well as in institutions of subnational governance. The legislature is thus also not the only branch of government to be constrained by constitutional principles and rights. With regard to environmental decisions, specifically, it has to be noted that many of these are taken not by the legislature but by the executive, and so, as Robyn Eckersley points out, "insofar as trade-offs must be made, it is better that they be made solemnly, reluctantly, as a matter of 'high principle' and last resort, and under the full glare of the press gallery and law reporters rather than earlier in the public decision-making process via the exercise of bureaucratic and/or ministerial discretion that is presently extremely difficult for members of the public to challenge."[8]

Furthermore, Waldron's suggestion that constitutionalizing a right is undemocratic because this indirectly disables citizens from debating or influencing its meaning or status requires some qualification. To be sure, Waldron's claim does not have to be seen as depending on any assumption, which in most contexts would likely be contentious, about the genuine representativeness of politicians; rather, his view takes as the standard of legitimacy the procedural principle of majoritarian rule. Because, in most jurisdictions, to effect a constitutional amendment generally requires more than a simple majority approval, the requirement contravenes that principle. However, this particular objection, that it is difficult to effect constitutional changes, cannot straightforwardly be applied to the initial constitutionalization of a right: precisely because a supermajority will be required to approve it, at the time of approval it would be "super legitimate" by majoritarian standards. Where his objection applies, though, is to the subsequent immutability of the provision. Circumstances change, as does the content of political will, and the problem lies in disabling future citizens from amending the provision by democratic, that is, simple majoritarian, means.

UNDEMOCRATICALLY BINDING THE FUTURE?

The focus of Waldron's concern here is the placing of binding constraints on future citizens, limiting their autonomy in policy making through principles developed on the basis of historically superseded exigencies.

Again, though, the objection appears to require some qualification. Although Waldron's argument purports to be directed against *any* canonical list of rights, it does not seem to apply, at least with the same force, to *all* kinds of entrenched rights. As was noted in relation to an earlier criticism, he appears to refer approvingly to "democratic rights," and it is hard to conceive of what it could mean for these to be effectively respected without a fairly complete catalogue of at least the standard liberal civil and political rights. The extension of such protections into the future can hardly be seen as an unwelcome binding constraint on future individuals, or as undemocratic, if they constitute "self-binding" commitments of democracy itself.

However, as we shall see in the next section, Waldron does not accept that any rights at all should be entrenched, if the aim is to preserve democracy. He does concede, though, that "if the people want a regime of constitutional rights, then that is what they should have: democracy requires *that*."[9] So he does not challenge the democratic legitimacy of a contemporary majority constraining future majorities, even if this amounts to "voting democracy out of existence, at least so far as a wide range of issues of political principle is concerned."[10] He does, however, seek to *dissuade* from such a course.

What Waldron's argument seems to come down to, then, is not that a decision to entrench rights is itself democratically illegitimate; nor does it (because it could not) seek to prove that entrenching rights necessarily harms democracy into the future; rather, the argument essentially amounts to a claim that rights proponents are imprudent and irresponsible in advocating the removal of protections for democratic decision making.

RIGHTS PROPOSALS HAVE AN
UNDEMOCRATIC MOTIVATIONAL STRUCTURE?

Waldron seeks to challenge the credibility of his opponents' case by suggesting that there is something fundamentally undemocratic, and perhaps even self-contradictory, in its motivational structure. He thinks that citizens might be dissuaded from following rights proponents if they consider what attitudes are exemplified by the latter.

> To embody a right in an entrenched constitutional document is to adopt a certain attitude towards one's fellow citizens. That attitude is best summed up as a combination of self-assurance and mistrust: self-assurance in the proponent's conviction that what she is putting forward really *is* a matter of fundamental right and that she has captured it adequately in the particular formulation she is propounding; and mistrust, implicit in her view that any alternative conception that might be concocted by elected legislators next year or the year after is so likely to be wrong-headed or ill-motivated that *her own* formulation is to be elevated immediately beyond the reach of ordinary legislative revision.[11]

However, this depiction is vulnerable to criticism on a number of grounds. In taking as its target the attitude of a *campaigner* for rights, the quoted claim about unwarranted assurance misses the mark it would need to hit in order to dissuade citizens from agreeing with "her." For in the event that citizens consider her arguments, and a majority agree that what she proposes is a matter of fundamental right, then her self-assurance would not be unwarranted in Waldron's terms. Waldron's remarks about "mistrust" similarly miss their target. It is certainly true that an element of mistrust can be assumed to animate proposals for constitutional rights: those in favor of constitutionalizing certain fundamental rights believe that this protects the interests the rights represent against the trade-offs they might otherwise be subject to under the pressures of expediency that affect ordinary politics. There is a mistrust in the inherent inequities that majoritarian decision making can generate and tolerate, and a mistrust of any assumption that a majority will always be sufficiently motivated to protect the interests of minorities. Such mistrust is not, in the rights proponent's view, unwarranted, and its implications are not necessarily undemocratic, for majoritarianism has to be justified by democratic criteria, not vice versa. The majoritarian decision-making procedure may be defended as the least worst decision-making procedure under circumstances of disagreement, but this defense would not suffice to establish that a majoritarianism qualified by the constraints of providing certain fundamental rights for everyone was, all things considered, less democratic. To establish this would require an account of the rationale and criteria of democracy that did not reduce, with circularity, to the majoritarian principle.

Here is not the place to offer even a sketch of a theory of democracy, especially since that could immediately arouse the suspicion that it was tailored so that my preferred view of environmental rights would fit into it. Nevertheless, I do think it is appropriate to indicate why the assumptions underlying the view of democracy informing Waldron's swinging critique of constitutional rights are uncompelling.

INTERNAL TENSIONS IN THE MAJORITARIAN CRITIQUE OF RIGHTS

Waldron objects to the presumption of proponents of constitutional rights in appearing to lay claim to a rationality superior to that which animates ordinary politics. His view is that there is no Archimedean point, no privileged vantage point, from which to affirm that superior rationality; and this is sufficient reason to leave matters open to ongoing democratic debate. Yet he is also ready to lament the unwisdom of a majority, or even of a supermajority, decision arising precisely out of ordinary democratic processes to entrench rights on the grounds that while these people currently have a view of certain fundamental values, and this may appear to them to get at the truth, it is really just one attachment in a likely series; any decision they take can in principle be viewed from the vantage point of a hindsight available to the theoretical commentator but not to them, and viewed, moreover, *as* but one of a likely series of temporary convictions. His own view therefore rests on a mere assumption of the radical mutability of social values that has no firmer ground than the view he opposes.

Indeed, his own view might be thought to be less firmly grounded when we consider the inconsistency manifest in the way he views disagreements among the citizen body. He claims that "if people disagree about basic rights (and they do), an adequate theory of authority can neither include nor be qualified by a conception of rights as 'trumps' over majoritarian forms of decision-making."[12] Yet in circumstances of disagreement, it is far from obvious why he thinks it more appropriate to "rely on a general spirit of watchfulness in the community, attempting to raise what Mill called 'a strong barrier of moral conviction' to protect our liberty."[13] The assumption of radical pluralism extending over time seems to be inconsistent with any appeal to a "general spirit" of a "community" or to a liberty that "we" unproblematically share. Such an appeal seems moreover to disregard basic sociological considerations about why people may not be able to realize their full potential as "moral agents endowed with dignity and autonomy" or to exercise political influence in the "processes by which decisions are taken in a community under circumstances of disagreement." It is precisely a concern that this potential may in many cases be held in check or suppressed by inauspicious socioeconomic or cultural circumstances that underpins the view of those who believe that aspects of social disadvantage are appropriately the substance of rights for the disadvantaged. Furthermore, in advocating reliance on ordinary rights generated by statutory or common law rather than constitutional rights, Waldron also requires us to share his assumption that the existing balance of ordinary rights is a result of, and reflects, majoritarian political will. We are expected to rule out a priori any suspicion—any *mistrust*—that the ordinary legal rights found in any liberal democracy might systematically favor the interests of any particular minority group of society, such as property owners, for instance.

Finally, against the various speculative objections Waldron raises we have to set the empirical historical evidence that tends to suggest that constitutional rights, wherever they have been effective, have served to enhance citizens' access to justice, both procedural and substantive.[14] This could only be considered a diminution rather than an increase in democracy on a view of democracy that was too impoverished to merit being taken as a benchmark of normative criticism.

SECTION CONCLUSION

In this section I have defended the general principle of constitutionalizing rights against charges that it necessarily runs counter to democratic principles. I have suggested that such charges can ultimately only be sustained on the basis of implausible assumptions at the level of political sociology and unwarranted assumptions at the level of normative theory. On the basis of more realistic and reasonable assumptions, by contrast, we are able to appreciate why existing democratic regimes, and their citizens, do as a matter of fact accord importance to constitutional rights, even taking these to be in important ways *constitutive* of democracy itself. Certainly, citizens' access to the institutions of justice is an important feature of any constitutional democracy, especially given that their effective ability to influence the legislature may be rather less than Waldron's position implies. Moreover, in order to sustain the claim that democracy is undermined by the attempt to constitutionalize rights, "democracy" itself has to be defined in terms such that effectively forfeit any claim for it to be a preemptive value.

So far, however, I have sought to show only that there is nothing inherently undemocratic about the constitutionalizing of rights in general; this does not imply that there could be nothing undemocratic about constitutionalizing any specific right; it also does not mean that any right could necessarily be considered a "democratic right" as opposed to being neutral with regard to principles of democracy. In the next section we consider why certain rights may be necessary for democracy, and ask whether these might include environmental rights.

Democratic Rights

It may be persuasively argued that a certain set of rights is necessary in principle for the functioning of democracy. As already noted, even Waldron refers approvingly to generic "democratic rights," and whatever force his objections may have against other constitutional rights, these, at least, might be thought to be immune. Yet that is not in fact his view. In order to get clear about the issues here it may be helpful, though, first to clarify what the expression "democratic rights" is itself to be taken to mean for the purposes of this inquiry.

The expression "democratic rights" is not to be taken to refer to rights that have been decided on or constitutionalized by democratic means. On the understanding informing this chapter, it is accepted with Waldron that the fact that a right may have a democratic genesis is neither a necessary nor sufficient condition for its being called a democratic right: it is not sufficient, since democratic decisions can have undemocratic outcomes, and one possible sort of outcome is the entrenchment of an undemocratic right; it is not necessary since democratic outcomes, and thus democratic rights, might be secured by undemocratic means.

The contrast between democratic and undemocratic rights, therefore, is drawn on the basis of a consideration of the effects or function of the rights: democratic rights are necessary to the functioning of a democracy whereas undemocratic rights would undermine its functioning. Of course, an indefinitely large variety of definitions are possible, but for present purposes it suffices to draw attention to a narrower and a broader sort of definition. On a narrow definition, democracy consists in a set of procedures for arriving at decisions; on a broader definition, democracy would be seen not simply as a set of procedures or mechanisms but as a type of society, complete with certain value commitments regarding not only the procedures for reaching decisions but also regarding desirable outcomes.

I propose to consider rights that are democratic according to the former conception of democracy as democratic rights in a strong sense: these are rights that are necessary to the very functioning of a democracy—of any democratic regime at all—and thus can be considered constitutive for democracy. Democratic rights in a weaker sense would be rights that happen to be necessary for (or even simply conducive to) the realization of the substantive principled goals of a given democratic regime, but which are not necessary for every conceivable regime that has a well-founded claim to be considered democratic in the stricter sense. For the moment, I shall be concerned only with the question of whether and how any constitutional rights can be considered democratic rights in the stronger sense.

DEMOCRACY'S "SELF-BINDING" RIGHTS: PROCEDURAL RIGHTS

It can fairly readily and, I think, persuasively be shown that certain rights are a part of what Michael Saward calls democracy's "self-binding commitments."[15] Such rights do not have a merely contingent relation to democracy, but are a necessary and constitutive part of it. Thus certain political rights, for quite evident reasons, would appear to be necessary for any democracy worthy of the name: if there were not a constitutionally assured and equal right of citizens to vote, the political system could hardly be considered democratic; nor could it be if there were not a right to stand for political office, or to associate and communicate with regard to elections, and so on. In general, then, certain rights of political participation can be conceived of quite readily as democratic rights.

These participatory rights can be distinguished in important respects from other types of constitutional rights. The rights that can be claimed to be strictly constitutive for democracy are essentially, or at their core, "rights of participation," or "rights of action." What is conceptually distinctive about this type of right is that it is fulfilled if and when its holder performs the action that he or she has a right to perform; no action of any other party is directly at issue in the basic specification of the right; if the right-bearer fails to perform the action, no duty has been violated. Its fulfillment does not immediately or directly depend on the fulfillment by any other of a duty to act or forbear. Rights of the other two types, by contrast, cannot even be intelligibly described as rights unless there is a determinate duty of another party that correlates with the right. These types of right have the form of what Hohfeld refers to as a "claim-right,"[16] the intelligible specification of which necessarily includes the specification of a correlative duty: in the case of "negative" rights, or rights of protection, the duty is primarily one of forbearance from certain actions; for "positive" rights, or rights of performance, the duty is primarily one of performing a certain action. By contrast, participatory rights, rights of action, are fulfilled if and only if their bearers exercise them, and it is conceptually impossible for such rights to be violated.

Yet while the actual exercise of participatory rights may depend entirely on the will or ability of the bearer, however, the possibility of exercising them—and indeed the very existence of them as rights—depends on the existence of the requisite institutions and procedures. If these institutions and procedures are ones that are required for democracy to function, then the rights exist for the same reason that the democracy does. Rights of participation can thus be argued to have the same justification as the corresponding democratic procedures within which they are exercised. They can be conceived of as *procedural* rights as distinct from *substantive* rights, as rights relating to procedural requirements for the functioning of democracy in general rather than substantive requirements that a particular democratic regime might seek to meet. It may therefore be thought that even if substantive rights might be vulnerable to criticism as undemocratic, procedural, participatory rights are not.

However, this argument has been resisted by Waldron. His root objection to what he dubs the "proceduralist gambit" is that the distinction between substance and democratic procedure is not a clear-cut one: "People disagree about how participatory rights should be understood and about how they should be balanced against other values."[17] "Many of the values we affirm in our opinions about democratic procedures are also values that inform our views about substantial outcomes."[18] To be sure, at the most fundamental level, the commendation of any procedure has to do with its fittingness as a means for achieving a certain sort of substantive outcome, otherwise it would have no point; it is also likely that the more detailed a specified procedure is, the more it may be taken to steer toward one particular sort of outcome rather than another. Nevertheless, the most basic procedural rights set out in quite general language at the constitutional level are likely to be indeterminate with regard to any controversial outcome involving a particular conception of justice or the good rather than the maintenance of a democratic system of government. Furthermore, even if no procedure could be completely indeterminate with regard to outcomes, it is not clear why Waldron thinks there may be any more democratic alternative to entrenching certain procedures, for, as Fabre points out, "[i]f constitutionally entrenching *any* procedure is undemocratic and therefore unacceptable, it logically follows that there should be no constitution at all."[19] Waldron simply does not address this implication.

It therefore seems to me that we can accept with Waldron that there can be no procedures that do not relate to a substantive purpose, and nevertheless argue that the substantive purpose of certain procedures can be to enhance democracy. While there may be disagreement about how well—or even whether—they achieve this, the disagreement does not have to be seen as one between defenders of democracy and their opponents, but as one between competing views of what democracy entails. Certainly, if we consider the actual purposes of certain procedural rights—which might include promoting public debate, extending the range of issues of which citizens have knowledge, and expanding the possibility of their exercising influence over those issues, for instance—there seems no overwhelming reason why they should be objected to in the name of democracy rather than supported by it.

If we are therefore entitled to assume that some procedural rights may be defended as functionally necessary for democracy, the question to consider now is whether that defense would extend to *environmental* procedural rights.

Environmental Procedural Rights

The most significant developments in actual environmental rights provision to date have centered on procedural rights with respect to matters of specifically environmental substance. These rights—of access to environmental information, participation in environmental decision making, and access to justice in environmental matters—have received widespread support from environmental campaigners, have been recognized as workable rights by legal commentators, and have been increasingly endorsed by governments. They have received a considerable impetus from what is probably the most significant agreement to date in the field of environmental rights protection, "The Convention on Access to Information, Public Participation in Decision Making, and Access to Justice in Environmental Matters," generally known as the Aarhus Convention, which was signed in 1998 by thirty-five states as well as by the European Union (EU).

The Aarhus Convention was conceived with the express aim of promoting democracy as well as protecting the right of everyone to live in a healthy environment. Rights of information are clearly a prerequisite of effective democratic citizenship; and democracy is enhanced by increasing government and industry transparency and accountability on environmental issues. Opening up access to justice in the environmental field to members of the public is a democratic necessity given that the implementation and enforcement of environmental protection laws is a task that governments alone cannot fully accomplish: in a democratic society based on the rule of law, individual citizens and their various associations have a role to play in this field too, and it is one that governments should recognize and support. If the aim of these rights is to improve citizens' effective access to justice as well as to democratic decision-making mechanisms, they would hardly fall foul of Waldron's concerns about rights that disable citizens.

It is worth noting that the agenda of Aarhus was in significant part determined by a concern to get newly independent states of Central and East Europe closer to EU standards of environmental protection, and the democratic component was considered crucial to this end. Drafters and commentators alike claimed that the experience of the former communist bloc testified to a direct correlation between deficits in democracy and in environmental quality. Access to reliable information on the environment and recognition of the role of NGOs in raising the level of public awareness of environmental issues were seen as prerequisites to developing a "civil society" of democratic citizenry.

It is also worth noting that the small number of governments that were obstructive in negotiations for the Aarhus Convention did not seek to justify their resistance with Waldron-style arguments about democracy; their concerns were rather substantive economic ones about how the proposed rights could be used to block development decisions and counter rights of economic freedom more generally. In thus seeking to reserve those substantive decision-making areas from the influence of citizens their aim could be seen as one of seeking in effect to *dilute* the convention's democratic content.

If the aim of such rights is to open up new areas of public debate, to bring an increased range of decisions into the sphere of influence of citizens, and to provide a counterbalance to the substantive values promoted by existing rights, then they have a prima facie claim, certainly not automatically invalidated by Waldron's general objections, to be considered democratic rights. It is therefore hard to deny the democratic legitimacy of procedural environmental rights.

However, it may be argued that they have this legitimacy only insofar as they are seen simply as a logical extension of existing democratic rights: hence the opening up of information and justice with regard to environmental decisions could be nothing other than a specific application of more general democratic principles. On this view, environmental rights would have no legitimacy other than that shared with other procedural rights. Yet it can be argued, and in the Aarhus convention it is explicitly stated, that those procedural rights are underpinned by a fundamental substantive right to live in an environment adequate for health and well-being. How democratic are that fundamental right and other substantive rights it might generate?

Substantive Environmental Rights as Democratic Rights

Substantive environmental rights—a fundamental "right to an adequate environment," and rights derivable from this—do not appear to be democratic rights in the sense that procedural rights can be claimed to be. It is in principle possible to offer a complete description of a democratic regime without necessarily making any reference to the quality of its physical environment. Many constitutions of the past omitted any such reference, without this being considered a source of democratic deficit; and even if no recently promulgated constitution omits reference to the importance of environmental quality, whether as a public policy objective or even as a right, this might still be distinguished from democratic objectives more strictly construed. Nevertheless, certain objectives of social policy are entrenched as constitutional rights, and, according to some theorists, this entrenchment can be defended by reference to the requirements of democracy. Their argument is not that such rights are necessary to democracy in the strict sense of being constitutive for democratic decision-making processes, but that they represent necessary preconditions for the effective functioning of a democratic regime. After briefly examining this argument we will consider whether it points to a democratic justification for environmental rights.

The preconditions argument seeks to establish democratic legitimacy for rights that are conceived as means to the ends of securing effective democratic rights rather than as rights that could be described as representing democratic ends in themselves. Such rights are not directly democratic rights in such a strict sense that a description of democracy which omitted reference to them would necessarily be an incomplete description. Nevertheless, they are rights that appear to be material requirements for the effective functioning of a fully developed democratic regime. For instance, it is widely accepted that a right to education, while not strictly necessary for the existence of democratic decision-making processes, is nevertheless a necessary condition for effective political participation: any conception of democracy that required or allowed the citizenry to be ill-informed and uneducated would not be a conception worthy of deployment as a benchmark of legitimacy. Some theorists extend this reasoning to argue that further substantive rights are necessary for the effective functioning of rights pertaining to democratic procedures. Thus rights to health, housing, and welfare (even including basic income) have been defended as necessary preconditions of democracy. Michael Saward, for instance, writes that

> a citizen may . . . be so lacking in basic human needs—food, shelter, clothing—that her or his possession of the right to basic liberties is so hollow as to be wholly symbolic. For this reason, I have included in the list of unambiguously democratic rights one to a basic income, sometimes referred to as a guaranteed minimum income. . . . The basic income is an essential condition for the effective exercise of other basic rights and freedoms of democracy.[20]

Saward's claim, then, is that the capacity to make effective use of democratic rights is undermined where certain basic social and economic rights are not met.

However, this line of argument has been considered problematic even by supporters of constitutional social rights. Cecile Fabre, for instance, has raised two doubts about it.[21] First, insofar as it rests on the suggestion that people have a right to food, housing, and so on in order that they can participate politically it seems to miss the real point of such rights: rights to health and welfare are important for reasons that have nothing to do with political participation. Second, the connection between meeting people's needs and their capacity to participate in public fora is too tenuous: rights to relief from extreme need might be justified on the grounds that they are necessary for political participation, but fully adequate welfare rights mean more than what is required simply to enable a person to haul oneself to a voting booth, and she doubts that these could be justified in terms of what is needed to enable people to participate politically.

So how do matters stand with regard to environmental rights? Robyn Eckersley has suggested that the preconditions argument can be used to support environmental rights:

> there are certain basic ecological conditions essential to human survival that should not be bargained away by political majorities because such conditions provide the very preconditions (in the form of life support) for present and future generations of humans to practice democracy. In one sense, they might be seen as even more fundamental than the human political rights that form the ground rules of democracy.[22]

However, as others have pointed out,[23] if certain ecological preconditions have to be met, there is no necessary reason why they have to be met by democratic means. Thus rights that flow from the ecological preconditions argument are not necessarily democratic ones, and could even in principle be antidemocratic. Ecological preconditions may be important (as a number of values other than democracy may be), and sensible people in a democracy may in fact agree that decisions to protect them need to be taken; but if they do not happen to agree with this, then it would be *un*democratic to have a right going against their express will and preferences. It would not be an adequate response to this objection to insist that ecological preconditions are so important—with human lives, and hence their democratic society, depending on them—that they simply must be protected by rights, since this would be to beg precisely the question that the democratic critic believes requires a democratic answer: for whether it is in fact so important is for the democratic participants to decide, and if they choose some other value, such as free choice, over survival, *that* is their democratic right.

It therefore appears that the preconditions argument is as problematic regarding the democratic legitimacy of environmental rights as it is for social rights.

However, a slightly different line of argument could be developed, adapting what Norman Daniels has put forward in the name of "relative rationality."[24] The basic argument would be that if it is rational for a democrat to affirm equal civil and political rights, then it is also rational for a democrat to affirm the equal worth of those rights. This argument can be invoked in support of social rights on the grounds that the effective enjoyment of civil and political rights is seriously compromised for the socially and economically disadvantaged sectors of society. So if democracy is recognized to imply certain self-binding rights, then these rights themselves imply further, substantive, rights.

Nevertheless, while the "relative rationality" principle itself may be persuasive, its deployment in the argument for social rights is problematic in that it depends on additional assumptions that are challengeable, namely, that assuring the equal worth of political rights depends on a redistribution of income and wealth such as is brought about by guaranteeing certain social rights. Against this, it could be argued that relative rationality could be respected by means of more rigorous procedures protecting political rights from heterogeneous influences,[25] for instance, rather than by supplementing them with social rights. Thus, whatever its merits as an argument for social justice, this argument is no stronger than the preconditions argument as a specifically democratic justification for social rights. The argument also shares with the absolute preconditions argument the problem of potentially yielding a conclusion about substantive outcomes that in practice might be democratically opposed.

Nevertheless, when we consider how the relative rationality argument might work in relation to environmental rights, matters may look a little different. It could be argued that if it is rational to affirm procedural environmental rights, then it is rational to affirm all the necessary conditions for achieving the ends for which they were introduced. Such ends would not be specific substantive environmental conditions, but an equal right of all to participate in establishing what those conditions should be. This seems an impeccably democratic principle. However, before seeing how this argument could be developed in favor of substantive environmental rights, it is necessary to indicate how these can be so conceived that they are not vulnerable to the kind of criticisms that have been seen to apply to social rights.

Environmental Rights as Negative Rights

Thus far have I have examined the case for substantive environmental rights on the assumption that they should be treated as a subspecies of social—or "positive"—rights.

I now address the question whether they might not also, or even instead, be assimilated to negative rights. If they can, this is potentially significant given that negative rights are generally considered to be more readily justifiable on democratic grounds than positive rights; the question of the democratic legitimacy of negative environmental rights will be examined more carefully, though, once the basic case for them has been set out and defended against foreseeable objections.

The basic reason for seeing a right to be free from environmental harm as a negative right is that, like negative rights generally, it would be fulfilled through the proscription of certain activities which others might otherwise engage in. Saward suggests that a green democratic right could be expressed as a negative right thus: "The state must not deprive citizens, or allow them to be deprived, of an undegraded environment." Thus, just as individuals have a right not to be subject to the kinds of harm wrought by practices of torture, unlawful detention, and so on, they may equally be thought to have a right not to be subject to comparable sorts of harm which might be wrought through practices which assail them, for instance, with toxic pollutants.

It therefore seems appropriate to view a right to an adequate environment as a negative right to the extent that the demand it implies is not that the government has to "provide" a clean environment, but that it prevent private parties—and its own agencies—from polluting or despoiling what would otherwise have been, without the need for any positive action, an adequate environment.

Nevertheless, a number of objections to this view have to be considered. An initial objection of a relatively minor sort is that, in practice, such a right might be advanced in circumstances where the environment has *already* been compromised, and so the demand based on it would not literally be preventative: the demand might be for rectification of or compensation for harm that has already been done rather than for prevention of some impending harm. Yet even in these circumstances it is possible to maintain, in point of normative principle, that the right should be classified as a negative one: compare, for instance, the case of a regime engaged in systematic torture or murder of its citizens; here the fact that the harm is already being done, and thus requires remedial rather than preventative action, does not in any way diminish the normative case for the citizens' right to be free from the harm.

It may be further objected, though, that the normative principle is an abstract one that simply does not carry through with regard to the implementation of the right by means of determinate duties. Thus whereas in the case of a regime engaged in rights abuses such as torture the demand is for restraints on actions occurring under the auspices of the state, in the case of protection from environmental harms, by contrast, the demand is for positive programs of action by the state. The thought is that in the former case the state needs only to cease what it is doing for the right to be fulfilled, whereas in the latter case the state has to undertake positive activities to fulfil the right, which can be more problematic in various ways. In particular, the environmental protection program may require the diversion of resources to its accomplishment. Yet while this may (sometimes) be the case, this in itself does not mark off environmental from more established negative rights, since any institutional protections are going to require resourcing. If there is a relevant difference between negative and positive rights on the question of resources, it lies in the fact that for negative rights an allocation of resources is necessary only as a means to the end represented by the right whereas for positive rights the redistributive allocation is itself inherent in the aim of the right. Thus typical positive rights such as welfare rights directly entail a redistribution of resources. The right to an adequate environment, however, is not a right to a particular share of resources, and so does not need to be seen as a positive right on this ground. While social rights necessarily presuppose the existence of a welfare state and developed economy, all that environmental rights necessarily presuppose are the existence of the natural world and a normative order which recognizes rights. It therefore seems appropriate to speak of a negative right to be free from interference effected in the medium of the environment.

It is difficult to envisage, though, that a negative environmental right could be an *absolute* right in the sense of requiring a complete absence of interference, where "interference" is measured as "degradation" of the environment. For one thing, a completely undegraded environment cannot be exactly what is at issue, since an environment may be degraded to some degree and yet still be adequate for everyone's health and well-being. In fact, it can be argued that a degree of environmental degradation is unobjectionable if it occurs through developments which are aimed at the *promotion* of people's health and well-being. As Joseph Sax argues, for instance, "leaving free from pollution" could entail unrealistic—and largely undesired—diminution or elimination of economic activity; and he thinks it implausible to suggest that unless a society hardly transforms its environment at all it should be branded transgressive of fundamental human rights.[26]

What about freedom from degradation of the environment to the point that it actually does cause *harm* to individuals, though? Should this, at least, not be considered an absolute normative imperative? The problem here, too, as Mark Sagoff has indicated, is that protection from environmental harms cannot be formulated as an absolute imperative in the way that protections of more established negative rights can. He notes that although laws aimed at protecting citizens from environmental threats do resemble, for instance, child labor, civil rights, and antidiscrimination statutes "insofar as they identify moral evils and seek to minimize or eliminate them,"[27] they nevertheless also differ in important respects.

> Pollutants and the risks they cause are evils, but unlike child labor and racial discrimination, they are to some extent necessary evils, because they inevitably accompany beneficial activities we are unwilling to do without. What is more, even a single instance of discrimination, voting fraud, or sexual harassment is a crime to which Americans are opposed as a society. . . . In controlling pollution and other risks, however, a conception of diminishing returns applies: As pollution levels approach zero, further reductions, as a rule, cost more to make but may be less important from a moral point of view.[28]

Environmental protection, then, is not an all-or-nothing matter. "We cannot entirely eliminate hazards created by people;" writes Sagoff, "rather, we must accept some risks that are insignificant, uncertain, or impossible to control; we must accept others because the costs of controlling them still further, *even from an ethical point of view*, are grossly disproportionate to the additional safety we gain."[29] Hence Sagoff argues that "No one has a right to a completely risk-free environment or to be protected from *de minimis* hazards even when they are caused by man."[30]

However, while I substantially accept this assessment of the less than absolute character of environmental rights, I would dispute that this is a peculiar feature of environmental rights that is not shared by the other rights mentioned. For instance, the unequivocal crimes that may be associated with discrimination, sexual harassment, and so on, have always to be distinguished from more minor sorts of offense that society requires individuals simply to live with; and the general point here is simply that in its actual implementation the "harm principle" always has to be set against a principle of *proportionality*. So if the negative environmental right neither could nor would need to be a right to be free from absolutely any harm or risk thereof, it could nevertheless be understood as a right to be free from "*unacceptable*" harm. This, after all, is the essence of established negative rights: even such a right as that to be free from torture conforms to this principle rather than to a principle of freedom from any harm whatever. Therefore the negative status of environmental rights cannot be denied on this ground either.

There are, of course, peculiar difficulties in arriving at serviceable definitions of "unacceptable harm" in the environmental field. There are certainly immense technical difficulties in trying to quantify harms and risks in a field that is so thoroughly permeated with uncertainties. However, the point about the criterion of "acceptability" is that, whatever the current state of scientific knowledge, certain risks, as currently perceived, either are or are not deemed to be acceptable on the basis of *political* decisions. The question that has to be asked in the present context is whether democratically legitimate decisions about acceptability of risk would be enhanced or compromised by constitutionalizing negative environmental rights.

The Democratic Legitimacy of Negative Environmental Rights

In a self-governing society a risk may be an acceptable one if it is knowingly and willingly assumed by those affected by it. As Sax observes, since "self-government is at the core of democratic government, and genuine choice is a key to self-government, assuring that risks taken are the product of such genuine choice is fundamental to the legitimacy of environmental decisions."[31] So what does it take to make a choice legitimate? "It is not necessary that each individual personally consent to every risk, nor that risks taken be equally imposed on every individual. No society could undertake any sort of activity if it awaited unanimity, or if it had to promise that the benefits and detriments of every program would be entirely equal across the population."[32] But if we cannot demand unanimity, there is a democratic case for insisting "that decisions be made under conditions of sufficient knowledge and consideration so as to reflect a true choice fully appreciative of the consequences." And if benefits and detriments flowing from decisions cannot be shared entirely equally, the parameters of acceptable inequalities at least must be democratically legitimated.

In ensuring that everyone has a say in the specification of acceptable environmental risks, the procedural environmental rights discussed previously clearly have an important role to play. However, procedural rights alone are not sufficient to this end. There are a number of reasons, in any complex and stratified society, why it would not in practice be possible for everyone to participate in the determination of acceptable risk. If it is not practically possible for all to exercise participatory rights with equal effectiveness, then decision-making processes should be so organized that some of the foreseeable consequences of the impossibility of genuinely universal participation are accounted for. That is to say, if some people, especially those from certain disadvantaged sectors of society, lack the knowledge, education, capacity, confidence, time, and so on, to participate effectively in pursuit of their own environmental interests, then, independently of considerations about the need to rectify socioeconomic disadvantages at source, there is a case for saying that their basic interests should in some way be represented in the deliberations of those who do participate.

At the least, as Sax suggests, the majority can be said to owe to each individual a basic right not to be left to fall below some minimal level of substantive protection against hazard. For it can and does happen that risks that are chosen by majoritarian democratic processes fall particularly heavily on certain groups or individuals. "The most tragic images of environmental harm are those involving hapless victims, those who without sufficient knowledge or involvement and without choice have had risk and damage imposed upon them."[33] It is also worth noting that sometimes people, particularly the poor, "assent" to a heightened risk of environmental harm, if this is the only way they can retain their livelihood; yet such a situation is not only unjust, but also undemocratic, since such people are under an effective material compulsion to accept, and bear the brunt of, decisions in a way that others are not. The basic democratic principle of equal autonomy would thus appear to be violated.

So I believe there is a case not only of justice, but also of democratic principle, that can be made for a basic norm, as suggested by Sax, that "the least advantaged individual is insulated against imposition of risk below some minimal threshold within his or her own society."[34] This norm is most appropriately conceived as a fundamental substantive environmental right. In formulating the relevant norm, one can imagine, for instance, a Rawlsian procedure whereby from behind a "veil of ignorance" rational agents would determine which risks they would wish to be protected against under any circumstances, and which risks they would be willing to run as a trade-off against certain attendant benefits. This procedure would in effect make it possible to distinguish protective rights, which are on a par with those protecting liberties, from provisions that may be subject to the trade-offs allowed by the difference principle. Rights relating to a minimum environmental standard would come under the same protection as basic liberties, and in this respect they would be akin to existing negative rights in not being liable to any trade-off. For having granted that some trade-offs of environmental quality against socioeconomic advantage might be considered permissible in a democracy, it is nevertheless arguable that certain basic limits to trade-offs are warranted, particularly in circumstances of environmental injustice whereby the economic benefits of some are traded against the environmental detriments of others.

Such a right is not vulnerable to the problem we noted earlier regarding attempts to argue for social rights as democratic rights, whereby opponents can claim that it is not irrational to assent to political rights (i.e., democratic rights in a strict sense) and yet to dissent from social rights if one can conceive of how procedures in the former sphere can be insulated against substantive disruptions in the latter sphere. For, by contrast, it would be irrational to assent to procedural environmental rights and yet dissent from substantive environmental rights if the sphere of the former cannot similarly be insulated from the sphere of the latter. And I have sought to indicate why it cannot—in particular, because in the very specification of *acceptable* environmental risks procedural and substantive dimensions intermesh.

At this point, however, it is open to a skeptic to respond, echoing Waldron, that if a commitment to procedural environmental rights does entail substantive rights then this is a reason for a democrat to resist entrenching that commitment in a constitution. Should democratic participants not retain a right to dissent from a commitment to such substantive outcomes? In reply to this critical question, the implications of conceiving the right as a negative one must be brought to the fore.

Negative rights are generally considered to be more readily justifiable on democratic grounds than positive ones are. Certain negative rights can reasonably be claimed to be implied by the core demands of democracy: thus civil rights, aimed for instance at protecting citizens' freedom of expression and association, follow with a clear substantive logic from the requirements of a properly functioning democracy. However, this direct connection does not seem to hold for negative environmental rights (for reasons already discussed). Interestingly, though, the connection by no means holds for a number of other negative rights, including some of those that have proven to be the least controversial in democracies. It would be implausible to suppose that rights not to be tortured or arbitrarily imprisoned, for instance, are only respected by democracies because of the practical difficulties of registering a vote under such proscribed circumstances. Indeed, if that were so, then arrangements could be made—such as temporary release on polling day—that would render torture and arbitrary imprisonment consistent with democratic imperatives. Rather than subscribe to this bizarre and abhorrent view, I think, most democratic theorists would accept that there is some stronger normative connection between a range of rights to be left alone and those rights that are more strictly associated with democratic procedures. In other words, democratic rights in what I earlier referred to as the weak sense of the term, are in practice as vital to a fully fledged democratic polity as rights pertaining to its formal constitution. Certainly, the counterintuitive results of following strict proceduralism to the extreme consequences noted force on our attention the issue of the extent to which procedural democracy has certain substantive normative presuppositions. If such wrongs as torture, servitude, slavery, and so on cannot be ruled out on any grounds other than that they impede political participation, then there can be no more democratic warrant for rights to protection against them than there is for rights to environmental protection. However, I think the appropriate view to take is that these rights can be justified not on the grounds that they are necessary for the effective functioning of democracy but rather on the *same* grounds that democracy itself is justified.

So it is appropriate to consider the more fundamental reasons why negative rights in general are more readily defensible in a democracy than positive ones are. A reason for this is that, as rights to be left alone or free from interference by the state or third parties, a presumption can be made in their favor in a democracy that cannot so readily be made for positive rights. To put it perhaps rather crudely: in a democracy, individuals have a presumptive right to do whatever they choose to do just as long as what they choose is not proscribed; in the absence of a proscription, they do not need to produce a justification for what they choose to do, and the onus is on those who would proscribe the action to produce a justification. If we then consider how the presumption itself is warranted, it suffices, I think, without going into the various justificatory explanations that may be given for democracy, to note that a common feature of them would be to deem that individuals have basic rights of autonomy or self-governance; without some such presupposition, even a descriptive account of democracy would be incomplete, and a normative one would be all but impossible.

I would therefore maintain that if substantive environmental rights can be conceived as negative rights, it is possible to argue strongly for their democratic legitimacy. The argument developed from the premise of democratic neutrality that is used to criticize positive rights can actually be deployed in support of negative environmental rights: if democracy requires individuals to be considered to have a basic right of self-governance this implies a presumptive right of individuals to be free of any interference that is either not democratically justified or necessary in order to maintain democracy. Unless some substantive reason to the contrary is provided, then, the presumptive right of noninterference can be deemed to hold with respect to interferences that occur in the medium of the environment as much as in any other medium where individuals' personal or bodily integrity is threatened.

Conclusion

Environmental rights can assume a variety of forms within a constitution, including the three broad types discussed in this chapter: procedural rights, positive rights, and negative rights; each type, I have suggested, can in principle be claimed to have democratic legitimacy comparable to that of more established rights of these types. Therefore if any constitutional rights at all can be considered to have democratic legitimacy, then a wide range of constitutional environmental rights can. Reasons have also been given for thinking that on any normatively elaborated conception of constitutional democracy it actually requires full recognition of these rights.

Notes

1. World Commission on Environment and Development, *Our Common Future* (The Brundtland Report) (New York: Oxford University Press, 1987).

2. For an overview of the issues see, for example, Tim Hayward, "Constitutional Environmental Rights: A Case for Political Analysis," *Political Studies* 48, no. 3 (June 2000): 558–72.

3. Robert Goodin, *Green Political Theory* (Cambridge, U.K.: Polity Press, 1992), 168.

4. Jeremy Waldron, "A Rights-Based Critique of Constitutional Rights," *Oxford Journal of Legal Studies* 13 (Spring 1993): 18–51. Waldron's specific concern in this article is to counter arguments in a British context for a Bill of Rights, particularly if this should be accompanied by U.S.-style provisions for judicial review. However, his arguments for the most part are couched in terms sufficiently general to be of applicability in other contexts too.

5. Ibid., 20.

6. Ibid.

7. Ibid., 27.

8. Robyn Eckersley, "Greening Liberal Democracy: The Rights Discourse Revisited," in *Democracy and Green Political Thought*, ed. Brian Doherty and Marius de Geus (London: Routledge, 1996), 229.

9. Waldron, "A Rights-Based Critique," 46.

10. Ibid.

11. Ibid., 27.

12. Ibid., 20.

13. Ibid., 18.

14. See, for example, Charles R. Epp, *The Rights Revolution: Lawyers, Activists, and Supreme Courts in Comparative Perspective* (Chicago: University of Chicago Press, 1998).

15. Michael Saward, *The Terms of Democracy* (Cambridge, U.K.: Polity Press, 1998), especially chapter 5.

16. Wesley N. Hohfeld, *Fundamental Legal Conceptions* (New Haven, Conn.: Yale University Press, 1919).

17. Waldron, "A Rights-Based Critique," 39.

18. Ibid., 40.

19. Cecile Fabre, *Social Rights under the Constitution: Government and the Decent Life* (Oxford, U.K.: Clarendon Press, 2000), 144.

20. Saward, *Terms of Democracy*, 99.

21. Fabre, *Social Rights*, 122–25.

22. Eckersley, "Green Liberal Democracy," 224.

23. For example, Andrew Dobson, "Democratizing Green Political Theory: Preconditions and Principles," in *Democracy and Green Political Thought*, ed. Brian Doherty and Marius de Geus (London and New York: Routledge, 1996).

24. Norman Daniels, "Equal Liberty and Unequal Worth of Liberty," in *Reading Rawls*, ed. Norman Daniels (Oxford, U.K.: Blackwell, 1975), 276.

25. For an argument along these lines see, for example, Michael Walzer, *Spheres of Justice: A Defense of Pluralism and Equality* (Oxford, U.K.: Blackwell, 1985).

26. Joseph L Sax, "The Search for Environmental Rights," *Journal of Land Use and Environmental Law* 6 (1993): 93–105, 95.

27. Mark Sagoff, *The Economy of the Earth: Philosophy, Law, and the Environment* (Cambridge: Cambridge University Press, 1988), 197.

28. Ibid., 197–98.

29. Ibid., 198, emphasis in original.

30. Ibid., 219.

31. Sax, "The Search," 97.

32. Ibid.

33. Ibid.

34. Ibid., 101.

CHAPTER 13

Deliberative Democracy and Environmental Policy

John O'Neill

Deliberative or discursive models of democracy have enjoyed a justifiable revival in political theory and public policy. Against the economic picture of democracy as a surrogate market procedure for aggregating and effectively meeting the given preferences of individuals, the deliberative theorist offers a model of democracy as a forum through which judgments and preferences are transformed through reasoned dialogue between citizens.[1] The recent revival of deliberative democracy has been expressed in policy practice through the development of a variety of "new" formal deliberative institutions that have been introduced alongside "older" democratic institutions and that are often presented as experiments in deliberative democracy. These include citizens' juries, citizens' panels, in-depth discussion groups, focus groups, consensus conferences, and roundtables.[2] As will be evident, these experiments in deliberative democracy have been particularly developed in the environmental sphere, as has the development of the theory of deliberative democracy.[3] In the context of public environmental choice the theory and practice of deliberative democracy has had particular power in criticism of standard economic approaches to environmental decision making represented by decision tools such as cost-benefit analysis (CBA). The deliberative critics have focused both on the reason blindness of cost-benefit analysis and its distributive implications.

Cost-benefit analysis as an approach to the resolution of value conflicts about the environment is reason blind. The strength and weaknesses of the *intensity* of a preference as measured by a person's willingness to pay at the margin for satisfaction do count in a decision; the strength and weakness of the *reasons* for a preference do not. Preferences are treated as expressions of mere taste to be priced and weighed one with the other. It offers conflict resolution and policy without rational assessment and debate. Politics becomes a surrogate market that completes by bureaucratic means what, within neoclassical theory, the ideal market is supposed to do—aggregate efficiently given preferences.[4] However, since environmental conflicts are open to reasoned debate and judgment that aim to change preferences not record them, it follows that different institutional forms are required for their resolution. Since conflict is open to reasoned adjudication, discursive institutions are the appropriate form for conflict resolution. The forum, not the market, becomes the proper institutional form.

The central point of the distributive criticism of cost-benefit analysis is not simply that it focuses on issues of efficiency rather than of distribution, but that the assumed logical independence of Paretian efficiency and distribution is mistaken. Existing costs and benefits themselves are the product of a set of property rights. If property rights are changed, so also is what is efficient. The treatment of efficiency as if it were logically independent of distribution is then at best misleading, for the determination of efficiency already presupposes a given distribution of rights. Since costs are not independent of rights they cannot guide the allocation of rights. Different initial distributions entail differences in whose preferences are to count. Hence, environmental policy and resource decision making cannot avoid making value choices that include questions of resource distribution and property rights.[5] In practice, cost-benefit analysis tends to conservatism by assuming a status quo distribution of rights. In particular since willingness to pay is income dependent the use of raw willingness to pay measures will give greater weight to the preferences of the rich—"the poor sell cheap."[6] Moreover, the interests of nonhumans and future generations cannot be directly captured at all through willingness to pay and they are indirectly captured at best precariously through the preferences of current consumers.[7] Deliberative institutions are often presented as responses to these distributive failings. The resolution of such conflicts requires deliberative institutions in which challenges to the legitimacy of given distributions of entitlements and outcomes are recognized. The distribution of resources and property rights is not presupposed as it is in market methods, but can itself be an object of public deliberation.

However, the deliberative alternatives have their own distributive problems. While these deliberative institutions are often presented as "facilitating" "inclusive" "dialogue" between equals, dialogue takes place against the background of large asymmetries of social, institutional, and economic power. This has implications for the ways in which deliberative fora themselves can operate. Within deliberative fora the capacity and confidence to speak and, more significantly, to be heard, differs across class, gender, and ethnicity. Just as "willingness to pay" in CBA is unevenly distributed, picking up inequalities of income, so also is willingness to say. Moreover, the two are related. Hence, there is power in the response to the deliberative critics: that it is a way in which those with the power of voice are able to exercise it over those who lack voice.[8] It is not just the internal workings of deliberative institutions that matters here but the context in which they operate. Deliberative institutions are open to being used strategically. Some of the new institutions that are claimed to be deliberative, in particular focus groups, are often employed in political practice not to allow deliberation to take place but rather to close it down. They are used to gather information of likely responses to different potential policies and actions not to open up debate but to anticipate and forestall it. The origin of the focus group technique in market research is not without its implications. Where deliberation is public, power can be exercised in the framing of issues prior to discussion and in the choice of the constituency for debate. If effectively captured by powerful institutions deliberative institutions potentially provide powerful legitimation tools—indeed much more powerful than expert based techniques like CBA, which lack democratic legitimacy. Correspondingly there are contexts in which dialogue may simply be a means through which those who lack social power concede to those who do not: in such contexts, for the powerless, dialogue might not be the appropriate response.

That the practice of new deliberative institutions can come apart from the theory is not surprising. Nor as far as the deliberative democratic theory is concerned need it be problematic. The deliberative theorist can respond that many of the potential problems in the practice of new deliberative institutions are ones that the deliberative theory of democracy would itself highlight. It is an internal feature of the most deliberative models that the deliberative institutions fail to the extent that such asymmetries of power and strategic action are present. Now that still raises real problems of how far any approximation to deliberative institutions is possible in existing or alternative social, economic, and political conditions, but that is as Habermas notes about "the possibility of effectively institutionalizing rational discourse"[9] and not about the account of rational discourse that deliberative democracy is taken to offer. The deliberative theorist can then claim that the potential problems with the practice of new deliberative institutions do not undermine the deliberative theory of democracy as such. Rather deliberative theory provides the normative basis from which an immanent criticism of the failings of putatively deliberative institutions can proceed. As such, the theory can be still said to have purchase. Hence Habermas's claim that while "the actual course of the debates deviates from the ideal procedures of deliberative politics . . . presuppositions of rational discourse have a steering effect on the course of the debates."[10] Thus goes the response for deliberative democracy.

I would like to make two general points about this response, before focusing on a particular set of problems raised by recent experiments in environmental deliberation. The first is that the deliberative criticisms of existing deliberative institutions in the end push beyond the purely political models of deliberative institutions that are defended in much of the literature. They point in the direction of traditional egalitarian claims about the structural conditions for democracy: formal equality in democratic rights is insufficient without equality in social and economic power. A rough equality in economic and social power is a necessary condition, and such equality requires shifts away from current patterns of ownership and control.[11] Second, any deliberative criticisms of existing experiments in deliberation rely on some account of what counts as good deliberation, which are themselves open to debate. The Habermasian model is particularly questionable in the intellectualist account of deliberation it offers. That model is particularly problematic in the environmental sphere, where the central questions of deliberation are more a matter of trust in testimony—of deciding *who* to believe—rather direct assessment of evidence and argument.[12]

However, recent policy experiments in environmental deliberation also raise more particular problems about the legitimacy of representation, some of which parallel some of the problems in market-based approaches. The problem of future generations and nonhumans is a recognized source of difficulty for deliberative theories of democracy.[13] Their direct voice is necessarily absent, and hence, as with market methods, consideration of their interests relies upon indirect representation. The absence of direct representation raises major problems concerning the ethical and political legitimacy of decisions made in the absence of their voice. At the same time it raises problems also for forms of environmental action and advocacy that are legitimized by appeal to the claim that protagonists are speaking and acting on behalf of those who are without voice. However, it is not just with nonhumans and future generations that the problems of representative legitimacy arise for deliberative theories. Many recent experiments in deliberative institutions—citizens' juries, in-depth discussion groups, consensus conferences, and the like—are small and hence raise issues about the source of their legitimacy as representative of larger populations. Moreover, this problem may be a necessary feature of deliberative institutions: the quality of deliberation requires smaller fora, the quality of representativeness requires larger fora, and the two demands pull in the opposite direction.

The Politics of Representation

Deliberative democracy faces significant problems about the nature of legitimate representation within deliberative fora. What makes for good representation—or at least adequate representation—for deliberative institutions? What institutional forms will suffice in what conditions? I want to start to answer those questions with a passage from a story by Borges, "The Congress":

> Don Alejandro conceived the idea of calling together a Congress of the World that would represent all men of all nations. . . . Twirl, who had a farseeing mind, remarked that the Congress involved a problem of a philosophical nature. Planning an assembly to represent all men was like fixing the exact number of platonic types—a puzzle that had taxed the imagination of thinkers for centuries. Twirl suggested that, without going farther afield, don Alejandro Glencoe might represent not only cattlemen but also Uruguayans, and also humanity's great forerunners, and also men with red beards, and also those who are seated in armchairs. Nora Erfjord was Norwegian. Would she represent secretaries, Norwegian womanhood, or—more obviously—all beautiful women? Would a single engineer be enough to represent all engineers—including those of New Zealand?[14]

The story ends with an echo of another of Borges's stories in which the development of cartography attains its highest point when the perfect map is identical to the area it maps: "the College of Cartographers evolved a Map of the Empire that was of the same Scale as the Empire and that coincided with it point for point."[15] Similarly the only adequate congress of the world is discovered to be the world itself.

> "It has taken me four years to understand what I am about to say" don Alejandro began. "My friends, the undertaking we have set ourselves is so vast that it embraces—I now see—the whole world. Our Congress cannot be a group of charlatans deafening each other in the sheds of an out-of-the-way ranch. The Congress of the World began with the first moment of the world and it will go on when we are dust. There's no place on earth where it does not exist."[16]

The characters go back out into the city "drunk with victory," to take part in the life of the congress in which all people and all things are represented perfectly by themselves.

It would be nice to think that don Alejandro had the last word on the subject, and in the design of institutions for representation the solution should be that we should simply go for a walk outside. Indeed one version of the idea represents a form of democratic anarchism that is attractive. However, I would not propose to use Borges's character Alejandro to design representative institutions anymore than I would use his cartographers to design maps. Maps are better when not identical to their original.[17] The congress of the world is not best represented by the world itself. In both cases, the solution rather misses the point of representation and the work it does in our lives. Borges's discussion remains important however. There is often a background assumption in discussions of representation that the perfect representation would be the person or object itself. Critics of "essentialism" sometimes complain that representatives do not map all the characteristics of those they represent.[18] They could not and this is not always a problem. Every representative institution is unrepresentative over some dimensions. No representation captures everything about those represented. I don't complain that my ordinance survey map fails to mark every stone. It doesn't matter that men with red beards lack a spokesperson in the United Kingdom. I do complain when my walking maps are indifferent to scale. There are proper complaints that large groups of the population lack any adequate representation in political life, for example, low-paid and retired workers.

What then are the criteria for saying who or what should be represented and whether representation is adequate? Here again, rather reluctantly, I want to depart from one suggestion in the Borges story. The problem is not one of a philosophical nature, at least in the sense that Twirl suggests, that of correctly fixing on Platonic forms. The reason why being "a man with a red beard who sits in armchairs" would normally be an irrelevant characteristic has nothing to do with appearing in a theory of forms. The problem of representation is political, not metaphysical.

Questions of legitimate representation have their own history in political theory.[19] They include the following:

1. Who is being represented in the political or decision-making process? Under what descriptions are they being represented? Is it as individuals, as members of particular functional groups or economic classes, as bearers of particular cultural, ethnic, or gender identities?[20] Is representation limited to current generations of humans or should it be extended to include representation of future generations or nonhumans? The answer to such questions requires appeal to normative criteria. What matters is who should count and under what description and for what ends, rather than simple statistical significance. Moreover, there are also descriptions under which representation might be objectionable in virtue of the attitudes they embody—consider, for example, the categories of "Norwegian womanhood" or "beautiful women" in the passage from Borges. Other categories are ethically irrelevant, for example, "men with red beards who sit in armchairs."

2. What is being represented? Are the particular interests of different individuals or groups to be represented? Or their common interests? Or are their values, their opinions, their preferences, their will, their discourses, or their identities to be the object of representation?

3. Who is doing the representation? What relation do representatives have to the represented? Does adequate representation require that the representatives of some class or group should share a common identity with those they represent, as some traditions of egalitarian thought suggest?

4. What is the source of the legitimacy of the representation?

   Three answers to that question have particular relevance here:

a. Authorization and democratic accountability: The claim that authorization is central to representation is given its starkest formulation in Hobbes, who makes it the whole of representation.[21] Representation is modeled on the legal attorney who speaks or acts on behalf of a client on being authorized to do so. However, in a number of democratic theories of representation authorization is embodied in democratic election.[22] As such, authorization is tied to the accountability of the representative to the represented, a feature absent in Hobbes's account of authorization. Thus on one liberal model of representation, the interests of individuals are represented through the act of authorization embodied in the vote. More radically, within socialist and egalitarian politics authorization is often associated with the representation of class interests through recallable delegates. Authorization is in itself agnostic on the question of who does the representing: the representative, when authorized, can be entirely different in characteristics from the person represented. A lawyer can represent children without being a child. In certain contexts you may prefer that X speaks for you, because of features you do not share—for example, they are more articulate say as a shop steward in an industrial tribunal.

b. Presence/shared identity: A feature of much feminist and socialist theory is that in the context of political representation a pure authorization model is rejected. Who does the representing matters. Exemplary is the following by women claiming a place in the Estates General in 1789:

> Just as a nobleman cannot represent a plebeian and the latter cannot represent a nobleman, so a man, no matter how honest he may be, cannot represent a woman. Between the representatives and the represented there must be an absolute identity of interests.[23]

The same thought underlay the principle in the socialist movement that the emancipation of the working class must be their own work, and correspondingly that its interests could not be represented by any other class. The thought that particular groups demand representation by those who share a common identity has become central to what Phillips calls "the politics of presence."[24] It underpins, for example, the demand for quota systems in modern electoral systems. While shared identity may be a necessary condition of adequate representation, there is still a requirement for authorization or accountability. That someone shares an identity with me under some description does not entail they can legitimately represent me in the absence of my authorization.

c. Epistemic values: A third source of appeal to legitimacy is the knowledge, expertise, or judgment that is taken to allow an individual to speak or act on behalf of some group. This argument is often developed in ways that are in tension with a representation legitimated through shared identity. Consider, for example, the view that there are certain individuals who, through knowledge, have a better grasp of the objective interests or good of some group than others in that group and that this knowledge legitimizes their representative status. Versions of that appeal are to be found in theorists as different as Burke, Mill,[25] and Lenin.[26] However, knowledge and presence need not always be in tension. One reason why a shared identity might be held to matter in representation is that similar experiences are a condition of proper knowledge of the interests and aspirations of that group.

Deliberative Democracy and the Sources of Legitimacy

What is the relation of deliberative institutions to the different answers to these questions about representation and its legitimacy? New deliberative institutions can be understood in part as experiments in deliberative democracy. In its minimal sense deliberative democracy refers to the view that democracy should be understood as a forum through which judgments and preferences are transformed through reasoned dialogue against the picture of democracy as a procedure for aggregating and effectively meeting the given preferences of individuals. Given this definition of deliberative democracy, certain answers to the question of *what* is being represented are ruled out, notably the given preferences of individuals.[27] Preferences or judgments are rather to be transformed through debate. Nor is deliberative democracy a modified form of interest-based pluralism. Deliberation in this context needs to be distinguished from processes of negotiation or bargaining between different particular interests, important as such processes are.[28] What is being represented has to be understood as judgments that are open to change through reasoned dialogue. Deliberative democracy has, then, implications for what is being represented.

However, when addressing the other questions I raised above, deliberative institutions are consistent with several different answers. In particular, deliberative democracy is compatible with competing answers to the question of the sources of legitimacy. For example, Edmund Burke's famous address to the electors of Bristol can be understood as offering a deliberative theory of democracy, underpinned by epistemic claims to legitimacy:

> Your representative owes you, not his industry only, but his judgement; and he betrays, instead of serving you, if he sacrifices it to your opinion. . . . [G]overnment and legislation are matters of reason and judgement, and not of inclination; and what sort of reason is that, in which the determination precedes the discussion; in which one set of men deliberate and another decide. . . . Parliament is not a *congress* of ambassadors from different and hostile interests; which interests each must maintain, as an agent and advocate, against other agents and advocates; but parliament is a *deliberative* assembly of one nation, with *one* interest, that of the whole.[29]

This is a deliberative model of political institutions in the sense that it sees political processes not as the aggregation of preferences or inclinations, nor as a process of negotiation between different private interests, but as a matter of arriving at common judgments on common interests founded on reasons and argument. However, this is clearly different from the model of deliberative institutions that informs the recent theory and practice of deliberative democracy. The difference from this older tradition is sometimes marked by the appeal to "inclusionary" processes for deliberation.

The addition of "inclusionary" to the concept of deliberative processes links the arguments about representation to some of the themes in the politics of presence, that is, that deliberative institutions should give equal access to all relevant voices by directly including representatives of different relevant identities. Wider inclusion is defended as a source of proper deliberation in which the widest range of different relevant views are heard.

> [D]eliberative processes will be improved, not undermined, if mechanisms are instituted to ensure multiple groups have access to the process and are actually present when decisions are made. Proportional or group representation . . . would ensure that diverse views are expressed on an ongoing basis in the representative process, where they might otherwise be excluded.[30]

The argument runs that a deliberative justification for the presence of different identities offers a more powerful defense than that based on a model of bargaining: "the primary purpose of access is not to allow each group to get 'its piece of the action'—though this is not entirely irrelevant—but instead to ensure that the process of deliberation is not distorted by a mistaken view of a common set of interests."[31] Preferences and judgments change through confronting a range of arguments and views. Inclusion, then, is justified by the nature of deliberation itself. Presence and deliberation can be consistent. The presence of different identities may be considered part of the ideal conditions in which consensus under the sole authority of the better argument emerges.

However, there are potential conflicts between deliberative democracy and a politics of presence.[32] Recent accounts of reasoned deliberation, especially those that have their roots in Habermas, define successful deliberation in terms of the convergence of judgments under ideal counterfactual conditions in which all have equal voice and "no force except that of the better argument is exercised."[33] There are tensions between this position and a politics of presence insofar as the latter has been recently related to a politics of difference.[34] Now the politics of difference has, I think, real problems, not least its tension with a politics of solidarity.[35] However, putting these issues aside, it remains the case that there may be no possibility for convergence even in ideal conditions.

One common argument against convergence is that for normative questions there are no truths of the kind found in science on which one could expect convergence through reasoned debate.[36] I remain unconvinced by this argument.[37] However, even if one rejects it, there are other sources of divergence that do have power. First, there can exist conflicts between different goods themselves, which give reasons for skepticism about the possibility of convergence even under ideal conditions. Different human goods fostered within distinct practices by different groups may themselves be in conflict. Consider, for example, the ways in which good husbandry of the land within a marginal farming community can come into conflict with the aims of conserving biodiversity.[38] Such conflicts may be unresolvable. Conservation does not have some lexicographic priority in such cases over the value of community or the internal goods of husbandry. Nor are there simple trade-offs between commensurable values. There are real human goods that demand realization but that conflict. Even under ideal conditions hard and sometimes irresolvable choices between values that contingently conflict cannot be eliminated from ethical and political life.[39] Second, many environmental problems involve conflicts of interests that are simply incompatible. For example, consider the conflict of peasant farmers and large seed companies over the control of agricultural biodiversity.[40] Third, under the nonideal conditions of actual deliberation in political and social life, the existence of consensus can be a sign of personal or structural power that is exercised to keep various voices and conflicts out of the realm of public discussion, rather than an indication of the exercise of the power of reasoned public conversation. For that reason there is as much a need for dissensus conferences as consensus conferences, for places where hidden conflicts are made explicit and silenced voices are heard.

The link between experiments in deliberative democracy and the politics of presence also raises a number of problems of legitimacy that echo Twirl's questions in the Borges story and have become increasingly pressing in arguments around representation in the politics of presence. Individuals have a complex set of identities under different descriptions. The questions of which of these is to count and under what descriptions different groups are included in deliberation, and of how particular individuals can be said to legitimately stand for or speak on behalf of others, becomes increasingly problematic:

> What . . . is an appropriate mechanism for dealing with political exclusion? Can Asians be represented by Afro-Caribbeans, Hindus by Muslims, black women by black men? Or do these groups have nothing more in common than their joint experience of being excluded from power?[41]

Or to take examples from recent examples of experiments in deliberation, in focus groups who are Blackburn Asian women or unemployed young men from Morecambe supposed to represent?[42] Whom should a retired worker on a citizens' jury about the recreation of a wet fen site be taken to represent?[43] The very descriptions used in these contexts by the social analyst force a representative status on participants that may be contested even by those individuals themselves. The contestation is proper. Simply being a member of a particular group does not entail that one is a representative of that group.[44] If these questions are combined with what is often called a radical "anti-essentialism," which denies the very idea that there are any characteristics that are shared by some group, then the subsequent "distrust [in] the notion that anyone can 'stand in' for anyone else"[45] may very quickly lead to an Alejandro solution in which representation by others is impossible. This in part points to problems in anti-essentialism, but I leave those aside here.[46] The problems of legitimacy of representation in recent deliberative institutions remain even if radical anti-essentialism is denied.

The problems are made more acute where authorization and accountability as sources of legitimation are absent. As the cases outlined in the last paragraph highlight, in many recent experiments in inclusionary deliberative institutions, such as citizens' juries, citizens' panels, consensus conferences, in-depth discussion groups, or focus groups, none of the participants are authorized to speak for any group they are taken to "represent," nor are they accountable to those groups. Indeed in most cases their status of being representative of some group is not chosen by the participants. For that reason, they appear to lack the sources of legitimacy that are appealed to for traditional democratic representative institutions.

There may, however, be other good reasons for taking at least some forms of the new deliberative institutions to be part of a democratic social and political order. One response is to insist upon a weaker role for such institutions within the democratic process, say to the formulation of options and possible recommendations, allowing for other forms of accountability to be retained in the decision-making process.[47] Another more promising argument in favor of a larger role for some forms of deliberative institution is to appeal to the Athenian practice of having political positions filled by lot as part of the democratic order.[48] The justification of the procedure lies in the idea of democracy as a social order of equals where citizens take turns in positions of power, in which, as Aristotle puts it, "they rule and are ruled in turn."[49] Among the main arguments in favor of the position is that, unlike most other institutional arrangements, power is not distributed to those who desire it and both power and responsibility circulate among citizens. In addition the approach offers a counterweight to the power of experts in decision making.[50] However, such Athenian solutions still require some institutional arrangements for the accountability of deliberative institutions to a wider public. Burnheim suggests otherwise: "Demarchic leaders would not be accountable because they would not be eligible for reappointment."[51] However, the reasoning here is unconvincing. The argument could and should run in the other direction; that is, because demarchic leaders are closed to reappointment, other forms of accountability need to be developed.

Giving Voice to the Voiceless: Nature and Future Generations

The problems of representativeness raised thus far are general problems for deliberative institutions that arise in any domain of choice, not problems peculiar to the environment. However, environmental decisions raise very particular problems for democratic theory concerning the nature and possibility of representation over and above those discussed so far. The central problem is that for many of those affected by decisions, two central features of legitimization—authorization and presence—are absent. Indeed for nonhumans and future generations there is no possibility of those conditions being met. Neither nonhumans nor future generations can be directly present in decision making. Clearly, representation can neither be authorized by nonhumans or future generations nor can it be rendered accountable to them. Hence, Hobbes, for whom authorization is all of representation, denies that "inanimate" or "nonrational beings" can authorize others to act for them.[52] The politics of presence that underlies much of recent literature in deliberative democracy is likewise ill suited to include future generations and nonhumans. In the case of current nonhumans this might be regarded as untrue. Something like an Alejandro solution is possible. Consider the success of Muir's strategy of taking Roosevelt out into the landscapes he aimed to preserve. There is a sense in which one might say that the strategy consisted in nature being represented by itself. However, while there is certainly a case more generally for taking deliberation into the places that are the object of deliberation, the articulation of any nonhuman interests or values here remains a human affair. The presence of nonhuman nature in deliberation about environmental choices requires human representation.

That neither authorization nor presence is possible is in one sense unproblematic—it could not be otherwise. The problem lies in the claims to legitimacy of those current humans who claim to speak on the behalf of future generations and nonhumans in the absence of sources of legitimation. The standard solutions offered to the problem are that current generations authorize or act as trustees on behalf of the interests of nonhumans and future generations. Thus the state (Pigou),[53] representatives from the environmental lobby (Dobson),[54] and citizens who have internalized those interests (Goodin)[55] have all been suggested as proxy representatives.

However, the solution of proxy representation has its own problems. These lie in part with the historical precedents of this form of representation. The idea that the interests of one group can be represented by those of others was used to justify the representation of women by husbands and servants by masters. It also underpinned the Whig notion of virtual representation employed to limit the extension of the suffrage and characterized thus by Burke:

> Virtual representation is that in which there is a communion of interests, and sympathy in feelings and desires between those who act in the name of any descriptions of people, and the people in whose name they act, though trustees are not actually chosen by them. This is virtual representation.[56]

The historical uses of the concepts of incorporated interests and virtual representation cast a shadow of illegitimacy over their revitalization in green political thought. Moreover, even granted their legitimacy, they appear ill suited to deal with the representation of nonhumans and future generations, since it is simply false to assert that their interests are identical to those of current generations of humans. Nonhumans and future generations are rather like the Catholics in eighteenth-century Ireland whom Burke claimed had no virtual representation since none with the same interests is "actually represented" in the political process.[57]

What response can be made for the virtual representation of nonhumans and future generations? First, it might be argued that the historical illegitimacy need not spill over to the representation of nonhumans and future generations. Such representation involves neither the relations of power and subordination that are involved in the illegitimate historical precedents, nor the failure to recognize the dignity of those denied direct representation. If individuals or groups can speak for themselves, then they should do so. However, where this is impossible there is no loss in dignity nor assumed power relations in others speaking for them: the representation of infants through the adults who care for them, while imperfect, is legitimate. Hence representing the interests of future humans and nonhumans through current persons is legitimate.[58]

What of the objection that there is no identity of interests between current humans and future generations and nonhumans? The main response is one that appeals to the publicness condition on deliberation, reasons must be able to survive being made public. The publicness condition is taken to force participants to offer reasons that can withstand public justification and hence to appeal to general rather than particular private interests.[59] Hence, reasons for action that appeal to wider constituencies of interest—including those of future generations and nonhumans—are more likely to survive in public deliberation than they are in private market-based methods for expressing preferences.[60] Goodin pushes this further and suggests that through such deliberation wider interests are internalized, to view democracy "as a process in which we all come to internalize the interests of each other and indeed of the larger world around us."[61] Through the internalization of interests of nature those interests can be virtually represented:

> Much though nature's interests may deserve to be enfranchised in their own right, that is simply impracticable. People, and people alone, can exercise the vote. The best we can hope for is that nature's interests will come to be internalized by a sufficient number of people with sufficient leverage in the political system for nature's interests to secure the protection they deserve.[62]

Goodin may be right here that this is the best one can hope for in terms of representing nature or future generations, but the idea of internalizing interests does not resolve the problems of legitimacy. The issue remains as to what, in the absence of authorization, accountability, or shared identity, can legitimate any particular individual or group making public claims to speak on behalf of the interests of others.

In the absence of authorization, accountability, and presence, the remaining source of legitimacy to claim to speak in such cases is epistemic. Those who claim to speak on behalf of those without voice do so by appeal to their having knowledge of the objective interests of those groups, often combined with special care for them. Thus, natural scientists, biologists, and ecologists are often heard making special claims "to speak on behalf of nature" where their claim to do so is founded upon their knowledge and interests. Environmental lobby groups make similar claims. However, such claims are also commonly disputed.

Two kinds of dispute are of particular significance here. First there are new versions of the traditional debate in political theory about the proper descriptions under which the representation should take place. Is it as individuals or as members of particular groups or as bearers of particular identities? The animal liberation and welfare movements are individualist: it is individual sentient beings that have moral considerability and it as such that they should be represented in our decisions. Those involved in the environmental movement and nature conservation are concerned primarily with the conservation of biodiversity, species, and habitats, and it is as members of particular species or as bearers of particular roles within an ecological systems that nonhuman nature is to be represented.[63] The dispute is normative. The debate is not primarily about particular knowledge claims as such, but rather about which knowledge claims are normatively relevant to the representation of nature—those concerning the welfare of individuals or those concerning the functioning of ecosystems and habitats. The conflict itself is in practice a real and important one. While it is often the case that what is good for habitats will also be good for individuals, there are a series of practical issues where the two come apart, for example, the culling by conservation authorities of feral animals or nonnative animals in order to preserve some particular habitat or the release by animal rights activists of caged animals into nonnative habitats. The spokespersons for nature speak in different voices.

A second set of disputes arises with direct challenges to the epistemic legitimacy claimed by putative scientific spokespersons for nature. These are of particular significance when representatives of nature have too much voice rather than too little, for example, when they conflict with communities speaking with an already marginalized voice who are policed in and excluded from "nature reserves" justified by natural scientists. Consider, for example, the Nagarhole National Park, where there have been moves from the Karnataka Forest Department to remove six thousand tribal people from their forests on the grounds that they compete with tigers for game. The move is supported by international conservation bodies—hence the remark of one of the experts for the Wildlife Conservation Society—"relocating tribal or traditional people who live in these protected area[s] is the single most important step towards conservation."[64] Or to take a European example consider the following comments of a local living by the natural park of Sierra Nevada and Alpujurra, a park that had been granted biosphere status by UNESCO and Natural Park status by the government of Andalusia:

> [Miguel] pointed out the stonework he had done on the floor and lower parts of the wall which were all made from flat stones found in the Sierra. I asked him if he had done this all by himself and he said "Yes, and look, this is nature" ("Si, y mira, esto es la naturaleza"), and he pointed firmly at the stone carved wall, and he repeated this action by pointing first in the direction of the Sierra [national park] before pointing at the wall again. Then, stressed his point by saying: "This is not nature, it is artificial (the Sierra) this (the wall) is nature" ("Eso no es la naturaleza, es artificial (the Sierra) esto (the wall) es la naturaleza").[65]

Conflicts sometimes exist between international conservation bodies speaking on behalf of the interests of nature seeking to protect "natural landscapes" and the socially marginalized groups whose lives and livelihoods depend on working within them. Places matter to such groups in ways that conflict with the goods defended by the representatives of nature. Such groups have particular local knowledge of place that gives them a distinct voice in its future different from that of the scientific expert who claims to speak on behalf of nature. The well-discussed arguments in political epistemology about whose knowledge claims count in environmental decision making is in part an argument about the legitimacy of representation founded purely on epistemic authority: Who can claim to speak on behalf of others, where the only claims for legitimacy are knowledge claims, and authorization, accountability, or presence are impossible?

Conclusion

I noted at the outset of this paper that deliberative democracy is often invoked as a response to the reason blindness and distributive failings of standard economic approaches to environmental decision making such as cost-benefit analysis. The problems I have raised in this paper do not, I think, give reasons to retreat from the claim that deliberative institutions do potentially offer a more defensible approach to environmental decision making. However, they do so only in certain conditions, in particular with a rough equality of economic and political power and social standing between different actors. And they bring their own unresolved and sometimes unresolvable problems of representative legitimacy. Recent experiments in deliberative democracy rely for their legitimacy as representative institutions on appeals to the presence of members of different groups. However, they often do so without clear sources of authorization and accountability from those represented. The representation of nonhumans and future generations in deliberative institutions raises deeper problems. Given the necessary absence of authorization, accountability, and presence, claims to speak on behalf of nonhumans and future generations are reduced to epistemic sources of legitimacy sometimes coupled with special claims to care. To raise these problems is not to claim that recent experiments in deliberative institutions lack democratic legitimacy. What it does point to is the need for a clearer account of their role within democratic institutions. My own view is that an account along Athenian lines offers the most likely answer to that need. It also highlights the sources of proper contestability of claims to speak on behalf of others within environmental deliberation. Given the limited sources of legitimacy for the representation of nonhumans and future generations, the contestability of claims to speak for those groups are, I suspect, ultimately ineliminable. However, such contestable forms of representation are the best we can hope for. Moreover a potential virtue of deliberative institutions is that in forcing reason to go public, they create the space for contesting representation. Hence, disputes about the legitimacy of representation will properly remain at the center of the deliberative politics of the environment.[66]

Notes

1. S. Benhabib, ed., *Democracy and Difference* (Princeton, N.J.: Princeton University Press, 1996); J. Bohman and W. Rehg, eds., *Deliberative Democracy: Essays on Reason and Politics* (Cambridge, Mass.: MIT Press, 1997); J. Cohen, "Deliberation and Democratic Legitimacy," in *The Good Polity*, ed. A. Hamlin and P. Pettit (Oxford, U.K.: Blackwell, 1989); J. Dryzek, *Discursive Democracy: Politics, Policy, and Political Science* (Cambridge, U.K.: Cambridge University Press, 1990); J. Elster, "The Market and the Forum: Three Varieties of Political Theory," in *Foundations of Social Choice Theory*, ed. J. Elster and A. Hylland (Cambridge, U.K.: Cambridge University Press, 1986); J. Elster, ed., *Deliberative Democracy* (Cambridge, U.K.: Cambridge University Press, 1998); J. Fishkin, *Democracy and Participation: New Directions for Democratic Reform* (New Haven, Conn.: Yale University Press, 1991); A. Guttman and D. Thompson, *Democracy and Disagreement* (Cambridge, Mass.: Harvard University Press, 1996); B. Manin, "On Legitimacy and Political Deliberation," *Political Theory* 15 (1987): 338–68; D. Miller, "Deliberative Democracy and Social Choice," *Political Studies* 40 (1992): 54–67; C. Sustein "Preferences and Politics," in *Contemporary Political Philosophy*, ed. R. Goodin and P. Pettit (Oxford, U.K.: Blackwell, 1997), 156–73.

2. For useful recent discussions, see J. Aldred and M. Jacobs, "Citizens and Wetlands: Evaluating the Ely Citizens' Jury," *Ecological Economics* 34 (2000): 217–32; A. Armour, "The Citizens Jury as Model of Public Participation: A Critical Evaluation," in *Fairness and Competence*

in Citizen Participation, ed. R. Goodin and P. Pettit (Dordrecht, The Netherlands: Kluwer, 1995); J. Burgess, M. Limb, and C. Harrisson, "Exploring Environmental Values through the Medium of Small Groups: Parts 1 and 2," *Environment and Planning A* 20 (1988): 309–26, and 457–76; J. Burgess, J. Clark, and C. M. Harrisson, *Valuing Nature: What Lies Behind Responses to Contingent Valuation Surveys?* (London: U.C.L., 1995); A. Coote and J. Leneghan, *Citizens' Juries: Theory into Practice* (London: Institute for Public Policy Research, 1997); S. Joss and J. Durant, *Public Participation in Science: The Role of Consensus Conferences in Europe* (London: Science Museum, 1995); J. Gordon, *Canadian Round Tables and Other Mechanisms for Sustainable Development in Canada* (Luten, U.K.: Local Government Management Board, 1994); P. Macnaghten et al., *Public Perceptions of Sustainability: Indicators, Institutions, Participation* (Lancaster, U.K.: Center for the Study of Environmental Change, Lancaster University, 1995); K. P. Rippe and P. Schaber, "Democracy and Environmental Decision-Making," *Environmental Values* 8 (1999): 75–88.

3. J. Dryzek, "Ecology and Discursive Democracy: Beyond Liberal Capitalism and the Administrative State," *Capitalism, Nature, and Socialism* 3 (1992): 18–42; R. Eckersley, "The Discourse Ethic and the Problem of Representing Nature," *Environmental Politics* 8 (1999): 24–49; R. Goodin "Enfranchising the Earth, and Its Alternatives," *Political Studies* 44 (1996): 835–49; M. Jacobs "Environmental Valuations, Deliberative Democracy, and Public Decision-Making Institutions," in *Valuing Nature?* ed. J. Foster (London: Routledge, 1997).

4. See J. O'Neill, *Ecology, Policy, and Politics: Human Well-Being and the Natural World* (London: Routledge, 1993); and M. Sagoff, *The Economy of the Earth* (Cambridge, U.K.: Cambridge University Press, 1988).

5. J. Martinez-Alier, G. Munda, and J. O'Neill, "Commensurability and Compensability in Ecological Economics," in *Valuation and Environment: Principles and Practices*, ed. C. Spash and M. O'Connor (Aldershot, U.K.: Edward Elgar 1999); M. O'Connor and E. Muir, "Endowment Effects in Competitive General Equilibrium: A Primer for Paretian Policy Analysts," *Journal of Income Distribution* 5 (1995): 145–75; W. Samuels, "Welfare Economics, Power and Property," in *Law and Economics: An International Perspective,* ed. W. Samuels and A. Schmid (Boston: Martin Nijohoff, 1981); A. Schmid, *Property, Power, and Public Choice* (New York: Preager, 1978).

6. See R. Guha and J. Martinez-Alier, *Varieties of Environmentalism* (London: Earthscan, 1997).

7. O'Neill, "*Ecology, Policy, and Politics,*" chapter 4.

8. W. Beckerman and J. Pasek, "Plural Values and Environmental Protection," *Environmental Values* 6 (1997): 65–86.

9. J. Habermas, *Justification and Application: Remarks on Discourse Ethics* (Cambridge, Mass.: MIT Press, 1993), 57.

10. J. Habermas, *Between Facts and Norms* (Cambridge, Mass.: MIT Press, 1996), 540.

11. J. O'Neill, "Socialist Calculation and Environmental Valuation: Money, Markets and Ecology," *Science and Society* (forthcoming).

12. O'Neill, "*Ecology, Policy and Politics,*" chapter 3; J. O'Neill, *The Market: Ethics, Knowledge, and Politics* (London: Routledge 1998), chapter 8; J. O'Neill, "Rhetoric, Science, and Philosophy," *Philosophy of Social Sciences* 28 (1998): 205–25.

13. Goodin, "Enfranchising the Earth," 835–49; Eckersley, "The Discourse Ethic," 24–49.

14. J. L. Borges, "The Congress," in J. L. Borges, *The Book of Sand* (Harmondsworth, U.K.: Penguin, 1979), 20–22.

15. "the craft of Cartography attained such Perfection that the Map of a Single province covered the space of an entire City, and the Map of the Empire itself an entire Province. In the course of Time, these Extensive maps were found somehow wanting, and so the College of Cartographers evolved a Map of the Empire that was of the some Scale as the Empire and that coincided with it point for point. Less attentive to the Study of Cartography, succeeding Generations came

to judge a map of such Magnitude cumbersome, and, not without Irreverence, they abandoned it to the Rigors of the sun and Rain. In the western Deserts, tattered Fragments of the Map are still to be found, Sheltering as occasional Beast or beggar; in the whole Nation, no other relic is left to the Disciple of Geography." J. L. Borges, "Of the Exactitude of Science," *A Universal History of Infamy* (Harmondsworth, U.K.: Penguin, 1981), 131. The idea of such a perfect map is one that Lewis Carroll anticipates in *Sylvie and Bruno Concluded*.

16. Borges, "The Congress," 32.

17. The point has more general relevance to questions around idealization in models and theories. As Joan Robinson notes, "A model which took account of all the variegation of reality would be no more use than a map at the scale of one to one." J. Robinson, *Essays in the Theory of Economic Growth* (London: Macmillan 1962), 33.

18. By the same token certain versions of the politics of difference—those that combine the need for the presence of all identities in political decisions with the denial of "essentialism" and with it of the claim that anyone can stand in for anyone else—very quickly tend to Alejandro solutions. I return to this point below.

19. H. Pitkin, *The Concept of Representation* (Berkeley: University of California Press, 1967); A. Birch, *Representation* (London: MacMillan, 1972).

20. The choice between individuals qua individuals and individuals qua members of groups was at the center of the associationalist criticisms of liberal representative democracy. Typical is G. D. H. Cole: "In the majority of associations, the nature of the relation is clear enough. The elected person . . . makes no pretension of substituting his personality for those of his constituents, or representing them except in relation to a quite narrow and clearly defined purpose or group of purposes which the association exists to fulfil. . . . True representation . . . is always specific and functional, and never general and inclusive. What is represented is never man, the individual, but always certain purposes common to groups of individuals." G. D. H. Cole, *The Social Theory* (London: Methuen, 1920), 105–6. For a discussion see P. Hirst, *Representative Democracy and Its Limits* (Oxford, U.K.: Polity Press, 1990). Cole's defense of associationalism has relevance for recent problems in the politics of presence. Cole's point is this: No one can represent me in my individuality. Someone may be able to represent me under a specific description for a specific purpose. My shop steward may not represent me in my gender, my ethnicity, my conceptions of the good life, and so on, but she may represent me as an employee in a particular firm. Under other descriptions I may need distinct forms of representation.

21. T. Hobbes, *The Leviathan* (Harmondsworth, U.K.: Penguin, 1968), chapter 16.

22. J. Plamenatz, *Consent, Freedom, and Political Obligation* (London: Oxford University Press, 1938); H. Pitkin, *The Concept of Representation* (Berkeley: University of California Press, 1967), 42ff.

23. Cited in A. Phillips, "Dealing with Difference: A Politics of Ideas or a Politics of Presence," in *Contemporary Political Philosophy*, ed. R. Goodin and P. Pettit (Oxford: Blackwell, 1997), 175.

24. A. Philips, *The Politics of Presence* (Oxford, U.K.: Clarendon Press, 1995); A. Philips, "Dealing with Difference," cf. W. Kymlicka, "Three Forms of Group-Differentiated Citizenship in Canada," and C. Gould, "Diversity and Democracy: Representing Difference," in *Democracy and Difference*, S. Benhabib, ed. (Princeton, N.J.: Princeton University Press, 1996).

25. "No government by a democracy . . . either in its political acts or in the opinions, qualities and tone of mind which it fosters, ever did or could rise above mediocrity, except insofar as sovereign Many . . . let themselves be guided . . . by the counsel and influence of a more gifted and instructed One or Few." J. S. Mill, *On Liberty*, ed. J. Gray and G. Smith (London: Routledge, 1974), 82.

26. "The history of all countries shows that the working class, exclusively by its own effort, is able to develop only trade union consciousness, i.e., the conviction that it is necessary to combine in unions, fight the employers, and strive to compel the government to pass necessary

labor legislation, etc. The theory of socialism, however, grew out of the philosophic, historical, and economic theories elaborated by educated representatives of the propertied classes, by intellectuals." V. Lenin, *What Is To Be Done?* (Oxford, U.K.: Oxford University Press, 1963), chapter 2.

27. Thus it rules out the kind of economic model of democratic representation offered by Downs according to which the function of representatives is to discover and transmit to their party information about the desires of their constituents. A. Downs, *An Economic Theory of Democracy* (New York: Harpers, 1957), 88ff.

28. J. O'Neill, "Value Pluralism, Incommensurability, and Institutions," in *Valuing Nature*, ed. J. Foster (London: Routledge, 1997), 84–85; J. Elster, "Introduction" in *Deliberative Democracy*, ed. J. Elster (Cambridge, U.K.: Cambridge University Press, 1998).

29. E. Burke, "Speech to the Electors of Bristol at the Conclusion of the Poll," in *The Works*, vol. 3, ed. E. Burke (London: Nimmo, 1899), 95–96.

30. C. Sustein, "Preferences and Politics," 169.

31. Ibid.

32. For a fine discussion of the tensions see Phillips, *The Politics of Presence*, chapter 6.

33. J. Habermas, *The Legitimation Crisis of Late Capitalism*, trans. T. McCarthy (Boston: Beacon, 1975), 108.

34. The tensions between convergence and dissent are usefully explored in the chapters in Benhabib, *Democracy and Difference*.

35. Andrew Collier puts the point forcibly: "the idea that each oppressed group ought to be fighting for itself rather than for the emancipation of all the oppressed, seems to me to be regrettable. . . . If we ever get the Left off the ground as a serious political force again, let it be academics who fight for the railways and railway workers who fight for universities, men who specialize in feminism, and whites who make it their priority to fight racism." A. Collier, *Being and Worth* (London: Routledge, 1999), 49. The concern is, I think, legitimate. However, a distinction needs to drawn between "acting in solidarity with" and "acting as a representative of." The former can only be done by those who do *not* belong to the same group, but its legitimacy requires accountability to self-organized groups with whom solidarity is expressed. A politics of presence becomes a problem when the two are confused, when "acting in solidarity with" and in this sense "on behalf of" a particular group is taken to involve acting "as a representative of" that group.

36. B. Williams, *Ethics and the Limits of Philosophy* (London: Fontana, 1985), chapter 8.

37. J. O'Neill, "Meta-ethics," in *Blackwell Companion to Environmental Philosophy*, ed. D. Jamieson (Oxford, U.K.: Blackwell, 2001).

38. J. O'Neill and M. Walsh, "Landscape Conflicts: Preferences, Identities, and Rights," *Landscape Ecology* 15 (2000): 281–89.

39. J. O'Neill, "The Good Life below the Snow-Line: Pluralism, Community, and Narrative" in *Cross-Cultural Protection of Nature and the Environment*, ed. F. Arler and I. Svennevig (Odense, Denmark: Odense University Press, 1997).

40. J. Martinez-Alier, "The Merchandising of Biodiversity," in *Justice, Property, and the Environment: Social and Legal Perspectives*, ed. T. Hayward and J. O'Neill (Aldershot, U.K.: Avebury, 1997).

41. Phillips, "Dealing with Difference," 181.

42. Macnaghten et al., *Public Perceptions*.

43. Aldred and Jacobs, *Citizens and Wetlands*.

44. Compare Gould: "[O]ne cannot argue that *any* member of a group can equally well represent *all* members of a group. It would be odd indeed to think that Clarence Thomas could represent all African-Americans or that Margaret Thatcher could represent all women." Gould, "Diversity and Democracy," 184.

45. Philips, "Dealing with Difference," 180.

46. I develop these in J. O'Neill, "Essences and Markets," *The Monist* 78 (1995): 258–75, and *The Market*, chapter 1. See also the comments in Cole, *The Social Theory*, quoted above.

47. Jacobs, "Environmental Valuations," 224.

48. For a defense of this position under the name of "demarchy" see J. Burnheim, *Is Democracy Possible?* (Cambridge, U.K.: Polity Press, 1985).

49. Aristotle *Politics* 2.2, trans. C. D. C. Reeve (Indianapolis, Ind.: Hackett, 1998).

50. Typical is Neurath's comment: "Democracy is . . . a continual struggle between the expert who knows everything and makes decisions, and the common man with just enough information to hold the power of the expert in check. Our life is connected more and more with experts, but on the other hand, we are less prepared to accept other peoples' judgement, when making decisions. . . . What is called democracy implies the rejection of experts in making decision, therefor[e] democracy in Athens was based on lot." O. Neurath, "Visual Education," in *Encyclopedia and Utopia: The Life and Work of Otto Neurath (1882–1945)*, ed. E. Nemeth and F. Stadler (Dordrecht, The Netherlands: Kluwer, 1996), 251.

51. Burnheim, *Is Democracy Possible?* 167.

52. Hobbes, *Leviathan,* chapter 16.

53. "There is wide agreement that the state should protect the interests of the future *in some degree* against the irrational discounting and of our preferences for ourselves over our descendants. The whole movement for conservation in the United States is based on this conviction. It is the clear duty of Government, which is the trustee for unborn generations as well as for its present citizens, to watch over, and, if need be, by legislative enactment, to defend, the exhaustible natural resources of the country from rash and reckless spoliation." A. C. Pigou, *The Economics of Welfare*, 4th ed. (London: MacMillan, 1932), 29–30.

54. A. Dobson, "Representative Democracy and the Environment," in *Democracy and the Environment: Problems and Prospects*, ed. W. Lafferty and J. Meadowcraft (Cheltenham, U.K.: Edward Elgar, 1996).

55. Goodin "Enfranchising the Earth," 835–49.

56. E. Burke, "Letter to Sir Hercules Langrishe," in *The Works*, vol. 4, ed. E. Burke (London: Nimmo, 1899), 293.

57. Ibid.

58. For a development of this line of argument see Goodin, "Enfranchising the Earth," 841–44.

59. The point is one that has roots in Kant for whom every moral principle must meet "the formal attribute of publicness": "'All actions affecting the rights of other human beings are wrong if their maxim is not compatible with their being made public.'" I. Kant, "Perpetual Peace," in *Political Writings*, appendix 2, ed. H. Reiss (Cambridge, U.K.: Cambridge University Press, 1991). The test rules out those arguments from principles that appeal to self-interests where this conflicts with just concern with the interests of others, since the persuasiveness of such arguments could not survive publicity. For developments of this point see Elster, "Deliberation of Constitution Making," in *Deliberative Democracy*, ed. J. Elster (Cambridge, U.K.: Cambridge University Press, 1998); and J. Rawls, *Political Liberalism* (New York: Columbia University Press, 1996), 66–71. The obvious rejoinder is that deliberation in this sense forces participants to mask private interests as public interests and in that sense to make the process less rather than more transparent.

60. See Goodin "Enfranchising the Earth," 846–47; and Jacobs "Environmental Valuations."

61. Goodin "Enfranchising the Earth," 844.

62. Ibid.

63. For discussions see J. B. Callicott, "Animal Liberation: A Triangular Affair," in *In Defense of the Land Ethic* (Albany, N.Y.: SUNY Press, 1989), and "Back Together Again," *Environmental Values* 7 (1998): 461–75; D. Jamieson, "Animal Liberation is an Environmental Ethic," *Environmental Values* 7 (1998): 41–58; K. Rawles, "Conservation and Animal Welfare," in *The*

Philosophy of the Environment, ed. T. Chappell (Edinburgh, Scotland: Edinburgh University Press, 1997); and M. Sagoff, "Animal Liberation and Environmental Ethics: Bad Marriage, Quick Divorce," *Osgoode Hall Law Journal* 22 (1984): 297–307.

64. Cited in R. Guha, "The Authoritarian Biologist and the Arrogance of Anti-Humanism," *The Ecologist* 27, no. 1 (1997): 17.

65. From Katrin Lund, "What Would We Do without Biodiversity?" Workshop "Contesting Nature: Anthropology and Environmental Protection," September 21, 1998.

66. Earlier versions of this paper were read at the seminar "Deliberation and Nature" in the ESRC-funded series, "Deliberative and Inclusionary Processes in Environmental Policy Making," at a workshop in Tampere, Finland, that formed part of the project "How Does Nature Speak?" and at seminars at Dundee University and Helsinki University. My thanks for the many helpful conversations on those occasions. Particular thanks are owed to Jacqui Burgess, Simon Niemeyer, and Clive Spash for their comments. I would like to acknowledge the support of the Arts and Humanities Research Board. Parts of this chapter appeared previously in J. O'Neill, "Representing People, Representing Nature, Representing the World," *Environmental Planning C: Government and Policy* 19 (2001), Pion Ltd.

Part IV

DEMOCRACY AND ENVIRONMENTAL MOVEMENTS

CHAPTER 14

Cycles of Closure in Environmental Politics and Policy

Robert Paehlke

Looking back at the latter part of the twentieth century we can see that advances in environmental protection have often been associated with relatively open and participatory modes of environmental decision making. This patterned outcome runs counter to assertions that environmentalism somehow promotes democratic closure in the service of the "antigrowth" predilections of a narrow elite.[1] That is, whatever the challenges to democratic implementation thus far encountered, in practice environmental initiatives have generally advanced democratic practice and enhanced greater openness and wider participation in decision making.[2] This democratizing thrust is evident, for example, in the development of environmental impact assessment procedures,[3] in the participatory provisions of most environmental legislation in the 1970s and since,[4] and most recently in the efforts by environmentalists and others to open up the decision processes of North American Free Trade Agreement (NAFTA), the World Trade Organization (WTO), and other international trade agreements and organizations whose decisions are now so central to environmental policy outcomes.

Nonetheless, the twentieth century witnessed at least three bouts of democratic closure in environmental decision making. The first might be called bureaucratic closure wherein the early preservationist thrusts of the conservation movement were gradually supplanted by scientific resource management and the "gospel of efficiency."[5] The second followed the considerable successes of the environmental movement in the late 1960s and throughout the 1970s. Even prior to the election of Ronald Reagan environmental protection no longer enjoyed "motherhood" status and soon came to be identified as an enemy of economic growth and, as such, a threat to "the American way of life." This second, "political," closure was short-lived for a number of reasons not the least of which were new environmental threats. A second wave of environmentalist concern arose in the late 1980s, only to be followed by yet another wave of closure that has continued—a closure bound up with globalization and the "cult of impotence."[6]

Prior to a detailed consideration of the three periods of closure it is worth making three broad observations regarding the pattern as a whole. The first observation concerns the motivation behind what might be called an ongoing thrust toward closure, a motivation best captured by Andrews when he noted that environmentalists have generally felt that "in closed or low visibility arenas the power of highly organized private interests is maximized."[7] This is consistent with Max Weber's dictum that: "Every bureaucracy seeks to increase the superiority of the professionally informed by keeping their knowledge and intentions secret. Bureaucratic administration always tends to be an administration of 'secret sessions': insofar as it can, it hides its knowledge and action from criticism."[8] Corporate bureaucracies are perhaps more successful than public bureaucracies in this regard as they are unencumbered by the ethos that underlies governance within liberal democratic states, but both forms of bureaucracy generally prefer to conduct their business in private.

Openness, participation, and "sunshine" are enemies of all concentrations of power. This is in part why, in my view, the decentralization of environmental decision making is fraught with problems.[9] Not only are smaller administrative units more easily overwhelmed by global-scale economic actors, but state and local governments are much more likely to escape serious media or NGO-based scrutiny than are national or global-scale forums. The former is especially true when economic diversification is lacking, as in many jurisdictions dependent on resource extraction. The latter is especially true when media ownership is highly concentrated and patterns of cross-media ownership prevail. The price of the present quest for media ownership "synergies" is the increasing deterioration of distinctive and effective local political coverage.

The second analytic observation is that closure in environmental decision making and less effective environmental protection are both frequently associated with economic downturns and with perceived threats to national security. Thus rising unemployment, high public deficits and debt, falling stock prices, recession, inflation, war, or serious political tensions can all push environmental protection off the public's list of leading concerns and thereby off the political agenda. Another way to put this is that unless enhanced environmental protection is a leading public priority *and* environmental NGO activity is at a high level, improvement is unlikely. In a phrase: Economic and security concerns almost always trump environmental concerns.

In recent times, political momentum for environmental action built during the 1960s and early 1970s, but was overwhelmed by the stagflation of the late 1970s and the economic difficulties of the early 1980s. That momentum returned strongly by the later 1980s as prosperity returned to North America. By then public opinion was highly oriented to environmental concerns and was accelerated by events including Chernobyl, the Exxon Valdez, and rising concern with the possibility of climate change. By 1992, however, public attention was again transfixed by economic issues, especially downsizing and deficits. Each upsurge in environmental opinion had, however, also created a thrust for participatory opportunities, just as each downturn in salience led to new forms of closure. In the Reagan years, participatory closure took many forms including mandatory cost-benefit analysis for all new regulatory initiatives. In the 1990s, even within regimes ostensibly disposed to environmental protection, environmental decisions migrated to the global level to be resolved behind closed doors and there were often resisted by the representatives of North American governments.

The third analytic observation concerns Anthony Downs' issue-attention cycle.[10] The observations made in Downs' noted article regarding environmental concerns remain relevant now thirty years later. In brief, Downs argued that most political issues face a systematic "issue-attention cycle" wherein "[E]ach of these problems suddenly leaps into prominence, remains there for a short time, and then—though still largely unresolved—gradually fades from public attention."[11] The fading is in part the result of stage three of the cycle—the gradual spreading of the realization of the cost of significant progress. At that point some in the public become bored, some get discouraged, and still others feel threatened by thinking about a problem that is not easily resolved (without significant costs). Downs argues, however, that environmental issues "will be eclipsed at a much slower rate than other recent domestic issues."[12] This is, in Downs' view, because environmental problems (especially air pollution) have "high visibility," because environmental problems directly affect a majority of citizens (almost everyone in Downs' estimate), and because pollution can be attributed to a small group of villains (industrial polluters, whom Downs judges to be "scapegoats").

Environmental issues have, it turns out, weathered the issue-attention cycle. Downs' reasons, however, have not held up so well. Some recent environmental problems are less literally visible than the forms of air pollution Downs had in mind. While climate change, for example, is alarming to those who understand its essential irreversibility, the detailed parameters of its future path are still uncertain and its most dangerous aspects are not yet manifestly obvious. As well, few citizens see the slowly shrinking habitat of endangered species. Most see only the gradual growth of seemingly benign suburbs, or healthy-looking agricultural and forest monocultures.[13] In general we have thus been better at dealing with (relatively visible) pollution issues than (less visible) habitat, climate, and sustainability issues.[14] Moreover, as the environmental justice literature makes clear and contrary to Downs' assumption, many environmental problems do not necessarily affect a majority of citizens equally.[15] Finally, in some now prominent issues, even the "scapegoats" are not so obvious—we all contribute to climate change and most of us would find our daily behavior affected directly by its remedies.[16]

Thus the issue-attention cycle may apply to environmental issues and may explain in part the waxing and waning of closure on environmental issues. We certainly will see the cyclical assertiveness of those threatened by the high cost of issue resolution. Downs, however, did not fully recognize that both the effects and the costs associated with environmental problems are unevenly distributed. Nor did he offer much insight into the relevance of the changing political economy of media on the issue-attention cycle. With hindsight we can see that these may all be contributory factors. Polluters are not "mere" scapegoats, but powerful economic actors. They command an array of public relations firms, lobbyists, lawyers, and media advisors—and have massive advertising budgets at their disposal. When they feel threatened they respond very effectively, so effectively that even visible perils are sometimes simply accepted as inevitable. The wonder is that once some of the most visible issues waned, environmental concerns returned to prominence, albeit fleetingly, in the 1980s. Accounting for that restoration of issue attention, and its subsequent re-decline, is a central concern of this chapter. But let us begin with the initial rise of environmental concern in the 1960s.

Earth Day Momentum Opens
a Window on Environmental Policy

North American political life changed irretrievably in the 1960s, but not only as a result of the civil rights movement, the Vietnam War, or sex, drugs, and rock and roll. The emphasis of the early environmental movement on pollution greatly broadened the appeal of conservation by shifting the focus from wilderness spaces to human settlements and from nonhuman species to the health of the urban majority of humans. Where the industrial age had previously been dominated by the two-dimensional politics of rich versus poor (wages, working conditions, wealth distribution, and the welfare state), the rise of environmentalism added a third dimension. Support for environmental issues was quite consistent across all previous divisions in capitalist industrial society.[17] Whether rich and poor, black and white, male and female individuals might well be concerned with some environmental issues. The two-dimensional politics typical of industrial society was on the way to becoming the three-dimensional politics, arguably the norm of postindustrial society.

The new politics of the environment, however, had an antecedent in the conservation movement from whose history the early environmental movement gleaned a crucial insight. The conservation movement had had an enormous faith in science, and in the ability and willingness of public officials to discern and to defend the "public interest." As Grant McConnell, writing in the 1950s regarding the U.S. Forestry Service, put it: "there is, first, an underlying assumption of some single correct balance of uses which 'is in the public interest'; second there is a bias toward *measurable* benefits. Obviously, the most practicable unit of measurement is the dollar."[18] The conservationist principal of multiple use, he went on to say, says nothing about how to determine which use is the "highest use" and in the end administrative discretion and a balancing of the political strength of competing interests is the real basis for resolution. Crucially to the outcome, this process of bureaucratic resolution dominated by politics took place, typically, behind closed doors. The managers of federal resource agencies presumed an objective public interest and imagined that they were its guardians. This often resulted in closed-door politics, allocation deals, and bureaucratic arrogance clothed in science and administrative objectivity.

The regulated industries and interests dominated the process. The predominant share of national forests was open to logging, rangelands were overgrazed, rivers were dammed, and downstream waters were divided among industrial, urban, and agricultural users. Said waters and forests were often sold below cost.[19] Moreover, mining interests typically had low-cost access to publicly owned resources.[20] The public interest is a political matter, not something to be objectively determined by experts. The "capture" of agendas and agencies by economically powerful interests is more often the result of closed administrative processes. Resource-use allocations are inevitably value-laden decisions and as such are more likely to be executed equitably and fairly by public officials listening to *all* interests, making their decisions, and asserting their reasons for those decisions in public settings. Needless to say, the process would work best when there is a high level of public attentiveness regarding such issues.

This perspective informed both Earth Day, an offshoot of the participatory Vietnam "teach-in" initiatives of the 1960s, and the National Environmental Policy Act (NEPA), the first new environmental legislation of the era. The level of active support for Earth Day (1970) surprised the Nixon administration, major conservation organizations, and the organizers of the event itself. *Time* magazine estimated that twenty million people took part in one of the major rallies or in events organized within 1,500 universities and colleges and some 10,000 schools.[21] Numerous activist environmentalist organizations arose out of the event, including Environmental Action, the Union of Concerned Scientists, and the Natural Resources Defense Council. NEPA literally forced governmental introspection, encouraging broad public involvement and requiring that all government agencies prepare statements reviewing the possible impacts of their initiatives on the environment. Several court cases in the early 1970s and the implementing regulations of 1978 resulted in a highly open and participatory environmental assessment process requiring public hearings, timely public notice, the availability of relevant documents, the participation of the full range of interests, and, in some cases, intervenor funding.

This process, as it evolved, was highly innovative in terms of governmental openness. The new environmental activists did not presume that science in-and-of-itself led to politically neutral outcomes, nor that public officials would automatically defend the public interest. Perhaps following the 1960s predilection to participatory democracy, the new environmentalist organizations, as well as the Congress, sought open-decision processes that involved the public, and public interest organizations, in regulatory decisions. Accordingly, there were public participation provisions in the Clean Air Acts of 1970 and 1977, the 1972 amendments to the Water Pollution Control Act, the Toxic Substances Control Act (1976), the Resource Conservation and Recovery Act (1976), the superfund legislation of 1980, and many other pieces of environmental legislation. Science was newly understood to be inherently contestative and sometimes self-interested and it was presumed that experts in general would disagree. Therefore the public interest should be determined within open processes with all views taken into account.

The public, it was presumed, had the capacity to understand complex arguments. Indeed, it might be argued that environmentalism itself was in part the result of rising educational levels in the postwar period. Educational level is in fact a predictor of environmental opinion, the higher the level of education the higher the level of environmental concern. Thus the new concern went hand in hand with demands for more openness and public involvement. Indeed, one of Rachel Carson's most effective assertions was that people were exposed to pesticides "without their consent, and often without their knowledge."[22] As knowledge of the possible effects of chemicals on health became more widely known there was a growing demand for a right to know both workplace and community exposures. The right-to-know was one of the few aspects of environmental openness to continue during the trend to environmental closure in the Reagan years.

The Energy Crisis, Reagan, and the Restoration of Closure

As the momentum of Earth Day waned, environmentalism soon lost motherhood status. Part of this decline was likely the normal working of the issue-attention cycle, including a growing sense, following the energy crises of 1973 and 1979, that environmental protection could affect the economy and everyday life in significant ways. Rejection of offshore drilling, nuclear power, and coal (and especially all three) was easier until this seemingly meant that someone might ride the bus, or that employment opportunities might be lost to rising energy prices. Until the complexities and importance of "soft energy path planning" were widely understood, it was easy for energy interests (in the context of an energy crisis) to convince the public that environmentalists stood in the way of all viable alternatives to dependence on imported oil.

Even after the work of Lovins and others became more widely known, many who were sympathetic and who worried about pollution were prepared to accept the Reagan right turn as a complete package. Some had concluded (not unreasonably) that energy shortages and rising energy prices were the prime cause of the economic difficulties of the day, and could be convinced that some aspects of "extreme" environmental protection were a luxury we could no longer afford. Others who voted for Reagan just were not thinking about environmental matters when they did so—they were concerned about national security, or were simply looking for "leadership" and "decisiveness" and were less concerned about the directions that it would take.[23] Until Lovins introduced the soft energy path, environmentalists seemingly opposed all solutions to perceived energy problems. After 1976 this new energy perspective was understood in some circles, but the tentative steps toward solar energy and energy efficiency taken by the Carter administration were threatening to many deeply entrenched economic interests. Moreover, the administration seemed unable to defend America's vital interests abroad, including especially secure access to Middle East oil.

It was widely known that a Reagan administration would have no particular sympathy for environmental concerns, but it can be argued that he was elected as much in spite of this well-known antipathy as because of it. Only after the election, however, was it fully clear that the new administration would not follow the approach of Republican environmental moderates such as William Ruckelshaus. All new environmental and resource administrative appointments were openly hostile to environmental protection and arrived with a transformation strategy that was well thought out in advance within conservative think tanks such as the American Enterprise Institute and the Heritage Foundation. These neoconservative organizations even supplied lists of acceptable environmental political appointees, administrative personnel, and science advisors.[24] Scientists appointed to administrative roles, for example, were expected to have a commitment "to high levels of proof about the harm of chemicals."[25] An open, participatory, balanced approach was no longer on the agenda.

Some of the agency heads most hostile to the environment such as Anne Gorsuch and James Watt were, of course, in office for only a few scandal-ridden years. Some of the less well-known appointments were, however, perhaps even more notable for their directness of purpose: "John Crowell, general counsel of the Louisiana-Pacific Corporation, the largest purchaser of timber from the national forests, became assistant secretary of agriculture in charge of the U.S. Forest Service. Robert Burford, a Colorado rancher and state legislator, became director of the Bureau of Land Management (BLM). Robert Harris, a leading critic of the new surface mining act and organizer of the litigation from Indiana challenging the new law, was placed in charge of the office administering it."[26] The signals being sent to industry were clear and the administrative reality that followed was systematic though sometimes surprisingly subtle.

Environmental legislation, for the most part, remained in place. Most actions were taken at the budgetary or administrative level, rather than at the political level. Programs were effectively limited as "too expensive" or enforcement was simply curtailed by imposing severe limits on the travel expenses of, for example, Occupational Health and Safety Administration (OSHA) inspectors. One of the most dramatic budgetary phaseouts was for funding to energy efficiency and solar energy initiatives, zeroed out within two years while subsidies to nuclear energy remained.[27] The Environmental Protection Agency (EPA) saw its budget cut (allowing for inflation) by one-third in the first two years of the Reagan administration.[28] There was, however, surprisingly little debate regarding these initiatives. They were presented as part of reducing the cost of government (and originated within a rapidly expanding Office of Management and Budget). President Reagan did label solar energy an exotic technology, hardly the sort of damnation that one might expect to accompany budgetary slashing, but politically effective in its understatement.

All of this is well known. What has been less widely discussed is the antidemocratic character of the Reagan administration regarding the environment, in effect the systematic "closure" of participatory opportunities and a return to the closed business-government norms of the preenvironmental era. In the 1970s it had been feared by some analysts that environmental scarcity might force antidemocratic initiatives against a resistant public, but as it turns out it was antienvironmentalism that required closure to achieve its ends.[29] The administration was as determined to roll back environmental openness and participation as it was to alter environmental policy outcomes. Nonetheless, no sooner had Reagan been elected than environmental organizations showed considerable growth in membership numbers and fund-raising capabilities, despite a relatively low ebb (in 1979–80) in environmental concern among the general public.[30]

From the outset the instincts of the Reagan administration, without necessarily being fully mindful of the history and consequences of such actions, were toward closure within the realm of environmental policy. The administration and the people that it put in place simply did not believe that most environmental problems were real, or if they were real were important. They just did not want to hear contrary views. At the conclusion of a meeting with environmental leaders (in early 1981) Secretary Watt "announced that there would be no more such meetings because there was nothing else to discuss." Similarly David Stockman, head of the Office of Management and Budget (OMB), had concluded while a member of the House Committee on Energy and Environment that "he had become convinced that pollution was no real problem; hence it could be ignored."[31]

Given these viewpoints of key environmental actors in the administration, it is not surprising that the participatory (and thereby visible) decision structures that had developed over the preceding decades were seen as not only an unnecessary expense, but with potential political costs given that many within the public—even Republican voters in considerable numbers—did not think that pollution could be ignored. Thus, the basic strategy of avoiding legislative change and concentrating on budgetary change so that legislative debate (and thereby visibility to the broad public) was minimized. The outcome on the ground (nonenforcement) was comparable. Profound environmental policy change was set in a context of spending and "red tape" reduction. Fifteen years later, in a new political context to be discussed below, an almost exact parallel strategy was seen through in Canada and Ontario.

Reductions in environmental public participation opportunities included the following: (1) little use was made of the participatory mechanisms within existing antipollution legislation regarding new regulated substances, because few new regulations were proposed; (2) the administration proposed "to curtail the rights of citizens to propose lands as unsuitable for mining, to participate in permit reviews, and to play a role in other aspects of the regulatory program"[32] (regarding surface coal mining); (3) forest management rules were proposed that sought to eliminate public participation in the forest planning process[33]; (4) reduced participatory oversight of Bureau of Reclamation decisions regarding water rights allocations increased the likelihood of favoritism to large landowners; (5) numerous EPA publications were destroyed and the rights of EPA scientists to publish their findings were curtailed[34]; (6) OSHA "right to know" rules were modified to favor industry's concerns with proprietary rights; (7) wildlife (as distinct from livestock) interests on BLM district advisory boards were reduced to one position; (8) intervenor funding was systematically opposed and the OMB sharply curtailed funding for public information programs in all agencies; and (9) even the requirement to label household appliances regarding energy efficiency was opposed both at both the federal and state levels.[35]

This list is by no means comprehensive. The last item is particularly interesting in two regards. One, it suggests that the administration was not inclined even to low-cost, nonregulatory alternatives when it had the option of completely ignoring an environmental problem. That is, the widely debated option to appliance labeling was appliance energy efficiency standards. The administration did not even wish to provide those consumers who cared enough about energy or pollution a convenient opportunity to make such choices when buying appliances. As we will see, in the "second wave" of environmentalism (1987–1992) such opportunities were emphasized even by industry. Two, the Reagan administration's much vaunted preference for decentralized federalism was highly selective.

One theory of federalism (and scale of governance generally) to which many environmentalists through the years have been inclined is the view that local and state government is "closer to the people and to the problems." Smaller-scale governance, this view holds, is more democratic and environmental protection more effective. There even appears to be potential here for a rare convergence of views between environmentalists and neoconservatives.[36] However, it would appear that in this instance at least neoconservative preferences for decentralized federalism endure only if lower levels of government are *less* inclined to interfere with the preferences of large landowners or industry. More often than not, it might be argued, state and local governments *are* less inclined to intervene because they typically deal with fewer powerful economic interests any one of which could cost the economy of their jurisdiction proportionately more than they would cost (or plausibly threaten to cost) national economies.

In any case, the Reagan administration sought to override state authority in environmental matters on many occasions. The EPA, under Gorsuch, "effectively exempted most new polluting industrial installations from state reviews."[37] Reagan proclaimed a "new (more decentralized) federalism" but while "responsibility for carrying the environmental laws was shifted from Washington to the states" the states were "starved of federal funds."[38] Federal funding allocations declined from $500 million in 1979 to $300 million in 1982 and did not increase significantly from that point until 1991. The EPA even ceased to keep accurate track of state environmental expenditures. However, other sources indicate that while state spending on air pollution programs remained unchanged as a proportion of federal funding, "according to the Congressional Budget Office, federal dollars accounted for only 33 percent of state spending on water programs in 1986 (down from 49 percent four years earlier) and 40 percent of hazardous waste programs (down from 76 percent)."[39] As Philip Shabecoff put it: "To the consternation of industry, state governments across the country beefed up their environmental budgets and staff to fill the vacuum created by the federal government."[40]

State level increases in environmental expenditures were, however, very uneven and industries concerned with tough standards could expand their operations in states with relatively low levels of protection and curtail, or threaten to curtail, investment in states that had tougher enforcement. In this regard, the decentralization of "new federalism" was a success and, arguably, would form the logic of 1990s antienvironmental initiatives at the global level. Hays aptly assessed the central dilemma of the Reagan administration regarding decentralization: "On the one hand their ideology called for a transfer of power to the states. On the other, their commitment to the business community led them to support the drive on the part of corporate leaders to use the federal government to override state policies to which industry objected. On some occasions the administration made it clear that whereas it might wish to override state authority, it did not wish to take a position contrary to its ideology if such action would create a media issue."[41]

Throughout the Reagan years regulations based on the scientific determination of health risks were replaced by a process that subjected such concerns to a largely administrative calculation of the economic benefits and costs of protecting human and environmental health. Human lives and health were thereby rendered as values on the same level as profits. Moreover, the resolution process was not a matter for open debate so much as a technical exercise carried out within a closed administrative process using data supplied by industry. The administrative, and government-business, determination of the public good had returned in the guise of a benefit-cost calculus.

Time and Events Partially Restore Environmental Openness

Just as environmental concern had waned somewhat by the late 1970s, it might be said that Reagan's antienvironmentalism had worn thin by the end of his second term (and had of course been considerably softened in order to achieve reelection in 1984). George H. Bush was only all too willing (and somehow able) to claim that he was going to be an environmental president. His campaign for president opened with an aggressive attack on pollution in Boston harbor, the home state of his democratic opponent. Credit for any semblance of plausibility in such assertions must go to the benignly competent William Ruckelshaus who had returned to the helm of EPA for Reagan's second term. Addressing environmental issues front and center allowed Bush to distinguish himself from his predecessor, but was also made necessary by a rising tide of public concern and the new set of environmental issues that had emerged.

The organizational strength of the environmental movement had of course never waned. Reagan and Watt led directly to increased movement in organizational strength. Broad public opinion regarding environmental issues may have waned, but those for whom environment was an important concern became more concerned and active. As Hays put it: "Reagan's policies actually strengthened public support for environmental organizations. Memberships, resources, and organizational capabilities grew. With larger staffs they could lobby more effectively in Congress on more issues, undertake more litigation, and mobilize members more fully. They were also able to pursue new activities, such as employing technical and professional staff who brought with them a higher degree of credibility and respect in the technical and professional world."[42]

This in turn kept the decision process from the complete closure that had been attempted in the early 1980s, but was not enough to reestablish momentum or launch significant new initiatives. But by the late 1980s a series of events and new issues helped to trigger a broad opinion shift toward environmental protection. The events included Bhopal (1984), Chernobyl (1986), and the grounding of the Exxon Valdez off the pristine coast of Alaska. The new issues included the inability of many municipalities to find suitable sites for disposing of a rising tide of solid waste, the expanding hole in the ozone layer, greenhouse gases and climate change, and the rapid cutting of tropical rainforests. The first of these issues was rendered highly visible by the meandering journey of a garbage barge from New York City, the latter by a highly effective campaign, featuring a parade of rock stars and compelling information about the enormous ecological diversity that was at risk.

Bhopal had a particularly significant effect on environmental openness and participation. The event provided considerable impetus to workplace and community right to know (RTK) initiatives that had been gaining momentum at the local and state levels since the late 1970s. By 1984 there were sixteen municipal RTK laws (Philadelphia being the first) and seventeen state laws (as well as some federal rules regarding workplace labeling of hazardous chemicals). Bhopal accelerated this process and, in combination with industry's discomfort with innumerable different rules in multiple locations, led to action by a reluctant federal government shortly before the 1986 congressional elections. The advocates of these initiatives included medical and emergency officials, including firefighters who feared entering industrial facilities without knowing if explosions and poisonous exposures were possible or where such risks were located. Advocacy of public information was, in this context, almost impossible to resist even by conservative state and federal regimes.

By the late 1980s public opinion polls (and media attention) indicated that the relative environmental quietude of the general public had ended. The Bush administration and the equally conservative Mulroney government in Canada, for example, felt compelled by the force of public opinion to reach an agreement requiring mutual action on acid precipitation. Even Margaret Thatcher claimed (at least in public) to be concerned about the environment. Action on this issue had long been resisted by the Reagan-Bush administration with endless calls for additional research over and above the massive array of studies long in hand. This new wave of public concern, and the changes that it triggered, was, however, significantly different from the events and outcome of the post–Earth Day period of the 1970s.

The environmental movement was itself considerably different though (and perhaps because) many of the same people were still involved. Where the movement of the late 1960s and early 1970s was often radical and even apocalyptic, and had instinctive doubts about capitalism, technology, and industrial society, the movement of the late 1980s and early 1990s was, as Shabecoff put it, pragmatic and professional. It was also more diverse and complex. By this time many more environmental organizations managed large budgets and staffs, organizational leadership was highly experienced in dealing with government and business, and many who worked in these organizations, as well as in government and business, had by this time had university training in new courses and programs in environmental science and policy. Confrontation and an either/or attitude regarding economy and environment was less often their first instinct. Thus, in this second wave of environmental concern, policy participation took new forms.

There were attempts at what came to be called environmental mediation.[43] The coal industry, for example, bargained with community and environmental organizations over the terms and conditions of open-pit extraction and the level and timing of restoration. Optimistically, it might be argued that both sides had learned something during the Reagan era—environmentalists that being shut out of decisions was risky, and business that even when the best leader one could hope for was in power environmental concerns just would not go away. The watchwords of environmental policy in this period were sustainable development, green products, economy-environment integration, roundtables, and (a little later) voluntary initiatives.

This new approach involved both more, and less, participation and openness. There was seemingly more openness on the part of business and government to consideration of environmental concerns, and to interaction with environmental organizations. At the same time, however, there was a continuing resistance to new environmental regulations, and a considerable increase in corporate expenditures on antienvironmental lobbying, public relations and media activities, and to the creation of antienvironmental "front" groups (made to appear as grassroots organizations).[44] In fairness, in part this was a matter of different industrial sectors, firms, and corporate actors being inclined to differing approaches. Nonetheless, the generalization holds— most businesses no longer publicly dismissed environmental concerns and some were more open to ongoing interaction, but at the same time they lobbied hard to maximize their freedom of action.

In this context, green products were an ideal "solution." Those people who were particularly concerned about the environment could buy (for a modest price premium) paint that contained fewer toxic chemicals or recycled toilet paper.[45] But, rules would not be imposed upon those industries that preferred to avoid such initiatives. Outcomes were not a matter of participatory versus nonparticipatory political processes, they were not political at all—one could be an environmental or a nonenvironmental consumer, but no one could be an environmental citizen. The majority view need not be ascertained; each person, in effect, could choose his or her own mix of values and science. You carpool or wait for a bus, if you want to, but I must get my tiger skin coat to the dry cleaners in a hurry—each to his or her own.

Some significant environmental protection innovations arose out of sustainable development and green product initiatives, including opportunities to grow organic produce. Sometimes, as well, a role for public authority emerged, as in those nations where governments took the certification of green products seriously.[46] But, for the most part, the openness and participation achieved was the openness of the marketplace, not of democracy.[47] In effect, individual rights (to do environmental damage) overwhelm the potential for majority rule on behalf of environmental protection. Moreover, it is not at all clear why those who prefer beneficial environmental outcomes should pay the price premium, rather than the other way around. Even with the costs of pollution aside, today's SUV rate of gasoline consumption elevates tomorrow's energy prices.

Also common within the second wave of environmental concern were sustainable development initiatives that frequently raised important questions new to public discussion, and involved mixes of participants that were new in terms of their multi-stakeholder complexity. But, typically these initiatives had the trappings of power (as in the case of the President's Council on Sustainable Development—PCSD), but not the actuality. Discussion covered the right questions, but strong policy initiatives were rarely forthcoming.[48] Given that a Gallup poll taken in 1989 indicated that 75 percent of Americans considered themselves environmentalists, a revised Clean Air Act could be obtained, but effective action on resource sustainability, climate change, and biodiversity would be resisted nonetheless.[49] Truth could again be spoken to power regarding such matters, and power would be polite in a pro-environmental political climate, but the rules of the game were rapidly changing.

Globalization and the Restoration of Closure

Where many environmental issues that arose in the 1970s were local or national in character, the issues of the late 1980s were increasingly international. Tropical rainforests and coral reefs are often a world away from local environmental concerns (though we in the wealthy nations may well be contributing significantly to the problem). Ozone depletion and climate change are irretrievably global in character. Acid precipitation is an international problem in both Europe and North America. Moreover, as authority for environmental decisions was increasingly decentralized to the state and local level, economic decisions, the organization of production, and product branding were moving rapidly to the global level. New forms of information organization and communications were at the heart of increased globalization and new political rules for the changing economic landscape soon followed: GATT begat WTO and FTA was born and quickly begat NAFTA.

These new trade agreements provide elaborate harmonization of economic and industrial policies among signatory nations. Rules are established to diminish the possibility of one nation providing "unfair" trade advantages for its exporters, or any unfair impediments to imports. Low wages and poor working conditions, however, are not necessarily seen as providing an unfair advantage to exports. Moreover, environmental rules regarding the processes used in the production of imports may be considered to be unfair impediments to imports. Thus, it is frequently argued, there is a systematic bias within these expanding trade systems to lower wages and reduced environmental protection.[50] Others have noted that there are also some pressures within global trading systems toward harmonization upward of environmental standards.[51] One aspect of this new reality that is clear is that global-scale, trade-related decisions regarding environment are less open, participatory, and democratic than are most comparable domestic decisions.

Irrespective of trade rules and rulings, a tendency to closure is inherent in the process of globalization itself. First and foremost, consumers increasingly do not know the environmental effects associated with the production of the product they are consuming and, indeed, do not even know where in the world the product was produced. Typically products are identified as to where they were assembled but information regarding the production of components and the extraction of raw ingredients is unavailable. Nor do global consumers have a parallel role as citizens that might influence the environmental and social rules regarding extraction and production. They (we) are implicitly thereby presumed to be indifferent to such matters, which are largely left to authorities of the producing jurisdiction. In effect, we have (as consumers) become citizens of the world within a global jurisdiction all-but-devoid of politics, let alone openness, citizen participation, and democracy. This is a new world where "economism" rules, where only economic issues are given weight within the trade negotiating and adjudication process. The ensuing void has been filled in part by the rise of global-scale environmental and social NGOs, but even basic information regarding wages in the garment industry of Vietnam or the environmental impacts of mining in Guyana are not readily obtained or widely communicated. Nor is it at all obvious how global consumer/citizens might act effectively in such matters.[52]

Moreover, lower wages and labor standards and less stringent environmental rules and enforcement within some nations producing for a global market create pressures on all nations to be more "competitive" and "flexible." These pressures are almost always applied outside the process of public discourse. Governmental officials are quietly informed that while corporate leaders have "always been concerned about the environment" and are "constantly making improvements" they simply cannot keep plant X open if enforcement of rule Y is not delayed until "competitive conditions improve." The regret may be genuine or it may not. Actual closures for environmental reasons alone are likely limited in number,[53] but there is no doubt that trade agreements sometimes induce diminished environmental protection.

One clear example of this is the shift in Canadian environmental policy in the 1990s. Once a world leader in environmental protection, since the establishment of the FTA and NAFTA, rollbacks in protection have become the norm.[54] Expenditures on environmental protection have been sharply reduced (both in highly industrialized

Ontario and federally), nonenforcement of existing regulations is now common in Ontario, international climate change agreements have been largely ignored (and implementation resisted), the federal government has been unwilling or unable to see through legal protection for endangered species despite a decade of explicit promises to do so, and public participation opportunities have been sharply curtailed (especially in Ontario where intervenor funding and most environmental advisory committees were eliminated).

FTA and NAFTA did not directly cause these particular outcomes, but the economic rationalization, albeit temporary, associated with those agreements led to sharp increases in unemployment and public deficits, especially in Ontario in the early 1990s. Ontario is crucial in Canadian environmental policy as it is economically equivalent to New York and California rolled together and the provinces, not the federal government, are generally dominant in environmental matters. These economic difficulties in turn produced a shift in political climate and a decline in the salience of environmental issues. A government was elected in Ontario in 1995 (and reelected in 1999) that, in terms of environmental and resource policy, has reenacted the early years of the Reagan administration as if it were following a guidebook.[55] The overarching goal of all policy initiatives in both the Reagan and the Harris governments was to enhance economic competitiveness. As with the Reagan administration, the political difficulties of the Harris government have been small, but have come as a result of environmental outcomes.[56] As with Reagan as well, this openly antienvironmental government has systematically undone consultancy mechanisms, and avoided public debate by foregoing the direct repeal of environmental legislation.

One difference between the two regimes has been that Harris has acted within a context of globalization and trade agreements that had advanced considerably by 1995. Relatively closed environmental decisions are more commonplace at the international level. Decisions by trade panels that environmental rules are really "hidden trade barriers" are essentially closed to citizens and even environmental organizations.[57] Indeed, the complex trade agreements themselves are negotiated in essentially closed sessions with input to trade negotiating teams coming overwhelmingly from corporations and business organizations, with perhaps limited contributions from labor. The climate of closure has been normalized.

Trade treaties can have profound environmental and social effects, but those involved in the process often contend that these agreements are "trade agreements only" The GATT (and its successor the WTO), for example: "explicitly prohibits a country from imposing countervailing duties on imports produced under lower environmental standards than its own. This restriction makes it impossible for 'greener' countries to protect more environmentally responsible producers from having to compete with less responsible foreign producers."[58] Just as Reagan in the 1980s foreclosed open discussion of environmental decisions, the economistic presumptions of the globalization process limits public discussion regarding such decisions.

It might even be argued that to the extent that domestic policy decisions are increasingly influenced by international factors, including policy-based competitive advantages of trading partners, democratic processes and institutions are rendered increasingly moot. Some governments may well prefer to have an excuse for failing to act contrary to the preferences of economic interests. This reality can, however, be masked through the use of increasingly effective data from polls and focus groups, skillful agenda management, and effective media relations. Generally compliant media allow governments to enhance competitiveness at the expense of policies a majority might prefer to see. The Harris government has combined such factors with splendidly effective media campaigns funded from the public treasury (and is also advantaged by divisions within the political opposition that allow reelection by plurality).

At the international level there has always been a largely unquestioned absence of openness and direct democratic participation. This closure has been acceptable to the public because international negotiations are fraught with complexities and because it is assumed that elected governments will defend the national interest as a matter of course. This doctrine, however, bears an uncanny resemblance to the "public interest" doctrine that early conservationists presumed would be apprehended and defended by public officials. However, neither the "public interest," nor the "national interest" has obvious, nonpolitical content. There are many ways to characterize either. The latter may be perceived to be almost wholly economic in character (as measured by GDP), or it may be seen multidimensionally as inclusive of economic gain, environmental protection, and social well-being—no one of which automatically results in gains in the others. Trade negotiators of all nations doubtless are in the habit of thinking in one-dimensional (economistic) terms and presume (perhaps disingenuously) that social policy and environmental policy are matters utterly outside their already arduous array of responsibilities. The overall result is a foreclosure of open, democratic processes.

In the end, however, global economic integration may all but require global-scale political action regarding environmental and social policy. These areas are no longer easily advanced in some nations (especially less economically competitive nations) without democratic participation in decision making at the global level. It is thus no longer acceptable either that the protection of the "national interest" is conceived as wholly economic in character, or that its protection is left in the hands of appointed officials who say very little in public. Trade treaties legislate both explicitly and implicitly—explicitly as regards economic policy, implicitly as regards social and environmental policy. Closure in the 1990s and since has thus come largely by default.

Michael Kidron, writing in 1968, was one of the first to observe the potential threat posed to democracy by the increasing transfer of the domestic political agenda to the international realm.[59] Until recently, within the international realm, media would dutifully report that there was "a frank exchange of views" and global television would show the toasts at the concluding banquet, but no ordinary citizen would ever know what happened behind the closed doors of the "negotiating process" regarding either trade or the environment. It was (and remains) typically unclear to the wider public what position one's nation was taking or why it was taking it. In this closed climate the power of economic interests is maximized. How else could one explain how it is that both a Democratic administration in the United States and a Liberal government in Canada consistently through the 1990s resisted every effort to even begin to deal with climate change?

The result of a now decades-long internationalization of the public policy agenda is thus far from open and participatory. Globalization itself is now widely resisted primarily because it is thus far fundamentally antidemocratic. Unfortunately, the visible alternatives within North American public discourse appear to be economic protectionism and neo-isolationism, hardly the wisest of courses. The option of conditioning trade access to North American and European markets on acceptance of social minima and the highest international environmental standards has not entered the realm of elite discourse. Nor has the possibility of setting an international minimum wage within industries producing for global markets. Without such steps, and others such as human rights (including the right to organize unions) and international workplace standards, democratic possibilities in every nation are undermined through the addition of (sometimes irresistible) global pressures to the existing array of domestic political forces.

Without such steps, the process of economic globalization will continue to reduce the salience of politics and policy for citizens everywhere. Environmental policy outcomes are now as often as not determined in some unknown place within a process peopled by international lawyers, anonymous international trade bureaucrats, and all-but-silent-in-public negotiators and diplomats. The core issues of political life become something beyond the influence of ordinary citizens and well beyond the influence of city halls that folklore already has it that one cannot fight. It is little wonder that political indifference and cynicism are increasingly the norm even within wealthy democracies.

Democratic theory has it that citizens must be informed and actively involved in civic life. A world that is integrated in terms of investment, economy, transportation, and communications cannot avoid a multidimensional political life at that level as well. Making that global political life open and participatory is the greatest challenge of the new millennium. This does not necessarily mean world government, but it does mean making the global politics that already now exists salient and accessible to citizen influence both within every nation and directly at the global level. Effective democracy at every level now requires such a change, a change that in turn requires rethinking science education, media control, the place of citizen organizations, and the design of our institutions of governance.

Science, Salience, and Democracy

Both science and values are central to the proper conduct of environmental affairs. Effective science requires openness, and democracy is necessary to achieve a widely acceptable and effective resolution of value-laden issues. Making effective environmental decisions is, then, difficult since it requires a broadly dispersed understanding of, and interest in, science. Everyday citizens have only limited time to devote to the full range of public affairs issues and few have a very detailed knowledge of environmental science. Even in the Reagan era, however, a substantial majority continued to favor vigorous environmental protection. How was it then possible for the Reagan administration to be elected and reelected despite holding views apparently out of step with the majority of citizens on these matters?

One obvious answer is that a substantial proportion of the U.S. population did not (and does not) vote. Another answer lies in a closer analysis of public opinion.

Roper polls, conducted between 1973 and 1982, which annually forced respondents to choose between "adequate energy" and "protecting the environment," are highly revealing. The proportion favoring "adequate energy" rose through the 1970s and peaked in the autumn of 1980 at 8 percent more than the proportion favoring "protecting the environment." Only following the election of the Reagan administration was there a reversal of this proportion.[60] Similarly, in 1979 the proportion feeling that environmental protection had "gone too far" at 24 percent came within 5 percent of those who felt it had "not gone far enough" (the closest ever), though by 1983 48 percent thought that regulations "did not go far enough" and only 14 percent felt that "they went too far" (with 30 percent feeling that the right balance had been struck). In other words, environmental opinion had, just prior to the 1980 election, softened in the face of energy and economic difficulties.

Even more important, however, is the fact that environmental issues have a limited salience. This reality is captured in the notion of a "permissive" consensus on environmental protection.[61] In other words, Americans (and Canadians) prefer a clean environment, but will allow an otherwise popular leader to hold, within some bounds, a different view on environmental matters. Reagan consciously tested those bounds, so too did Harris in 1990s Ontario. Had Reagan not dumped Watt and Gorsuch and softened the outright attack on environmental protection there might have been political damage. But, given those limited actions (hardly a reversal), he was reelected overwhelmingly on the strength of economic recovery. As Dunlap reported, two polls in 1982 got at the heart of the salience of environmental issues. When asked which issues would change their votes, or had actually influenced their votes, only from 1 percent to 3 percent of Americans identified "environment."[62] In other words, other issues overwhelm environmental issues in terms of electoral influence (at least in the political context of the early 1980s).

What is the long-term significance of this finding? It is difficult to avoid the conclusion that a majority preference for environmental protection of relatively low intensity and salience does not ensure that anything like consistent protection will be secured. Particularly at risk are those aspects of the environment that must be protected continuously and that would be essentially lost forever if lost but once. Also likely vulnerable are those parts of the environment that appear to limit energy security. In a contemporary U.S. context, the Alaska Wildlife Refuge comes to mind on both counts. In the longer term, the low salience of public environmental concern suggests a need to find ways to enhance the functioning of democracy so that the majority's, albeit limited, concern will be attended to at least in part.

This is hardly the only reason for significant action to improve contemporary democracy. Arguably, democracy itself is threatened on several fronts. As Putnam and others have documented, democratic participation is in radical decline.[63] Global economic integration contributes to this new reality by removing, or seeming to remove, much environmental, economic, and social policy decision making from the hands of elected governments. It is simply not obvious to many citizens that government is worth influencing because government itself is perceived to have minimal influence over societal outcomes. More basically, declining participation in civic organizations coincides with the increasing normality of two-parent working families and the rise of television (which as a media form has consistently substituted entertainment for information) with a resulting loss of time available for all "nonessential" activities including civic participation. The combination of reduced time and rising complexity does not bode well for the future of democratic life.

Environmental issues may suffer especially from these shifts (to global-scale decision making and declining participation) given their complexity, low salience, and the need for broadly based scientific sophistication to offset tendencies to closure. There are, however, many possibilities for coping with these challenges. They include: (1) some democratization of science research communication and education; (2) the partial decommercialization of electronic media; (3) work-time reductions as a means of civic, community, and family restoration; and (4) some beginning of cooperative, multidimensional global governance.

The Reagan administration was able to buy time with assertions that more research was needed before we were sure that acid deposition was a real problem long after there was a scientific consensus on this point. Today, others put forward comparable assertions regarding climate change and biodiversity protection. Both the science of legitimate environmental concerns and science itself continuously evolve while both sides of most controversies continuously lay claim to "sound science." It is difficult to deny that effective environmental decisions require lifelong science education for both citizens and decision makers. This task has been partially addressed by environmental NGOs, popular publications such as *Scientific American*, and some universities, but we are a very long way from mass environmental science education and public debate, without which relatively closed decisions may well become the norm.

Could scientific public education be significantly enhanced through the use of electronic media? At present such efforts only rarely take place outside of small-audience public broadcasting outlets and cable channels. It is also difficult to imagine that mass channels dependent on advertising dollars would be willing to risk lower ratings or in any case to be able to treat controversial subjects with any reasonable degree of neutrality. What can be done with complex and controversial issues, given sufficient funding, is apparent, however, from the recent work of Ken Burns and the scale of audience that he has reached. Is there not such potential for the newer realms where science meets ethics such as biodiversity, biotechnology, and new reproductive technologies? Or, sustainability, prosperity, and climate change?[64] Surely there are imaginative ways to ensure that a reasonable proportion of what transverses the public airwaves intelligently addresses issues of consequence to a democratic society. A modest tax on the order of 10 percent on advertising revenue would be more than sufficient to the task.

The other two possibilities are more indirect. Anders Hayden has meticulously documented the importance of work-time reductions (WTR) to the quality of contemporary life.[65] Historically, workweeks were reduced through the first half of this century, but not since despite the fact that for more than three decades the proportion of the parents in the workforce has risen sharply. The price is paid, he argues, in terms of civic, community, and family life, and the environment. There is, of course, no guarantee that WTR would ameliorate all of these challenges—people might choose to continue to opt out of civic life in favor of more hours of television or engage in wanton environmental destruction on ever more elaborate off-road vehicles. One simply must trust that this would not be everyone's first choice and that WTR does have the potential to partially restore Putnam's reported decline.

This chapter as a whole suggests that any decline in civic participation carries profound risks for both democratic effectiveness and environmental protection. Most important in the present political context, WTR raises the possibility of a blend of economic and noneconomic benefits arising from the enhanced productivity of global economic integration. It also poses a political challenge to economism. It further undermines the illusion that trade is a technical subject, largely separate from social and environmental decision making. It allows citizens of all nations to see that democracy is vulnerable everywhere when economic integration proceeds without some social and environmental minima. The third wave of closure will be with us until this is widely understood.

Notes

1. The assumption that environmental protection is based within an antigrowth "elite" is not supported by opinion polling data. Even when asked directly if economic growth should be sacrificed to achieve environmental protection, citizens have consistently concurred more often than they took the opposite view, even while electing Ronald Reagan. See, for example, Riley E. Dunlap, "Polls, Pollution, and Politics Revisited: Public Opinion on the Environment in the Reagan Era," *Environment* 29 (July/August, 1987): 11.

2. Robert Paehlke, "Democracy and Environmentalism: Opening a Door to the Administrative State," in *Managing Leviathan: Environmental Politics and the Administrative State*, ed. Robert Paehlke and Douglas Torgerson (Peterborough, Ontario, Canada: Broadview Press, 1991), 35–55.

3. Lynton Caldwell, *Science and the National Environmental Policy Act* (Tuscaloosa: University of Alabama Press, 1982).

4. Paehlke, "Democracy and Environmentalism," 42.

5. Samuel P. Hays, *Conservation and the Gospel of Efficiency* (Cambridge, Mass.: Harvard University Press, 1959).

6. Linda McQuaig, *The Cult of Impotence* (Toronto: Penguin, 1999).

7. Richard N. L. Andrews, "Class Politics or Democratic Reform: Environmentalism and American Political Institutions," *Natural Resources Journal* 20 (1980): 237.

8. Max Weber, "Bureaucracy," in *From Max Weber: Essays in Sociology*, trans. and ed. H. H. Gerth and C. Wright Mills (New York: Oxford University Press, 1946), 233.

9. See Robert Paehlke, "Spatial Proportionality: Right-Sizing Environmental Decision-Making," in *Governing the Environment*, ed. Edward A. Parson (Toronto: University of Toronto Press, 2001), 73–123.

10. Anthony Downs, "Up and Down with Ecology—The 'Issue-Attention Cycle,'" *The Public Interest*, no. 28 (summer 1972): 38–50.

11. Ibid., 38.

12. Ibid., 50.

13. Habitat loss only sometimes comes as a dramatic forest clear-cut; it more evolves over decades or centuries into a human settlement lacking ecosystemic complexity. Measures of how far we have come are the absence of large predators from Europe and the decline of even butterfly and frog populations in North America.

14. Kenneth Arrow et al., "Economic Growth, Carrying Capacity, and the Environment," *Science* 268 (April 28, 1995): 520–21.

15. See, for example, Robert Bullard, *Dumping in Dixie: Race, Class, and Environmental Quality* (Boulder, Colo.: Westview, 1991); and Robert Paehlke and Pauline Vaillancourt Rosenau, "Environment/Equity: Tensions in North American Politics," *Policy Studies Journal* 21 (winter 1993): 672–86.

16. Unless sequestration can carry more of the burden than would appear to be the case.

17. Paehlke and Rosenau, "Environment/Equity."

18. Grant McConnell, "The Conservation Movement—Past and Present," *Western Political Quarterly* 7 (1954): 471.

19. David Malin Roodman, *Paying the Piper: Subsidies, Politics, and the Environment* (Washington, D.C.: Worldwatch, 1996).

20. Again see Roodman who notes that since 1873 the U.S. government has foregone nearly $250 billion in mineral royalties on public lands.

21. Robert Paehlke, "Earth Day," in *Conservation and Environmentalism: An Encyclopedia*, ed. Robert Paehlke (New York: Garland, 1995), 185–86.

22. Rachel Carson, *Silent Spring* (Greenwich, Conn.: Fawcett Publications, 1962), 22.

23. Polls consistently showed that issue by issue, voters and Reagan were not on the same page, but nonetheless voters liked him "as a whole package."

24. Samuel P. Hays, *Beauty, Health, and Permanence: Environmental Politics in the United States, 1955–1985* (New York: Cambridge University Press, 1987), 494.

25. Ibid., 496.

26. Ibid., 494.

27. Friends of the Earth, *Ronald Reagan and the American Environment* (Andover, Mass.: Brick House Publishing, 1982), 70–78.

28. Norman J. Vig, "Presidential Leadership: From the Reagan to the Bush Administration," in *Environmental Policy in the 1990s*, ed., Norman J. Vig and Michael E. Kraft (Washington, D.C.: Congressional Quarterly Press, 1990), 38.

29. See Paehlke, "Democracy and Environmentalism."

30. Vig, "Presidential Leadership," 45–46.

31. Hays, *Beauty, Health, and Permanence*, 504.

32. Friends of the Earth, *Ronald Reagan*, 15, 25.

33. Ibid., 18.

34. Ibid., 33.

35. Hays, *Beauty, Health, and Permanence*, 519.

36. See Paehlke, "Spatial Proportionality," for further discussion.

37. Friends of the Earth, *Ronald Reagan*, 9.

38. Philip Shabecoff, *A Fierce Green Fire: The American Environmental Movement* (New York: Hill & Wang, 1994), 227.

39. John DeWitt, *Civic Environmentalism* (Washington, D.C.: Congressional Quarterly Press, 1994), 54.

40. Shabecoff, *Fierce Green Fire*, 230.

41. Hays, *Beauty, Health, and Permanence*, 518.

42. Ibid., 505.

43. Douglas J. Amy, in *Managing Leviathan: Environmental Politics and the Administrative State*, ed. Robert Paehlke and Douglas Torgerson (Peterborough, Ontario, Canada: Broadview Press, 1991), 59–79.

44. See Sharon Beder, *Global Spin* (White River Junction, Vt.: Chelsea Green Publishing, 1998), 27–46.

45. John Elkington and Julia Haines, *The Green Consumer Guide* (London: Victor Gollancz, 1988).

46. They were not taken seriously in Canada. See David S. Cohen, "Subtle Effects," *Alternatives Journal* 20 (September/October, 1994): 22–27.

47. The distinction between markets and democracy is best made in Mark Sagoff, *The Economy of the Earth* (New York: Cambridge University Press, 1988).

48. The PCSD, for example, languished during the Clinton administration and the Ontario Roundtable disappeared with the election of 1995.

49. Polling figures are reported in Shabecoff, *Fierce Green Fire*, 233.

50. See, for example, *The Case against the Global Economy*, ed. Jerry Mander and Edward Goldsmith (San Francisco: Sierra Club Books, 1996).

51. David Vogel, *Trading Up* (Cambridge, Mass.: Harvard University Press, 1995).

52. There are possibilities, however. See, for example, Ronnie D. Lipschutz, *Global Civil Society and Global Environmental Governance* (Albany, N.Y.: SUNY Press, 1996).

53. V. D. McConnell and R. M. Schwab, "The Impact of Environmental Regulation on Industrial Relocation Decisions," *Land Economics* 66 (1990), 67–81.

54. Detailed in Paehlke, "Spatial Proportionality."

55. Robert Paehlke, "Environmentalism in One Country: Canadian Environmental Policy in an Era of Globalization," *Policy Studies Journal* 28 (2000): 160–75.

56. Most important were the events at Walkerton, Ontario, where seven deaths and thousands of illnesses resulted from contaminated drinking water following privatization of water testing.

57. Regarding global trade and democracy see, for example, Mander and Goldsmith.

58. David Vogel, "International Trade and Environmental Regulation," in *Environmental Policy in the 1990s*, ed. Norman J. Vig and Michael E. Kraft (Washington, D.C.: Congressional Quarterly Press, 1997), 348.

59. Michael Kidron, *Western Capitalism since the War* (London: Penguin, 1970).

60. Riley Dunlap, "Paradox at the Polls: Environmental Concern in the 1980s," *Environment* 29 (July/August, 1987): 6–11, 34–37.

61. For a discussion of how the salience and strength of environmental opinion affected the Reagan administration see Robert Cameron Mitchell, "Public Opinion and Environmental Politics in the 1970s and 1980s," in *Environmental Policy in the 1980s*, ed. Norman J. Vig and Michael E. Kraft (Washington, D.C.: Congressional Quarterly Press, 1984), 54–57.

62. Dunlap, "Paradox at the Polls," 35; Vig, "Presidential Leadership," 44; Mitchell, "Public Opinion," 66–67.

63. Robert D. Putnam, *Bowling Alone: The Collapse and Revival of American Community* (New York: Simon & Schuster, 2000).

64. One excellent program is *What's Up with the Weather?* (WGBH Boston).

65. Anders Hayden, *Sharing the Work; Sparing the Planet* (New York: Zed Books, 1999).

CHAPTER 15

The People, Politics, and the Planet

WHO KNOWS, PROTECTS,
AND SERVES NATURE BEST?

Timothy W. Luke

This chapter reconsiders the claims for Nature being made in the name of locality, people, or sustainability by many environmental activists around the United States of America. Whether it is Earth First! sympathizers, neighborhood antitoxics campaigners, environmental justice organizers, or experimental green technologists, one often finds images of locality and the people residing there being linked in environmental protection efforts. These essentially populist expressions of ecological concern also mobilize special claims on behalf of the people living in specific bioregions or at particular sites, because they allegedly possess greater awareness, care, or wisdom about what should be done in these environments to safeguard their ecological integrity.

Such claims are difficult to defend to many others, because the everyday operations of the current world economy increasingly are organized to delocalize individuals and communities by integrating them into globalized networks of exchange. In turn, the professional-technical experts who construct and control these networks for global exchange constantly seek to improve the efficiency of this highly complicated system for world trade. At the same time, some experts cast suspicion upon most attempts to preserve local autonomy, even for sound ecological reasons, as a conservative defense of positional goods by small special interests that would bar others from enjoying what they have by accidents of birth or previous migration. This chapter will question the motives and goals of these expert globalizers in order to defend the positions taken by local environment activists, who usually make the best efforts to defend their environments from further destruction.

In surveying briefly the actions of many individuals and groups in the United States during the 1990s and 2000s, this chapter tries to show how democratic values and populist practices are being reactivated in many unusual environmental movements today. These movements are best suited to know, protect, and serve Nature inasmuch as their efforts, first, are pitched against the values of global efficiency adopted by transnational firms staffed by professional-technical experts, and, second, are opposed to the subpolitical forms of power those experts wield against everyone in their efforts to manage corporate exchange and technological growth on a global scale. While these experts pretend to have special reliable knowledge about the world's economy and environment, populist resistances against their authority persistently point out the failures of, and gaps in, this expertise.

Of course, many populist movements are led by dissident experts, many environmental movements play one expert scientific study off against others, and many populists are invested in other kinds of capital, expertise, or services that big transnational firms no longer operate. So this story is not a starkly simple study of the local white hats valiantly fighting global black hats. Nonetheless, there are many indications that local activists and groups are closer to the environments that need protections, while transnational firms and remote experts can always move on to not yet contaminated areas once they have despoiled their existing sites of operation. Therefore, the chapter will outline some of the larger forces creating these basic conditions of contention as well as focus upon a few specific examples that begin to indicate why the people closest to where the planet is being threatened will best know how to serve and protect it.

Globalization and Postmodernity

The ties between greater global corporate control and renewed populist local resistance have acquired considerable importance, because so much of the world's ecology, and many segments of the global economy, have deteriorated so badly during the past ten or fifteen years.[1] This deterioration also has spread quickly during the 1990s and 2000s—a time of unabashed Western triumphalism. After the Industrial Revolution, no place in the world holds out against machines: technology is everywhere. After the two world wars, few places around the world hold on to traditional formulas of authority: democracy is spreading everywhere. After the Cold War, no part of the world seriously holds forth as a real alternative to the market: capitalism is everywhere. Only a few truly critical alternatives stand out in opposition to these trends, like democratic populist local movements. Most importantly, these movements are working hard to unravel how technology, democracy, and capitalism interact so adversely, while trying to correct the ecological and economic destruction these interactions promote.

Therefore, much of what exists at this moment in the United States and most other advanced capitalist economies, whether one looks at economic structures or political practices, embodies long-standing inequalities in wealth, power, and knowledge that benefit a few to the detriment of the many.[2] Such loosely constrained concentrations of authority and affluence, in turn, prevent the democratic promise of more broadly based popular empowerment and enrichment from being realized. If the economy and society were organized otherwise, it could make possible even more prosperity, greater harmony, and better governance.[3] Furthermore, most efforts to change are being thwarted continuously by entrenched elites intent upon preserving their power, position, and privilege.[4] Other more democratic, equitable, and popular expressions of modernity, however, are possible. And, it is this potential that many new local, regional, and national populist resistances against globalized inequality and disempowerment are hoping to attain.

From the election of Margaret Thatcher in the United Kingdom in 1979 to the collapse of the USSR under Mikhail Gorbachev during 1991, many things changed in the world's economy and state system. First and foremost, the social contract drawn up during the Industrial Revolution essentially has been abandoned. New technologies, globalization, and ideological splits have enabled neoliberal ideologies to discredit the welfare state and its social democratic culture of collective concern for the well-being of everyone.[5] The "winner take all" mentality of markets during this time has pushed most new income gains into the top 20 percent of many societies, while the bottom 80 percent's incomes have stagnated or shrunk.[6] Scientific expertise also has increasingly lost much of its former credibility through self-interested associations with big business or big government. And, many states now find it difficult to maintain the integrity of their borders, sustain economic growth, or attain control over all the technical, environmental, demographic, and cultural influences affecting their populations from abroad.[7] A handful of countries are benefiting disproportionately from these transformations, a few others are struggling desperately to keep what they have had from being lost entirely, but most others are losing what industrial democracy once guaranteed to their populations. To protect what remains, ordinary people are left fighting neoliberal reforms to preserve valued ways of living against free trade, global governance, and high technology.[8] These conflicts are also what lie, in turn, at the heart of local, regional, and national popular movements for greater democracy.[9]

For many, these political trends are simply one more expression of postmodernization.[10] To explore this possibility, Lyotard offers some useful insights into postmodernity. Basically, he describes "a modern era that dates from the time of the Enlightenment and that now has run its course: and this modern era was predicated on the notion of progress in knowledge, in the arts, in technology, and in human freedom as well, all of which was thought of as leading to a truly emancipated society: a society emancipated from poverty, despotism, and ignorance. But all of us can see that the development continues to take place without leading to the realization of any of these dreams of emancipation."[11] These contradictory readings of a "postprogressive" notion of progress or an "adevelopmental" type of development follow from the rising popular distrust in once widely shared metanarratives of truth, enlightenment, or progress.

Because they lack once trusted ideological trappings, science and technology increasingly fall under the sway of "another language game, in which the goal is no longer truth, but performativity—that is, the best possible input/output equation."[12] Expertise often is expected to do little more than continuously accelerate the processes of production and consumption. As a result, many professional-technical experts essentially adopt an empty, and also troubling, ideological standpoint: "the State and/or company must abandon the idealist and humanist narratives of legitimation in order to justify the new goal: in the discourse of today's financial backers of research, the only credible goal is power. Scientists, technicians, and instruments are purchased not to find truth, but to augment power."[13]

Performativity, then, becomes the central value of the social machines behind the technical machines in globalization's informational revolution, which also turn upon continuously defining, developing, and then deploying specialized systems of expertise. These power/knowledge codes now constitute a new worldwide regimen for managing resource scarcities, rent seeking, and social reward systems. Globalization rests upon new technologies; still, it is not so much technology that matters but rather "the human skill and social organization which lie behind it. . . . it is the professional experts who have constructed the system, which in turn has created them."[14] The labor performed through many diverse and divided disciplines of expertise, in turn, generates most of the productive power driving contemporary economies and societies. The action of expert elites inside of formal organizations, at the same time, remakes old class contradictions by presuming the inaction of lay populations outside of these complex organizations.[15] The elites' presumptions about mass acquiescence before their scientific and managerial authority, however, have never entirely held true. Many different oppositional forces always have tested the power of professional-mechanical experts from above, below, and within. Rule by shifting variegated blocs of expert elites over mass consumer society also brings along with it resistance from ever-changing, unorganized populist oppositions.

The power/knowledge behind economies of signs and space in transnationalized informational society, however, does not spring into being on its own. Fast capitalist markets, which anchor and underpin global informationalization, coevolve within complex networks of technical expertise defined and dominated by new professional elites. As Lasch observes, these elites include "not only corporate managers but all those professions that produce and manipulate information," and with their commitment to making, mastering, or monitoring informational assets—or "the lifeblood of the global market"—they are "far more cosmopolitan, or at least more restless and migratory, than their predecessors."[16] In ways that most democratic populist resistances do not appreciate, the social forces in search of greater performativity already "think locally and act globally," because this slogan perfectly captures not only an ecological ideal, but also the basic realities of performativity-maximizing transnational commerce within and between informationalizing societies.

Perkin ties such economic and cultural processes back to the institutionalized hegemony of professional expertise, arguing that experts transform society from top to bottom by mobilizing power through their special knowledges. The expert class rules because

> It raises living standards not just for the few but for every member of society. It puts most of its man- and woman-power into services rather than agriculture and manufacturing. It substitutes professional hierarchy for class as the primary matrix of the social structure. It recruits to those hierarchies by means of meritocracy, entailing an increase in social mobility from below. It extends this to women, thus ensuring their (admittedly limited) emancipation. It entails the massive growth of government, including the universal benefits of the welfare state, which enlarges and moralizes the concept of citizenship. It expands the provision of higher education in order to create human capital. It concentrates production of both goods and services in large business corporations whether private or state-owned, in a new structure of corporate neo-feudalism. And, paradoxically perhaps, it threatens to erode the nation state by internationalizing corporate neo-feudalism and creating a global economy.[17]

Perkin concludes that all contemporary informationalizing economies and societies are now controlled "by those who control the scarce resource of expertise in its manifold forms."[18]

Ecological populists are troubled by the false promises made by professional-technical experts about attaining higher standards of living from realizing greater measures of performativity. The distrust in narratives of truth, progress, or enlightenment also leaves many people wary about the merits of "the best possible input/output equation." On the one hand, these equations often mean that more people lose employment, more communities incur ecological damage, and more localities suffer economic hardship. On the other hand, a society organized around professional-technical experts relentlessly pursuing perfection through performativity leads out into very tough terrain of "the risk society."

The fusion of professional-technical expertise and performativity in most quarters of the economy and society validates Ulrich Beck's vision of "the risk society." That is, at this juncture in history the social production of wealth is systematically accompanied by the social production of *risks*, and, as a result, it is now the case that "the problems and conflicts relating to distribution in a society of scarcity overlap with the problems and conflicts that arise from the production, definition, and distribution of techno-scientifically produced risks."[19] Modernization is forcing many agencies and structures to become more reflexive because the performativity underlying this era's postprogressive growth already has remade technology/democracy/capitalism into new global background conditions. While the classical narratives of economic rationalization, which have underpinned the modernization project, did presume that greater command, control, communication, and intelligence would come from applying more rational decision making to life, the realities of risk society find everyone living amid far too many irrational consequences of rational decision making that now are beyond anyone's command, control, communication, or intelligence. Hence, local populists continuously highlight how the allegedly growing calculability of instrumental rationality also actually brings greater measures of incalculability—which are unintended and unanticipated but rooted, ironically, in instrumental irrationality—along with it.

Nevertheless, professional-technical experts still derive power, prestige, and privilege in the collective quest for greater performative results from "their possession of specialized knowledge, based on education, competitive merit, and experience on the job—in a word, on their human capital."[20] As Lasch argues, they also constitute an essentially postmodern class that incarnate the values of neoliberalism in almost everything they do. Living without metanarratives, they are symbolic analysts, technical experts, and managerial specialists. They also are often deterritorialized souls, "who live in a world of abstract concepts and symbols, ranging from stock market quotations to the visual images produced by Hollywood and Madison Avenue, and who specialize in the interpretation and deployment of symbolic information."[21] As postmodern times become focused on the work of nations, as Reich asserts, the silent majorities of "routine producers" and "in-person servers" are now becoming very restive over losing both their metanarrative meanings and most social control over their future to such abstract mobile minorities of systems-thinking "symbolic analysts."[22]

Moreover, as Reich suggested a decade ago, the successful can "secede" from the body politic because their greater performativity permits those with the skill, capital, or contacts to build private telecommunications systems, patronize private schools, trade globally, reside within gated communities, employ private security guards, and tax themselves in private systems of protective covenants.[23] The less able, however, are left seeking entitlements from a weakened national regime no longer coasting on the momentum of its traditional authority, no longer assured of an unlimited power to tax, borrow, and spend, and no longer able to guarantee complete territorial sovereignty.[24] Those who cannot find a place in the performative organization of world trade, in turn, frequently must join local populist movements, accept the narcocapitalist economy, or find some other escape from the ravages of neoliberal globalization symbolized to many by the World Trade Organization.

Populism and the Subpolitical

The diverse blocs of professional-mechanical experts working behind global neoliberalism do not understand how much their project actually can contradict and confound democracy in countries like the United States. Expert management of public affairs by the state may appear to guarantee "individual values," but these precepts often are only the values of neoliberal experts who believe they are empowered to keep "the people" equal by impelling them to pursue individuality in an open society, to secure various abstract enactments of individual rights, and to assist the needier elements of society. Such agendas of enlightened managerialism from above and without frequently conflict with those of self-reliant people struggling to rule themselves as fully functioning democrats in fulfillment of goals chosen by/for/of "people," and not by liberal statists.[25] Many local and regional movements, then, ask a troubling question: who actually sets the rules of governance, and for whom?

A proliferating panoply of experts, who once meant to support the good life for individuals in states, has come to constrain real democratic choice as well as reduce communal self-governance to the ratification of expert decisions taken elsewhere. Populist movements point to troubling tendencies: real people in many actual communities might choose through open and free democratic means to *not* accept economic growth through globalization, to *not* endorse toxic dumping in their region, to *not* pay for expensive tax concessions for foreign companies, or to *not* lose local employment to back global free trade, and all for many important local reasons. Yet, experts continue to intervene in their lives to force such policies down their throats as "the state of the art" they must accept.[26] The worries of populists are compelling because people sense how rapidly the ever-changing demands of performativity in technical and economic infrastructures are degrading life in most localities. Turbulent worldwide webs move matter, energy, and information from everywhere to anywhere, while at the same time piling up most "goods" in a few places to the detriment of most other places that accumulate only higher piles of more "bads." These operations work underneath, above, and apart from the polis, but they are also structures of power, systems of exchange, and signs of culture. Such subpolitical systems, as Beck indicates, are often misrepresented as the black boxes of "science" and "technology," but their power effects, social values, and cultural practices lie at the center of the "economy," "society," and "state."[27]

No one can make much sense out of the current crisis without acknowledging how fully the subpolis, which is the collective assemblies of economic and social rationalization practices in technoscience, underlies it. Indeed, the subpolitical "preprograms the permanent change of all realms of social life under the justifying cloak of techno-economic progress, in contradistinction to the simplest rules of democracy—knowledge of the goals of social change, discussion, voting, and consent."[28] It represents the continuous workings of tremendous operational authority layered under politics, occluded in technologies from ordinary political understandings, hidden from politicians by the mechanics of markets or the elisions of experts. Like the polis, the subpolis is a built environment, but its constructs all too often are massively depoliticized by professional-technical rhetorics embedded in the practices of civil engineering, public health, corporate management, scientific experiment, technical design, and property ownership.[29] Populists worry about increasing the quasi objectivity of subjects as they engage in most economic or technical activities, because these activities cannot be separated from the growing quasi subjectivity of objects circulating en masse in globalized economies of scale.[30]

The subpolis reveals itself in the vast sprawl congealing in suburbia, the gridlock clogging flows of traffic, the maldevelopment rising out of rapid growth, and the toxic by-products coming from desired products. Like most populists, Beck worries about how "the possibilities for social change from the collaboration of research, technology, and science accumulate," as economies and societies find the locus of social order and disorder "*migrates from the domain of politics to that of subpolitics*."[31] In the subpolis, what begins at an individual level as a rational plan combines at a collective global level into the irrational, unintended, and unanticipated. Yet, it is difficult to resist these plans inasmuch as the workings of modern technics and markets become "institutionalized as 'progress,' but remain subject to the dictates of business, science, and technology, for whom democratic procedures are invalid."[32] Unlike the polis, which is a more stable collective of people situated in a specific fixed locality or particular nation–state, the subpolis patches itself together out of ever-shifting assemblies of different persons and diverse technics that interoperate with many other technical assemblies and people elsewhere in multi/trans/supernational time as well as within inter/infra/intralocal space.

Within the world's comparatively fixed geopolitical order, there are many much more fluid techno-economic systems that continuously revolutionize humanity's built environments. Networks of industrial production and by-production, then, construct a transnational subpolis of technoscience acts and artifacts beneath, within, and above each territorial polis as this latter entity is still being composed out of political acts.[33] This technified mode of mounting revolutionary changes in everyday life is work conducted in the subpolis and it underscores how thoroughly

> now the potential for structuring society migrates from the political system into the sub-political system of scientific, technological and economic modernization. A precarious reversal occurs. *The political becomes non-political and the non-political political.* . . . The promotion and protection of "scientific progress" and of "the freedom of science" become the greasy pole on which the primary responsibility for political arrangements slips from the democratic system into the context of economic and techno-scientific non-politics, which is not democratically legitimated. *A revolution under the cloak of normality occurs*, which escapes from possibilities of intervention, but must all the same be justified and enforced against a public that is becoming critical.[34]

Democratic publics in the territorial polis ordinarily must accept these changes without much contestation, because such technoscientific revolutions are believed to bring the good life, albeit at times with a few risks. For those unwanted, but still allegedly quite controllable, noxious by-products of technological innovation, democratic publics are encouraged to resist regulation by the state or to wait for new technical innovations in the subpolis to mitigate their adverse effects. In fact, however, the subpolis of techno-scientific artifacts seriously abridges the decisive authority promised by conventional political institutions, and here is where new populist movements intervene.

Like democratic populists, Beck frets about the unintended effects of radical in-novations from the subpolitics implied by continuous change in advanced industrial technics. That is, the political system, on the one hand,

> is being threatened with disempowerment while its democratic constitution remains alive. The political institutions become the administrators of a de-velopment they neither have planned for nor are able to structure, but must nonetheless justify. On the other hand, decisions in science and business are charged with an effectively political content for which the agents possess no legitimation. Lacking any place to appear, the decisions that change society become tongue-tied and anonymous. . . . What we *do not* see and *do not* want is changing the world more and more obviously and threateningly.[35]

Because of the subpolis, ordinary processes of democratic legitimation begin to fail. Modern industrial revolutions with all of their negative ecological and economic by-products are highly technified forms of collective action. The vital infrastructure sup-porting everyday life "remains shielded from the demands of democratic legitimation by its own character" inasmuch as "it is *neither politics nor non-politics*, but a third en-tity: economically guided action in pursuit of interests."[36] The agitation of democratic populists is aimed at bringing the clients of this globalized subpolis to realize how fully "the structuring of the future takes place indirectly and unrecognizably in research lab-oratories and executive suites, not in parliament or in political parties. Everyone else—even the most responsible and best informed people in politics and science—more or less lives off the crumbs of information that fall from the tables of technological sub-politics."[37]

As Beck's insights confirm, governments now try to reduce risk—to themselves and their constituents—by using subpolitical maneuvers to reduce the dangers of dem-ocratic governance into the more predictable certainties of expert rulings.[38] Politics de-velops into "sub-politics," insulating real political choices from the democratic hurly-burly of popular elections or partisan wrangling, while empowering small networks of experts to make decisions on the basis of their professional-technical disciplinary codes in networks of professionalized interest articulation/aggregation where more networks of other experts make/enforce and interpret the rules. Hence, the main political con-flict zones today are no longer necessarily those between labor and capital, left and right, racial majorities and minorities, or women and men. Rather they break along other axes of authority, namely, between those who know and those who do not, those who can and do participate in elitist managerial decision taking and those who cannot, or those who intervene in the personal spheres of others and those who cannot.[39]

Populist Efforts to Protect Nature Best

By opposing these destructive tendencies with new alternative values, democratic populists push to renew nonhierarchical social relations, technical simplicity, small-scale economies, political decentralization, reasonable science, and cultural vitality within the free spaces of present-day national society. Unlike most expert programs for greater corporate managerialism, many democratic populists favor mobilizing the immediate producers and consumers to reconsider how crucial decisions about their relations to Nature can change rather than surrendering this prerogative to state and corporate technocrats.[40]

The contestation of expert managerialism by populist movements puts ecology at the center of a new critical sensibility to revitalize political debates over the key issues of who decides, who pays, and who benefits in the complex economic and technological relations of people with Nature.[41] A sense of Nature, as ecologically constituted free space for self-created being, could reorder the relations of the individual to the collective, of personality to society, and of these dual social relations to Nature.[42] This ecological sensibility could also reinvest individuals with the decision-making power to construct their material relations to the environment in smaller-scale, nonhierarchical, ecologically sound technical relations between independent producers in local and regional commonwealths. Most people now know states and businesses will not act responsibly in many instances. Therefore, democratic populist movements typically reaffirm the responsibility of all individuals for preserving their ecological inheritance and passing it on to future generations.

There are innumerable examples of all these trends across the United States, so it is difficult to privilege any by discussing them specifically in any detail. Nonetheless, a few examples can bring these ideas into a tighter focus. Most important, these examples underscore how ordinary people are trying to assert greater control over their lives through direct action and democratic organizing.[43] In today's global economy, professional-technical experts work very hard to make competent people and communities more and more incompetent at controlling their own lives, but populist resistances essentially are about reclaiming a competence for the individual and locality against transnational systems of production and consumption.

Popular anticorporate movements spring up continuously in many quarters of American society. Many of them fade away quickly, some of few gain a media attention and public support, and a few of them persist in their struggle to actively resist corporate control and exploitation in their localities. Most movements tend to be single-issue protest efforts aimed at blocking corporate maneuvers with regard to only one or two pressing concerns.[44] These tactics, however, often fail, because, as James MacKinnon of AdBusters suggests,

> The error is in naming the enemy—which is neither trade nor globalization. The real target is corporate rule. The fact that the Seattle protest was neither left nor right, reform nor revolution, only shows the breadth and depth of the rebellion against corporationization.[45]

The loosely organized antiglobalization coalitions that have disrupted WTO, IMF, and WEF meetings in Seattle, Washington, D.C., and Davos, Switzerland, are learning to name the enemy and target the problem more astutely in their direct action campaigns at home or on the world stage at these big global summits.

An excellent example on the opposite end of the political scale is Alternatives for Community & Environment (ACE) in Boston. ACE began in Roxbury, Massachusetts, to defend this economically depressed area of the larger Boston metropolitan area from experiencing greater environmental injustice.[46] The site of the old South Bay incinerator and illegal dump sites, the neighborhood faced the construction of an asphalt batching plant on one illegal dumping ground as an economic development project. ACE negotiated agreements with the commonwealth to clean up the incinerator, end illegal dumping, and launch new environmentally sound economic development initiatives in the neighborhood.[47] This environmental justice group, like hundreds of others around the nation, is dedicated to resisting the arrogant abuse of local neighborhoods by people elsewhere who would impose economic and ecological hardships on others in order to escape these evils themselves. This overtly political movement articulates a populist agenda inasmuch as it seeks to build competencies for ordinary people amid a system of expert power that rests upon generating more and more incompetence to perpetuate itself.[48]

Frequently, these populist activities are misidentified by outside observers as merely being experiments in alternative technology, community outreach, or sustainable development.[49] Sometimes their activities can be described in such terms, but in other instances they actually do constitute an attempt to break new ground technologically, economically, or culturally. These pioneering practices provide the basis for a new politics and economy: one that is locally theorized, enacted, and shared. Because they respect how fully the economy must also be ecological, the self rests within the spatial articulation of society, and politics can only be redirected through practices, many democratic populists work away at subpolitical sites and spaces to repoliticize discourses and practices that most experts would continue to monopolize as a region for professional-technical discretion or to regard as the space for prerogatives of property.[50] Whether this work is done by entrepreneurs, community activists, inventors, or dissident professionals, it provides a concrete alternative to continuing to accept what is simply because it exists.

Not all populist efforts to resist corporate power, then, are focused upon resisting, reforming, or regulating the business activities of large firms. Many populists instead take direct action against transnational commerce by pushing experimentation at the local level with new types of innovative small business. The revitalization of farmers' markets in the 1970s has enabled farmers to reintegrate local food production with local and regional food consumers outside of the standardized food regime of large transnational firms. California had only 4 farmers' markets in the late 1970s; it now has around 300, and there are more than 2,500 nationwide.[51] The tendency for large supermarket chains to not build new stores in certain neighborhoods as well as to pull out of declining areas moved activists in low-income urban areas to develop the Community Food Security Coalition to develop linkages among farmers' markets, neighborhood activists, urban food banks, and sustainable agriculture movements in many major American urban areas in the 1990s.

Other offshoots of this populist economy building are movements like the Urban Agriculture Network and Chefs Collaborative 2000. By using vacant labor, community labor, and pooled household demand, Urban Agriculturalists try to demarketize food production by growing foods in neighborhoods for local consumption.[52] Nearly 14 percent of all food already is grown in cities, and far more food could be produced on ground devoted to lawns or ornamental plantings. Chefs Collaborative 2000 was begun in a few large American cities by chefs who were committed to building urban agriculture, sustaining farming, and supporting antihunger organizations.[53] By contracting with urban agriculturalists or sustainable farming operators, this group uses noncorporate food sources to alter their own menus and patrons' awareness of food production.

Community currency systems are another means for building populist institutions against larger corporate and state interests. Paul Glover in Ithaca, New York, created the Ithaca HOURS currency system by pegging intracommunity exchange to hourly units of labor that residents exchange for goods and services among themselves and at 300 local businesses.[54] Instead of existing actual paper currency, computer-based credit/debit systems enable similar exchanges in many American and Canadian communities. Such LETS, or local exchange trading systems, are popular because this sort of local currency cannot circulate outside of the community that creates and uses it, "so it ensures connections between people exchanging skills, goods, and services."[55] Starr notes, "in almost every locality, small businesses now face competition from powerful multinational corporations, who use huge advertising budgets to homogenize preferences (in the guise of 'choice'), cut prices based on their socially costly comparative advantage, eliminate inconvenient regulations and protectionist policies of all kinds, and now have the very definition of competition legally defined in their interests."[56]

The punk DIY, "Do It Yourself," movement also is creating anticorporate popular economic and cultural institutions as it "has evolved into a self-conscious enclave industry of bands, independent labels, zines, publishers, art venues and small businesses."[57] Although it too is mostly a pop culture movement, DIY explicitly condemns the products and consumer habits of corporate pop culture producers in order to provide an alternative lifestyle to individuals that is pitched more on their own self-defined and locally enjoyed terms. This sort of enclave economics also has echoes in many ethnic, racial, and religious communities. Whether they are connected with the new transnational diasporas of Cold War era, older communities of racial minorities, or religious groups, such markets also are organized around meeting needs that larger corporate producers ignore as well as redistributing the benefits of exchange more locally or justly.[58]

Democratic populists, however, do not always limit their efforts only to overtly political movements on a local or world scale. Ordinary individuals are among the first to recognize how transnational corporate firms and big state bureaucracies fail them, but they do not always sit on their hands, waiting for some other private company or government agency to make things better. Instead these individuals start working on their own at the local level to cope with economic irrationality and social inequality through direct action at a subpolitical level.

In Falmouth, Massachusetts, for example, John Todd experiments with "living machines" to treat municipal sewage flows by running them through greenhouses filled with various plants, animals, and microorganisms.[59] The organic elements consume nutrients in the sewage, while they also either degrade or store many toxic chemicals found in these waters. Once the waste waters are released from the greenhouses, they are essentially safe for human use. In Chicago, Illinois, Scott Bernstein's Center for Neighborhood Technology works to enlarge the city's affordable housing opportunities, enhance these dwellings' energy efficiency and environmental sustainability, and explore the creation of new high-wage sustainable employment opportunities in the city's neighborhoods.[60] By creating coalitions among residents, businesses, and government offices, Bernstein has built urban gardens, lessened neighborhood waste streams, and provided jobs with no ecological impact. In New York City, Paul and Julie Mankiewicz have developed new technologies to grow food on top of city high-rises in hydroponic gardens to promote employment, save energy, enhance food stocks, and enrich urban living.[61] By using urban food waste for compost, discarded Styrofoam packaging for soil, and empty roof space on high-rises, the Mankiewiczs have developed an outstanding system to empower people economically and technologically where they live now, namely, inside of conventional housing stock located in major metropolitan areas by permitting them to grow a large amount of their food needs.

The prevailing arrangements of authority in conventional corporate organization trust managers to find the most profitable type of products to produce, while engineers and technicians are also expected to uncover the most efficient means of manufacturing and distributing these products. As long as stockholders receive rising rates of return, and customers are satisfied with their product purchases, these arrangements usually continue undisturbed. Unfortunately, there typically are other variables in these arrangements, like the environmental impacts, community benefits, social costs, or political implications of production, that can affect adversely the lives of many ordinary people. The presumptions of subpoliticization quite often neutralize these worries by transposing them into questions of technical expertise and/or prerogatives of property ownership. Yet, not everyone easily accepts the efforts by big businesses or the state to subpoliticize the central concerns of their personal lives or their community's well-being. This resistance shows up in many different ways, and at a variety of locations. However, the local economic revitalization campaigns, new sustainable development attempts, and alternative technology experiments do provide some examples.

An excellent case in point is Spencer Beebe's Ecotrust organization in Portland, Oregon, which works at revitalizing local communities across the Pacific Northwest hard hit by declines in the fishing, timber, or mining industries.[62] Ecotrust identified the Willapa Bay area, with its multiple agroindustrial enterprises in oystering, fishing, timbering, and cranberry cultivating, as a stressed ecosystem and declining community that needed a new focus in order to restore its ecological integrity and economic viability. Beebe brought together local entrepreneurs and some conservation-minded economists, business planners, and financial backers to come up with new strategies to economically revitalize the region. Alana Probst, an environmental economist, moved to the Willapa Bay area, and started the Willapa Alliance to protect the environment by building better business models.[63] Probst found ways to disengage local people from low value-adding circuits of big time corporate production by helping townspeople build small sawmill operations, a cranberry product mail order business, forest product gleaning businesses, a natural fisheries business, and a local business services exchange. All of these enterprises aimed at producing goods and services in an ecologically sensitive fashion, while keeping profits, decision-making authority, and control at the local level as much as possible.

This commitment to individual initiative and local well-being is reflected in the sustainable development work done by the Practical Farmers of Iowa (PFI), founded by Ron Rosmann and several other farmers across Iowa in the 1980s. Along with two neighbor's farms, Rosmann's 480-acre farm near Harlan, Iowa, is part of a 1,200-acre block of herbicide-free farmland, and 320 of Rosmann's acres are certified as organic farmland by the Organic Crop Improvement Association.[64] By using different crop rotation, integrated pest management, and ridge tillage methods, Rosmann has escaped the monocrop/monoculture system of chemical-dependent agricultural methods. He did this to save money on artificial fertilizers, herbicides, and insecticides, to bring the land back to a healthier organic condition, and to restore his decision-making power as a businessman and landowner. As he maintains, "the very definition of sustainable farming involves the preservation of the community itself. If the farm is sustainable, it will sustain people to work and, by extension, the local community."[65] Rosmann and PFI stage field days many times a year to popularize their practices among other farmers, and they also push their principles, through the Campaign for Sustainable Agriculture, to change the policy frameworks that reward farmers for remaining stuck in monoculture modes of production.[66]

In her own way, Sally Fox of Natural Cotton Colors, Inc., is an innovative sustainable agricultural producer, but she also is an alternative technology pioneer who has entirely rethought the production cycle of cotton textiles in a challenge to today's high-polluting and resource-wasting cotton industries.[67] Fox obtained a master's degree from the University of California-Riverside in integrated pest management after studying entomology at California State University-San Luis Obispo, but she also has been a weaver and spinner since childhood. After seeing some naturally colored cotton from Guatemala at a handweavers conference, she became fascinated with the possibility that such cotton could be more pest resistant, more environmentally benign to grow, and less wasteful to turn into cloth because one could dispense with expensive dyeing processes. After experimenting on her back porch in 1982 with some brown cotton seed from old Mexican and Central American cotton strains, Fox succeeded in selecting out some strains with the longest fiber lengths and greatest variety of natural color. By 1988, she had found plants that produced machine-spinnable cotton with good natural color, and she contracted with a Japanese mill to provide a ton of her cotton at $5 a pound, as opposed to 70 cents a pound for ordinary white cotton grown with traditional techniques.

By 1989, she was growing 500 tons, had secured trademark protection for her Fox Fibre textiles, and won plant variety protection certificates for three different varieties of her cotton.[68] Fox's organic fields, however, were troubling to other conventional growers in California, so she moved her operations to a site near Wickenburg, Arizona, in 1992. Her products are an important innovation because of the outrageously expensive and polluting methods of growing cotton. Indeed, nearly one-quarter to one-half of all pesticide applications in the United States are put on cotton plants, which contaminates soil and pollutes groundwater in many localities. Fox's cotton costs about $2.50 a pound to produce versus 72 cents a pound for conventional white cotton, but the latter product then costs $2.40 a pound to dye.[69] Once woven into cloth, however, dyed cotton fades with each washing; but, washing Fox's natural fibers actually darkens and fixes the color. Eliminating the dyeing process also saves up to 85 percent of the energy used in conventional cotton textile production, while eradicating the need for heavy metals, volatile organic chemicals, and nonbiodegradable surfactants.[70] Fox's innovations, of course, undercut conventional monoculture cotton producers, but these cycles of production are heavily invested in big corporate networks of control. In addition, she has made possible the creation of entirely new product lines from comparatively cleaner green organic cottons.

The work of Seeds of Change, a small organic seed supply company that began in southwestern New Mexico by preserving a diverse array of food-stock crops, is another good case in point.[71] Big agricultural corporations have not been interested in preserving biodiverse stocks of seed with small strains of heirloom foodstock varieties, because it is unprofitable and inefficient for them. As a result, the American seed market by the 1990s had devolved to the point that only about 3 percent of the food variety available in 1900 was still available, and almost 100 percent of what was available was not grown organically.[72] Moreover, big companies mostly sell hybrids that do not reproduce well, and growers are forced to buy new seed every year. Home gardeners, small farmers, and local communities, then, are being prevented from farming local food varieties as freely as they could simply to sustain the profits of large firms. As Starr observes, "international agribusiness reduces formerly independent farmers to agricultural workers, or simply dominates the purchase of export crops, reducing farmers to serfs on their own land."[73]

To correct this situation, Kenny Ausubel organized Seeds of Change in 1989 to sell open-pollinated seed types, preserve local heirloom food varieties, and empower small growers to produce the plant types they wish to cultivate. Because fewer than ten major seed, chemical, and pharmaceutical companies control more than 70 percent of the world's seed trade,[74] this work is highly significant. Local communities need to eat, but big companies desire to make greater profit. In this contradiction, one finds firms pushing the world to consume only twenty or so plant types for 90 percent of human food needs, even though there are 80,000 known edible plants.[75] Little companies, like Seeds of Change, in many places around the nation aim to preserve individual freedom and local choice by protecting strains of seed.

Even something as prosaic as the flow of trash is claimed by professional-technical experts as a stock of exploitable material for incineration or land filling under their astute care. The possibilities that reducing, reusing, and recycling present to every household are purposely ignored or even aggressively prevented in many areas to keep private investments in dumps and incinerators profitable. Local activists, who either want to live more simply or hope to avoid having a landfill, dump, or incinerator nearby, constantly agitate against having to coexist with such facilities, but they rarely have workable alternative solutions.

Against this backdrop, local activists, like Daniel Knapp of Urban Ore, Inc., in Berkeley, California, David Gershon of Woodstock, New York, and Christopher Nagel and William Haney III in Fall River, Massachusetts, are working to provide options for individuals and communities.[76] Knapp works hard against "wasting" in favor of the reuse approach to discarded material, recycled building supplies, and dumped goods. Contractors save money by depositing useable recycled building supplies to his reuse center as well as by purchasing reusable lumber, fixtures, and bricks.[77] Gershon's not-for-profit operation provides four-month-long programs of behavior modifying routines to individuals, companies, and municipalities to cut their consumption of goods and services, which reduces the waste stream and saves money.[78] Nagel and Haney are entrepreneurial environmental engineers who have developed new molten metal technology (MMT) systems to extract saleable gases, metals, and ceramics catalytically from otherwise toxic industrial wastes.[79] None of these efforts entirely eliminate waste, so dumps, junkyards, incinerators, and landfills will continue to be needed. Nevertheless, these local initiatives are all pitched at resisting the subpolitical system of waste creation and management that angers and frustrates millions of people everyday all around the nation.

Recognizing how things should be otherwise, these popular local initiatives are attempts to demonstrate how and why they could be otherwise in very specific concrete ways. Many people recognize how severely inequality plagues contemporary economies and societies, but workable alternatives for overcoming these inequities are few and far between. Experiments such as these briefly discussed here attempt to address this scarcity by finding ways to build individual and community competencies. Rather than viewing environmental disasters as isolated incidents of untidy waste disposal or inefficient management of natural processes, these populist initiatives would make Nature an equal partner with people to avoid such tragedies as the unreasoning abuse of the environment. The living and inorganic constituents of Nature could be entitled to rights and privileges as worthy of defense as any human rights and social privileges.[80] Guarantees of ecological security should ramify, in turn, into greater freedom, dignity, and reasonability for the human beings whose own autonomy suffers in Nature's abusive indenturement to corporate enterprises' instrumental rationality.

Conclusion

Today's local popular resistances confront tremendous powers as they face the unfolding of globalization. Built environments, global webs of trade, and basic ecologies of human existence, as they now are being restructured by globalization, all favor the agendas and prerogatives of state bureaucracies or corporate enterprises. Experts in those institutions usually seek to reduce individual autonomy and communal freedom in a global competition to rerationalize national governments in neoliberal ways and entrench Fortune 500 companies more centrally in the civic life of nations. As states and firms shed their one-time responsibilities for ensuring social services in waves of restructuring, new movements of populist communitarian resistance are forming. With the tactics of "industrial democracy," big businesses decisively undercut both American Populism and European socialism with the managerial welfare state and economic growth.[81] Yet, those victories were won only to the degree that the social contracts of the welfare state delivered mass satisfaction in exchange for political passivity.[82]

The New World Order of the twenty-first century is an inviting subject for an astute ecological analysis. Transnational corporate capitalism, aided and abetted by the richer Organization for Economic Cooperation and Development (OECD) states, has entirely distorted both the urban-industrial and rural-agricultural ecologies underpinning ordinary everyday life.[83] Consequently, a few dozens of vast monoculture, monoproduct, monoservice networks now supply most of the matter, energy, and information needs for billions of people in most countries at virtually unsustainable and mostly ungeneralizable levels of output. Without the work of these networks, life itself as most people know it in its urban-industrial or suburban-consumer forms is impossible. As the Cold War has ended, the welfare state and consumer capitalism, which emerged hand in hand during the Second Industrial Revolution to oppose socialism, either are being reimagined by neoliberal codes for global performativity, which challenge old narrowly focused national benefits and markets or their being resisted by populist movements—from NIMBYistic site defense groups to right-wing militias to multicultural environmental justice fronts—as citizens begin opposing the performativity imperatives of globalization.[84]

Populists may be caught within the performativity of the global system, but they refuse to submit to their entrapment. Populist resistances arise out of an advanced marketplace, but they do not have to be for it. Populist resistances against performativity, as the examples briefly discussed here suggest, are about respecifying how the global market either brings together or keeps apart people and things, by finding alternative modernities to existing forms of modernity that serve more people, more fairly, more locally.[85] Even the most system-affirming corporate technologies contain self-subversive moments within their makeup. Populists are working to exhume and exploit those subversive potentials by revealing the unseen flexibilities, unknown possibilities, and untested alternatives when used locally that contemporary technologies contain for developing an ecologically sound and ethically fair economy.[86] Societies of bureaucratically controlled consumption, as a whole, can be undone. Yet, their revolutionary "undoing" will be attained only by destructively reconstituting pieces and parts of existing institutions, technologies, and values in a new antiperformative way of "doing"—reorganized on a smaller scale, less-hierarchical, far less-centralized basis in new forms of real community building in specific localities outside the reach of corporate global experts.

There is no definitive program for local democratic populists that articulates what to do. Populism does not provide a fail-safe recipe for the future or a surefire method for realizing a successful local commonwealth.[87] Rather this new populism only starts to outline tactics for the present by elaborating clearly what to undo in the subpolitical systems of expert decision making. Taking back into the community, populace, and government issues that have been consigned to technical experts or corporate managers is only a beginning.[88] The ordinary person's vision of the WTO, IMF, or WEF as a bloc of state and business executives working to serve very narrow bureaucratic and technical interests by rationalizing globalization makes these organizations a likely target for popular resistance. By taking the practices of democratic governance back from professional-technical experts, and integrating this resistance with an ecological and ethical critique of corporate capitalism, local, regional, and national movements are working to protect Nature best in testing alternatives to contemporary consumerist society.[89]

Notes

1. See Andrew Goudie, *The Human Impact on the Natural Environment*, 4th ed. (Cambridge, Mass.: MIT Press, 1994); and J. R. McNeill, *Something New under the Sun: An Environmental History of the Twentieth-Century World* (New York: Norton, 2000).

2. See Timothy W. Luke, *Screens of Power: Ideology, Domination, and Resistance in Informational Society* (Urbana: University of Illinois Press, 1989); and Michael Perelman, *Class Warfare in the Information Age* (New York: St. Martin's, 1998).

3. See William A. Shutkin, *The Land That Could Be: Environmentalism and Democracy in the Twenty-First Century* (Cambridge, Mass.: MIT Press, 2000); and Michael Sandel, *Democracy's Discontent: America in Search of a Public Philosophy* (Cambridge, Mass.: Harvard University Press, 1996).

4. See Linda Stout, *Bridging the Class Divide and Other Lessons for Grassroots Organizing* (Boston: Beacon, 1997); and Charles Derber, William Schwartz, and Yale Magrass, *Power in the Highest Degree: Professionals and the Rise of the New Mandarin Order* (New York: Oxford University Press, 1990).

5. David Harvey, *The Condition of Postmodernity* (Oxford, U.K.: Blackwell, 1989); and Ulrich Beck, *The Reinvention of Politics* (Cambridge, U.K.: Polity Press, 1997).

6. See Hans-Peter Martin and Harald Schumann, *The Global Trap: Globalization and the Assault on Democracy* (London: Zed Books, 1997).

7. Richard Falk, *Predatory Globalization: A Critique* (Cambridge, U.K.: Polity Press, 1999); and Susan Strange, *The Retreat of the State* (Cambridge, U.K.: Cambridge University Press, 1996).

8. See Ulrich Beck, *The Brave New World of Work* (Cambridge, U.K.: Polity Press, 2001); and David Korten, *When Corporations Rule the World* (West Hartford, Conn.: Kumarian Press, 1995).

9. See Kirkpatrick Sale, *Rebels against the Future: The Luddites and Their War on the Industrial Revolution* (Reading, Mass.: Addison Wesley, 1995); James C. Scott, *Domination and the Arts of Resistance: Hidden Transcripts* (New Haven, Conn.: Yale University Press, 1990); and Daniel Kemmis, *Community and the Politics of Place* (Norman: University of Oklahoma Press, 1990).

10. See Douglas Kellner and Steve Best, *The Postmodern Turn* (New York: Guilford, 1997); and Fredric Jameson, *Postmodernism, or the Cultural Logic of Late Capitalism* (Durham, N.C.: Duke University Press, 1992).

11. Jean-Francois Lyotard, *The Postmodern Condition: A Report on Knowledge* (Minneapolis: University of Minnesota Press, 1984), 39.

12. Ibid., 46.

13. Ibid.

14. Harold Perkin, *The Third Revolution: Professional Elites in the Modern World* (London: Routledge, 1996), 2.

15. See Scott Lash and John Urry, *Economics of Signs and Space* (London: Sage, 1994); and Alvin W. Gouldner, *The Future of Intellectuals and the Rise of the New Class* (New York: Seabury, 1979).

16. Christopher Lasch, *The Revolt of the Elites and the Betrayal of Democracy* (New York: Norton, 1995), 5.

17. Perkin, *Third Revolution*, 8.

18. Ibid., 1.

19. Ulrich Beck, *The Risk Society* (London: Sage, 1992), 19.

20. Perkin, *Third Revolution*, 1.

21. Lasch, *Revolt of the Elites*, 35.

22. For more articulation of these circumstances in an informationalizing global economy, see Robert B. Reich, *The Work of Nations: Preparing Ourselves for 21st-Century Capitalism* (New York: Knopf, 1991).

23. Reich, *Work of Nations*, 171–84.

24. See Timothy W. Luke, "Discourses of Disintegration, Texts of Transformation: Re-Reading Realism in the New World Order," *Alternatives* 18 (1993): 229–58.

25. See Zygmunt Bauman, *Legislators and Interpreters: On Modernity, Post-Modernity and Intellectuals* (Ithaca, N.Y.: Cornell University Press, 1987).

26. See, for example, Kevin P. Phillips, *Staying on Top: The Business Case for National Industrial Policy* (New York: Random House, 1984); James Fallows, *More Like Us: Making America Great Again* (Boston: Houghton Mifflin, 1989); or Robert Reich, *Work of Nations*.

27. Beck, *Risk Society*, 183–236.

28. Ibid., 184.

29. See Timothy W. Luke, *Capitalism, Democracy, and Ecology: Departing from Marx* (Urbana: University of Illinois Press, 1999), 2–24.

30. See Bruno Latour, *We Have Never Been Modern* (London: Harvester Wheatsleaf, 1993).

31. Beck, *Risk Society*, 223.

32. Ibid., 14.

33. Luke, *Capitalism, Democracy, and Ecology*, 58–82.

34. Beck, *Risk Society*, 186.

35. Ibid., 187.

36. Ibid., 222.

37. Ibid., 223.

38. Ibid., 230–36.

39. Luke, *Capitalism, Democracy, and Ecology*, 217–46.

40. See Andrew Szasz, *Ecopopulism: Toxic Waste and the Movement for Environmental Justice* (Minneapolis: University of Minnesota Press, 1997); Richard Hofrichter, *Toxic Struggles: The Theory and Practice of Environmental Justice* (Philadelphia: New Society Press, 1993); and Vandana Shiva, *The Violence of the Green Revolution: Third World Agriculture, Ecology, and Politics* (London: Zed Books, 1991).

41. See Amory Starr, *Naming the Enemy: Anti-Corporate Movements Confront Globalization* (London: Zed Books, 2000); James R. Beniger, *The Control Revolution: Technological and Economic Origins of the Information Society* (Cambridge, Mass.: Harvard University Press, 1986); James Burnham, *The Managerial Revolution* (Bloomington: Indiana University Press, 1960); David Noble, *America by Design: Science and Technology and the Rise of Corporate Capitalism* (New York: Knopf, 1977); and Robert Vance Presthus, *The Organizational Society* (New York: Knopf, 1962).

42. For additional consideration, see Cheryll Glotfelty and Harold Fromm, *The Ecocriticism Reader: Landmarks in Literary Ecology* (Athens: University of Georgia Press, 1996). Also see Robert Gottlieb, *Forcing the Spring: The Transformation of the American Environmental Movement* (Washington, D.C.: Island Press, 1993); and Kenneth M. Stokes, *Man and the Biosphere: Toward a Coevolutionary Political Economy* (Armonk, N.Y.: Sharpe, 1994).

43. See Carl Boggs, *Social Movements and Political Power: Emerging Forms of Radicalism in the West* (Philadelphia: Temple University Press, 1986); and Harry C. Boyte, *Community Is Possible: Repairing America's Roots* (New York: Harper, 1984).

44. See Mark Dowie, *Losing Ground: American Environmentalism at the Close of the Century* (Cambridge, Mass.: MIT Press, 1995), 207. For more discussion of such groups, see Robert D. Bullard, *Dumping in Dixie: Race, Class, and Environmental Quality* (Boulder, Colo.: Westview, 1990); Kirkpatrick Sale, *Dwellers in the Land: The Bioregional Vision* (Philadelphia: New Society Publishers, 1991); Roger Gottlieb, *Forcing the Spring: The Transformation of the American Environmental Movement* (Washington, D.C.: Island Press, 1993), or Bunyan Byrant, ed., *Environmental Justice: Issues, Policies, and Solutions* (Washington, D.C.: Island Press, 1995).

45. Cited in Starr, *Naming the Enemy*, 65.

46. See Slutkin, *The Land That Could Be*, 4–8.

47. See Steve Lerner, *Eco-Pioneers: Practical Visionaries Solving Today's Environmental Problems* (Cambridge, Mass.: MIT Press, 1997), 322–24.

48. These "globalization from below" tactics are discussed by Falk, *Predatory Globalization*, 127–36; and William K. Tabb, *The Amoral Elephant: Globalization and the Struggle for Social Justice in the Twenty-First Century* (New York: Monthly Review Press, 2001), 161–79.

49. Some good examples of efforts to reposition ecological concerns centrally in economics, politics, and society can be found in: Murray Bookchin, *Post-Scarcity Anarchism* (New York: Ramparts Books, 1971); Alexander Cockburn and James Ridgeway, eds., *Political Ecology* (New York: Quadrangle Books, 1979); Barry Commoner, *The Poverty of Power* (New York: Bantam, 1976); Richard C. Dorf and Yvonne L. Hunter, *Appropriate Visions: Technology, the Environment and the Individual* (San Francisco: Boyd and Fraser, 1978); Hazel Henderson, *Creating Alternative Futures: The End of Economics* (New York: Berkley Publishing, 1978); Amory Lovins, *Soft Energy Paths* (Cambridge, Mass.: Ballinger, 1977); and E. F. Schumacher, *Small Is Beautiful: Economics as if People Mattered* (New York: Harper and Row, 1973).

50. See *The Ecologist, Whose Common Future: Reclaiming the Commons* (Philadelphia: New Society, 1993).

51. J. Michael Kennedy, "A Healthy Crop," *Los Angeles Times*, April 19, 1996, E1–2.

52. Starr, *Naming the Enemy*, 124–27.

53. Ibid.

54. Ibid., 129.

55. Ibid., 130.

56. Ibid., 10.

57. Ibid., 131.

58. See Arjun Appadurai, *Modernity at Large* (Minneapolis: University of Minnesota Press, 1995).

59. Lerner, *Eco-pioneers*, 47–66.

60. Ibid., 81–90.

61. Ibid., 159–70.

62. Ibid., 232.

63. Ibid., 234–42.

64. Ibid., 287–93.

65. Ibid., 295.

66. Ibid., 267–97.

67. Ibid., 101–6.

68. Ibid., 103–4.

69. Ibid., 111.

70. Ibid., 110.

71. Ibid., 309–15.

72. Ibid., 310.

73. Starr, *Naming the Enemy*, 10.

74. Lerner, *Eco-pioneers*, 312.

75. Ibid., 314.

76. Ibid., 13–17.

77. Ibid., 115–28.

78. Ibid., 341–52.

79. Ibid., 143–58.

80. For additional discussion, see Timothy W. Luke, *Ecocritique: Contesting the Politics of Nature, Economy and Culture* (Minneapolis: University of Minnesota Press, 1997). Another approach

to the "constructedness" of Nature is in Klaus Eder, *The Social Construction of Nature: A Sociology of Ecological Enlightenment* (London: Sage, 1996).

81. For more discussion of "industrial democracy" and "suburban consumerism" as forms of life, see Stuart Ewen, *Captains of Consciousness: Advertising and the Roots of Consumer Culture* (New York: McGraw-Hill, 1976); Thomas Hine, *Populuxe* (New York: Knopf, 1986); and Stuart Ewen, *PR! A Social History of Spin* (New York: Basic, 1996).

82. See David A. Hounsell, *From the American System to Mass Production, 1800–1932* (Baltimore, Md.: Johns Hopkins University Press, 1984).

83. See Ben Agger, *Fast Capitalism* (Urbana: University of Illinois Press, 1989); Stanley Aronowitz, *The Crisis in Historical Materialism: Class, Politics and Culture in Marxist Theory* (New York: Praeger, 1981); and Trent Schroyer, *The Critique of Domination: The Origins and Development of Critical Theory* (Boston: Beacon, 1975).

84. See, for example, Jeremy Rifkin, *The End of Work* (New York: Viking, 1995); and Daniel A. Coleman, *Ecopolitics: Building a Green Society* (New Brunswick, N.J.: Rutgers University Press, 1994).

85. As Wendell Berry notes on page 63 in "Out of Your Car, Off Your Horse," *Atlantic Monthly* 267, no. 2 (February 1991): 60–63, some localities will never be sustainable. "New York City cannot be made sustainable, nor can Phoenix" but many others can be and should be. Also see Philip Shabecoff, *A New Name for Peace: International Environmentalism, Sustainable Development, and Democracy* (Hanover, N.H.: University Press of New England, 1996); David Morris, *Self-Reliant Cities: Energy and the Transformation of Urban America* (San Francisco: Sierra Club Books, 1982); and Richard Register, *Ecocity Berkeley: Building Cities for a Healthy Future* (Berkeley, Calif.: North Atlantic Books, 1987).

86. For more discussion, see Philip Shabecoff, *Earth Rising: American Environmentalism in the 21st Century* (Washington, D.C.: Island Press, 2000); and Paul and Percival Goodman, *Communitas: Means of Livelihood and Ways of Life* (New York: Random House, 1960).

87. Harry C. Boyte, *Community Is Possible*, 213.

88. See Paul Piccone, "Beyond Pseudo-Culture: Reconstituting Fundamental Political Concepts," *Telos* 95 (spring 1993): 3–14.

89. See David Dickson, *Alternative Technology and the Politics of Technical Change* (Glasgow, Scotland: Fontana, 1974); and Ivan Illich, *Energy and Equity* (New York: Harper and Row, 1974).

CHAPTER 16

Linking Movements and Constructing a New Vision

ENVIRONMENTAL JUSTICE AND COMMUNITY FOOD SECURITY

Robert Gottlieb

Establishing a Community Focus

During the 1980s and 1990s, environmental justice emerged as a powerful new voice within the environmental movement. While tracing lineage to a rich history of twentieth-century social movements that had linked the social and the ecological, the contemporary forms of environmental justice have been at once more focused and singular. Environmental justice groups have challenged the mainstream environmental movement's limits (perceived or otherwise) as a white middle-class movement dedicated to securing and maintaining various environmental amenities. They have done so by utilizing a language that is rooted in civil rights discourse, including the focus on risk discrimination. In the process, environmental justice has become an important influence in reconstructing the environmental argument to incorporate considerations of equity and justice, enabling the environmental movement to partially break out of its white middle-class confines.

Environmental justice's greatest strength has been its ability to become rooted in issues of everyday life. This community- or place-based focus suggests opportunities for expanding environmental agendas and linking the movement to an array of other social movements. To do so, however, community movements like environmental justice need to contend with broader social and economic forces contributing to community and environmental decline. These include issues of both production and consumption, many of which are increasingly framed by globalization influences. One compelling example of a critical global production system shaping consumption patterns and community outcomes involves food—how it is grown, manufactured, and reengineered, distributed, sold, and consumed.

In the past few years, a new type of community-based, yet global-focused politics has emerged, including in the area of community food politics. This chapter describes how environmental justice-oriented community food movements, challenging the structures and outcomes of a globalized food system, can help extend the environmental justice discourse and ultimately the language, agendas, and values of environmentalism itself. We will also see how these movements challenge and expand existing understandings and practices of democracy.

321

Seeds of Change

In the spring of 1992, a group of my students prepared to launch a year-long, environmental justice-related research project. The students were most interested in identifying how environmental issues connected to social and economic concerns in low-income neighborhoods and how an environmental justice approach effectively addressed community needs. The discussions at first seemed rather abstract. But then the riots or civil disorders of April 30–May 2, 1992, in Los Angeles erupted. These events reoriented the students' discussion and made the choice of topic and the outcome of any research process immediate and compelling.

The 1992 events made clear the importance and immediacy of assessing—and addressing—community needs. The background to the riots during the previous two decades had been the restructuring and eventual decline of the region's manufacturing industries that had been the source of higher paying jobs. Those industrial changes had in turn extended Los Angeles's social and economic gaps between communities and racial and ethnic groups. The concept of environmental discrimination or environmental racism had begun to be applied to the myriad of "negative land uses" and disproportionate risk burdens experienced by low-income communities or communities of color, adding the environmental gap to an already widening divide that had opened up between communities and regions. If the widening divides and risk burdens were becoming endemic, then the riots became both the occasion and the cautionary explanation of the powerful social, economic, and environmental insecurities that were unraveling the social fabric and further exacerbating the divisions between communities and neighborhoods within the region.[1]

Deeply affected by the riots and wanting to be more purposeful about their research, the students sought to select a set of core community issues, through a case study approach, that could identify both problem areas and opportunities for community action. For the case study, they selected a neighborhood in South Central Los Angeles that reflected the region's evolving demographics (more immigrants, increasingly Latino, especially Central American) and widening divide characteristics (lack of jobs, inadequate transportation, etc.). The students then undertook a needs assessment (an evaluation of core problems and community needs) in conjunction with community and church groups. They asked residents to identify their most urgent issues, and assumed, despite their own environmental orientation, that it would more likely be in the area of community economic development.

The needs assessment produced surprising results. Above and beyond the need for jobs or even housing or transportation, *food issues* were identified by many of the residents as their most immediate and widespread concern. This included problems of food access, food quality, and food price. At the same time, the residents and community groups surveyed revealed a strong interest in developing alternative approaches, such as a neighborhood farmers' market, a community or school garden, or a new community-oriented supermarket for the area. These were approaches that potentially encompassed a set of alternative strategies for how a neighborhood or a community could meet its food-related needs. And what the students were discovering about this significant interest in food issues also paralleled what other needs assessment surveys of low-income communities were indicating in Los Angeles and elsewhere.[2]

The report that was produced, "Seeds of Change: Strategies for Food Security for the Inner City," provided three key insights, similar to the concepts found in other studies addressing the link among food, environment, and justice. First, the way food issues are experienced at the community level, such as those identified by the South Central Los Angeles case study area residents, constitutes, in its broadest context, the overarching concept of *community food security*. Second, such issues need to be evaluated through a *food systems analysis* capable of identifying the structures and outcomes related to how food is grown, processed, and manufactured, distributed, marketed, and sold. Third, the issues associated with community food security and a food systems analysis in turn have *powerful environmental implications*.[3]

While community food security refers to the problems and possibilities for action at the regional, local, or neighborhood scale, food systems analysis identifies the environmental, economic, and macro- as well as micro-related issues and policies that have shaped the way those problems are experienced. Community food security as an action strategy and food systems analysis as a conceptual framework point to a more dynamic environmental approach, integrating issues around land use, sustainability, production, and community life. Indeed, each of these areas—community food security and food systems analysis and their implications for a broadened environmental agenda—can also be seen as potentially contributing to the development of a new kind of environmental discourse.

The concept of food security first emerged in the 1970s and early 1980s in the international development field. In the Third World setting, the ability to achieve food security was often used interchangeably with the need for hunger intervention in communities and nations experiencing high poverty rates. But *community* food security emerged as a different type of concept, both in the Third World context and increasingly during the late 1980s and early 1990s in the U.S. context as well. Community food security, for one, was primarily community rather than individually focused, the way most hunger intervention programs tend to be oriented. Community food security definitions (e.g., "all persons obtaining, at all times, a culturally acceptable, nutritionally adequate diet through local, non-emergency sources") have been careful to distinguish the goal (culturally acceptable, nutritionally adequate, local sources) as well as the form (nonemergency) of intervention. Community food security came to be seen as a strategy for community empowerment and social justice (with its focus on increased access, cultural specificity in food choice, and food self-reliance) and prevention (with its focus on dietary and nutritional considerations and sustainable food production). Community food security analysis has also sought to evaluate the nature of the resources available, both community and personal (the "basket of strategies" for sustainable livelihood that development analyst Robert Chambers identified in the Third World context), as well as how such resources can be made available. Community food security indicators can include income levels, transportation factors, availability of storage and cooking facilities, food prices, nutritional and dietary issues, and the cultural appropriateness of food choices. Community food security issues might also refer to food safety, environmental hazards, patterns of ownership, production and processing methods, food sources, and the nature of the food product itself.[4]

Achieving community food security, as a number of its advocates already began to argue by the early 1990s, could best be accomplished by building what sociologist Harriet Friedmann has termed *alternative food regimes*, or what has more popularly become known as community food systems. Food systems analysts have contrasted regional or local food growing and marketing arrangements, or "food regimes," with what has emerged as the dominant, long-distance, industrialized, highly concentrated, and globally reorganized system of food growing, processing, manufacturing, marketing, and selling. Food systems analysis has also explored the shift from the local to the global, where corporate restructuring has increasingly come to influence and alter the very definition of what is meant by food. And both community food security and a food systems analysis potentially provide, in environmental terms, a broader community-based focus for environmental justice.[5]

By the time the Seeds of Change group published its results in 1993, interest among U.S. groups in a community food security approach oriented toward building regional or community food systems had grown considerably. This was magnified by the realization that the indications of community food *insecurity* had increased almost exponentially during the 1980s and 1990s in the United States as well as in Third World regions and communities. The Seeds of Change study, for example, indicated that the case-study area, the majority of whose residents were recent immigrants from Central America and Mexico, was significantly food insecure. Twenty-seven percent of the residents surveyed through a random sample said they experienced hunger an average of five days every month—in effect, continually dropping in and out of hunger. A food price survey reinforced earlier findings that these residents paid more for food than their middle-class counterparts, even as they paid a much higher percentage of their available income for food.[6] The study also identified a lack of fresh and high quality food. It indicated that diet and nutrition and physical health issues were prominent (obesity among school-age children has in fact come to be defined as an "epidemic" according to a number of recent studies). Children are sometimes eating not enough calories and more often calories without sufficient nutrients or with excessive fat, salt, or sugar content.[7] The Seeds study pointed to food access problems (which had become even more severe with the steady abandonment of low-income communities by full-service food markets). This latter problem is especially exacerbated in those neighborhoods where average car ownership is substantially lower than region-wide averages.[8] This changing food system is also subject to a range of negative environmental impacts—from pesticide use and pollution and waste problems, to urban sprawl and loss of farmland.

As part of their evaluation, the Seeds of Change group traced the rise nationally of a new type of movement addressing community food security issues and the corporate restructuring of the food system. This food movement first exploded on the scene in the late 1960s and early 1970s as part of the search for alternative lifestyles and a more radical approach to the problems of agriculture and the rural economy. The food movement subsequently shifted its attention to questions of hunger and poverty and the continuing decline of the small family farm during the Reagan era. By the 1990s, the food movement began to focus more directly on issues at the regional and community level. Several of these regional groups talked about sustainable food systems and community approaches to meeting food needs, and had identified a new kind of community food security politics as central to their agenda for action.

During the mid-1990s, a number of these groups began to coalesce in an effort to establish a community food security agenda. These efforts at coalition building sought to identify a new type of politics among social justice, sustainable agriculture/small farm, and environmental constituencies. This included a focus on global food system–related issues, such as the rapid growth and even more rapid challenge to the introduction of genetically modified foods. The antiglobalization demonstrations at the WTO meetings in Seattle in December 1999 had, for example, particularly strong participation among the new food/environmental groups. And perhaps most significantly, a tentative alliance of the new food groups and inner city community groups such as the Los Angeles-based Community Coalition also began to take shape. Indeed, the type of issues identified in the Seeds of Change report—lack of food access, food quality concerns, and the interest in alternative, community food system type programs such as farmers' markets and urban agriculture—provided a baseline for building these new kinds of alliances. The possibility that a common ground could be located between community food security and environmental justice not only extended the agendas of those particular movements, but also identified potential new pathways for environmental and social change. And it could seek to describe and challenge the dominant food system, the better to know how to change the production and consumption patterns that so heavily influenced the quality of the environment and of daily life.

Broadening the Agenda:
The Case of the 1996 Farm Bill

In August 1994, thirty environmental, community development, sustainable agriculture and antihunger activists, and food system analysts met in a rather barren room in the Hilton Hotel in downtown Chicago. They had been invited by the organizers of the meeting to try to identify a common approach to food system issues and community food security action, using the venue of the upcoming Farm Bill legislation. The group identified three key objectives: to pass new community food security legislation as part of the Farm Bill, to stimulate new alternative food system and community food security programs, and to focus public attention and initiate a dialogue among movements about this new community food security approach.[9]

The Farm Bill seemed a useful focus for this new approach. For nearly fifty years the omnibus Farm Bill legislation, introduced approximately every five years, had been structured as a set of subsidy and price support programs for various commodity groups to address their continuing concerns about overproduction. Beginning with the 1981 legislation, three different sets of players—the emerging sustainable and organic agriculture groups, the small family farm advocates, and environmentalists focused on soil erosion and pollution concerns—came together to seek revisions and new directions for the legislation. Discussions focused on ways to reduce the intensity of production and link the cost of production to prices, as well as to identify conservation reserves that could take fragile land out of production. These ideas were subsequently introduced as part of a set of "alternative farm bill" amendments during the 1985 and 1990 Farm Bill legislative debates. There were also efforts to link the environmental and rural farm approaches (associated with the growing of food and rural economic development issues) to a fourth crucial "alternative food" player—antihunger groups. These groups were focused on protecting and possibly expanding the Farm Bill's food assistance provisions such as food stamps and the school lunch program.[10]

The alternative farm bill amendments introduced during the 1981, 1985, and 1990 legislative debates were associated with various coalition-related efforts to influence overall food policy and help consolidate the myriad of alternative or sustainable agriculture groups into a more coherent political force. The coalition initiatives had also provided a forum for mainstream environmental organizations like the Natural Resources Defense Council to raise such issues as nonpoint source pollution from pesticides and fertilizers and to link the problem of agriculture-related toxics with concerns about land and wildlife contamination. Since the sustainable agriculture groups also focused on pesticide use, an environmental/sustainable agriculture alliance seemed possible. A common position regarding rural environments, land use, and, at least for some, farm worker health and safety was also conceivable. And while the antihunger groups were not directly a part of this coalition-building process, the sustainable agriculture groups were now including issues of food access and availability for the rural and urban poor as an important dimension of their own advocacy.[11]

But during this process of Farm Bill–related coalition building, political tensions also emerged, including unresolved differences in emphasis between environmental groups and rural development advocates. During each of the Farm Bill debates, those differences were never fully resolved by the alternative farm bill initiatives, nor did a fully articulated environmental-rural coalition approach successfully emerge. Rural development advocates remained concerned about the economic squeeze on small farmers and the complex yet critical area of price supports. The concern about economic survival, in turn, was compounded by the continuing economic pressures on farmers to produce, which potentially undercut the environmental initiatives regarding soil conservation, crop rotation, and the land use focus on habitat and open space. The environmentalists, in turn, tended to avoid issues of economic security for farmers and generally ignored broader food system changes. Farmworker issues also tended to be avoided.[12]

Ultimately, each of these alternative food players had established a set of arguments and carved out an arena for legislative action that addressed only one set of discrete outcomes in relation to food system changes. It had also become clear by the 1994 Hilton Hotel meeting that a broader, more integrated rural-to-urban approach was needed that could address related social, economic, and environmental problems associated with food system outcomes.

Was such an approach possible, given the stresses in the coalition process and differing perspectives on agendas and constituencies? One of the research questions posed by the Seeds of Change report had been whether and how a rural-to-urban or regional food systems approach might emerge. The report had pointed to the development of groups around the country that promoted such an integrated approach, such as the Hartford Food System (HFS) in Connecticut. First established in the late 1970s through the initiative of a progressive city government, the HFS had initially focused on food access and the abandonment of the inner city by full-service supermarkets. One of the few urban food advocacy groups formed in the 1970s able to survive into the Reagan-Bush era, the group had evolved into an independent nonprofit organization, though it maintained an influential role among municipal and statewide policy makers. During the 1980s and 1990s, it had expanded its agenda to include a broader set of food issues, including those impacting farmers as well as urban residents. It promoted and helped stimulate farmers' markets, food cooperatives, community gardens, and new community-based enterprises. By the early 1990s, this more expansive approach of the Hartford group had come to be shared by a number of other food system–oriented groups in places like Austin, Texas, and Minneapolis–St. Paul. What most connected these groups was their desire to respond to the urgency of the myriad of urban food problems, particularly those faced by low-income communities. This urban-oriented food advocacy was primarily community oriented (and included the use of the term *community food security*). Several of the community food security groups also sought to address the increasing stresses of small and local farmers, as well as the goal of achieving a more sustainable food system.[13]

Joining their sustainable agriculture, environmental, and antihunger counterparts, the community food security groups had begun to emerge as the new players within the food advocacy arena. Partly in the hopes of cementing this role, the groups meeting in Chicago agreed that the Farm Bill offered an important opportunity to make more visible their concepts of community food security and local food systems change. Farm Bill–related campaigns, it was felt, could aid in eventually coalescing a wide range of groups and constituencies around such concepts. The challenge, nevertheless, was formidable. Just four months after the Chicago meeting, with efforts to draft a "Community Food Security Act" under way, the Newt Gingrich-led Republicans swept to power in the 1994 elections. The Republican ascendancy meant that each of the constituencies previously engaged in Farm Bill initiatives—mainstream environmentalists, small-farm advocates, and antihunger constituencies—were placed on the defensive. The Gingrichites were hostile to environmental measures such as soil conservation and crop rotation programs as well as pesticide-use reduction measures. They challenged key small-farm support programs, such as the various price support programs, and spoke instead of reducing government intervention and unleashing the market and creating a "freedom to farm," as the new Farm Bill came to be known. And the Gingrichites were also focused on reducing food assistance programs as part of a broader assault on "welfare" and "entitlements" that would culminate two years later in passage of the welfare reform legislation.[14]

For the community food security advocates, the triumph of the Gingrichites further underlined the importance of being able to establish a stronger, more integrated approach and a more inclusive advocacy language about food system changes. Not only would the conservative backlash need to be countered, but programs and approaches that provided an alternative to the antigovernment (and anti-poor people) pro-market rhetoric that was sweeping Washington also had to be identified. The language used to advance such programs—community empowerment, neighborhood and local action, strengthening farmer-to-consumer links—proved powerful. And the examples available to illustrate those approaches—farmers' markets, community gardens, greater food access, greater food choice, maintaining agriculture in the shadow of, if not within the city—resonated in terms of the most powerful arguments associated with environmentalism and among other social movements. These included the attachment to place, the search to create livable communities, and the desire for justice.

Passing new legislation—a legislative amendment or additional program to be added on to the Farm Bill—was further complicated by initial skepticism of the other coalition advocates. Some antihunger groups feared that the language of community empowerment and neighborhood action associated with community food security would be used against the traditional antihunger arguments that had relied on a food assistance and emergency relief framework. Mainstream environmental groups, while not opposing the initiative, remained aloof and never directly associated with the community food security campaign. The mainstream environmentalist position was focused on environmental impacts from the growing of the food, not what happened to the food itself (with the exception of pesticide residues on produce that had been sprayed, which had come to be seen as a winning, middle-class consumer-related issue). Sustainable agriculture groups were more sympathetic from the outset, and the concept of community food security, beginning with the 1995–96 Farm Bill debates, became increasingly embraced by these groups as an important urban link to their approach.

The markup of the Farm Bill ultimately included a small item—a Community Food Projects program with authorization and funding for the next seven years—that became the successful outcome of the process that had been launched at the Hilton Hotel in August 1994. A new organization—the Community Food Security Coalition (CFSC)—was formed in the process, and hundreds of new programs, organizations, and policies were established at the local level. Already by 1998, one Web site listing indicated more than fifty major conferences or workshops to be held in the course of just a single month by local, regional, or statewide community food security groups related to various community food security themes. There continued to be a proliferation of projects and programs, policy initiatives, and new kinds of democratic organizations and enterprises, primarily at the local and regional levels, but that could be directed at national and even global food agencies and issues. In 1999, in response to this outburst of activity, the USDA launched its own Community Food Security Initiative. In developing this program the department had borrowed liberally from some of the core policy recommendations put forth by community food security advocates during the 1995–96 Farm Bill campaign.[15]

Community food security had clearly emerged as a new type of political and social language, and a new kind of policy focus. It provided, in part, a new framework that potentially broadened the agenda of both the new food movements as well as the environmental justice groups seeking to respond to pressing community needs. And it helped establish new forms of participation and democratic activity where the issues of food or environment could be engaged at the community level, challenging the presumption that who determined what food we eat—or what air we breathe and water we drink—were solely the dictates of a global economy.

The New Framework: Environmental Justice/Community Food Security Links

As they have evolved, community food security and environmental justice movements have come to share a set of common assumptions, conceptual frameworks, and movement-building strategies. These include:

CREATING A MULTICLASS, MULTICOMMUNITY APPROACH, WITH A STRONG FOCUS ON THE NEEDS OF LOW-INCOME COMMUNITIES

Both community food security and environmental justice have focused on meeting the needs of low-income communities, which are the most food insecure and environmentally degraded. Such issues involve questions of *community resources*. Community food security goals tend to extend beyond a focus on food insecurity (defined as an individual not having enough to eat), and include such objectives as job training, business skill development, urban greening, farmland preservation, and community revitalization. Environmental justice groups have not only fought unwanted facilities and negative land uses, but have also raised issues of brownfields' redevelopment, open space and recreational opportunities, transportation needs, and a "healthy schools" program. Many of those "food" and "environmental" issues are also crossover issues in terms of building a multiclass, multicommunity approach.

BUILDING COMMUNITY

One of the great strengths of the community food security approach is that it offers a vision based on the development of viable alternatives to the dominant global food system. That system currently marginalizes urban consumers and low-income communities through poor access and a lack of affordable, nutritious food, and presents enormous barriers for small family farmers to have any control over access to markets for their products (which in turn marginalizes rural communities). Direct farmer-consumer relations, grow-your-own, and other community-based production and distribution arrangements create new kinds of economic spaces for farmers and consumers and urban and rural communities, while establishing new kinds of alternative models to a food system that has become increasingly transnational and corporatist in how it functions. Community food security projects have the potential to offer food system alternatives as a vehicle for community economic development, and can also help build community identities by encouraging neighborhood activities, such as co-ops, community gardens, and farmers' markets.

Similarly, by their nature as community-rooted groups, environmental justice organizations have the capacity to identify and promote community-building type initiatives. *Community identity* becomes significant as an *environmental identity;* the two tend to merge. Thus, environmental justice groups have begun to explore core community needs and themes, whether housing, transportation—or food. The concept of community building becomes essential to this approach, and helps expand a risk discrimination or equity framework into a broader and potentially alternative agenda of developing and strengthening community institutions.

EMPHASIZING EMPOWERMENT AND SELF-RELIANCE STRATEGIES

Community food security projects emphasize the need to strengthen the ability of individuals, as potential community actors, to more effectively provide for their own and for their community's food needs rather than to be fully dependent on outside sources, such as food banks or public assistance programs. While recognizing the importance of food assistance and charitable programs in a period of enormous, intractable food insecurity, community food security emphasizes community development and empowerment strategies for individuals as community participants. It also seeks more systemic, structural change in the food system and at the community scale to more effectively establish conditions of self-reliance. By emphasizing empowerment and self-reliance, community food security seeks to establish new forms of democratic organization and participation, whether cooperatives, new marketing arrangements, or the creation of new kinds of public spaces, like farmers' markets or community gardens.

While the starting point for environmental justice tends to focus on unwanted burdens and negative risks for both individuals and communities, nearly all environmental justice struggles have raised issues of participation and decision making. Environmental justice groups have also pointed to the importance of direct community participation and engagement in various land-use and development planning processes. Environmental justice struggles have perhaps been most successful as *empowerment strategies;* that is, extending the initial focus on what is not wanted to the community's right to decide what it does want. Environmental justice movements are noteworthy in their enabling new leadership to develop at the neighborhood or community level, including women and people of color who have often felt disempowered from participating in core community decisions. Similar to community food security, environmental justice can be considered a movement seeking to renew and extend democratic life. As my colleague Margaret FitzSimmons once commented, environmental justice tells us that you don't have to be an expert to be a citizen.

PLACE-BASED FOCUS

Both community food security and environmental justice tend to focus on specific geographic communities or places, including a crucial, though not exclusive focus on the needs of low-income communities. While both environmental justice and community food security activists struggle against negative land uses or system-related inequities, both are increasingly oriented toward new place-based relationships; that is, how to overcome the lack of positive land uses in a community (e.g., supermarket redlining resulting in poor food access or siting of facilities that increase the environmental burdens within an area). This geographic or place-based focus gives both sets of struggles cohesion and a sense of identity. Community building becomes both a process and a goal. It ensures greater participation in community life, critical to broadening the concept of democracy, so central to both movements.

COMMUNITY HEALTH AND PREVENTION-ORIENTED HEALTH

Both environmental justice and community food security are concerned about the health of communities and community members. Environmental justice advocates identify and struggle around issues of community health that are associated with multiple environmental burdens. Community food security activists focus on food and nutrition as community health concerns, including such problems as anemia, obesity, cancer, and hypertension, related to high rates of hunger and poor access to healthy foods. Moreover, both movements focus on a prevention approach, by developing strategies that provide alternatives and that seek to eliminate hazards and health-related burdens before they are created.

FOCUS ON CORPORATE DOMINANCE/SYSTEM-RELATED ISSUES

Both environmental justice and community food security activists act in opposition to, or at least challenge the role of corporate interests and their practices in the environmental and food system arenas. By shifting from justice and inequity concerns to a focus on the problems of community and economic development, both movements necessarily address and/or come in conflict with powerful system-related industrial forces. Both sets of movements also encounter issues associated with the flow of capital as well as the role of government (for example, investment decisions, control and uses of technology, land uses, and so forth).

SUSTAINABILITY AND LIVABLE COMMUNITIES

Both of these approaches identify a vision of sustainable institutions and livable communities. This vision is linked to a search for alternative practices and modes of development. With environmental justice, it may mean implementing pollution prevention practices that identify the design of new types of products and processes as well as institutional and community arrangements that address the root of an environmental problem or set of linked problems. For community food security, it may mean such practices as community supported agriculture (which attempts to create a nonmarket framework for economic activity), farmers' markets, co-ops, and/or gardens. These practices and programs, in turn, can form the nucleus of a sustainable food system, an alternative economic space in which small producers and distributors can thrive.

Conclusion: Creating New Agendas

The similarities between community food security and environmental justice suggest opportunities for creating new coalitions, broadening agendas, and enabling what are often characterized as different movements to learn from each other's experiences and analyses of system-based problems. For the community food security movement, environmental justice offers important lessons about the tactics of place-based organizing, the need to confront powerful urban and industrial forces in bringing about community changes, and the importance of political empowerment. For environmental justice advocates, community food security offers a strategy of system-based *transformation* that seeks to create healthier and more livable communities, which in turn can provide a natural extension of all environmental justice activity.

This type of linkage still requires a *politics* where different movements don't simply meet halfway from their separate spheres but have become joined through the construction of a common vision, based on the powerful claims of justice and democratic participation. It is this common vision that can also help liberate environmentalism from its confines as a bounded movement, where it has largely been defined. Such a bounded environmentalism refers to discrete, separate, issue-based or "interest-group" movements, as well as the separation of the social and the ecological. To extend the argument, part of the historical dilemma for environmentalism has been its lack, as Fred Buttel argues, of a "'natural' or enduring constituency that anchors its base of support." But that "absence of constituency" may also reveal a potential strength of environmentalism by its capacity to establish what Hilary Wainwright describes as a "totalizing vision." If "environmental issues are ubiquitous in [the sense] that there is scarcely a social relationship that does not involve some implication for resource use, pollution, ecosystem processes, or the biosphere," Buttel argues, then environmentalism needs to see itself as a social movement with a broad view and a broad agenda.[16] Similarly, when any environmental issue can be seen as socially determined, whether resource use, pollution, ecosystem processes, the biosphere . . . or the food we grow, process, sell, and eat, then environmentalism's great task will also be to see itself as a primary agent of social change.

When the social and the ecological are joined, and different movements begin to identify their common ground and construct a common vision, then movements for change have the capacity to become more powerful actors in the struggles to come. Linking environmental justice and community food security can help point the way.

Notes

1. Eulalio Castellanos et al., Research Group on the Los Angeles Economy, *The Widening Divide: Income Inequality and Poverty in Los Angeles* (Los Angeles: UCLA Graduate School of

Architecture and Urban Planning, 1989); Cynthia Pansing, Hali Rederer, and David Yale, "A Community at Risk: The Environmental Quality of Life in East Los Angeles," Los Angeles: Graduate School of Architecture and Urban Planning, 1989; see also, Edward W. Soja, Allan D. Heskin, and Marco Cenzatti, "Los Angeles: Through the Kaleidoscope of Urban Restructuring," Los Angeles: UCLA Graduate School of Architecture and Urban Planning, 1985.

2. See, for example, *RLA Grocery Store Market Potential Study* (Los Angeles: Rebuild LA, October 1995).

3. Linda Ashman et al., "Seeds of Change: Strategies for Food Security for the Inner City," UCLA Graduate School of Architecture and Urban Planning, 1993.

' 4. Robert Chambers, *Sustainable Livelihoods: Environment and Development; Putting Rural People First*, IDS Discussion Bulletin No. 240 (Brighton, U.K.: Institute for Development Studies, 1988); see also Amartya Sen, "The Political Economy of Hunger: On Reasoning and Participation." Paper presented at the conference "Overcoming Global Hunger," Washington, D.C., World Bank, December 1, 1993.

5. Friedmann, "After Midas's Feast: Alternative Food Regimes for the Future," in *Food for the Future: Conditions and Contradictions of Sustainability*, ed. Patricia Allen (New York: Wiley, 1993), 213–33. See also Harriet Friedmann, "The Political Economy of Food: A Global Crisis," *New Left Review* 197 (1997): 29–57. See also Robert Gottlieb and Andrew Fisher, "First Feed the Face: Environmental Justice and Community Food Security," *Antipode* 28, no. 2 (1996): 193–203.

6. Ashman et al., "Seeds of Change," 167–73, 161–65. See also Philip R. Kaufman et al., *Do the Poor Pay More for Food? Item Selection and Price Differences Affect Low-Income Household Food Costs*, USDA Agricultural Economic Report No. 759 (Washington, D.C.: USDA, November 1997); *The Poor Pay More: Food Shopping in Hartford* (Hartford Conn.: Citizen's Research Education Network, February 1984); Judith Bell and Bonnie M. Burlin, "In Urban Areas: Many of the Poor Still Pay More for Food," *Journal of Public Policy and Marketing* 12, no. 2 (fall 1993): 268–70; James M. McDonald and Paul E. Nelson Jr., "Do the Poor Still Pay More? Food Price Variations in Large Metropolitan Areas," *Journal of Urban Economics* 30 (1991): 344–59.

7. A. H. Mokdad, M. K. Serdula, W. H. Diets, B. A. Bowman, J. S. Marks, and J. P. Koplan, "The Spread of the Obesity Epidemic in the United States, 1991–1998," *JAMA* 282 (1999): 1519–22; Charlotte Neumann et al., *Prevalence of Hunger and Malnutrition among Los Angeles Elementary School Children*, UCLA School of Public Health, A Report for the Los Angeles Unified School District, 2000.

8. The concept of "transit dependent" has been defined as an area where car ownership is less than 80 percent of the population in a given census tract. See Robert Gottlieb and Andrew Fisher, "Food-Related Transportation Strategies in Low-Income and Transit-Dependent Communities," University of California Transportation Center, Working Paper No. 957, Berkeley, 1996.

9. Andy Fisher, "Community Food Security: A Food Systems Approach to the 1995 Farm Bill and Beyond: A Policy Options Paper." Paper presented to the working meeting on Community Food Security, Chicago, August 25, 1994.

10. Jeffrey A. Zinn and A. Berry Carr, "The 1985 Farm Act: Hitting a Moving Target," *Forum for Applied Research and Public Policy* (summer 1988): 17–18; Ken Cook, "Pinch Me. I Must Be Dreaming," *Journal of Soil and Water Conservation* (March/April 1986); Center for Resource Economics, *1990 Farm Bill: Environmental and Consumer Provisions, Volume II: Detailed Summary* (Washington, D.C.: Island Press, 1991).

11. Garth Youngberg, Neill Scaller, and Kathleen Merrigan, "The Sustainable Agriculture Policy Agenda in the United States: Politics and Prospects," in *Food for the Future: Conditions and Contradictions of Sustainability*, ed. Patricia Allen (New York: Wiley, 1993); David Ostendorf and Dixon Terry, "Toward a Democratic Community of Communities: Creating a New

Future with Agriculture and Rural America," in *Environmental Justice: Issues, Policies, and Solutions*, ed. Bunyan Bryant (Washington, D.C.: Island Press, 1995), 157–58; Barbara Meister, "Analysis of Policy Options for Promoting Sustainable Rural Development in the 1995 Farm Bill" (Master's thesis, JFK School of Government, Harvard University, 1994).

12. Valerie B. Straus, "The Farm Crisis of the 1980s and the Neopopulist Political Response," UCLA Graduate School of Architecture and Urban Planning, 1993; Andrew Fisher and Robert Gottlieb, "Community Food Security: Policies for a More Sustainable Food System in the Context of the 1995 Farm Bill and Beyond," Working Paper No. 11, Lewis Center for Regional Policy Studies, UCLA School of Public Policy, May 1995; Patricia Allen and Carolyn Sachs, "Sustainable Agriculture in the United States: Engagements, Silences, and Possibilities for Transformation," in Youngberg et al., *Food for the Future*.

13. On the Hartford Food System, see Dawn Biehler, Melissa Sepos, and Mark Winne, *The Hartford Food System: A Guide to Developing Community Food Programs* (Hartford, Conn.: Hartford Food System, 1999).

14. Author's notes, proceedings of the Community Food Security Coalition meeting, Philadelphia, February 9, 1996.

15. Community Food Security Coalition, *The Community Food Security Empowerment Act* (Los Angeles: Community Food Security Coalition, January 1995); Mark Winne, *Food Security Planning: Toward a Federal Policy* (Hartford, Conn.: Hartford Food System, 1994); A number of the policy recommendations in the Community Food Security Coalition proposed legislation were subsequently incorporated into the USDA Community Food Security Initiative Action Plan released in August 1999 in advance of the USDA Community Food Security Summit in October 1999. See also, *USDA's Community Food Security Initiative Roll Call of Commitments* (Washington, D.C.: USDA, October 1999).

16. Frederick H. Buttel, "Rethinking International Environmental Policy in the Late Twentieth Century," in *Environmental Justice: Issues, Policies, and Solutions*, ed. Bunyan Bryant (Washington, D.C.: Island Press, 1995), 191; Hilary Wainwright, *Arguments for a New Left: Answering the Free-Market Right* (Oxford, U.K.: Blackwell, 1994), 212.

CHAPTER 17

Civic Environmentalism

Charles T. Rubin

Some three decades of United States environmental policies built more or less on a "command and control," centralized model have produced a mixed record. Most of the indicators relevant to what these policies were intended to do show at least some improvement.[1] Air and water throughout most of the country are cleaner than they once were, there are fewer sites where toxic chemicals represent a risk, and there is more careful handling of toxins. But no one has declared victory. The improvement has been slower than many hoped, more expensive than others believe is justified. Meanwhile, the luxury of achieved gross improvements has allowed and perhaps even encouraged greater sensitivity to whole new classes of finer problems and risks. More and more refined, attention to threats to the well-being of nature has, not surprisingly, produced a new and frequently changing list of items that can arguably merit the attention of new government regulatory policies.

So much is generally understood. Many also appreciate how this situation has created a certain fluidity or flexibility in discussions of what is to be done next. Even leaving aside the wide divergences that exist among those who primarily attempt to *theorize* about the nature of environmental problems does not dramatically reduce the diversity of approaches that can be found. Should command and control give way to market mechanisms, or seek to incorporate marketlike mechanisms? Should national environmental policy making take a back seat to international efforts? Should regulators seek more cooperative relations with the regulated? Should the legal system be more open to common-law claims of environmental damage? Should there be a greater place for risk-benefit, risk balancing, and/or cost-benefit considerations in the regulatory process? Should rescue of the environment be the "central organizing principle for civilization?"[2] Should we aim at ecosystem management, or the restoration and sequestration of wildlands? Are some of these approaches more appropriate to some kinds of environmental problems than others?

Such a rich brew of competing problem definitions and policy options may represent a maturing of the environmental issue. There has been a great broadening of environmental concern since the main elements of the present regulatory regime were put into place. Then, a relative few were highly motivated, and these few had a relatively clear idea of the main dangers and appropriate governmental responses. We are all environmentalists now, but our large and diverse republic practically guarantees that we have different priorities, concerns, and solutions in mind.

Among all the various contenders for what should come next, something called "civic environmentalism" stands out for claiming to attempt to think through the changing political landscape for environmental protection and the practical consequences of the very diversity that makes it possible for it to get a serious hearing in the first place. While far from monolithic, a first defining characteristic of civic environmentalists is that they have come to understand that there are many different kinds of environmental problems in the world, and many different points of view on those problems. This complexity is only augmented by the fact that as important as environmental goods are understood to be, they are acknowledged not to be the only goods that are appropriately sought through public or private action.

In the second place, civic environmentalism claims to be a peculiarly appropriate approach to policy making because its insight into human and social diversity encourages it to take federalism and decentralized decision making seriously. Some of its proponents seem therefore to have made their peace with American liberal democratic institutions far more than an earlier generation of environmental authors, who were prone to grave doubts about the adequacy of that framework for saving the world. Others see decentralization as a challenge to a political realm that has not lived up to its democratic potential.

Finally, civic environmentalist authors claim to take the entire realm of politics and citizenship quite seriously, at least in terms of the way they understand those realms. Some seem stung by hoary charges of environmental elitism. Others are disenchanted with claims of the virtues of centralized technical expertise, or recognize that politics and society have their own delicate ecology that cannot simply give way to the claims of nature. For whatever reason, there is an anxious willingness to bring new and hitherto undervalued players into the environmental policy arena.

In what follows, these three themes will be examined as they are developed by some of the key thinkers behind the civic environmentalism movement: William Shutkin, DeWitt John, and Marc Landy. This examination will suggest that understanding the nature of and prospects for civic environmentalism means appreciating the manner in which it raises fundamental questions about both politics in the United States, and about the meaning of political activity more broadly.

Whatever their similarities, we will see that there is no lack of differences among those who write about civic environmentalism. Since William Shutkin has published the most extended treatment of a political theory of civic environmentalism, his work can serve as a benchmark against which to compare other versions.

Shutkin sees civic environmentalism as having the capacity not only to achieve goals of environmental improvement, but to make good on too-long deferred promises of American democracy. Three times he quotes Langston Hughes's lines:

> O, let America be America again
> The land that never has been yet
> And yet must be—the land where every man is free

Our failure to fulfill this promise thus far is deeply connected with the environmental degradation that we see all around us. When people are socially and economically unequal, too much focused on private property and the private realm, and politically disenfranchised, they cannot properly look after the places in which they live, leaving them prey to rapacious forces of wealth and political power, whether national or international in scope. Built on such faulty foundations, even previous attempts at environmental improvement can readily become misguided. They focus on national targets rather than those that affect most directly the lives of individuals in their particular places, protect parks and wildernesses that are far removed from the lives of most people, or encourage cynical bargaining between government and powerful businesses and industries about what the proper goals of environmental policies are in the first place.

Shutkin proposes a restructuring of the terms of environmental concern and American politics from the ground up. What is necessary is a "systems approach" to politics and nature, a "holistic approach" that appreciates how environmental "problems . . . and their solutions are . . . inextricably linked to social, political, and economic issues."[3] Such an approach is necessary due to the great truth that undergirds environmentalism: "the interconnectedness of all things and life systems . . . the inexorable faith in the wholeness of nature."[4]

It is clear to Shutkin that this interconnectedness of all things is strong indeed. "The civic elements in a community—the education system, the rates of poverty and unemployment, the level of political participation—and the physical environment are thus reciprocating conditions."[5] "Indicators of civic health in a community" like "strength of social networks and association, rates of employment and poverty, the degree of participation in political and civic affairs, and the income gap between professionals and managers and wage earners . . . can serve as a useful proxy for more traditional environmental indicators such as the Toxic Release Inventory, the number of ozone alert days in a year, or the level of pollutants in fish tissues. They are a touchstone by which environmental progress can be measured."[6]

So the shape of political life takes on great importance for Shutkin. He draws his theory of "civic democracy" from a variety of sources, including Benjamin Barber's notion of "strong democracy."[7] He seeks the "real democracy" of "self-governing communities" (not individuals)[8] in which "the ruled and the rulers are one."[9] He endorses John Dewey's view that "democracy is not an alternative to other principles of associated life. It is the idea of community life itself. . . . It is a name for a life of free and enriching communion."[10]

These broad goals turn out in practice to mean that Shutkin favors highly participatory planning processes at the local and regional level. The problem with traditional national command and control regulations is that they are "'premised on the fiction of an omniscient center' capable of dealing with all environmental problems in a centralized and uniform manner."[11] National standards are not good at dealing with the very sorts of pollution and land-use problems that have the most impact at the local level; indeed, they can preempt appropriate local efforts. That result should not be surprising given the extent to which American democracy is undemocratic in its results and perhaps even in its basic assumptions. "The special interest groups that dominate environmental decision making tend to be associated with wealthy corporations, whose profits derive from continuous, if not rapacious, economic growth, which is a function of development, production and consumption, the same factors that lead to environmental harm."[12] The fact that there is therefore little or no "meaningful participation by ordinary Americans"[13] in the political system reflects and exacerbates an inherent and deeply problematic tendency to look first to private affairs, which in turn is linked to the troublesome stress on private property to be found in our Lockean regime.[14]

In the end, too many environmentalists fall prey to this situation; "[w]ith its emphasis on legal and technical solutions, mainstream-professional environmentalism has failed to encourage active political and civic participation."[15] The net result of all these defects is a civic culture in decline, which, as noted, allows for environmental degradation. The problem is serious everywhere, but particularly severe in poor, minority, urban neighborhoods. Hence, what has come to be called environmental justice is of particular concern to civic environmentalism.

The participation of a broad array of "stakeholders" in a planning process has the obvious initial advantage of circumventing existing but almost certainly unrepresentative political authorities, or of making them simply one among a number of those who come to the table. Stakeholders develop ideas about what they want their communities to look like. Those ideas are turned into comprehensive planning documents, generally with the assistance of professional planners who presumably can bring the necessary systems orientation to the task—the second major advantage planning has over politics as usual. Finally, there is need for some sort of enforcement mechanism for these plans; Shutkin presents a variety of such mechanisms, private, quasi public, and governmental.

Shutkin devotes four chapters to case studies of his brand of civic environmentalism: Boston (a project to develop urban agriculture in the economically distressed Dudley neighborhood), Oakland, California (a transit village in the Latino Fruitvale district), Colorado (rural land conservation in Routt county), and New Jersey (land-use planning in Randolph township and Morris county). All are emphatically works in progress, so Shutkin's use of these examples suggests just how important in and of itself the development of a comprehensive and authoritative plan is, independent of any "final" results. For not only is the historic American mistrust of urban planning a major source of present ills ("development patterns have tended to defy coherence or planning"[16]), planning itself is a road not taken for contemporary environmentalism. "The ideas of visionary planners, from Frederick Law Olmsted, Lewis Mumford, and Jane Jacobs, to Benton MacKaye, Ian MacHarg [sic] and Robert Yaro, have remained outside the sphere of mainstream-professional environmental advocacy, resulting in a largely after-the-fact approach to environmental problem-solving."[17] That plans have come to exist at all, particularly plans that aim at what are in Shutkin's eyes the proper substantive goals, and that those plans appear to have some kind of enforcement mechanism or at least broad local legitimacy, goes a long way to allowing Shutkin to suggest the success of civic environmentalism.

There are, however, some problems with Shutkin's picture of civic environmentalism. To start with, there is some reason to wonder how he makes the transition he does from "strong democracy" to planning, which is often and understandably taken to be anything but democratic. Shutkin has an initially easy answer to this question. His conception of planning is not predicated on centralized expertise; as we have seen, plans arise out of public or private efforts at the grass roots. But how do these stakeholder visioning processes reach their conclusions? Shutkin himself notes that in Colorado, "[g]iven all the brainstorming and dialogue that gave rise to these plans, many county residents joked that people were 'blinded by vision' and enervated by the seemingly endless visioning sessions."[18] It would hardly be a surprise if under these circumstances only those most committed to the process prevailed, and indeed Shutkin seems to celebrate the way the ranchers, who saw themselves as having the most to lose by further recreational development, largely got the protection they sought for their operations. However sympathetic one might be with this result, it is not entirely clear that it represents a departure from the domination of decision making by those with the greatest economic interests that Shutkin otherwise laments.

Or again, one might wonder about the role that professional planners continue to play in the processes that Shutkin describes. These planners have learned to eschew the overtly antipolitical language of their forebears such as the notorious statements by Le Corbusier: "plans are not politics" and "the plan must rule."[19] But the stakeholder model of decision making, in seeking to bring together as diverse a selection of interested parties as possible, is a model that readily opens the door to decision making by supposed facilitators. One of Shutkin's favorite authors, James Howard Kunstler, documents apparently with no irony the way in which planners enter communities, tell participants what is wrong in those communities, and ask them how they would like their communities to be. Lo and behold, people want what they've been told they can have instead of the conditions they have been told they should abhor.[20] And then, of course, further determination of outcomes is possible because it is up to the planner-facilitators to translate the inchoate suggestions of the many participants into concrete architectural plans, zoning codes, vision statements, and so forth.

The point here is not to encourage cynicism or paranoia about visioning processes and planners, but to suggest that the tension between democratic politics and planning may be harder to overcome than Shutkin admits. Stakeholder visioning presents itself as something that can circumvent politics as usual and thereby be more inclusive, but that claim may be overstated. It may simply shift the arena of decision making and thereby redefine relevant inequalities of knowledge, power, wealth, and so on. Shutkin might be prepared to accept that shift if it favors those who have hitherto been non- or minimal participants in decision making, as he suggests is happening in Fruitvale and Dudley, but it is hard to see how that is the situation in the New Jersey and Colorado cases. He acknowledges that in these cases the actual stakeholders, all of whom seem to be more at the privileged end of the spectrum, have to make special efforts, generally in the form of guarantees of "affordable housing," on behalf of those who are still not at the table.

If in practice stakeholder visioning is not quite so fine an example of democratic politics as Shutkin would like it to be, we might chalk that up to the imperfection of any decision-making arrangements, were it not for the fact that it does not seem so much more democratic in principle either. The question of who decides who is a stakeholder is not a small one; a facilitating organization is clearly free to choose stakeholders in a way that will produce a desired result. Yet even if we assume a very open process where stakeholders are entirely self-defined, are they not likely to be people who by their interest in and willingness to participate in such a potentially arduous process are not entirely representative? The very idea of a stakeholder, taken literally, does not seem that far removed from "special interest." There are times when justice is said to demand that decisions be made by people who do not have a stake in the outcome. Furthermore, we can readily see how the term "citizen" can be conceptualized in terms of an abstract equality, which then might tend to percolate into concrete arrangements related to suffrage, law, and opportunities to govern. But to speak of stakeholders already seems to require that we acknowledge that some people have more "at stake" in a given outcome than others. Of course, part of an open visioning process might be to define just what the relevant "stakes" are; we might even expect disputes on that topic, for example, how to weigh the stake families have in playable open space versus the stake an owner has in developing the land in question. Such disagreements over substantive vision of how the world ought to be are the stuff of all politics, including the politics-as-usual that Shutkin so distrusts. If stakeholder vision processes cannot escape them, then we need to know more about their superior ability to deal with such disputes over the formal system of electoral politics. For Shutkin, the grounds of preference seem to be the fact that they include a different selection of people in the process, and that they produce particular results that he supports.

Shutkin articulates a high-toned civic ideal, where high degrees of participation are intended to produce high degrees of unity. Because he looks to self-governing *communities* rather than *individuals*, however, he can be satisfied with recommending a process that has every potential for allowing small and potentially unrepresentative groups of people to make authoritative decisions on behalf of the entire community. In one sense, this result may be democratic, for it comes rather close to the actual operations of small democracies even if it does not fully accord with democratic rhetoric. The outcome is the less problematic the more the community in question is homogeneous, but how often are even relatively small communities this uniform in today's United States? Whether the kind of widespread environmental education that Shutkin stresses would be enough to conduce to the necessary unity is likewise an open question.

Shutkin could surely turn this criticism around; politics-as-usual in our liberal democracy can be dominated by small groups of unrepresentative citizens, and not even have the advantage of producing substantive results that meet his criteria for a healthy environment and community. But there is an important difference between the two situations that illustrates a problematic aspect of Shutkin's enterprise. Because liberal institutional arrangements start from self-governing individuals rather than communities, their politics is not predicated on such high expectations for unity. The goal is less likely to be a plan-based solution to certain determinate problems that are assumed to be clear to all. To the extent that they do not have "communion" as their assumption or goal, liberal arrangements have more room for politics even than Shutkin's (unintendedly?) political planning process, for they rest content with higher degrees of contingency with respect to the outcome of a decision-making process.

To put the point another way, the more Shutkin stresses genuine give-and-take among competing visions, the less the process he describes seems likely to be different from politics-as-usual, except for its ability to do an end run around existing institutions and authorities that have not been responsive to what Shutkin believes they should be doing. The advantage of the process, then, is that the right people win. That is a long way from his stress on community self-governance, communion, planning, and a systems approach. But the more those attributes are brought to the fore, the less he seems to be talking about a process that conforms to the realities of genuine political life, which would not even have to exist if there were the unity of understanding and purpose that he supposes.

So it seems only too likely that Shutkin's picture of civic environmentalism ultimately depends more on its achievement of a substantive vision than it does on the local empowerment that is the formal basis for his definition. In the New Jersey case, for example, genuinely local decision making readily gives way to the necessities of regionalism and regional planning because of course everything is supposed to be strongly interconnected. But then it is the state that, it seems properly in Shutkin's view, mandates the land-use planning process at the local and regional level. But surely there is no ecological justification for such planning to stop at the borders of New Jersey either, and stakeholding likewise crosses conventional political boundaries. At this point, we have to wonder what becomes of the smallness of strong democracy, and how the life of free and enriching communion is to be sustained on a large scale.

By setting such a high standard both socially and ecologically, then, Shutkin's picture of civic environmentalism raises important questions about its basic goals and assumptions. The tensions we have noted within his account point to the possibility that he has not yet come to grips with the specifically political elements necessary to any effort to decentralize decision making and give people more of a stake in making their own communities better. His vision of planning and democracy under the rule of ecological necessities is, it seems, deliberately apolitical or even antipolitical (e.g., the transformation of democracy into a free and enriching community). He simply assumes the self-evidence of environmental problems, mistrusts existing political institutions in the United States, and in the "land that could be" supplies a substantive vision to replace the ongoing debate over the shape of public (and to some extent even private) life that is necessarily the stuff of politics.

DeWitt John provides a picture of civic environmentalism that is more at home with some of the basic facts of American political life and as a result is far more modest in its expectations than Shutkin's. The subtitle of his book, *Civic Environmentalism: Alternatives to Regulation in States and Communities*, already begins to tell the story. John sees civic environmentalism as a more decentralized mode of environmental decision making, but he does not have the extremely high expectations for local empowerment that Shutkin presents. The focus of his case studies (of Colorado's efforts to encourage energy conservation, attempts in Iowa to reduce agricultural chemical use, and developing plans for the restoration of the Florida Everglades) is, for the most part, on state- and national-level legislatures, bureaucracies, and organizations. Civic environmentalism from his point of view is not an alternative to existing governmental structures, but a new kind of behavior or a new set of expectations *within* these structures. "Civic environmentalism is not a replacement for traditional regulatory policies; it is rather a complement to those policies."[21]

These new behaviors and expectations are possible, or even necessary, for two kinds of reasons. On the one hand, "[c]ivic environmentalism is possible because the struggle to put regulatory laws in place has been at least partially successful. Polluters know that if they do not somehow reduce emissions, there may be political pressure for regulation."[22] Furthermore, this same national regulatory system has contributed to a change in attitudes in the broad public and also in business and government agencies. Tellingly, John speaks of the way in which corporations and government agencies "have hired large staffs of professionals whose careers are built on identifying and reducing environmental problems. As we shall see, these *insiders* play an important role in making civic environmentalism work."[23] Note then that some of those about whom Shutkin has serious reservations, the professional environmental insiders, are a crucial support for John's civic environmentalism.

On the other hand, civic environmentalism is necessary because it is a means by which to address various kinds of environmental problems with which the old command and control regulations did not by and large concern themselves. There is a good deal of "unfinished business" for which civic environmentalism is a more appropriate approach than national command and control regulation: restoring and protecting ecosystems, combating nonpoint pollution, and pollution prevention.[24] In other words, a large part of what makes civic environmentalism what it is for John is not merely *how* a problem is addressed, but what *kind* of problem is being addressed.

Thinking about the requirements for dealing with these different kinds of problems, John suggests, leads to seeing how different tools are necessary to address them, "such as technical assistance to farmers and small businesses, subsidies, public education, and new approaches to investing in public services and facilities."[25] And while command and control regulation has tended to produce a confrontational political style, civic environmentalism aims at "fewer confrontations between black hat polluters and white hat protectors of the public trust, and there is more bargaining among a diverse set of participants. Civic environmentalism is a more collaborative, integrative approach to environmental policy than traditional regulation."[26]

John's rich and detailed case studies show how these various elements can all come together, but at the same time it should be acknowledged that their very richness and detail can also obscure just how civic environmentalism works in practice. Although he selects the cases for the kinds of environmental problems they represent, John does not otherwise edit his stories in such a way as to bias them toward elements he is most interested in seeing. While there are certainly moments of black hat/white hat conflict in the Everglades case, for example, there is also extended negotiation among the parties to restoration efforts. New methods of utility regulation in Colorado, designed to enhance energy conservation, are shown to bring some new players to the table, and the case of agricultural chemicals in Iowa shows how a state can take the lead in developing new methods of pollution prevention. While in none of these cases can it be said that grassroots players take center stage for long, the decision-making methods illustrated are perhaps more open than usual to citizen intervention, even if (as he promised) the professionals, whether in politics, law, government, or business, play the largest parts. For example, "the political forces behind Iowa's initiatives has been a relatively small group of insiders, including employees of state agencies and the land grant university, some federal officials, and a few key legislators. These people are linked by ties of friendship and long-term collaboration and by a common commitment to environmental values."[27]

The case studies, then, show a serious appreciation for real-world politics in a variety of ways. They are very attuned to basic issues of who does what to whom, and the importance of particular personalities in the way conflicts are developed or resolved.[28] They illustrate the importance of institutional structures and roles in setting the terms for how problems develop or are settled. John understands that there are many reasons why participants in a decision-making process can come into conflict or make agreements, reasons not always directly related to the matter at hand.

Precisely because John is not as committed to a community based, grassroots civic environmentalism as Shutkin is, the federal role in making civic environmentalism what it is is a theme that he returns to repeatedly. In all the cases he presents, the federal role is restrained, and that obviously opens the door for something different from traditional command and control regulation. Yet his account of the relationship between center and periphery is certainly nuanced, and perhaps confusing.

We have already seen how he places civic environmentalism as a complement to, rather than a substitute for, national regulation, and also seeks to mark its distinctive contribution to a certain problem set as much as to nonregulatory methods. These methods themselves, summarized in a schematic flowchart as the "carrots" of information, funding, education, services, and subsidies rather than the "sticks" of regulation, do not have to be decentralized. The hierarchy suggested by this chart, which places environmental groups and federal policy entrepreneurs over the EPA, EPA over states, states over polluters, might indeed serve just as well to illustrate centralized command and control at the highest level of generality were it not for the fact that the chart includes both carrot and stick, and highlights the carrot lines by making them much wider than the stick lines.[29]

Yet John also claims at the beginning of the book that "civic environmentalism is inherently a bottom-up way of doing the public's business because it uses a different set of tools than classic regulation. Certainly the federal government can play an important supporting role, but most decisions, and most often the leadership, must come from the state and local levels."[30]

The apparent tension between these two pictures of civic environmentalism is somewhat resolved by John's observation that as an empirical matter "states that have the toughest regulatory climates also have the most nonregulatory and hybrid initiatives."[31] His case studies confirm that civic environmentalism depends on there being what he sometimes calls, following William Ruckelshaus, "a gorilla in the closet"[32] in the form of potential federal action, even if the gorilla is doing its best to appear as "a partner who can bring specialized resources into decisions made at the state and local levels."[33] Toward the end of the book he suggests that "[r]ather than simply saying that civic environmentalism is bottom-up, and thus implying that states and localities go it alone, we might say that civic environmentalism is a new kind of alliance between the national level and the state or local level."[34]

But the nature of that alliance remains ambiguous. While John says that there "must" be local leadership, his case studies do little more than show there *has* been local leadership. It is not clear that the issues themselves could only be dealt with at the state or local level, and the very fact that there *is* a gorilla in the closet suggests that the federal government could at any time step in to determine outcomes. He often cites local diversity as a barrier to drafting solutions in Washington, but admits that at any time the federal government could step in with groundwater regulations of the sort Iowa was trying to develop, particularly if larger-scale efforts are not forthcoming,[35] and that it did act in important ways in the Everglades case.[36] In fact, on the basis of his case studies John concludes that civic environmentalism depends on three kinds of top down support: the stick, cash, and expertise.

In general, John's analysis of his own case studies has a curious feature. He wants to show how they exhibit five characteristics that are distinctive to civic environmentalism: focus on unfinished business, use of nonregulatory tools, interagency and intergovernmental cooperation, attempts to find alternatives to confrontation, and federal government as coparticipant in decision making. That he finds all these characteristics more or less in his cases is not so surprising, given that he selected the cases. He has really shown that environmental issues exist that have the features he regards as central to civic environmentalism, and that policies can indeed be made when these features are present. That is something that people who think that all environmental policy must be made in Washington surely need to know.

But are there not other questions that should be asked at that point? Are the decisions made with these features better or worse decisions, by some specified measures or qualities? Are they reached faster or slower? Do they have more or less legitimacy, stronger or weaker technical merits? If there is more cooperation and less confrontation, is that because of other features of civic environmentalism, or is it just something that happens to be so in these cases, and that one might aim at in others? These are issues about which John has little to say. In contrast to Shutkin, at first glance, the features of the process seem more important to him than outcomes. His explanation of how civic environmentalism is possible is far stronger than his explanation of why it should be emulated.

This apparent avoiding of substance brings civic environmentalism back down to earth, but perhaps too abruptly. It is hard to find in John's argument much principled concern with federalism or with local empowerment on Shutkin's model. Indeed, he is sympathetic to one of his interview subjects, who notes that "[p]eople don't care about federalism; they just want to win, and they use whatever tools they have at hand."[37] On this basis, John early exhibits a certain pragmatic outlook; a "central theme of this book" is that "some tools are handier at the state and local levels than in Washington, D.C."[38]

John presents a case that states have a comparative advantage in using nonregulatory tools, because they are smaller and less diverse than the nation as a whole. (He is quick to add that this "does not make state governments better or worse than the federal government, just different."[39]) States can more easily customize initiatives, they can engage citizens more readily. State bureaucrats might find it easier to work with each other across agencies because they are more likely to know each other; the same can be said of citizen involvement.[40]

Yet none of these attributes means that states will necessarily act more effectively than the federal government. Questions of capacity still remain; while states may be far more professionalized and have greater expertise on hand than in the past, they still are unlikely to match the resources of the federal government. But then neither are they as likely as the federal government to be plagued by the inefficiencies of massive bureaucracies.[41]

John suggests that in theory one could reasonably expect that most of the same arguments about the strength of state governments in comparison with the federal government could be applied to local governments with respect to state governments. In practice, things do not work out quite so neatly. The size of local governments varies much more widely than state governments; "[o]ver three-quarters of local governments are actually zero-employee governments."[42] Similarly, local governments vary widely with respect to authority and "may not have enough diversity of expertise and opinion to organize a process that is truly open."[43] Or as he puts it later, "[s]mall town politics can be nasty."[44]

At every level, then, John ends up with a basically pragmatic justification for and description of civic environmentalism. The basic line of defense is that a new class of environmental problems that can (not must) be treated in a decentralized way can (not must) take advantage of some degree of decentralization in the political process. It works when it works.

But who judges when it works? To the extent that civic environmentalism is about keeping the gorilla in the closet, the success of local efforts will be judged, actually or potentially, by those beyond the local level, as we saw in his analysis of the future of Iowa's efforts. Because he is not terribly concerned with federalism or local empowerment, he does not consider the possibility that civic environmental success could be defined by a failure to decide definitively an issue causing significant local division, or even to decide that issue in such a way that does not conform to what some wider view of environmental quality might suggest is the correct decision. So despite his overt emphasis on process, John more subtly than Shutkin comes to associate civic environmentalism with certain substantive outcomes that lead to an underestimation of the significance of political processes that John describes so well.

For an account of civic environmentalism that is most sensitive to the nature of both nature and politics, we turn to the work of Marc Landy, writing on his own and with others. There is much agreement between Landy and John on the context in which civic environmentalism needs to operate, but there are some important differences with respect to goals. Like Shutkin, Landy looks to serious empowerment of local citizenries. Yet because he is more apt to consider people as citizens rather than stakeholders, his sense of how that empowerment will work is less bound to particular expectations about desirable outcomes. Like John, Landy stresses that civic environmentalism departs from the centralized, command and control model yet it "rejects national divestiture in environmental matters."[45] What is aimed at is a greater degree of cooperation among the levels of government. But that goal requires us to recognize that the "marriage between the levels of government will never be a love match."[46] There will always be causes of mistrust and different perceptions. The possibility for "a stable and productive union" in spite of these differences rests, it would appear, on the fact that ultimately all governments are working with the same material—people who live in specific places. That is why "the essence of civic environmentalism is public participation."[47]

The same conclusion is reached by way of another point of agreement with John. Civic environmentalism is about a new class of environmental problems for which the command and control model is inappropriate, and flexibility and collaboration necessary, for example, "point sources of water pollution, habitat protection, and the redevelopment of toxic waste sites."[48]

Civic environmentalism is appropriate to such problems not only because they are "complex and often diffuse" with respect to their natural components. In fact, the argument is rooted in two key points. First, the "common thread of these problems is the important role of land-use decisions and the interplay of public objectives with private property rights." In the second place, "'non-point sources' is just a euphemism for 'us.' It is the sum total of the wide variety of often small-scale activities that cause pollutants to run off the land and into the water."[49]

These two characteristics of second generation problems point in the same direction: the necessity for citizens to think of themselves as "pollution fighters" not in some abstract sense of saving the world, but in terms of what is going on in their own backyards, literally and figuratively.[50] If people are "to become active and creative partners in environmental improvement" there needs to be both public participation and a corresponding sense of obligation.[51]

Landy and his coauthors recognize that with respect to sites for participation, "the geography of environmental problems rarely meshes with existing political boundaries."[52] But it does not follow from that fact that all such problems must be nationalized; neither does it appear to be the case that some radical reworking or avoidance of existing political institutions is required. Rather, we should look for "individualized institutional designs enlisting the various affected jurisdictions in a manner that enables each to make the most useful contribution."[53]

Similarly, the strong component of self-interest that will inevitably be part of any focus on one's own backyard is not something to be lamented, but rather properly focused and contextualized. When it comes to private property owners, the "key is to enable them to act responsibly in ways that do not threaten their sense of entitlement. Their civic spirit is free to flourish when their private interests are made more secure."[54]

Clearly, from Shutkin's point of view arguments such as these have a serious flaw: they ignore the corrosive effects of private property on environmental policy decisions, and (given the close relationship he attempts to establish between civic well-being and environmental quality) they might well seem to overestimate the civic capital that is available in order to deal with environmental problems.

Landy and his coauthors have a variety of answers to this objection. The first is to be found in the case studies of The Chesapeake Bay Program, the CALFED-Bay-Delta Program in California (both remediation projects), the Sandhills Safe Harbor program in North Carolina and Coles Levee in California (habitat conservation), and the Gilbert-Mosley brownfield site in Wichita. Although like all civic environmental case studies we have seen (and indeed most case studies generally?) these instances are works in progress, they suggest that multilayered but place-based efforts that engage a wide variety of citizens on the basis of both private and public interests are indeed possible and (within the limits of the time covered) successful at moving toward their goals—

although the conditions that allow them to succeed vary widely, which is part of the point.

In the second place, while it is clear that Landy too has concerns about a civic culture in decline, his account of the causes differs somewhat from Shutkin's. While he does not "deny the wisdom of much of the centralization of policy that occurred between 1935 and 1965," he observes that "[i]f policy flows centrally, so will politics." That shift "has dire consequences for citizenship. Centralized politics inevitably means mass politics. . . . Citizenship is reduced, for the most part, to the relatively petty act of voting."[55] Without "the opportunity and the inclination to take part in civic life, the 'muscles' needed for good citizenship atrophy."[56] So, increased opportunity to deliberate locally can lead to increased capacity to do so.

Finally, however, it appears that Landy's civic environmentalism may have lower expectations than Shutkin's about the extent to which we need to aim at an intensely communitarian political culture. Like Shutkin, Landy relies on Tocqueville, but to different effect, noting that for Tocqueville American democracy was built on "self interest rightly understood," on a sense that doing good for myself means doing good for others. For Landy, then, the sphere of public decision making is properly limited because there is a natural impulse that can lead people to act both autonomously and responsibly.

Such limitations may not sit well with those who start from the strong interconnectedness of all parts the environment, and/or a strong interconnectedness between the state of the environment and civic culture. In fact, Landy sees that part of the defense of civic environmentalism as he understands it requires willingness to suggest that interconnectedness is not a fact but a metaphor, and as such "neither true nor false."[57] But he believes that it does significantly understate "the robustness of local environments"[58] and clearly predisposes to centralization. It thereby becomes consistent with another aspect of modern American politics, the creation of "programmatic rights" that require government to establish "programs and policies to secure those rights" and "ensure their universal applicability"[59] by centralized control.

So some basic assumptions about nature and the purposes of politics have to be confronted in order for Landy's civic environmentalism to make sense. Having come so far, however, it is necessary to acknowledge what is likely to be seen as one of the most problematic consequences of civic environmentalism—one that it is not clear Landy is willing to tackle head on. We have seen how he does not see civic environmentalism as requiring a divestiture of national authority. In the case studies, we see how the impetus for the efforts described comes from nationally mandated priorities. Yet one might think that the understanding of politics he lays out within that framework is subversive of such authority, and not unreasonably so. For if there is a class of genuinely local environmental problems, and if we are not to take programmatic rights that support national environmental policies for granted, then it would appear to be problematic to encourage and allow the development and exercise of civic muscles only in those cases where they are exercised to the liking of some higher authority. In other words, Landy's account of civic environmentalism raises most clearly the question of the degree to which national authority can allow a more or less unconstrained diversity with respect to local environmental problems, even unto the right of local efforts to make what may be widely perceived as wrong decisions.

Of course, we have a constitutional and legal order that is quite accustomed to dealing with this situation. To allow a higher degree of diversity in local efforts, what may be necessary is less systemic changes than changes in our expectations. It is to some extent business as usual for local, state, and federal governments to have to adjust their spheres of action in cases of conflict. Once we overcome the dogmatic assumption that environmental policy is somehow inherently appropriate to national (or larger) decisions, then accustomed routes of bargaining, litigation, passive resistance, and compromise will not have to look like failures, but may represent the way things ought to be.

In this respect Landy's civic environmentalism opens the door to a more nuanced understanding of the politics of environmental policy, where the term "politics" no longer is an abusive indicator of a failure to achieve some putatively obviously proper result, but instead reflects a normative commitment to no small degree of uncertainty and openness. A nice indication of the shift in perspective required comes from looking again at the significance of the fact that civic environmentalists are so inclined to case studies. To complain that they are all "works in progress" and therefore do not clearly demonstrate the success of civic environmentalism seems not unreasonable. However, what that complaint fails to see is that political decisions and the policies that result from them are nearly always quite properly works in progress, incomplete, and subject to revision.

From this point of view, the civic education that is necessary for civic environmentalism is not only related to ins and outs of ecology or environmental science, with the hope that with sufficient technical and scientific background citizens can be trusted to reach the right decision. More important would be an education in the civil treatment of the divergent opinions and interests that create differences over environmental issues in the first place. That would be an education in citizenship. As Landy notes, "It is utopian to expect to educate citizens about matters that require a great deal of expertise or are too abstract. But citizens can come to understand the issues at stake in concrete matters that affect them directly. Also, because the number involved is small, they can participate directly and therefore learn the actual arts of governing." They can "learn the deliberative skills and develop the appropriate level of personal responsibility necessary to preserve their freedom."[60] Notice that nothing here requires that we judge the success or failure of a particular policy-making effort by its achievement of particular substantive outcomes.

As we had occasion to note above, then, it would be more in tune with the implications of his own argument if Landy and his coauthors had avoided speaking about the solutions to environmental problems that are sought or achieved by civic environmentalism, as that language too readily implies that the goal is particular substantive outcomes. To put the point in terms that Bertrand de Jouvenel used, rather than see civic environmentalism as a means of solving finite problems, it should be viewed from the perspective that political decisions are necessary precisely when the terms of a problem are sufficiently contradictory to preclude finite solutions. The vacant land in my community cannot both remain green space and be subject to development. Given such a dispute, politics properly understood provides only contingent and often temporary *settlements*.[61]

Civic environmentalism may require that we be willing to accept that for some environmental problems, the fate of the earth is not in the balance, that there are cases where one can think locally and act locally.[62] There may be threats to global well-being that cannot be solved in our backyards, even if dealing with them might influence what we do in our backyards. For these, civic environmentalism is obviously not appropriate. All our authors, then, have rightly observed that an important part of civic environmentalism is definition of the problem set appropriate to it.

But having focused on problems of properly confined scope, it remains necessary to think about the problems in terms appropriate to state and local *politics*. That is not necessarily easy. Some four decades of environmental crisis have entrenched the rhetoric of emergency action where our existence and the existence of nature are at stake. An advantage of civic environmentalism's shift in scope is that if a change of outlook is possible at all, it would seem to be more possible in the more locally oriented problems whose nature and complexity are most likely to be evident to us. People care passionately about what is close to them, of course—civic environmentalism to some extent depends on that fact. But the need for trade-offs, compromises, and incrementalism is likely to be clearer the closer we are to seeing how and why they are necessary. Extreme problem definitions along with "simple" solutions are most likely to sell the less that we know about the matter in question. When things touch us directly, we are most likely, even if out of selfish motives, as Landy acknowledges, to see the complexities of issues.

The result of this shift may be a restoration of a sense of normal politics that was all too rare in the twentieth century. If normal politics is about settlements that provide the often temporary and contingent means of dealing with inherently contradictory claims, then confining the locus for disputes may have significant advantages in finding the accommodations that are appropriate to given circumstances. And we might expect that as circumstances change over time the experience of reaching such settlements may lead to the broader political consensus that eases decision making.

Civic environmentalism, then, would be about more decentralized settlements to more decentralized problems, settlements that acknowledge that the reason these problems enter into the political arena at all is that not everybody sees them as problems, or sees them in the same way as problems. But an implication of that outlook is that we acknowledge that sometimes a failure to decide is itself a decision, not doing anything the best that can be done. In war, Winston Churchill once noted, decisions must be swift, unified, and decisive. We have grown accustomed to thinking that all environmental problems require warlike action because we have too long been at war with nature. The urgency placed on environmental concerns often seems to make them the moral equivalent of war, and we therefore seek appropriate measures with a rhetoric, at least, of no compromises. But in peace, Churchill said, politics is quite different. "Many an apparently insoluble political problem solves itself or sinks to an altogether lower range if time, patience and phlegm are used."[63] The biggest challenge of a genuinely civic environmentalism may be to know when making peace with the world around us can be achieved by making our peace with the limitations and imperfections of peaceful political activity.

Notes

1. See, for example, Steven Haywood, *Index of Leading Environmental Indicators*, 6th ed. (San Francisco: Pacific Research Institute for Public Policy, 2001).

2. Al Gore, *Earth in the Balance: Ecology and the Human Spirit* (New York: Plume, 1993), 269.

3. William A. Shutkin, *The Land That Could Be: Environmentalism and Democracy in the Twenty-First Century* (Cambridge, Mass.: MIT Press, 2000), 22.

4. Ibid., 21–22.

5. Ibid., 47.

6. Ibid., 27–28.

7. Ibid., 28.

8. Ibid., 29.

9. Ibid., 28.

10. Ibid., 29.

11. Ibid., 101.

12. Ibid., 78.

13. Ibid.

14. Ibid., 42.

15. Ibid., 122.

16. Ibid., 55.

17. Ibid., 123. It seems quite unlikely that Jane Jacobs, a great critic of city planning, would be pleased to be included in this list of "visionary planners."

18. Ibid., 204.

19. Le Corbusier, *The Radiant City* (New York, Orion Press, 1964), iii, 8.

20. James Howard Kunstler, *Home from Nowhere: Remaking Our Everyday World for the 21st Century* (New York: Simon & Schuster, 1996), 225–26, 231–32.

21. DeWitt John, *Civic Environmentalism: Alternatives to Regulation in States and Communities* (Washington, D.C.: Congressional Quarterly, 1994), 14.

22. Ibid., 14.

23. Ibid., emphasis added.

24. Ibid., 10.

25. Ibid.

26. Ibid.

27. Ibid., 119.

28. See, for example, John's treatment of the contrasting personalities and roles of Dexter Lehtinen and Timer Powers in the Everglades case, Ibid., 138, 162.

29. Ibid., 15.

30. Ibid., 17–18.

31. Ibid., 79.

32. Ibid., 5.

33. Ibid., 18.

34. Ibid., 268.

35. Ibid., 120.

36. Ibid., 192.

37. Ibid., 17.

38. Ibid.

39. Ibid., 272.

40. Ibid., 272–74.

41. Ibid., 274–76.

42. Ibid., 272.

43. Ibid.

44. Ibid., 276.

45. Marc Landy, Megan Susman, and Debra Knopman, *Civic Environmentalism in Action: A Field Guide to Regional and Local Initiatives* (Washington, D.C.: Progressive Policy Institute, 1999), 3, <www.ppionline.org/ppi_ci.cfm?knlgAreaID=116&subsecID=151&contentID=1059>.

46. Landy et al., *Civic Environmentalism in Action*, 4.

47. Ibid.

48. Ibid.

49. Ibid.

50. Ibid.

51. Ibid.

52. Ibid., 3.

53. Ibid.

54. Ibid., 5.

55. Marc K. Landy, "Local Government and Environmental Policy," in *Dilemmas of Scale in America's Federal Democracy*, ed. Martha Derthick (Washington, D.C.: Woodrow Wilson Center Press, 1999), 228–29.

56. Landy, *Civic Environmentalism in Action*, 5.

57. Landy, "Local Government," 239.

58. Ibid., 254.

59. Ibid., 236, 237.

60. Ibid., 234.

61. Bertrand de Jouvenal, *The Pure Theory of Politics* (Indianapolis: Liberty Fund, 1963), 265–76.

62. Landy, "Local Government," 260.

63. Winston S. Churchill, *The World Crisis 1911–1918*, vol. 2 (New York: Barnes and Noble, 1993), 1131.

INDEX

About the Contributors

John Barry is reader in the School of Politics, Queen's University Belfast, Northern Ireland. He has written extensively on normative aspects of environmental politics. His books include *Rethinking Green Politics: Nature, Virtue, Progress, Environment and Social Theory* (with John Proops), *Citizenship, Sustainability and Environmental Research* (coedited with Marcel Wissenburg), *Sustaining Liberal Democracy* (coedited with Gene Frankland), and *The International Encyclopedia of Environmental Politics*.

Joe Bowersox is associate professor of politics at Willamette University, where he teaches courses in environmental politics, policy, and law. His publications include articles and chapters on western water policy, environmental ethics, and environmental political theory. He is coeditor (with John Martin Gillroy) of the forthcoming book, *The Moral Austerity of Environmental Policy*.

J. Baird Callicott is professor of philosophy and religion studies in the Institute of Applied Sciences at the University of North Texas. He is author of *Earth's Insights: A Multicultural Survey of Ecological Ethics from the Mediterranean Basin to the Australian Outback*, *In Defense of the Land Ethic: Essays in Environmental Philosophy*, and *Beyond the Land Ethic: More Essays in Environmental Philosophy*, and he is editor or coeditor of a number of books, including *Companion to a Sand County Almanac: Interpretive and Critical Essays* and *The Great New Wilderness Debate*.

Robyn Eckersley is a senior lecturer in the Department of Political Science at the University of Melbourne, where she teaches global politics, environmental politics, and political theory. She has published widely in the field of environmental politics, including *Environmentalism and Political Theory: Toward an Ecocentric Approach* and the edited volume *Markets, the State and the Environment: Towards Integration*.

Robert Gottlieb is Henry R. Luce Professor in the Urban and Environmental Policy Institute at Occidental College. He teaches courses on environmental history, environmental politics and policy, and urban and environmental issues. He is the author of *Forcing the Spring* and, most recently, *Environmentalism Unbound*.

Tim Hayward is a reader in the Department of Politics at the University of Edinburgh, United Kingdom. He is author of *Ecological Thought: An Introduction* and *Political Theory and Ecological Values*. He has published various journal articles on environmental and political philosophy and has coedited (with John O'Neill) *Justice, Property and the Environment: Social and Legal Perspectives*. He is currently completing a book on constitutional environmental rights.

Andrew Light is assistant professor of environmental philosophy and director of the Environmental Conservation Education Program at New York University, as well as research fellow at the Institute for Environment, Philosophy & Public Policy at Lancaster University (United Kingdom). He is editor or coeditor of a number of books, including *Environmental Pragmatism, Social Ecology after Bookchin, Beneath the Surface: Critical Essays in the Philosophy of Deep Ecology*, and *Moral and Political Reasoning in Environmental Practice*.

Timothy W. Luke is University Distinguished Professor of Political Science as well as codirector of the Center for Digital Discourse and Culture at Virginia Polytechnic Institute and State University in Blacksburg, Virginia. His research interests are tied to the politics of information societies, environmental affairs, and ecological criticism. He has just completed a new critical study of ideological politics at a number of major museums in the United States, which is entitled *Museum Pieces: Probing the Powerplays*. His most recent books are *Capitalism, Democracy, and Ecology: Departing from Marx; The Politics of Cyberspace* (coedited with Chris Toulouse); and *Ecocritique: Contesting The Politics of Nature, Economy, and Culture*.

Ben A. Minteer is assistant professor of environmental studies at Bucknell University. He has written widely on the intersection of environmental values and American pragmatic thought and is currently coediting (with Robert Manning) an anthology of papers on the philosophy and history of conservation, *Reconstructing Conservation*. He is also working on a monograph exploring the intellectual history of environmental pragmatism.

Bryan G. Norton is professor of philosophy in the School of Public Policy, Georgia Institute of Technology. He is author of *Why Preserve Natural Variety?, Toward Unity among Environmentalists*, and *Searching for Sustainability* (forthcoming). He is editor or coeditor of a number of books, including *The Preservation of Species, Ecosystem Health: New Goals for Environmental Management*, and *Wolves and Human Communities*. His current research concentrates on sustainability theory and community involvement in setting sustainability goals.

John O'Neill is professor of philosophy at Lancaster University. He has written widely on political theory, the philosophy of economics, ethics, environmental philosophy, and the philosophy of science. His publications include *The Market: Ethics, Knowledge and Politics* and *Ecology, Policy and Politics: Human Well-Being and the Natural World*.

Robert Paehlke is professor of political science at Trent University. He is the author of *Environmentalism and the Future of Progressive Politics*, several shorter monographs, and more than 100 journal articles and book chapters. He served as editor of *Conservation and Environmentalism: An Encyclopedia* and coeditor of *Managing Leviathan: Environmental Politics and the Administrative State*.

Bob Pepperman Taylor is associate professor of political science and director of the John Dewey Honors Program at the University of Vermont. He is also the author of *Our Limits Transgressed: Environmental Political Thought in America* and *America's Bachelor Uncle: Henry Thoreau and the American Polity*.

Charles T. Rubin is associate professor of political science at Duquesne University and graduate faculty in the Center for Social and Public Policy and the Center for Environmental Research and Education. His research and publications focus on political theory of environmentalism and urban planning and issues in science, technology, and policy. He is author of *The Green Crusade: Rethinking the Roots of Environmentalism* and editor of *Conservation Reconsidered: Nature, Virtue and American Liberal Democracy*.

Catriona Sandilands is associate professor in the faculty of environmental studies, York University (Toronto). She is the author of *The Good-Natured Feminist: Ecofeminism and the Quest for Democracy* and numerous other publications on ecological and feminist theory, green politics, sexuality and ecology, and, most recently, the struggles over nationalism in the Canadian national park system.

Luis A. Vivanco is assistant professor of anthropology and director of Latin American studies at the University of Vermont. His research focuses on the cultural politics of nature conservation, ecotourism, and sustainable development in Costa Rica and Oaxaca, Mexico. He has published several articles on ecotourism and environmentalism based on his dissertation research in Monte Verde, Costa Rica, and he is coeditor of *Talking about People: Readings in Contemporary Cultural Anthropology*.

Peter S. Wenz is professor of philosophy and legal studies at the University of Illinois at Springfield and adjunct professor of medical humanities at Southern Illinois University School of Medicine. His major intellectual interests concern how society can manage changes needed for environmental reasons with minimal harm to human beings, especially the poor and vulnerable. His current writing centers on global warming. His books include *Environmental Justice, Abortion Rights as Religious Freedom, Nature's Keeper*, and *Environmental Ethics Today*.